Classifying Entities and the Meaning of 'Tax Transparency'

Classifying Entities and the Meaning of 'Tax Transparency'

The UK Perspective

Michael McGowan

Wolters Kluwer

Published by:
Kluwer Law International B.V.
PO Box 316
2400 AH Alphen aan den Rijn
The Netherlands
E-mail: lrs-sales@wolterskluwer.com
Website: www.wolterskluwer.com/en/solutions/kluwerlawinternational

Sold and distributed by:
Wolters Kluwer Legal & Regulatory U.S.
920 Links Avenue
Landisville, PA 17538
United States of America
E-mail: customer.service@wolterskluwer.com

ISBN 978-94-035-3724-5

e-Book: ISBN 978-94-035-3744-3
web-PDF: ISBN 978-94-035-3765-8

About the Author

Michael McGowan is a visiting professor at the Dickson Poon School of Law, King's College, London. He is a graduate of the University of Oxford (MA, BCL) and of the Free University of Amsterdam (PhD). He teaches postgraduate students United Kingdom (UK) Business Taxation and European Union Tax Law, besides working as a tax adviser. For many years, he was a tax partner in major UK and United States law firms where his practice covered a very wide range of corporate, financing and other transactions, including fund formation and executive remuneration arrangements. His work regularly involved entity classification and tax transparency issues.

Table of Contents

Foreword

It is a pleasure to welcome this important contribution to tax literature. The expression 'tax transparency' has a variety of meanings depending on the circumstances and the tax involved. The topic is important to how the UK tax system categorises domestic (including Scots partnerships) and foreign entities.

The book is unusual in covering the full range of topics from loan relationships to trusts, as well as the full range of taxes from income and corporation taxes to VAT and stamp duties, and it even includes EU law. One could describe the book as adopting a practical approach, fully taking into account HMRC's practice, examined in a rigorous academic manner.

Categorising foreign entities is a topical and unsolved issue particularly following *Anson v HMRC* [2015] STC 1777 that the Supreme Court decided on the basis that it could not upset a finding of fact by the First-Tier Tribunal, which means that the decision is not much help to anyone else. The Tribunal was faced with deciding which of the conflicting experts on Delaware law was right, who were in turn faced with trying to apply their law to HMRC's somewhat vague list of questions on how the UK categorised entities. The real problem was that only someone familiar with both systems of law was qualified to do this. I enjoyed the author's comment that it illustrates that 'The UK approach to classifying non-UK entities risks basing important distinctions on abstract points with little real-world relevance.' Surely we could do better.

Having critically examined the state of UK law and compared it to how the US and the Netherlands solve the same problems, the author makes suggestions for improvement. The one that particularly appeals to me is a modified version of 'check-the-box'. One's first reaction is that anything would be better than check-the-box, but one needs to read the author's suggestions for avoiding the main problems of the US rule.

John Avery Jones

Preface

It is alleged that in 1939, Winston Churchill described the Soviet Union as 'a riddle wrapped in a mystery inside an enigma'. While the knock-on effects are less dramatic, this is also a fair summary of the UK tax rules for classifying entities, especially non-UK ones. Much the same can be said of 'tax transparency', an expression much bandied about but whose meaning remains contested and obscure.

All of this is strange because these are key concepts underpinning the UK tax system and how it operates in a globalised economy.

This book seeks to unravel the riddle/mystery/enigma and to go beyond the limited commentary in this area. Much of that commentary has understandably focused on the few UK judicial decisions to date. These raise as many questions as they answer. In any case, they only cover limited aspects of the entity classification/tax transparency conundrum. Discussion of these UK decisions has become bogged down in rather minor and (in the author's view) often irrelevant distinctions between UK and non-UK entities. While considering these decisions and their implications, this book aims to break free from this earlier approach. In particular, it does not contain lists or tables comparing particular features of UK and non-UK entities.

Considerable time is spent considering how tax treaties and EU law deal with entity classification and tax transparency issues. The comparative law angle is highlighted, with particular focus on the US and Dutch approaches to entity classification. Last but not least, there are suggestions about how UK law and practice in this area could be improved.

The book grew out of a PhD thesis which the author successfully defended in 2021 at the Vrije Universiteit van Amsterdam (VU), under the supervision of Professor Frank Pötgens of the VU and Dr John Avery Jones CBE. Successful research often consists of standing on the shoulders of giants. That has certainly been true in this case. In particular, John Avery Jones requires no introduction as a distinguished tax judge, tax practitioner and an academic of international repute with a prolific, heavily cited and ever-growing list of publications. He is also a pathfinder in the area covered by this book. The author is heavily indebted to him and to Professor Pötgens.

A number of friends, colleagues and former colleagues have offered considerable support and valuable insights throughout the process. While naming names may seem invidious, particular thanks are due to Dr Leopoldo Parada of the University of Leeds, to Nick Thornton of Fried Frank Harris Shriver and Jacobson LLP and to Malcolm Gammie KC.

Thanks are of course due to Lisa Zoltowska and her colleagues at Kluwer Law International. They have shown great flexibility and patience, successfully keeping the author on the straight and narrow. Any remaining faults are those of the author.

On the subject of patience, especial thanks are due to my wife, Christine, and to my three daughters, Victoria, Alice and Charlotte. They have lived and breathed this project, especially Charlotte who was born a few weeks after it began.

While this work should be of interest to academics and practitioners, both within and outside the UK, it is not and may not be relied upon as a substitute for tax advice. The law is stated as at 1 September 2022. All statements are made in the author's personal capacity and should not be regarded as those of any organisation.

Finally, the book is dedicated to my brother, Stephen, and to my uncle and godfather, William Greenway, two stars in my life who shone brightly but too briefly.

CHAPTER 1

Introduction

1.1 ENTITY CLASSIFICATION

'Entity classification' is the process whereby the United Kingdom (UK) tax law identifies and defines taxable persons, other than natural persons (i.e., individuals). A key part of this process is deciding whether a legal body is a 'company' or a 'partnership' for UK tax purposes. This is mainly because 'companies' are taxable persons in their own right, whereas 'partnerships' are not, at least when taxing their own income and gains.

'Entity classification' is not limited to identifying and defining only those non-natural persons with the necessary physical link to be taxable in the UK. It may also involve identifying and defining persons outside the UK with no such link. However, other UK taxpayers may have relevant connections with such entities (e.g., a UK-resident person may own shares in a United States (US) corporation). In order to tax that other UK taxpayer correctly, it is essential to understand what kind of entity that taxpayer has a relevant connection with.

1.2 TAX TRANSPARENCY

Entity classification raises the related question of whether a particular entity is 'tax transparent', and if so, what this means. Entities which are not 'transparent' are often referred to as 'opaque'. The answer to the transparency question often has a major impact on the UK taxation of the entity itself and of those with an interest in it.

'Transparency' is usually a non-technical shorthand for situations where: (i) an entity (e.g., a partnership or trust) is not a primary taxpayer in its own right in respect of income and gains[1] and (ii) its members/those with a relevant interest in it are taxed

1. It may still have liabilities to account for and collect tax on behalf of others, e.g., operating the UK payroll withholding system known as PAYE ('Pay As You Earn') on the earnings of directors and employees.

on distributed and undistributed income and gain as if they were directly interested in the entity's underlying assets and revenues.[2] However, as will become clearer, 'transparency' is not a concept with a single meaning nor does it only relate to taxing an entity's income and gains.

Typically, 'partnerships' are regarded under UK tax law as 'transparent' in the sense described above. Hence it is essential to define a 'partnership'. However, entities other than partnerships can be 'transparent'. This is true of some trusts and is discussed in Chapter 4. It is also typically true of contractual joint ventures and co-ownership arrangements which fall short of being partnerships. Therefore, an arrangement or entity can be 'transparent' without being a partnership.

Even if an arrangement is 'transparent', the precise mechanics for achieving this may vary. Hence 'transparency' for income tax purposes differs mechanically from 'transparency' for capital gains tax purposes. Crucially, a 'transparent' entity is rarely, if ever, a 'nothing' for tax purposes. Therefore, it is likely to modify the tax treatment of those connected with it, even if its members are taxed as if they were directly interested in its underlying income and gains.

In a globalised economy, questions of entity classification and tax transparency have become more common, especially when UK taxpayers have claimed double taxation relief for non-UK income tax when they invest in non-UK entities. The result has been major litigation in the last twenty-five or so years.

When defining 'transparency', one needs to take account of other rules which attribute undistributed income and gain from a UK or non-UK entity or arrangement to a UK-taxable person. That person will have a defined connection with the arrangement, e.g., a shareholder in a company or the settlor of a trust. These attribution rules are broadly drafted and in particular limit deferral of UK tax on income and gains accumulating within the entity or arrangement. Good examples are the 'controlled foreign company' rules;[3] the 'transfer of assets abroad' rules;[4] and the income and capital gains tax 'settlement' rules.[5] The effect of these rules is often similar to tax transparency but they differ in concept. Hence they are not discussed in detail. Such rules are structured so that, typically, income or gain of an entity or arrangement is not attributed to a person outside the UK tax charge so as to make it non-taxable.[6] To do so

2. A rare statutory definition of a 'transparent' entity appears in the UK corporate interest restriction rules in section 447(6) Taxation (International and Other Provisions) Act 2010 (TIOPA 2010). There it is simply defined as an 'entity' (otherwise unspecified) which 'is not chargeable to corporation tax or income tax as a person (ignoring any exemptions)'. Nothing is said about the tax treatment of those with an interest in the entity.
3. Part 9A TIOPA.
4. Part 13 Chapter 2 Income Tax Act 2007 (ITA).
5. Part 5 Chapter 5 Income Tax (Trading and Other Income) Act 2005 (ITTOIA); and sections 77-98A Taxation of Chargeable Gains Act 1992 (TCGA).
6. *See Becker v Wright* 42 TC 591, now reflected in section 648(1) and (2) ITTOIA. UK-source income can be attributed under the income tax 'settlement' rules to a non-UK-resident: *see IRC v Countess of Kenmare* 37 TC 383. Such attribution of UK-source income from UK-resident trustees to a non-UK-resident settlor may reduce the UK tax charge, which for a non-UK-resident is often limited to (any) tax deducted (or treated as deducted) at source at 20%: *see* sections 810-828 ITA and also Mark Brabazon: 'International Taxation of Trust Income: Principles, Planning and Design'. Cambridge University Press 2019, at 40 (hereinafter 'Brabazon').

would defeat their anti-deferral purpose, whereas such a purpose is irrelevant when dealing with 'transparency'. Such attribution rules are asymmetrical in other ways: income and gain may be attributed to the relevant UK taxpayer, but underlying losses of the entity or arrangement are almost never attributed in this way. There is often no such asymmetrical treatment of income and losses when dealing with classic cases of 'transparency' such as partnerships, some trusts and simple co-ownership arrangements.[7]

So how does the UK classify entities for tax purposes and, consequently, when and how does it regard an entity as being 'tax transparent'? Is the UK's approach to entity classification satisfactory, especially taking into account its double taxation treaties and European Union (EU) law? Is an alternative approach to be preferred? This work aims to address these issues in detail. The law is stated as at 1 September 2022.

7. Some anti-deferral rules do not even impute actual underlying income but create a stand-alone UK tax charge on a notional amount measured by reference to the actual underlying income of the entity. This seems to be the case with the UK 'controlled foreign company' rules: *see Bricom Holdings Ltd v IRC* [1997] STC 1179, a decision on the predecessor of Part 9A TIOPA.

CHAPTER 2

The Current UK Approach to Classifying Entities and Establishing Whether They Are 'Transparent'

2.1 INTRODUCTION

The UK treats an individual as a taxable person in respect of income and gains.[8] However, complications immediately emerge when trying to identify a 'company'. In other words, the type of entity which is subject to UK corporation tax on its income and gains so long as: (i) it is not acting in a 'fiduciary or representative' capacity;[9] and typically (ii) it is UK-resident or trading as a dealer in or developer of UK land or is trading through a UK 'permanent establishment'.[10] What does 'company' mean?

2.2 SECTION 1121 CORPORATION TAX ACT 2010

The key definition of a 'company' for UK corporation tax purposes is in section 1121 Corporation Tax Act 2010 (CTA 2010). This is based on predecessor wording in section 832 Income and Corporation Taxes Act 1988 (ICTA 1988). Section 1121 is an exhaustive definition:

> (1) In the Corporation Tax Acts, 'company' means any body corporate or unincorporated association, but does not include a partnership, a co-ownership scheme (as defined by section 235A of the Financial Services and Markets Act 2000), a local authority or a local authority association.

8. Although an individual can be taxable on income and gain in different ways, depending on the capacity in which that individual is acting: on his or her own account, as a guardian, trustee or as an executor or administrator of a deceased person's estate.
9. Sections 3(2) and 6 Corporation Tax Act 2009 (CTA 2009).
10. Sections 5-5B CTA 2009.

(2) Subsection (1) needs to be read with section 617 (under which the trustees of an authorised unit trust are treated for certain purposes as a UK resident company).

2.3 SECTION 1121: CORE CONCEPTS

The special UK tax treatment of an 'authorised unit trust' (a form of regulated collective investment scheme (CIS)) is discussed in Chapter 4. Co-ownership schemes are a form of 'transparent' collective investment vehicle. Both types of entity are specialised, limited exceptions to the general rule in section 1121(1). A 'local authority' is a UK local government administrative unit, as is a 'local authority association'. These entities are also specific exceptions to the general definition of 'company' in section 1121(1). Crucially, this general definition includes a 'body corporate' and an 'unincorporated association' but excludes any entity which is a 'partnership'.

2.4 SECTION 288(1) TAXATION OF CHARGEABLE GAINS ACT 1992

There is a similar definition of 'company' for capital gains tax purposes in section 288(1) TCGA, which is non-exhaustive:

> 'Company' includes any body corporate or unincorporated association but does not include a partnership, and shall be construed in accordance with Section 99.[11]

The next step is to analyse 'body corporate', 'unincorporated association' and 'partnership'. Before doing so, it is worth mentioning that the word 'entity' sometimes appears in UK tax legislation. Its use is fairly peripheral, e.g., the definitions of 'generally accepted accounting practice' in section 997 ITA and section 1127 CTA 2010. Section 417(6)(e) and section 429(6) TIOPA say that '"entity" includes anything which is treated as an entity in the financial statements of the worldwide group (regardless of whether it has a legal personality as a body corporate)'. So an entity seems to be any 'body' which is more than a mere contract but need not have the fully fledged legal personality of a body corporate. Hence it could include a body corporate, an unincorporated association, a partnership and a trust.

2.5 UNINCORPORATED ASSOCIATION

An 'unincorporated association' is usually regarded, for corporation tax purposes, as a contractually based (not trust-based) entity which lacks legal personality and exists for

11. Section 99 treats a unit trust scheme as a company with issued share capital for capital gains tax purposes, although this is now subject to section 103D TCGA: *see* Chapter 4. The definition in section 288(1) applies 'unless the context otherwise requires'. The context does otherwise require in section 170(9) TCGA. This defines a 'company' more narrowly for the purposes of defining a corporate group, when taxing chargeable gains. Section 170(9) includes in particular a 'company' (other than a UK LLP), wherever incorporated. It does not include an 'unincorporated association'.

non-business purposes. As Lawton LJ said in the Court of Appeal in *Conservative and Unionist Central Office v Burrell*:[12]

> I infer that by 'unincorporated association' in this context [i.e. the statutory predecessor of section 1121(1) CTA 2010] Parliament meant two or more persons bound together for one or more common purposes, *not being business purposes*, [emphasis added] by mutual undertakings each having mutual duties and obligations, in an organisation which has rules which identify in whom control of it and its funds rests and on what terms and which can be joined or left at will. *The bond of union* between the members of an unincorporated association *has to be contractual* [emphasis added].

A good example is a club which is not a separate legal person but an aggregation of members based on a contract, formed to provide members with the benefits of club membership and which aims to cover costs via membership fees.[13] Of course, some clubs take the form of a 'body corporate', a concept discussed further in section 2.6.

'Unincorporated associations' are in practice rare for tax purposes. Historically, this was not so. Until it became much easier to incorporate a company by registration and the Bubble Act of 1720 was repealed, many 'companies' with business purposes were in fact unincorporated associations: in effect, a form of partnership with a large and fluctuating body of members and whose business property was held on trust for those members. Hence they were often referred to as 'deed of settlement companies'. The Joint Stock Companies Act 1844 prohibited the formation of *new* unincorporated bodies with more than twenty-five members (reduced to twenty from 1856).[14] The 1844 Act did not apply to existing bodies. From 1857, such 'deed of settlement companies' with more than twenty members could carry on a trade or business but each member was severally liable for the debts of the organisation without a right of contribution from the other members. This incentivised such organisations to incorporate under the 1844 Act.[15]

The UK tax authorities (His Majesty's Revenue and Customs or HMRC) do not agree with Lawton LJ's comments. They regard them as not strictly necessary for the decision in *Burrell*. This is correct. They also regard them as defining 'unincorporated

---

12. [1982] 2 All ER 1 at 4b.
13. In *Blackpool Marton Rotary Club v Martin* 62 TC 686, a rotary club argued that it was a partnership subject to income tax, and not an 'unincorporated association' subject to corporation tax. Hoffmann J (as he then was) disagreed: 'The members of a club are not individually entitled to share in any profits which may arise from its activities. Their entitlement is to whatever privileges are conferred on them by the rules, and no more. Equally, they are under no liability to share in the losses of the club. Their liability is to pay the subscriptions and whatever other dues they may be responsible for under the rules, but nothing more. Those are vital distinctions between a partnership and a club. ...' These remarks are broadly consistent with Lawton LJ in *Burrell*.
14. This provision of the 1844 Act eventually became section 716(1) Companies Act 1985, which was finally repealed in 2002. It had already ceased to apply to professional partnerships.
15. For further discussion, *see* John F. Avery Jones CBE: 'Defining and Taxing Companies 1799 to 1965'. Studies in the History of Tax Law: ed. John Tiley, Volume 5 Hart Publishing 2012, at 28.

associations' too narrowly, not least because historically, 'unincorporated associations' *have* existed for business purposes. In their published guidance,[16] they state that '[t]here is no reason why an unincorporated body should not have trading or business objects, or carry on significant commercial activities'.[17] In particular, HMRC regard some forms of joint venture which fall short of being a partnership as being 'unincorporated associations' for UK tax purposes. However, they clearly do not regard all such joint ventures as 'unincorporated associations', and it is unclear where the dividing line falls.[18]

Others have queried the remarks of Lawton LJ in the *Burrell* case.[19] Peter Harris explores the origins of the definition of 'company' for corporation tax purposes which is now in section 1121(1) CTA 2010. Various formulations (covering other entities besides 'bodies corporate') were used prior to the 1965 introduction of corporation tax. Furthermore, in their (non-public) Notes on Amendments to Clauses in the 1965 Finance Bill, the then Inland Revenue (HMRC's predecessor) indicated that 'unincorporated association' was intended to cover any 'grouping [other than a partnership] of individuals in any form which has some recognisable existence for tax purposes apart from its individual members'. Or, to quote Harris, 'the broadest possible range of "bodies" from political to religious to educational to commercial'.

This expansive reading of 'unincorporated association' (with the related uncertainty about its scope) seems to be what Lawton LJ was seeking to avoid, even if his formulation jarred with the broader earlier idea of an 'unincorporated association'.[20] In essence, Lawton LJ was saying that, *for corporation tax liability purposes*, unincorporated arrangements *for business purposes* should either be regarded as partnerships (and hence outside corporation tax altogether) or, if they were not partnerships, should be subject to direct taxation only at the level of the participants in the arrangements. In particular, such arrangements (e.g., co-ownership of commercial property) should not be separate taxable entities (or 'companies') for corporation tax purposes.

This is a practical approach. Otherwise, a contractual joint venture falling short of partnership could be subject to corporation tax as an 'opaque' entity. This would

16. Company Taxation Manual CTM41305 (accessed 15 May 2020). *See also* Victor Baker: 'Conservative and Unionist Central Office v Burrell (1981): A Case of Hidden Significance'. Chapter 12. Landmark Cases in Revenue Law: eds John Snape and Dominic de Cogan. Hart Publishing 2019, at 267.
17. Nor do they think that the tie between the members of such an association need be a contract. However, there must be an organisation of persons with an identifiable membership bound together for a common purpose by identifiable rules, and the organisation must be distinct from those who would be regarded as its members. That organisation must not be some other form of association recognised in law, e.g., a body corporate or a partnership. Nor will it include trustees whose role is fiduciary and who in any case are not subject to corporation tax on profits accruing in a fiduciary capacity: section 6(1) CTA 2009.
18. *See* Part F of Baker *supra*.
19. *See* Peter Harris: 'Company, Person, Body of Persons, Entity: What's the Difference and Why?' [2011] British Tax Review 188 and especially at pp. 203-208 (hereinafter 'Harris').
20. As noted in Part H of Baker *supra*, there are other non-tax contexts in which modern UK statutes indicate that an unincorporated association *can* carry on a trade or business, with or without a view to profit: see section 1161 Companies Act 2006. This no doubt reflects thinking from the era of 'deed of settlement' companies. Similarly, unlike section 1121(1) CTA 2010, section 1173(1) Companies Act 2006 appears to treat a partnership as a form of unincorporated association.

have very unwelcome consequences for parties who have entered into a non-partnership business venture where they share certain costs but not profits.

A set of barristers' chambers is a good example. Each member of chambers only shares chambers' costs (e.g., rent) but otherwise operates as a sole trader and would expect to be taxed as such on his/her profits as they arise. Similarly, a member would expect to claim relief for any losses from practising as a sole trader. This is the expected outcome even though there is a formal business relationship between members of chambers. Moreover, each set of chambers typically has a recognisable identity distinct from its members from time to time.

Treating such an arrangement as an 'unincorporated association' risks economic double taxation (corporation tax at entity level and then income tax at member level on a subsequent profit distribution). This would not reflect the underlying commercial reality where the participants are a fairly loosely integrated group of sole traders. It would also be a worse outcome than in a full partnership where the partners alone are directly taxed on their shares of partnership income and gains and can claim relief for underlying partnership losses. Lawton LJ's formulation preserves broad tax parity between partnerships and unincorporated commercial joint ventures falling short of partnership. It treats both types of arrangement as taxable only at member level. Furthermore, his formulation avoids losses of such a joint venture becoming trapped within it and unusable by its members. Trapped losses could well result if that venture were subject to corporation tax as an 'unincorporated association'.[21]

The HMRC interpretation of 'unincorporated association' makes more sense in other contexts where the question is not what entities are subject to corporation tax. The tax legislation contains other references to an 'unincorporated association' in contexts far removed from whether an entity is liable to corporation tax. For example, Chapter 8 Part 2 Income Tax (Earnings and Pensions) Act 2003 (ITEPA 2003) sets out situations in which workers who are made available to clients by 'intermediaries' can be taxed as employees, even if they would not otherwise be regarded as employees. The result is that the 'intermediary' (or often the client) must operate PAYE, and account for social security contributions ('National Insurance') in respect of the worker.

Section 51 ITEPA 2003 makes clear that a 'company' can be an 'intermediary' for these purposes. Section 61(1) defines a 'company' exhaustively as 'a body corporate or unincorporated association, and does not include a partnership [which is treated as an "intermediary" separately under section 52 ITEPA 2003]'. The definition of a 'company' in section 61(1) seems to resemble section 1121(1) CTA 2010 closely. Yet in relation to Chapter 8 Part 2 ITEPA 2003, it makes sense to treat as an 'unincorporated

21. Since *Burrell*, there have been major changes to the corporation tax computation rules (e.g., the loan relationship, derivative contract and intangible fixed asset rules in Parts 5-8 CTA 2009). Those changes do not apply to income tax. Hence the interpretation of 'unincorporated association' favoured by HMRC would mean that a very different basis of tax computation could apply to a partnership of individuals, compared to an unincorporated commercial joint venture made up of individuals which fell short of partnership. This divergence in computing tax is hard to justify because the two situations may be very similar. Lawton LJ's narrow definition of 'unincorporated association' sidesteps this difficulty.

association' a commercial joint venture which falls short of partnership. This purposive interpretation avoids a major loophole in the definition of 'intermediary'.

Lawton LJ in *Burrell* was focusing directly on whether the Conservative Party was a 'company' subject to corporation tax on its investment income. The rough-and-ready line he drew leads to a sensible outcome. As discussed, in other contexts where tax legislation uses the term 'unincorporated association', a broader meaning than that proposed by him may be appropriate.[22]

2.6 A 'BODY CORPORATE'

2.6.1 What Is It?

A 'body corporate' is a separate legal person clearly distinct from its members which can acquire rights and incur obligations. It typically comes into being because of a publicised state-sanctioned act of creation. Incorporation by registration (e.g., under the UK Companies Act 2006) is the most common method of such creation. However, it is far from unique. For example, many such legal persons have been incorporated in the UK by Royal Charter or private act of parliament, e.g., the East India Company as well as canal and railway companies in the eighteenth and nineteenth centuries.[23]

For these purposes, an 'act of creation' must be a legally recognised and publicised step by a government or government-sanctioned body whereby a new legal person is brought into being and notified to third parties as such. A simple contract between the members of a legal person is not enough, even if that may be a precondition for the act of creation to occur. Hence under modern UK company registration procedure, the founding member or members of a company must submit a signed memorandum and articles of association to the Registrar of Companies. The new legal person only comes into being when the Registrar accepts those documents and formally admits the company to the public Register of Companies.

For UK corporate and tax purposes, a 'body corporate' need not always have more than one member. For example, a single shareholder suffices for a private limited

22. In such contexts, the legislation has sometimes moved away altogether from the 'unincorporated association' concept, which helps avoid confusion. A good example is the definition of 'securities' in ITEPA 2003 for the purposes of taxing employment-related securities. The first limb of that definition, in section 420(1)(a), refers to 'shares in any body corporate (wherever incorporated) or in *any unincorporated body* [emphasis added] constituted under the law of a country or territory outside the United Kingdom'.
23. There are also strong arguments (*see* Gerald F. Montagu: 'Is a Foreign State a Body Corporate?' [2001] British Tax Review 421) that a non-UK state is a form of 'body corporate', although in such cases it may not always be possible to identify a clear publicised act of creation, e.g., when a new state (for example, the USSR) emerges from the chaos of revolution and civil war. The same point may apply to corporations created by English common law such as the Crown or a 'corporation sole' such as a bishopric. In July 2022, the UK Treasury published a consultative document aimed at restricting sovereign immunity from UK direct taxation: 'Sovereign immunity from direct taxation: consultation on policy design' – GOV.UK (www.gov.uk) (accessed 18 July 2022). One of the proposals is that non-UK sovereign, non-natural persons (including non-UK states) will be treated as non-UK-resident companies liable to corporation tax on any income and gain from which they are not exempt.

company. A 'body corporate' need not have a business purpose: many UK charities are UK private companies limited by guarantee, and a number of non-profit-making clubs are structured as 'bodies corporate'. The example of a company limited by guarantee shows that members' interests in a body corporate do not always take the form of transferable shares representing paid-in capital. Lastly, for UK corporate and tax purposes, membership of a 'body corporate' need not carry with it limited liability (although limited liability is commonplace). UK company law expressly permits the incorporation of a private unlimited company.[24] Its members (at least two) have unlimited liability to make good any excess of liabilities over assets if the company goes into liquidation. However, the members are not directly liable to the company's creditors. Even if they must make good any shortfall, the company's obligations are its alone. This is consistent with it being an entirely separate legal person from its members (unlike, e.g., a Scottish partnership which is also a separate legal person, but whose partners can be directly sued as guarantors of the partnership's obligations by partnership creditors: *see* section 2.9).

2.6.2 Spotting a Body Corporate

The UK courts can be expected to treat as a 'body corporate' for UK tax purposes any legal person brought into being by an official publicised step either in the UK or elsewhere, so long as the relevant governing law indicates that the new legal entity, as well as being a separate legal person, is also a 'body corporate' whose identity, assets, liabilities and activities are clearly distinct from those of its members. This will not always be the case. Incorporation does not simply mean legal personality. It will be necessary to look at the rules bringing the separate legal person into being to decide if it is to be raised to the status of a 'body corporate' or, as one famous judge put it, if there is a 'manifest intention to incorporate'.[25] In *Maclaine Watson & Co Ltd v Department of Trade and Industry and related appeals,*[26] the House of Lords ruled that the UK had by statutory instrument treated the International Tin Council as a separate legal person with the legal capacities of a body corporate without it actually being a UK domestic body corporate. As Lord Oliver, giving the main judgment, put it, at page 547:

> [T]he effect of the grant of the legal capacities of a body corporate was that in United Kingdom law the [International Tin Council], though not formally incorporated, was invested with a legal personality distinct from its members.

He noted that there were good reasons for conferring separate legal personality without creating a UK domestic corporation. The members of the International Tin Council were sovereign states which would be reluctant to submit the internal

24. Section 3(4) Companies Act 2006. An unlimited liability company can be either a company with share capital or one whose members do not hold share capital but who provide a guarantee to the company instead.
25. Atkin LJ in *Mackenzie-Kennedy v Air Council* [1927] 2 KB 517 at 534, citing Littledale J in *Conservators of the River Tone v Ash* (1829) 10 B&C 349. On the facts, Atkin LJ found out that there was no such intention.
26. [1989] 3 All ER 523 at 547.

workings of the entity to the domestic jurisdiction of one of the council's members and especially to its domestic winding-up jurisdiction.[27]

It has also been argued that a 'body corporate' must have 'perpetual succession', which means that, before it is wound up, its membership can change without affecting its continued existence, rights and liabilities.[28] As discussed in section 2.9.7, it is not clear that 'perpetual succession' is confined to entities which are 'bodies corporate'.

2.7 UK LLPS AND EEIGS

Sometimes, an entity which is a 'body corporate' will be expressly excluded from the UK corporation tax charge, even if it has a territorial connection with the UK. In particular, the Limited Liability Partnerships Act 2000 sets out the procedure for creating, and the structure of the entity known as a 'UK LLP'. The 2000 Act describes the UK LLP as a 'body corporate', to maximise the chance of members' limited liability being respected in non-UK jurisdictions. A UK LLP needs two members or else a member's limited liability may be restricted under the 2000 Act. Those members have no direct contractual relationship with third parties who deal with the UK LLP. However, section 863 ITTOIA, section 1273 CTA 2009 and section 59A TCGA *treat* a UK LLP as if it were a 'partnership' where it carries on a trade, profession or business 'with a view to profit'.[29] Therefore, its income and capital gains are taxed only in the hands of its members. They are typically treated as partners in a partnership rather than mere members or employees of a body corporate.[30]

---

27. For further discussion of *Maclaine Watson, see Arab Monetary Fund v Hashim and others (No 3)* [1991] 1 All ER 871. For an earlier example of a court recognising the existence of a separate legal person with 'an existence apart from its members', which was nevertheless not a 'body corporate', *see* the majority of the House of Lords in *Bonsor v Musicians' Union* [1955] 3 All ER 518. This related to a registered trade union which was being sued by a former member for damages for wrongful expulsion.
28. *See The Conservators of the River Tone v Ash* (1829) 10 B&C 349, cited by Atkin LJ in *Mackenzie-Kennedy v Air Council* [1927] 2 KB 517. *See also* Montagu *supra.* where that author's 'fundamental use' test for whether an entity is a 'body corporate' requires it to have 'perpetual succession'.
29. In *Ingenious Games LLP and others v HMRC* [2021] STC 1791, the Court of Appeal ruled (at 1830-1831) that 'with a view to profit' has the same meaning as 'with a view of profit' in section 1(1) Partnership Act 1890 and requires the entity's members to have a purely subjective intention to make profits. The court also noted that since Partnership Act 1890, the *sharing* of profits is not an essential feature of a partnership. Similar statements were made in *M Young Legal Associates Ltd v Zahid Solicitors (a firm)* [2006] EWCA Civ 613, where doubts were raised about whether sharing profits was an essential feature of partnership before the 1890 Act.
30. UK pension funds do not benefit from this 'look through' treatment if they are members of a LLP which mainly invests in land and most of whose income is derived from land investments: *see* section 186(2) FA 2004 and section 1004 ITA. The treatment of a UK LLP for VAT, stamp duty, stamp duty reserve tax and stamp duty land tax is discussed in Chapter 5. Where a UK LLP ceases to carry on a trade, profession or business 'with a view to profit', it continues to be taxed as a partnership if the cessation is only temporary or during a winding-up following a permanent cessation. That cessation must not take place for tax avoidance reasons and the winding-up must not be 'unreasonably prolonged'. If a liquidator of the UK LLP is appointed or the court makes a winding-up order (or non-UK equivalent), then the LLP will cease to be taxed as a partnership. The transparency of UK LLPs under section 863 ITTOIA was considered in *Bayonet Ventures LLP and another v HMRC* [2018] UKFTT 262 (TC). The judge (following *Peter Vaines v HMRC* [2018]

An older example of a body corporate being carved out of UK corporation tax is the European Economic Interest Grouping (EEIG). EEIGs were originally an EU legal concept, being largely modelled on the French 'groupement d'intérêt économique'. EEIGs are created in EU Member States under Council Regulation (EEC) No. 2137/85 ('the 1985 Regulation') which has direct effect in Member States. Post-2020, the EEIG concept survives in the UK as the UK Economic Interest Grouping. EEIGs and their UK equivalent are permitted to engage in certain ancillary economic activities, e.g., research. Their purpose (unlike a UK LLP) must not be to make profits, although their activities may still generate profit. The comments below focus on EEIGs created within the EU.

EEIGs are formed by their members entering into a contract which is then registered: Articles 1(1) and 6 of the 1985 Regulation. There must be at least two members from different EU/European Economic Area Member States. Article 1(2) confers full legal capacity on a EEIG, but Article 1(3) provides that each Member State has a choice whether to regard a EEIG as having legal personality. A UK lawyer would regard legal personality as the inevitable result of the EEIG having full legal capacity. However, this is not the case in some civil law jurisdictions (notably Germany) where the fact that EEIG members are liable for the entity's debts means that it cannot have full legal personality in that jurisdiction, even though it has full legal capacity.[31]

In some Member States, EEIGs are not just legal persons but are formed as bodies corporate. EEIG members have unlimited joint and several liability for the debts of the EEIG (Article 24 of the 1985 Regulation), like Scottish partners. An EEIG member's liability can extend to debts incurred by the EEIG before that person became a member.

Article 40 of the 1985 Regulation states simply that 'the profit or losses resulting from the activities of a grouping shall be taxable only in the hands of its members'. So it must be treated as 'transparent' when taxing its income and gains and when allowing relief for losses, although not for the purposes of other taxes (notably Value Added Tax (VAT)). Article 40 gives no further detail on how direct tax 'transparency' is to be achieved. In particular, can any UK 'permanent establishment' of a EEIG formed outside the UK be treated as that of the EEIG members so as to subject those members to UK tax? Moreover, Article 40 says nothing about the tax treatment of members if they assign their interests. Is an assignment to be treated as a part-disposal of underlying EEIG assets or is the EEIG interest to be taxed as a separate asset (and if so, what kind of asset)?

UK legislation further develops the transparency provided for in Article 40 of the 1985 Regulation. Sections 842 ITA, 990 CTA 2010 and 285A TCGA all ensure that, for UK direct tax purposes, income and gains of a EEIG, wherever formed, are taxed at the level of the EEIG members and not at EEIG level. To achieve this, the EEIG is treated as the agent of its members or, if it carries on a trade or profession, as a partnership.

STC 297) ruled that section 863 does not disregard the LLP altogether and treat all its activities as carried on directly by its members. It merely assimilates the position of LLP members to that of partners in a partnership.

31. *See* John F. Avery Jones et al.: 'Characterisation of Other States' Partnerships for Income Tax' (hereinafter 'Avery Jones: Partnerships') [2002] British Tax Review 375 at 393-394.

Section 285A(1) Rule 5 TCGA 1992 also treats the interests of EEIG members as comprising shares in the underlying EEIG assets, rather than as a separate asset. Those shares are usually determined by reference to a member's share of any EEIG profits under the founding contract. This UK rule may go beyond what Article 40 strictly prescribes.[32]

2.8 UK 'BODIES CORPORATE'

Despite the exceptions in section 2.7, it seems clear that for UK corporation tax purposes, the following types of company formed by registration under the UK Companies Act 2006 will be 'bodies corporate' within section 1121 CTA 2010: private companies limited by shares or guarantee, private unlimited companies, and public limited companies limited by shares. Such entities cannot elect out of corporation tax.

This leaves the much harder question of which non-UK entities will be 'companies' within section 1121 CTA 2010 and which entities are 'partnerships', and hence not 'companies', for section 1121 purposes.

2.9 PARTNERSHIPS

2.9.1 What Is a Partnership?

So what entity constitutes a 'partnership', which section 1121 CTA 2010 then excludes from the definition of a 'company', as does section 288(1) TCGA?[33]

The classic English law definition of a partnership is in section 1(1) Partnership Act 1890 (*'the 1890* Act'). This defines partnership as the relationship between persons (plural) carrying on 'a business in common with a view of profit'.

32. Section 285A TCGA is a clearer 'lookthrough' than the normal capital gains tax rule applying to partnerships under section 59 TCGA: *see* Appendix A. For further discussion of the UK tax treatment of a EEIG, *se* Christopher J. Wales: 'European Economic Interest Groupings: Finance Act 1990' [1990] British Tax Review 335; and Tarlochan Lall: 'Taxation and the European Economic Interest Grouping' [1993] British Tax Review 134.
33. This exclusion can be read as indicating that, without it, certain types of 'body corporate' or 'unincorporated association' can be 'partnerships'. The authors of Avery Jones: Partnerships *supra*, at p. 394 fn 79 believe that the carve-out was to counteract the default classification of Scottish partnerships as 'companies'. However, Scottish partnerships have not generally been regarded as 'bodies corporate': *see* Paul Sutton and Jane McCormick: 'Scottish Limited Partnerships' Tax Journal, Issue 916, 26. According to Baker *supra*, at p. 276, the express exclusion of partnerships in section 1121 CTA 2010 was 'to avoid doubt'. This interpretation makes sense. As a general matter, the concept of a 'partnership' is meant to be distinct from that of a 'body corporate': the latter has legal personality but, more importantly, its identity, assets, liabilities and activities are clearly separate from those of its members in a way which is not the case in relation to a partnership, where the members are inherently involved in the underlying business, even if the partnership is a legal person. Section 1(2) Partnership Act 1890 also seems to have been included to avoid doubt, by stating that the members of a UK-incorporated company do not thereby form a partnership. If section 1(2) meant more than this, presumably non-UK-incorporated companies would be partnerships. This was presumably not intended: *see* Peter Harris: 'Corporate Tax Law: Structure, Policy and Practice'. Cambridge University Press 2013, at 30.

As already mentioned, 'with a view of profit' only requires a subjective aim of making a profit. 'Business' is in practice interpreted broadly, not least to include passive investment by a partnership so long as this investment is sufficiently 'managed' to distinguish it from mere co-ownership. In practice, that management can be supplied by an external manager, notably in the case of investment limited partnerships (LPs).

The 1890 Act applies to the entire UK and consolidated much (but not all) of the existing common law of partnership when it was enacted.

This 1890 Act definition has consistently influenced (and indeed over-influenced) judicial thinking on the meaning of a 'partnership' for tax purposes, especially when considering whether non-UK entities are partnerships.

Because a partnership is a collaboration 'with a view of profit', 'partnership' and 'unincorporated association' are usually mutually exclusive in English law (at least if one accepts the thinking of Lawton LJ: *see* section 2.5). Furthermore, there can be no overlap between a 'partnership' and a 'body corporate' where (as is possible) the latter has only one member. Section 1 1890 Act requires at least two members of a partnership. In any case, section 1(2) states (presumably to avoid residual doubt) that the relation between the members of a UK-incorporated company is not a partnership.

So what distinguishes a 'body corporate' from a 'partnership' if the relevant entity (which may be non-UK) has at least two members and pursues profit-making activity?

2.9.2 Problems of Definition

The answer has become harder because the substantive difference between a 'body corporate' and a 'partnership' has been watered down. Many modern 'partnerships', especially in professional and financial services, are hard to distinguish from private limited companies in the way they are structured and run. It is worth considering a number of other factors which potentially differentiate partnerships from bodies corporate.

2.9.3 Limited Liability

Limited versus unlimited liability of an entity's members cannot be a conclusive difference between a partnership and a body corporate. UK company law permits the creation of private unlimited liability companies (ULCs), which are clearly a 'body corporate' for tax purposes. The form of unlimited liability of members of such companies has already been discussed. Partners in a classic English or Scottish law general partnership have unlimited joint liability for partnership debts. That liability is owed directly to the creditors of the partnership. However, such unlimited liability partnerships are increasingly rare.

UK LLPs, despite their name, are a form of body corporate. Hence, their members' limited liability is not directly relevant to that of partners in a true partnership. However, under the Limited Partnerships Act 1907, a new or pre-existing partnership can register as a LP with the UK Registrar of Companies. If it does so, then liability is limited (with caveats) to the extent of partners' capital contributions, for those partners who do not participate in the management of the partnership.[34] There must be at least one general partner in such a LP, with unlimited liability for partnership debts. The general partner manages the LP. To limit liability further, the general partner is often a purpose-formed, lowly capitalised UK private limited company or (to limit accounting disclosure obligations) a UK LLP.

Looking abroad, a number of non-UK entities style themselves as 'limited liability partnerships' (LLPs) and are treated by HMRC as partnerships for UK tax purposes. The liability of a member for the debts of the entity is generally limited to the member's capital contribution even if the member takes part in the entity's management.[35]

US law firms operating in the UK are a good example of such LLPs. Unlike UK LLPs, these are not 'bodies corporate' benefiting from a special UK tax status. They are non-UK 'LLPs' (typically formed in Delaware or New York) which usually have a separate legal personality, yet regard themselves as partnerships for UK tax purposes on general principles. This seems to be broadly accepted by HMRC, even though section 301(1) of the US Revised Uniform Partnership Act typically makes each partner an agent of the partnership entity, rather than of each of the other partners. This differs from an English law partnership - which lacks legal personality - and, possibly, a Scottish partnership.[36] The precise extent of member limited liability in a US LLP will depend on the state where it was formed: *see* section 7.2.4.2.

Hence the limited liability of partners in a partnership is now both well established and extensive, even if such partners take part in running and managing the partnership business. Limited liability is a weak basis for differentiating a partnership from a 'body corporate', even though member liability in a LP or LLP may still be somewhat greater than that of a shareholder in a limited company.

---

34. The 1907 Act was amended in 2017 to make it even easier to use a LP as a tax transparent venture capital investment fund. The revised 1907 Act now permits (*see* section 8D) the designation of a LP as a 'private fund limited partnership' (PFLP) if the partnership agreement is in writing and the partnership is a 'collective investment scheme' for regulatory purposes. The meaning of 'collective investment scheme' is discussed in section 4.3.6.1. A limited partner in a PFLP need not make a capital contribution, unlike a limited partner in a 1907 Act LP which is not a PFLP. The liability of a PFLP limited partner is limited by the partnership property available to the general partner(s) to meet the debts and obligations of the LP. Section 4(3A) allows a limited partner in a PFLP to withdraw any capital contribution it makes from the LP without compromising its limited liability. This option is not available to a limited partner in a non-PFLP, although an equivalent effect can be achieved if most of a limited partner's capital contribution takes (as it usually does) the form of a profit-linked, subordinated loan. Section 6A contains a non-exhaustive list of activities which a PFLP limited partner may undertake without compromising its limited liability. This list part-clarifies a grey area in LP law. There is also no obligation to publicise in the London Gazette the transfer of a PFLP limited partner's interest.
35. This limitation may not apply if there is a direct default of the member, such as becoming liable to a third party for negligence.
36. *See* paragraph 6.10, and the corresponding footnote 8, of the 2003 Joint Report on Partnership Law of the English and Scottish Law Commissions (Law Com 283; Scottish Law Com 192) (hereinafter '*the Law Commission*') www.scotlawcom.gov.uk/publications/reports/2000-9.

2.9.4 Transferability of Interests

The free transferability of membership interests cannot be a fundamental difference between a 'body corporate' and a 'partnership'. Partnership rights can be transferred, in whole or part. However, without the consent of the other partners, a partnership interest typically cannot be transferred so as to confer full partner status on the transferee. Absent such consent, the transferee has at most the right to the economic fruits of the partnership interest and must accept the account of profits agreed by the partners. It has no right to vote as a partner nor to take part in firm management nor to inspect the partnership books.[37]

However, the articles of association of private companies typically place very severe restrictions on the transferability of members' interests. These restrictions are typically enforceable by the directors of the company. They are often reinforced with restrictions directly enforceable among the members themselves and set out in a confidential shareholders' agreement. All these private company transfer restrictions are likely to be at least as strict as those applying to interests in partnerships. They may even prevent a transfer of any of the economic benefits of a shareholding.

While a partner may be unable unilaterally to transfer the right to full partnership status to a purported transferee of its interest, the would-be transferor remains a full partner with rights as such, e.g., to vote on management issues. In a private company, the would-be transferor of a company share can be in no better position than the proposed transferee because its shares only entitle it to an ownership interest in the company but not to take part in management. This reflects the formal split between ownership and management which is a more obvious feature of a 'body corporate' than of a partnership, although most partners in large modern partnerships have little real say in entity management matters.

Overall the ability to transfer full interests in an entity is not a strong indicator of whether it is a partnership or a body corporate.

2.9.5 Legal Personality and Members' Entitlement to Profits as They Arise

Legal personality is not necessarily a key difference between a 'body corporate' and a 'partnership'. A 'body corporate' is by definition a legal person, and one which is distinct from its members, with full capacity to acquire rights and incur obligations on its own behalf, thanks to its incorporation. A UK LLP is a type of 'body corporate', but with a special tax status.

By contrast, an English law partnership is an aggregate, with no legal personality distinct from that of the partners. This lack of legal personality is a feature of partnerships found in a number of British Commonwealth jurisdictions. It does not mean that the partnership is a 'nothing'. English law recognises the concept of

37. Section 31 1890 Act. However, section 6(5)(b) Limited Partnerships Act 1907 provides that 'A limited partner may, with the consent of the general partners, assign his share in the partnership, and upon such an assignment *the assignee shall become a limited partner with all the rights of the assignor* [emphasis added].'

'partnership property'.[38] Such property (which is not always easy to identify in practice) is segregated from the personal property of the partners, even though the partnership is not a legal person. It must be held and applied exclusively for the purposes of the partnership and in accordance with the partnership agreement. An English law partnership is a contract under which each partner is both a principal and agent for the other partners when acting in the usual course of partnership business.[39] Hence the partners carry on the required 'business in common' together directly and co-own the 'partnership property' in the manner required by the partnership agreement and the 1890 Act (including the rules on 'partnership property').

By contrast, a partnership (limited or otherwise) formed under Scottish law has separate legal personality even though it too is formed purely by contract.[40] Section 4(2) of the 1890 Act clearly indicates that a Scottish partnership is nevertheless a 'partnership' for the purposes of that Act.

The nature of a Scottish partnership has been explored in tax litigation. *Major v Brodie*[41] is discussed in detail below. Scottish partnerships were further explored in *Memec* (*see* section 2.12) and *Anson* (*see* section 2.14). Although their legal personality probably does not give rise to 'perpetual succession',[42] it means that the Scottish firm can be the debtor or creditor (and perhaps the employer) of one of its partners. The partners together with the Scottish firm carry on the required 'business in common', although there is debate (*see* section 2.9.6) whether the partners do so purely as agents of the partnership entity (the view of the Law Commission) or both as agents of the partnership and as principals in their own right. Scottish partners are concurrently liable, jointly and severally, with the partnership itself, for partnership debts (effectively acting as guarantors). The Scottish partnership is not a nominee or trustee for the partners. Hence it can own partnership property, and partnership assets are not commingled with the personal assets of a partner. Overall, the legal personality of a Scottish firm is a less absolute form of legal personality[43] than that of a 'body corporate', which is a distinct 'legal person' entirely separate from its members from time to time. Hence it, not they, carries on its activities, acquires rights and incurs liabilities to creditors, even if it is an unlimited company. The members of a body

---

38. As defined in section 20 of the 1890 Act.
39. Section 5 of the 1890 Act.
40. *See* Lord President Cooper giving the leading judgment in *Mair v Wood* 1948 SC 83.
41. [1998] STC 491.
42. Paragraph 2.8 of the Law Commission *supra* doubts whether the legal personality of a Scottish partnership can continue on a change of partners. No conclusive answer has been reached about whether a partner can be the employee of a Scottish partnership, given its separate legal personality: *see Allison v Allison's Trustees* (1904) 6 F 496 and *Fife County Council v The Minister of National Insurance* 1947 SC 629. A member of an English partnership cannot be its employee, arguably because the partnership, not being a legal person, cannot be both employer and employee but, more importantly, because a partner is a 'co-adventurer not an employee': *see* Lord Carnwath in *Clyde & Co v Bates van Winkelhof* [2014] 1 WLR 2047 in paragraph 59.
43. Similar issues arise in Canada in relation to partnerships (sociétés de personnes') created under Quebec law, which is derived from pre-1789 French law. Views differ about whether such partnerships are fully fledged legal persons or merely exhibit elements of juridical personality such as a 'separate patrimony': *see* Nathan Boidman and Michael N. Kandev: 'Foreign Entity Classification and the Meaning of "Corporation"/"Société" in the Income Tax Act' (2009) Canadian Tax Journal, Volume 57, Issue 4, 800 and especially at 894 and 902.

corporate have no interest in its assets nor in its underlying profits. The same is apparently not the case with a Scottish partnership, although there is debate about the degree of separateness between the partnership entity (which is not a nominee or trustee) and the partners.[44] This is an important reminder that the concept of legal personality may contain different gradations of such personality. That exhibited by a Scottish partnership is not the same as the legal personality of a 'body corporate' incorporated under Scottish law.

As Peter Gibson LJ said in the Court of Appeal in *Memec v IRC* [1998] STC 754 at 765:

> Even a Scottish partner has an (indirect) interest in the profits of the partnership as they accrue as well as in the assets of the partnership. In a real sense the profits and assets are the profits and assets of the partners, the firm, their collective alter ego,[45] merely receiving those profits and holding those assets for the partners who are the firm. They are jointly and severally liable for the firm's debts.

Peter Gibson LJ in particular refers to Scottish partners having an indirect interest in partnership profits 'as they accrue'. A member of a company has no such interest in company profits which belong to the company alone as they accrue. Instead, it must await a company resolution to distribute, at which time the member acquires a right to a separate income stream: dividends.

The right of a member to underlying profits as they arise is a key difference for UK tax purposes in deciding if an entity is a 'body corporate' or a partnership, even where the latter has separate legal personality (as in Scotland). Put another way, a very valuable identifier of a 'business in common' within section 1(1) of the 1890 Act is the putative partners' right to profits as they arise.[46] This is more important than the mutual agency of the partners, unlimited joint liability for partnership debts or a

44. The Law Commission note (in paragraph 2.25 of their final report *supra*) that the separate personality of a Scottish partnership prevents any partner suing for damage to partnership property or having an insurable interest in such property. However, a partner joining a Scottish partnership is not liable for debts of the partnership before joining because (despite the firm's separate personality) those debts are regarded as the debts of other partners: *see* Avery Jones: Partnerships *supra* [2002] British Tax Review 375 at 405.
45. The 'alter ego' comment needs to be treated with caution. It is not the observation of a Scottish lawyer and should not be read as meaning that a Scottish partnership holds partnership assets on trust for the partners. In the Supreme Court in *Anson v HMRC* [2015] STC 1777, Lord Reed (a distinguished Scottish judge) observed that a partner in a Scottish partnership has an incorporeal movable right (a partnership share) but no direct proprietary interest in partnership assets. This is consistent with the view noted in fn 44.
46. The 1890 Act codifies the existing common law of partnership, which is not displaced by it unless inconsistent with it: *see* section 46 of the 1890 Act. A number of pre-1890 cases suggest that a partnership is primarily defined by the right of members to profits: *see Holme v Hammond* (1872) LR 7 Ex 218 at 234; and *Pooley v Driver* (1877) 5 Ch 458 at 473-476. In *Holme v Hammond,* Martin B (at pp. 228-229) and Cleasby B (at p. 234) indicated that the entitlement to profits must be accompanied by a voluntary contribution to capital of the putative partnership (although not all partnerships in fact require capital). In *Pooley v Driver,* Sir George Jessel MR relied on the criterion of profit entitlement to conclude that a so-called profit-linked loan in fact created a relationship of 'dormant and active partners' between the lender and the borrower (who was actively carrying on the business which was being funded). The lender was effectively a limited partner in a case which, however, predated the Limited Partnerships Act 1907. A similar case was *Lindsay Woodward & Hiscox v IRC* 18 TC 43, although the factual basis for concluding that

partner's proprietary interest in the assets of the partnership. It is also a more reliable criterion for determining whether entities formed outside the UK are 'partnerships' for the purposes of section 1121 CTA 2010. Section 1121's reference to a 'partnership' is not limited to UK entities. Hence this concept should not be applied to non-UK entities in a manner which is too heavily tied to English partnership law (under which partnerships are not legal persons but are contracts based on mutual agency).

The previous paragraph does not mean that entitlement to profits as they arise is the only litmus test of whether a particular person is a partner in an entity which is clearly a partnership. Especially in relation to English law-type partnerships conducting an active business, not investment, there may be a 'business in common' within section 1(1) of the 1890 Act, and a person may be a partner even where only entitled to a fixed sum regardless of the profits of the business.[47] This is especially true where each putative partner is agent of the other(s) for all acts done in the course of the business.

The separate legal personality of a Scottish partnership reflects French civil law's influence on Scottish law.[48] In other jurisdictions (notably those influenced by civil law), entities regarded as partnerships often have legal personality (or at least, as in Germany, full legal capacity which English law would regard as equivalent to legal personality). As discussed later (e.g., section 3.8), the legal personality of civil law partnerships is closely linked to the fact that the law of agency works differently in civil law jurisdictions from English and Scottish law.

Most partnerships formed under state law in the US have separate legal personality (although Delaware permits opting out of this separate personality).[49] This legal

there was a partnership, rather than a loan carrying a profit-linked return, was more marginal. There may also be cases (*see* fns 29 and 47) where entities are partnerships even if profits are *not* shared.

47. *See* the Court of Appeal in *Tiffin v Lester Aldridge LLP* [2012] IRLR 391. This concerned the employment rights of a 'fixed share partner' in a law firm which was a UK LLP. The individual in fact had a share of profits. Rimer LJ, giving the sole reasoned judgment, nevertheless considered (at paragraphs 19-24) earlier authorities on the 1890 Act, all of which appear to have related to English law general partnerships providing professional services, e.g., *Stekel v Ellice* [1973] 1 All ER 465 and *M Young Legal Associates v Zahid Solicitors (a firm)* [2006] EWCA Civ 613. He concluded that all that was needed after the 1890 Act was an overall aim to make a profit coupled with a 'business in common', namely one where each putative partner is the agent of the others for all acts done in the course of the business. In such cases, a person could be a partner even if only entitled to a fixed sum. This decision seems most relevant when deciding if a particular person can be a partner in an entity which is clearly a partnership based on mutual agency (as under English law) and where partners are not effectively excluded from acting as agents of the other partners (as would be standard in a LP). The need for at least some members to be entitled to profits remains a hallmark of partnership: *see* fn 13. Hence in the *M Young Legal Associates* case, the *Blackpool Martin* case was seen as one where there was no 'carrying on of a business' at all by the rotary club for the purposes of the 1890 Act.
48. In *Mair v Wood supra*, Lord President Cooper dated to the seventeenth century the separate legal personality of a Scottish partnership.
49. 6 Delaware Chapter 15-201(a). There seems to be no explicit facility to opt out of separate personality in the case of a Delaware LP: *see* S. 17-201(b) Delaware Revised Uniform Limited Partnership Act, although the contrary is suggested at Part 98.26.1 in James Kessler QC: 'Taxation of Non-residents and Foreign Domiciliaries'. 18th edition, Key Haven Publications Ltd 2019-2020 ('Kessler'). One commentator has queried whether 15-201(a) would be effective to deny a Delaware general partnership legal personality: *see* Kimberly Blanchard: 'The Tax

personality reflects the US Revised Uniform Partnership legislation, which accentuates the 'entity theory' of partnership, not least to avoid legal problems which could otherwise arise from membership changes giving rise to a 'new' partnership.[50] Therefore, in the US, legal personality goes hand in hand (unlike Scottish law) with a form of perpetual succession for partnerships.

To summarise, the presence or absence of legal personality is not a key difference between a 'body corporate' and a 'partnership', but the quality of that separate personality may be highly relevant, especially if it affects whether members are entitled to the entity's profits as they arise. The Scottish partnership illustrates how partners can be entitled to profits as they arise even if the separate personality of the firm means that it, not the partners, beneficially owns the partnership's assets. Assets (a property law concept) and profits (an accounting concept) are two different things, as will be further discussed in section 2.14.

2.9.6 *Major v Brodie*

At this point, it is convenient to consider *Major v Brodie.*[51] This was a successful taxpayer appeal in the English High Court against a decision to deny two individuals a tax deduction for interest paid by them on business loans. The individuals were partners in a Scottish general partnership A. Partnership A then became a partner, with an unrelated individual, in another Scottish general partnership, B. It was agreed that the two Scottish partnerships were separate legal persons. Therefore, it was possible for A to be a partner in B. The key question was whether B was carrying on its business of farming alone (being a separate entity) or whether A was also carrying on that business because it was a partner of B. The UK tax authorities argued that only B was carrying on the farming business because of its separate entity status. Therefore, the tiered partnership structure meant that no relief was available because the interest was being paid by partners in partnership A, which was not doing any relevant farming.

The court rejected this argument and decided in favour of the taxpayer. Distinguished experts opined on Scottish partnership law and what the separate personality of a Scottish partnership entailed. The lowest court, the Special Commissioner of Income Tax, made the all-important findings of fact on the Scottish legal position. It preferred the testimony of the expert appointed by the taxpayer and found that the business of partnership B was being carried on both by the partnership entity itself and, crucially, by its partners which of course included partnership A.

When classifying entities for UK tax purposes, Scottish partnerships are a helpful UK domestic example of how an entity with legal personality is not automatically a 'body corporate'. However, Scottish partnerships are in a somewhat different position to putative 'partnerships' with separate legal personality formed outside the UK. The

Significance of Legal Personality: A US View'. New York University School of Law 2015 Colloquium on Tax Policy and Public Finance, at 51-52.

50. *See* Gerald Montagu: '*Anson* and Entity Classification Revisited in Light of Brexit: Can an LLC Constitute a "Body Corporate"?' [2016] British Tax Review 466 at 488-489.

51. [1998] STC 491.

1890 Act applies UK wide and makes clear that its concept of partnership applies to partnerships formed under Scottish law.[52]

Section 4 provides:

> (1) Persons who have entered into partnership with one another are for the purposes of this Act called collectively a firm, and the name under which their business is carried on is called the firm-name.
> (2) *In Scotland a firm is a legal person distinct from the partners of whom it is composed* [emphasis added].

Section 5 then provides:

> Every partner is *an agent of the firm and his other partners* [emphasis added] for the purpose of the business of the partnership; and the acts of every partner who does any act for carrying on in the usual way business of the kind carried on by the firm of which he is a member bind the firm and his partners. ...

These rules apart from section 4(2) are meant to apply across the UK. The court in *Major v Brodie* was mindful of that. It was also keen to ensure that the tax rules on interest relief should produce a uniform outcome in England and Wales on the one hand and in Scotland on the other, despite differences in partnership law. This approach reflects the earlier decision in *R v General Commissioners of Income Tax for the City of London, ex parte Gibbs,*[53] regarding rules (now superseded) on computing English partnership profits where the make-up of the partnership changed. Three judges in the House of Lords made comments about how taxing statutes applicable to both England and Scotland should be applied uniformly, despite differences between the English and Scottish law of partnership. Those comments were not strictly necessary for the decision but they are clear. Viscount Simon L.C. said:[54]

> So far as English law is concerned, it is indisputable that a partnership firm is not a single person, though a different view obtains in Scotland, and in construing a taxing Statute which applies in England and Scotland alike, it is desirable to adopt a construction of statutory words which avoids differences of interpretation of a technical character such as are calculated to produce inequalities in taxation as between citizens of the two countries.

With this in mind, the court in *Major v Brodie* preferred the expert testimony put forward by the taxpayer. It ruled that while a Scottish partnership, and not its members, owns partnership assets beneficially, both the partnership (in that case, B) and its partners (including A) carry on the partnership business. This creates the necessary 'business in common' required by section 1(1) and is consistent with section 5.[55]

---

52. The bill giving rise to the 1890 Act was in existence for fifteen years and apparently, the provisions regarding Scottish partnerships were inserted at the eleventh hour, at the instigation of Lord Watson: *see* paragraph 6.6 and footnote 5 of the Law Commission *supra*.
53. 24 TC 221.
54. 24 TC 221 at 243-244.
55. The findings of the English court regarding Scottish partnership law are not Scottish legal precedent but merely findings of fact regarding the law of another jurisdiction (Scotland), based on contested expert evidence. In particular, the two experts disagreed. There was a similar clash

It is not easy to analogise from the tax treatment of a Scottish partnership when classifying a non-UK entity, even if both have separate legal personalities. A Scottish partnership is an amalgam of civil and common law influences. Besides, the special factors prompting the court to treat it as within section 1(1) of the 1890 Act do not apply to a non-UK 'partnership'. There is no equivalent for non-UK entities of section 4(2). *Ex parte Gibbs*[56] is equally inapplicable.[57]

A Scottish partnership's legal personality also has a different quality from the full juristic personality of a body corporate, as was made clear in the expert evidence in *Major v Brodie*. For example, the partners are directly entitled to the firm's profits and are liable for its debts along with the firm itself. In effect, they act as guarantors (unlike the shareholders of a UK unlimited company who cannot be sued directly by company creditors). Furthermore, a Scottish partnership probably lacks perpetual succession. Whether these are characteristics of other non-UK 'partnerships' with separate personality will depend on the facts and especially the relevant non-UK law.

Nevertheless, a Scottish partnership is a UK domestic entity where, despite its separate legal personality, partners are entitled to profits as they arise. That entitlement, which is fully respected for UK tax purposes, does not stem from partners having a proprietary interest in the Scottish partnership and its assets. Scots law has no concept of equitable proprietary rights. It simply divides rights between rights 'in rem' and contractual rights. As was pointed out in *Anson v HMRC* [2015] STC 1777,[58] the rights of a partner in a Scottish partnership are a 'ius crediti' or incorporeal movable right, not a right in rem.[59] Other entities in other jurisdictions (especially civil law jurisdictions) which purport to be partnerships may well have similar characteristics: *see* section 2.14.

---

of expert opinion on Scottish partnerships before the Supreme Court in *Anson v HMRC* [2015] STC 1777. Both sides were invited to make submissions on the nature of a Scottish partnership, because the taxpayer sought to analogise between the legal personality of a Scottish partnership and that of a Delaware LLC. The taxpayer (unlike in *Major v Brodie*) argued that a partner in a Scottish partnership was only an agent of the partnership, which alone (being a separate legal person) was carrying on the partnership business. Taxpayer counsel also argued that section 5 of the 1890 Act effectively did not apply in Scotland to the extent it made a partner agent for fellow partners, rather than for the firm. Scottish counsel for HMRC argued the opposite, i.e., that a partner in a Scottish partnership was both a principal and an agent of the Scottish firm, when carrying on that firm's business. The position of the taxpayer that a partner is only an agent of a Scottish partnership finds some support in paragraph 2.11, p. 8 of the Law Commission *supra* but seems inconsistent with *Major v Brodie*. There is no further discussion of these points in the judgment of the Supreme Court in *Anson*. The author gratefully acknowledges the assistance of the UK Supreme Court staff when accessing the archived recordings of the oral argument in *Anson*.

56. 24 TC 221.
57. Somewhat similar arguments are made in Angelo Nikolakakis: 'Anson v HMRC: Sour Grapes and Maple Syrup – Has the UK just adopted Check-the Box?' [2015] British Tax Review 538, especially at 549-550.
58. *See* section 2.14.
59. Section 20 of the 1890 Act, which deals with partnership property, may give Scottish partners, like English partners, additional statutory rights to ensure that partnership property is held and applied in accordance with the partnership agreement. However, it is still the Scottish partnership itself which owns that property, unlike an English partnership.

Major v Brodie also shows how one Scottish partnership can itself be a partner in another partnership, because a Scottish partnership is a person. If the Scottish partnership is a partner in another partnership, its own partners from time to time are also partners in that other partnership, but only in their capacity as partners in the Scottish partnership.

Recently, the Upper Tribunal, in *BCM Cayman LP, Bluecrest Capital Management Cayman Limited v HMRC* [2022] STC 1586, has considered whether a Cayman limited partnership can become a partner in an English limited partnership. English and Cayman limited partnerships are not legal persons. So the question boiled down to whether, if the corporate general partner of the Cayman partnership became a partner in the English partnership (and indeed signed the English partnership deed in the name of the Cayman partnership, not just its own name), would the other partners from time to time in the Cayman partnership also become partners in that English partnership?

The answer partly depended on the formal documentary procedure for admitting partners to the English partnership. The Upper Tribunal ruled that only the corporate general partner became a partner in the English partnership. The other Cayman partners did not. This seems too restrictive. The corporate general partner of the Cayman partnership had clearly joined the English partnership in its capacity as general partner of the Cayman partnership. It had in fact executed a new English partnership deed under which the Cayman partnership (despite its lack of legal personality) was 'admitted' by the other partners. The documentation indicated that the parties never intended the general partner to join as a purely stand-alone entity.

The decision also opens up an unwelcome gap between partnerships with and without legal personality. Had a Scottish partnership joined the English partnership, it would have been very hard to dispute that all the Scottish partners also became partners in the English partnership. However, this should not create a fundamental difference with a Cayman partnership 'joining' an English partnership. While a Scottish partnership is a legal person, its personality differs from that of a body corporate, as discussed above. The Scottish partnership and its partners are two sides of the same coin. A body corporate and its shareholders are not.

2.9.7 Perpetual Succession

The relevance of 'perpetual succession' when defining a 'body corporate' has already been mentioned in section 2.6. If an entity lacking 'perpetual succession' cannot be a 'body corporate', does the presence of 'perpetual succession' prevent an entity from being a 'partnership' for UK tax purposes? Probably not.[60] 'Perpetual succession'

60. Section 6(2) Limited Partnerships Act 1907 already provides that a LP registered under that Act shall not be dissolved because of the death or bankruptcy of a limited partner. In paragraph 3.16 of their final report, the Law Commission *supra* recommended that all English law partnerships should in future be legal entities with a presumption of their continuity on a change of partners. They saw this as remedying a major flaw in the 1890 Act, which provides no such continuity. They did not regard such a change as preventing an entity being a partnership. Indeed, such a change would better match commercial reality because third parties contract with a major partnership as it exists from time to time and pay little heed to changes in its membership. Such

should not be a key distinction between a 'body corporate' and a 'partnership'. Besides, many modern UK partnerships are in fact UK LLPs which, being a form of body corporate, exhibit 'perpetual succession'. It would therefore be discriminatory if 'perpetual succession' in respect of a non-UK entity (e.g., a US LLP) meant that it could never be treated as a partnership for UK tax purposes. It can in fact be largely a matter of legal drafting whether an entity has or lacks 'perpetual succession'.[61] Section 2.10 relates to a French entity now accepted by HMRC as a 'partnership' which nevertheless has 'perpetual succession' unless agreed to the contrary.

2.9.8 Public Recognition

Another perceived distinction between a 'body corporate' and a 'partnership' is that the former is brought into being by an official public step (e.g., registration or a legislative act), whereas the latter is essentially a creature of contract, with little or no overlay in the form of public official approval. While this may reflect the way in which companies and partnerships are formed in the UK, there is no necessary reason why this should be so in other jurisdictions. Again, the example of the French entity in section 2.10 is instructive.

Overall, it is increasingly difficult to find clear substantive differences between a partnership and a 'body corporate'. The best available distinguishing feature is whether members have a legal entitlement to underlying profits of the entity as they arise, even if this entitlement is only contractual.[62] If so, this highlights a degree of member involvement and interest in the entity's underlying business which differs from the classic split between management and members in a 'body corporate' and is consistent with the 'business in common' concept in section 1(1) of the 1890 Act.[63]

---

a change would also align English law with the US Revised Uniform Partnership Act of 1994. The Law Commission's proposal has yet to be turned into law.

61. *See* the discussion at 478-484 in Montagu: 'Anson and Entity Classification Revisited in Light of Brexit'.
62. The author has read arguments that entitlement to profits as they arise cannot be the litmus test of whether an organisation is fiscally transparent because partners in a Scottish partnership do not have 'that kind of property' in firm profits. However, this seems hard to reconcile with the nature of a Scottish partnership, as per sections 4(2) and 5 of the 1890 Act. Besides, as already discussed, Scottish partnerships are a special case and the same point may not apply to other non-UK entities. The same commentator also said that the key factor determining 'transparency' is the ability of members to remove profits from the organisation without any other person restricting that ability. 'Profit' is an accounting concept, not a property law concept. It is an abstract measure of the health of a business. Therefore, what is meant by 'removing profits', if profits are not a legal asset which can be owned? Is 'removing profits' referring to distributions of assets to entity members in respect of profit entitlements (e.g., 'drawings' in a partnership)? If so, it would be odd for transparency to hinge on an automatic entitlement to such distributions: any business organisation (including a partnership) will wish to restrict distributions from time to time, in order to manage cash flow prudently.
63. There is still an element of unreality about drawing such fundamental distinctions between entities on the basis of whether members are entitled to underlying profits as they arise. This entitlement may be largely a legal and drafting fiction, whether or not the entity has separate legal personality. Given the tight and secretive management of many modern partnerships, including wide management discretion to adjust profit shares and retain cash, the idea that partners are entitled to profits as they arise is often theoretical.

With that provisional conclusion in mind,[64] the next step is to review the limited case law which has attempted to classify various non-UK entities (apart from trusts) and to determine if they are 'tax-transparent'.

2.10 DREYFUS

2.10.1 Background

In the late 1920s, the Court of Appeal heard *Dreyfus v IRC*.[65] This was not connected to the infamous case which convulsed France at the start of the twentieth century. Rather it involved the UK income taxation of the grain trading activities of a French 'société en nom commandite' or SNC based in Paris but carrying on business in the UK. The SNC had two members, the Dreyfus brothers, who also managed it. They were non-UK-residents. The case predated corporation tax. Hence the SNC was subject to UK income tax on its UK trading profits. It had paid this tax. The question was whether the Dreyfus brothers could also be assessed to 'supertax' on their putative shares of SNC profits. 'Supertax' was a predecessor of the higher rates of UK income tax and was payable only by 'individuals'. The UK tax authorities argued that the Dreyfus brothers were assessable to supertax because they were partners in a partnership, i.e., the SNC. Then as now, partnerships were 'transparent' for the purposes of taxing their income (although assessment mechanics were different). Hence, an individual partner paid supertax on his or her share of the underlying income of the partnership, whether or not that income was distributed. The Dreyfus brothers successfully appealed against the supertax assessment on the basis that the SNC was not a partnership for UK tax purposes. The Court of Appeal agreed. It did not definitively decide what kind of entity the SNC was, although there are hints in the judgments that it was a type of 'body corporate'.

2.10.2 Significance

Dreyfus is so far the only significant UK tax case in which entity classification and 'tax transparency' issues have been considered in respect of inbound UK investment. It also illustrates the approach of the UK courts when classifying non-UK entities. This differs from their approach when classifying UK entities. The non-UK tax treatment of the entity is not relevant. Its nature is ascertained by reference to the non-UK law under which it is formed and the specific facts of the case, including any documentation

64. There was oblique legislative support for this conclusion in the definition of 'corporate entity' in the (now repealed) 'worldwide debt cap' rules in Part 7 TIOPA. Section 340 defined a 'corporate entity' as a UK or non-UK 'body corporate' *or any other entity meeting conditions A and B*. Condition A was that those with an interest in the entity must hold 'shares in the entity, or interests corresponding to shares'. Condition B was that the profit entitlement of each person with an interest in the entity 'depends upon a decision that is taken by the entity or members of the entity, and is taken after the period in which profits arise'. Part 7 was replaced by the more stringent corporate interest restriction rules in Part 10 TIOPA.
65. 14 TC 560.

governing the entity. Therefore, classifying non-UK entities is very fact-sensitive. Evidence of the relevant non-UK law governing the entity will often be crucial. Ascertaining that law requires a finding of fact by the UK court, usually based on expert evidence. Once the entity's nature has been worked out, one classifies it for UK tax purposes by seeking analogies with relevant UK entities. In short, the UK uses a 'resemblance' approach to classify non-UK entities.

2.10.3 Findings

In the light of the expert evidence, the court regarded the SNC as too structurally dissimilar from an English law partnership for it to be a 'partnership' for UK tax purposes. Hence its members were not partners, and no supertax was payable. Particular points were as follows:

(a) The SNC did not come into being simply because its members agreed to form it, unlike an English or Scottish partnership. It came into being by virtue of public registration. This was very different to the process for forming a partnership in the UK.
(b) Once formed, the SNC was not the nominee or 'alter ego' of its members. It and not its members carried on the business (unlike an English or, arguably, a Scottish partnership). So there was no 'business in common'. The SNC owned the assets and earned the income of the business. It incurred the liabilities in its own name and for itself alone. In short, its legal personality was more absolute than that of a Scottish partnership, although members of the SNC could, like Scottish partners, be directly liable for its debts if the SNC failed to satisfy them.
(c) SNC members had no automatic entitlement to its profits as they arose, unlike partners in an English or Scottish partnership. A prior resolution of the SNC was required before a member's entitlement to profit could crystallise. In that sense, the member's position was similar to a shareholder in a company.
(d) Members were not agents for each other, as in an English partnership. At most, they were agents of the SNC itself.[66]

2.10.4 Judgments

The following passages from the two fully reasoned judgments are illuminating.

Lord Hanworth MR stated:[67]

> ... we must respect the foreign entity properly established ... it is a matter of the status which an entity brings over here with it. Now this being the case, how can it be said that in respect of this trade ... it can be dealt with as the individual profits

66. This point overlooks the fact that in a Scottish partnership (a separate entity), partners are also agents of the entity and arguably not of each other (*see* expert evidence of Professor Gretton in *Major v Brodie* [1998] STC 491). Yet a Scottish partnership is still a 'partnership' for UK tax purposes, although its status is 'sui generis'.
67. 14 TC 560 at 577.

> or individual trade of the two partners, when we are told in plain and clear words that the 'société' does not owe its existence to the combination of the parties, that it is a legal person distinct from the individuals of which it is composed? ... it seems to me quite plain ... that [the profits] are being earned for the 'société' or the French entity, and not for these men, and that these men ... are not entitled to, and would not know what was their interest in the business over here unless and until that declaration had been made, according to the resolutions of which we have a translation in the case. ... *We have to recognise that it is not the business of these persons, they are not the persons who are carrying on the trade, and there is not merely an imaginary, but a legally constituted entity which is carrying on the business* [emphasis added].

Lawrence LJ said:[68]

> Without going through all the findings [of fact] in the case, I would point out one or two which to my mind really decide this case, the first being this, that *on complying with certain formalities, which, as I understand it, consisted of depositing a document with the Registrar of the Commercial and Civil Court and publishing a notice in the paper, an entity, to use a neutral term, springs into existence, and that entity is one which owns the property of the [SNC], and which incurs the liability in respect of the debts of the concern, and which has the sole right to receive the earnings of the concern, and has the control of the distribution of the profits. Added to that, it is plain on the findings that a member of that entity is not an agent for the others in carrying on the business of the concern* [emphasis added]. Without going into other findings ..., those facts alone seem to me to be wholly inconsistent with the notion of a partnership as existing in this country, and that being the only question to be decided in the case, I think that is all that need be said. It is quite true that the position of persons who are members of such a Society as this may be likened more or less to that of shareholders in a limited or unlimited company in England, and also more or less to the position of partners in a partnership firm. But whatever be their position, they are not ... partners within the meaning of the Income Tax Acts.

Lawrence LJ clearly saw some parallels between the position of a SNC member and a shareholder in a UK unlimited company. The judgments at no point referred explicitly to Scottish partnerships.[69] However, there appeared to be significant differences between this SNC and a Scottish partnership, even though both were separate legal persons.

2.10.5 The Impact of *Dreyfus*

Dreyfus has barely been discussed in subsequent cases, perhaps because those cases mainly concerned 'transparency' questions in relation to outbound investment from the UK, where the narrow issue did not require the court to decide whether a non-UK entity was a 'partnership'.

68. 14 TC 560 at 579.
69. Although Lord Hanworth MR may have had a Scottish partnership in mind when he alluded to an 'imaginary entity'.

The judges worked from an English law paradigm of what a partnership is and how it is formed. Yet for UK tax purposes, there is no reason why the concept of 'partnership' should be limited in this way. The Court of Appeal's approach seems too parochial. Other jurisdictions, especially civil law jurisdictions such as France, have different legal cultures and constructs. The legal form and formation procedure of a 'partnership' under French law may therefore differ significantly from the UK equivalent. A less parochial approach underlies the Supreme Court decision in *Anson*, discussed in section 2.14.

A less parochial application of UK tax concepts to non-UK legal structures was also recommended by the Court of Appeal only a few years after *Dreyfus* in *Ryall v The DuBois Company Ltd.*[70] The key question was whether a UK taxpayer could claim the favourable 'remittance' basis in respect of distributions to it as a member of a German GmbH (the German approximation of the UK private limited company). If its member's interest constituted 'stocks' or 'shares' in the GmbH, then the remittance basis was not available, under the law as it then stood. On the evidence, there were significant differences between the concept of a 'share' under UK company law and the rights and liabilities attaching to a member's interest in a GmbH. However, as Romer LJ said:[71]

> Here it is quite plain that the words 'stocks' or 'shares' cannot be used in their ordinary meaning as the words are used in this country, because, under the Rule in question, they have to be used in connection with foreign companies and, therefore, it is a question of law as to what their meaning is.[72]

70. 16 TC 431.
71. 16 TC 431 at 443. The last part of this statement is a reminder that all UK entity classification and tax transparency questions boil down to the correct legal interpretation of the relevant UK tax rule or concept. In *Dreyfus*, the relevant concept was that of 'partner'. However, interpreting that rule or concept requires a full understanding of the relevant non-UK arrangement in the light of its governing law and, in the author's view, taking full account of the role that the entity plays in its legal system of origin.
72. *Ryall* was not cited in *South Shore Mutual Insurance Co Ltd v Blair* [1999] STC (SCD) 296. There, the court ruled that so-called founder members' deposits of an English company limited by guarantee were not 'issued share capital (by whatever name called)' within what is now section 1119 CTA 2010. Therefore, they were not 'ordinary share capital' for the purposes of creating a corporation tax 'group'. The company had been formed before the 1980 prohibition on companies limited by guarantee having a share capital. It had also been formed without an explicit share capital and the court was not prepared to treat the 'founder members' deposits' as such. They had not only some features of capital but also subordinated debt-like features. They had not been subscribed pursuant to the company's 'memorandum of association'. Overall, this non-binding decision defines 'ordinary share capital' quite conservatively, in a purely UK context and relying quite heavily on UK company law formalities. *Ryall* sensibly suggests a different approach when dealing with non-UK entities. Maybe that approach is now reflected in section 259NE(4)(a) TIOPA, which defines a 'partnership' as 'includ[ing] an entity established under the law of a territory outside the United Kingdom *of a similar character to a partnership* [emphasis added]'. This definition only applies for the purposes of Part 6A TIOPA, which counteracts the UK tax benefits of certain hybrid mismatches. HMRC do not accept this definition as covering a US LLC. To cover a LLC which is 'transparent' in the US, the concept of a 'relevant transparent entity' has been inserted for limited purposes in Part 6A: *see* section 259GB(4C) TIOPA. This new concept is not a general acceptance by HMRC that a US LLC is 'transparent' for UK tax purposes!

In reality, HMRC do not follow *Dreyfus* and typically regard a SNC as 'transparent' for UK tax purposes.[73] Apparently, they believe that the expert evidence was flawed and that under French law, SNC members *are* entitled to profits as they arise. Hence the SNC is 'analogous to a partnership' for UK tax purposes, despite the way in which it is formed (by registration), the more developed nature of its legal personality, the lack of mutual agency and the manner in which it conducts its business.[74]

These revised views on *Dreyfus* are consistent with the earlier discussion about the most important distinction between a 'partnership' and a 'body corporate' for UK tax purposes. Admittedly, paragraph 1673 of the (archived) International Tax Handbook muddies the waters: 'We look for indicators as to whether the Association carries on the business itself or whether the participators do so jointly; and whether the profits accrue directly to the participators or whether they accrue to the association which then distributes them to the participators.' The first part of this quotation jars with the earlier HMRC statement that the SNC in *Dreyfus* was 'analogous to a partnership'. In particular, that SNC carried on the business itself, and there was no mutual agency between its members.

Ultimately, the UK tax status of a particular SNC will depend on its detailed structure, and especially on the legal form of a member's interest in it. Those details may differ from SNC to SNC. In that sense, *Dreyfus* is a decision limited to its specific facts.

As discussed in section 2.13 below, HMRC have a list of criteria which they regard as relevant when deciding whether a non-UK entity is 'transparent'. The status of that list following the Supreme Court decision in *Anson* is unclear. However, if it is applied to the facts of *Dreyfus* (and HMRC's concerns about the expert evidence are put to one side), the Court of Appeal's conclusion seems correct[75]!

Dreyfus remains unsatisfactory because the court never developed a full understanding of where a SNC fits into the French law of business organisations. The forms which partnerships take under civil law systems largely reflect key differences between the law of agency under those systems compared to English law. This is discussed in more detail in section 3. For present purposes, under French law, a SNC is a 'formal' partnership[76] whose creation as a separate fully disclosed entity by registration ensures that the activities of partners bind the entire partnership. Under English law, this would

73. Their detailed position is set out in paragraph 1673 of the old International Tax Handbook (now archived) published by the UK tax authorities.
74. The case stated in *Dreyfus* (*see* 14 TC 560 at 564) suggests that the death or legal incapacity of a partner would not always lead to the SNC's dissolution. In short, there was 'perpetual succession'.
75. *See* John F. Avery Jones CBE: 'The English Dreyfus Case: Categorisation of a French SNC for Tax Purposes in the UK'. Fiscalité et entreprise: politiques et pratiques: eds Mélanges en l'honneur de Jean-Pierre Le Gall. Dalloz 2007, at 325.
76. *See* Avery Jones: Partnerships *supra* [2002] British Tax Review 375 at 380 fn 26, 381, 389 and 394-396. That article also highlights the differences *between* civil law jurisdictions regarding the way in which 'formal' partnerships are created and what form they take. A French 'formal' partnership is regarded as a legal person under French law. This is not necessarily so elsewhere. The Dutch position is closer to the English law position. Registration gives information to third parties about the entity. It confers no particular status on a 'vennootschaap onder firma' or VOF, which lacks legal personality under Dutch law, although it has extensive legal capacity – *see*

not be necessary because the law of agency is different. In other words, the SNC's registration under French law is not about creating an entity where there is a rigid separation between the activities of the entity and those of its members. Hence analogising with the process of incorporating a UK body corporate seems faulty.[77]

2.11 OXNARD

2.11.1 Background

The nature of a civil law partnership was considered by the Court of Appeal in a non-tax case, *Oxnard Financing SA v Rahn and others*.[78] *Dreyfus* was not cited, and the case considered a Swiss general partnership,[79] not a French SNC.

The issue was the procedure for suing, in the English courts, the Swiss partnership and its members. If the entity were a corporation, then it would have been correct to sue the entity itself and not its members.

Uncontested evidence of Swiss law was provided. The court concluded that the entity was a general partnership enjoying a high degree of legal personality enabling it to contract in its own name and to own assets. It was not, however, a corporation and consequently did not have legal personality under Swiss law, which (unlike English law) does not always treat an entity with full legal capacity as being a legal person. Creditor claims against the entity were primarily enforceable against the entity itself, with the partners having full direct liability to creditors on a secondary basis. This is similar to the position of Scottish partners. There was no consideration (unlike *Dreyfus*) of when and how the partners were entitled to the entity's underlying profits, nor the way in which it carried on business.

In reaching its decision, the court relied on an earlier Court of Appeal decision on litigation procedure in *Von Hellfeld v Rechnitzer and Mayer Freres*.[80] That case did concern a French SNC and the court concluded on the basis of expert evidence that the SNC was a partnership. As Phillimore LJ stated at 754-755:

> [The expert evidence is] not enough to shew … that a société en nom collectif is like a corporation in this respect, not merely that it has a separate persona, but that it has separate ownership of property and separate liability from the ownership or liability by or of the persons composing the aggregation.

---

section 7.3.2. In Germany, a 'formal' partnership can have full legal capacity, but not legal personality if its members have liability for the entity's debts.

77. Although an incoming member of a SNC is liable for existing debts of the SNC, which is regarded as carrying on the business itself. This differs from the position regarding an incoming Scottish partner or an incoming member of a Dutch VOF: *see* Avery Jones: Partnerships *supra* [2002] British Tax Review 375 at 405.
78. [1998] 3 All ER 19. *See also* Robert Kent [1999] British Tax Review 125.
79. For further detail, *see* Avery Jones: Partnerships *supra* [2002] British Tax Review 375 at 381 fn 26, 394. Apparently, as in Germany, a Swiss partnership can have legal capacity, but not legal personality, if its members can be directly liable for the entity's debts. This distinction between full legal capacity and legal personality is alien to an English lawyer.
80. [1914] 1 Ch 748.

Again there was no consideration (unlike *Dreyfus*) of when and if the SNC members were entitled to its underlying profits, nor of how the entity was formed or carried on business. The conclusion was the opposite of *Dreyfus*. This highlights how much such cases turn on questions of fact and especially the expert evidence on relevant non-UK law.

2.11.2 Conclusions

Not being tax cases, it is not clear how much weight can be placed on *Oxnard* and *Von Hellfeld*. Details of the expert evidence were sparse. Nevertheless, both cases show that the UK courts have been willing to treat as partnerships non-UK entities with separate legal personality (or, in the case of a Swiss general partnership, full legal capacity consistent, for UK tax purposes, with separate legal personality). The courts in these cases also understood that it is important to evaluate what legal personality does and does not entail, in the circumstances. Both entities had a legal personality which was apparently more developed than that of a Scottish partnership. In particular, the SNC carried on the relevant business. However, as Phillimore LJ makes clear, there was not a sufficient distinction between the rights and liabilities of the entity, versus those of its members, to treat it as a body corporate. The latter is a special kind of legal person where there is a much more absolute dividing line between the entity and its members.

In both these cases, the non-UK entities were respected as 'partnerships' without relying on the special factors bringing a Scottish partnership within section 1(1) of the 1890 Act.

2.12 *MEMEC V IRC*

2.12.1 Introduction

In the late 1990s, the High Court and the Court of Appeal considered a tax transparency question in *Memec plc v IRC*.[81] The question arose in relation to outbound investment by a UK-resident company which owned German subsidiaries. In order to reduce German corporation tax paid by its subsidiaries, the UK-resident company entered into a 'stille Gesellschaft' (or 'silent partnership')[82] agreement with the German subholding company which directly owned the other German subsidiaries. Under that agreement, the UK-resident company obtained the right to be paid 87.84% of the annual profits of the 'silent partnership'. In return, it paid a capital contribution to the German subholding company.

81. [1996] STC 1336, followed in [1998] STC 754.
82. 'Gesellschaft' does not always mean 'partnership' in German. It can also mean 'company' or 'society', in much the same way that in the past, English has used 'company' to refer to both incorporated and unincorporated bodies, as well as to groups of people.

2.12.2 Silent Partnership

In the High Court, Robert Walker J (as he then was) described a 'silent partnership' as follows:[83]

> The essential points are that the silent partner (stille Gesellschafter) makes a capital contribution to a commercial enterprise run by another person who is designated as the owner (Inhaber). The owner remains the owner of the business assets and of the income from those assets as it accrues. The silent partner has no proprietary interest in the assets but has a contractual right to payment of his share of the annual profits (if any) as shown by the partnership accounts, and can sue for damages in the event of any misappropriation. The owner runs the business, though the silent partner has access to information about it. The silent partner is not responsible for liabilities of the partnership beyond the amount of his contribution, but his share of any loss will be debited to his contribution and must be made good out of his share of the profits of later years before any share of profits is distributed to him. On termination of the partnership, the silent partner gets a return of his capital contribution, so far as it has not been lost. A silent partnership has no separate legal personality under German law. Its existence is often unknown to customers dealing with the owner.

The 'silent partnership' in *Memec* was[84] the more common 'typical' silent partnership, created under Article 230 of the German Commercial Code.[85] A rarer variant is the 'atypical' silent partnership. This distinction between 'typical' and 'atypical' is a German tax law distinction, although it reflects certain commercial differences. In particular, in an 'atypical' silent partnership, the silent partner may also be given a vote in partnership affairs and a share of goodwill[86] or of appreciation in the assets of the partnership.[87] Its interest more closely resembles that of a co-entrepreneur, while a 'typical' silent partnership more closely resembles a profit-participating loan. However, such loans ('partiarische Darlehen') are themselves a separate concept under German commercial law. They are not created under Article 230 of the Commercial Code but are governed by section 607 of the Civil Code. Moreover, the lender does not participate in losses nor in the value of assets, unlike a silent partner.[88]

The share of profits payable by the German subholding company in *Memec* to the UK-resident company was deductible within the German subgroup for German corporation tax purposes. It was not, however, deductible for the purposes of the German municipal 'trade tax' on the subgroup's income. To ensure that the whole arrangement did not create additional UK corporation tax, a UK foreign tax credit for this 'trade tax'

83. [1996] STC 1336 at 1345.
84. *See* John F. Avery Jones: 'Memec plc v IRC' [1997] British Tax Review 188.
85. *See* Avery Jones: Partnerships *supra* [2002] British Tax Review 375 at 381 fn 27.
86. *See* Avery Jones: Partnerships *supra* [2002] British Tax Review 384 at fn 38.
87. *See* Bureau Francis Lefebvre, Loyens &Volkmaars, Oppenhoff & Rädler: 'Hybrid Financing'. IBFD Publications BV, Editions Francis Lefebvre 1996, at 4.6.2.2.
88. *See* 'Hybrid Financing' *supra*, at 4.5.2.1.

had to be available to the UK-resident company. Otherwise, the German corporation tax saving would be neutralised by increased UK corporation tax.[89]

2.12.3 No UK Foreign Tax Credit

Various unsuccessful arguments were put forward to show that a UK foreign tax credit for 'trade tax' was available. The first argument was that the 'silent partnership' was 'transparent' for UK tax purposes. If so, what the UK-resident company received from the 'silent partnership' was a share of the very dividend income received by its German subholding company from its own German subsidiaries. If the UK-resident company was receiving a share of those dividends, it could claim a foreign tax credit for the 'trade tax' on the German profits which funded those dividends. It was not strictly necessary to decide whether the 'silent partnership' was a 'partnership' for UK tax purposes, although if it was, then it would be easier to treat it as 'transparent' because of how the UK taxes partnerships.

2.12.4 The High Court

In the High Court,[90] the judge noted the special circumstances of a Scottish partnership but stressed that the key issue was whether the 'silent partnership' was 'transparent' and not whether it was a 'partnership' within section 1(1) of the 1890 Act. Even though the 'silent partnership' lacked legal personality, it was not transparent because the 'stille Gesellschafter' had no proprietary interest in the shares owned by the German subholding company nor in the dividends to which they gave rise. Therefore its right to a share of those dividends was a separate income source, and not dividends from the German subsidiaries.

The judge added:[91]

> Transparency is normally associated with a situation where the ultimate recipient of the income in question has a beneficial interest in it from the start, and moreover the income is not transmuted at some intermediate stage by the need for trustees to exercise a discretion or by its being packaged so as to reach the ultimate recipient in the form of a fixed annuity.

2.12.5 The Court of Appeal

Unlike the High Court, the Court of Appeal focused much more closely on whether the 'silent partnership' fell within section 1(1) of the 1890 Act and was therefore 'transparent' for UK tax purposes. The main judgment was given by Peter Gibson LJ. On the 'transparency' issue, he commented at length:

89. The whole arrangement was a cross-border hybrid financing, the aim being that an additional German tax deduction did not correspondingly increase the tax liability of the UK finance provider.
90. For a discussion of the High Court decision, *see* John F. Avery Jones: 'Memec plc v IRC' [1997] British Tax Review 188.
91. [1996] STC 1336 at 1353j.

The relevant characteristics of an ordinary English partnership are these: (1) the partnership is not a legal entity; (2) the partners carry on the business of the partnership in common with a view to profit (see s 1(1) of the Partnership Act 1890 (the 1890 Act)); (3) each does so both as principal and (see s 5 of the 1890 Act) as agent for each other, binding the firm and his partners in all matters within his authority; (4) every partner is liable jointly with the other partners for all debts and obligations of the firm (see s 9 of the 1890 Act); and (5) the partners own the business, having a beneficial interest, in the form of an undivided share in the partnership assets, including any profits of the business.

A limited partnership differs relevantly only in the following respects: (a) characteristics (2) and (3) above are modified in that the limited partner takes no part in the management of the partnership business (see s 6(1) of the Limited Partnership Act 1907), the ordinary partners acting on his behalf as well as on their own behalf; and (b) the limited partner on entering the partnership is obliged to make a contribution of a sum or sums as capital or property of a stated amount and characteristic (4) above is modified in that the limited partner is only liable up to, but not beyond, the amount so contributed.[92] ...

[A] Scottish partnership differs in the following respects: (a) characteristic (1) above does not apply: the partnership is a legal entity distinct from the partners of whom it is composed, but an individual partner may be charged on a decree of diligence directed against the firm, and on payment [by that partner] of the firm's debts is entitled to pro rata relief from the firm and his other partners (see s 4(2) of the 1890 Act); (b) characteristic (3) above is also modified in that the partner is not a principal but is an agent of the firm and his partners;[93] (c) characteristic (4) above is modified in that the partner is not only jointly but also severally liable; (d) characteristic (5) above is modified in that the assets of the partnership are vested in the partnership legally and beneficially, the interest of each partner in the partnership property being described ... as 'a pro indiviso right in the stock or common fund vested in the partners, firstly for payment of the company debts and then for the partners themselves'. ... However, the partner has an interest [in the partnership] which may be arrested (or seized) by his separate creditors, but only in the hands of the firm, and specific property of the partnership cannot be arrested by such creditors. ...

The justification for treating a Scottish partnership as transparent, though it may be less obvious because of the interposition of the partnership as a legal entity ..., can be perceived in that in substance the position of the partners in relation to the profits is the same as in an English partnership: those profits are earned by the partners carrying on business in common together[94] and are shared in the same way and the partners, whilst not directly owning the business and assets, indirectly do so and have an indirect interest in them which is capable of being arrested by the creditor of a partner.

A silent partnership, whilst ... not being a separate legal entity, differs from both English and Scottish partnerships in a number of respects. [Robert Walker J] considered the decisive point to be the absence of any proprietary right, legal or equitable, enjoyed by [the UK-resident taxpayer] in the shares of the [German]

92. The rules on limited partner contributions have been modified since 2017 in relation to 'PFLPs': *see* section 2.9.3.
93. The expert evidence produced by the taxpayer in *Major v Brodie* [1998] STC 491 suggests that this remark about the Scottish partner not being a principal is questionable. It was also doubted by Scottish counsel for HMRC in *Anson v HMRC* [2015] STC 1777, who had appeared as junior counsel for the taxpayer in *Memec*.
94. This to some extent conflicts with the judge's earlier comment that partners in a Scottish partnership are only agents of the firm, not principals.

> subsidiaries or in the dividends accruing on those shares. That is certainly a strong point of distinction from an English partnership, though it is less obviously so in the case of a Scottish partnership. But even a Scottish partner has an (indirect) interest in the profits of the partnership as they accrue as well as in the assets of the partnership. In a real sense the profits and assets are the profits and assets of the partners, the firm, their collective alter ego, merely receiving those profits and holding those assets for the partners who are the firm.[95] They are jointly and severally liable for the firm's debts. In contrast, though a silent partner is indirectly interested in those profits, in that his entitlement to a share of the profits (or his obligation in respect of the losses) will be computed by reference to the profits of the owner at the end of the year, his interest is purely contractual. A clearer distinction is the point advanced by [counsel for the UK tax authorities] that, *unlike in an English or Scottish partnership, in the silent partnership no business is carried on [by the UK-resident taxpayer and the German subholding company] in common with a view to profit* [emphasis added]. ... The liabilities of the business are those of [the German subholding company] alone, though [the UK-resident company] can be called on by [the German subholding company] to bear its share of losses computed at the end of the year to the extent of its capital contribution. *To a third party, [the UK-resident taxpayer's] role in the silent partnership is irrelevant and may not be known* [emphasis added].
>
> The position of [the UK-resident taxpayer] seems to me to be that of a purchaser who, for a consideration consisting of the contribution of a capital sum and an undertaking to contribute to losses of the owner of a business up to the amount of the contribution, purchases a right to income of a fluctuating amount calculated as a share of the annual profits of the business. Neither in English or Scottish law would that leave [the UK-resident taxpayer] a partner with the German subholding company.

2.12.6 Critique

As in the High Court, *Dreyfus* was not discussed. However, the Court of Appeal was correct to focus on the 'partnership' issue. If there were a 'partnership' by UK standards, then income tax transparency should have followed whether or not the taxpayer had a proprietary interest in the shares owned by the German subholding company and the dividends from them.

The court sought to demonstrate how partners of both an English and Scottish partnership have an 'interest' in partnership income and assets. This reasoning is less convincing, at least as it relates to Scottish partnerships. Furthermore, it is of limited relevance when dealing with a non-UK entity. The most obvious reasons for treating Scottish partnerships as tax transparent 'partnerships' are Scotland-specific: the definition of 'firm' in section 4(2) of the 1890 Act, plus the judicial desire to apply UK-wide tax legislation uniformly across the UK. As *Major v Brodie* illustrates, Scottish academic opinion is not uniform on whether a partner in a Scottish partnership is both a principal and an agent, rather than just an agent of the firm. It is therefore not that easy to

95. If this comment is meant to suggest that a Scottish partnership holds its assets as a trustee or nominee for its partners, then it is not correct.

analogise from Scottish partnerships when classifying non-UK entities which claim to be partnerships.

Functionally, the 'silent partnership' was quite similar to an English LP formed under the Limited Partnerships Act 1907. It lacked legal personality; the silent partner took no part in management; and the silent partner's effective liability was limited to its capital contribution, which it made in exchange for a predefined share of the underlying income of the arrangement. The silent partnership was not identical to an English LP. The silent partner had no direct obligations to creditors of the underlying business, and its identity may well not have been known to them. Nor was the silent partnership officially registered, unlike an English LP.[96]

Germany has other forms of LP such as the Kommanditgesellschaft (KG) and the GmbH & Co KG[97] or indeed the 'atypical' silent partnership. These bear an even closer resemblance to an English LP than a 'typical' silent partnership. Yet that should not prevent a 'typical' silent partnership from being classified for UK tax purposes as another form of LP, structured differently from its UK analogue because German civil law (and especially the civil law of agency) differs from the English common law.[98] A less insular approach to the meaning of 'partnership' for entity classification purposes, with less emphasis on UK paradigms, would be consistent with *Ryall v The DuBois Company Ltd.*[99] Such an approach requires a closer examination of where a 'silent partnership' fits into the range of German legal entities or arrangements.

Since *Memec*, it is even clearer that a 'partnership' is normally 'transparent' for direct tax purposes. For income tax, section 848 ITTOIA states that 'Unless otherwise indicated (whether expressly or by implication), a firm is not to be regarded for income tax purposes as an entity separate and distinct from the partners.'[100] For corporation tax, section 1258 CTA 2009 is effectively identical. Section 59 TCGA performs the same function for both capital gains tax and corporation tax on capital gains: *see* Appendix A.

96. There was presumably no need for such registration (whose sole purpose is to trigger the limited liability of limited partners in an English LP). The silent partner had no direct obligations to creditors of the underlying business anyway.
97. This is a LP where the general partner is a purpose-formed private company, usually with limited net assets of its own. German law even contains a hybrid entity comprising both partnership and company features called the Kommanditgesellschaft auf Aktien or KGaA. The interests of limited, but not general, partners in a KGaA take the form of share capital. There is no clear UK analogue for a KGaA, which is taxed as a body corporate in Germany: *see* 'Hybrid Financing' *supra*, at 4.6.1.
98. For more on this, *see* section 3.8 below.
99. 16 TC 431.
100. This is the 2005 rewrite of section 111 Income and Corporation Taxes Act 1988. Equivalent language was inserted as section 111(1) of the 1988 Act, on the 1994 switch to income tax self-assessment. That led to separate income tax assessments on individual partners (rather than a joint assessment on all partners in the partnership name, which section 111 required pre-1994). A partnership therefore became even less 'entity-like' for UK tax purposes when individual self-assessments replaced joint assessments: *see* Henderson LJ in *Peter Vaines v HMRC* [2018] STC 297, where he stresses that in a partnership, there is a single business carried on by all the partners. Indeed, since the inception of income tax, the underlying partnership business (and not the partnership itself) has always been the 'source' of a partner's income.

Memec needs to be reconsidered in the light of *Anson*: *see* section 3.8 below. *Memec* also prompted the UK tax authorities to publish a list of criteria which they regarded as key when classifying non-UK entities as 'transparent' or not. That list is discussed next.

2.13 THE HMRC LIST

2.13.1 What Does It Say?

This list is in HMRC's International Tax Manual.[101] It has no statutory force but purports to provide guidance on how to classify a non-UK entity as opaque or transparent, taking relevant judicial decisions up to and including *Memec* into account. HMRC stress that the expressions 'opaque' and 'transparent' are not coterminous with 'body corporate' and 'partnership'. That is clear from *Memec* where the opaque 'silent partnership' lacked legal personality so could not be a body corporate. Furthermore, as discussed in Chapter 4, certain trusts can be transparent for UK tax purposes. Transparency is not limited to partnerships, although it may take a different form in relation to other entities.

The six items mentioned 'in particular' on the list are:

(1) Does the foreign entity have a legal existence separate from that of the persons who have an interest in it?
(2) Does the entity issue share capital or something else, which serves the same function as share capital?
(3) Is the business carried on by the entity itself or jointly by the persons who have an interest in it that is separate and distinct from the entity?
(4) Are the persons who have an interest in the entity entitled to share in its profits as they arise; or does the amount of profits to which they are entitled depend on a decision of the entity or its members, after the period in which the profits have arisen, to make a distribution of profits?
(5) Who is responsible for debts incurred as a result of the carrying on of the business: the entity or the persons who have an interest in it?
(6) Do the assets used for carrying on the business belong beneficially to the entity or to the persons who have an interest in it?

All six items are apparently to be considered in the light of the non-UK commercial (but not tax) law governing the entity. No one item is conclusive although (3) and (4) apparently carry particular weight.

101. INTM 180010 www.gov.uk/hmrc-internal-manuals/international-manual/intm180010 (accessed 24 May 2022).

2.13.2 Critique

The status of this list[102] is unclear following *Anson*, which is discussed in section 2.14.

The phraseology of some items is curious and the questions posed are too binary. For example, Scottish partnerships and French SNCs show that there can be varying degrees of separateness between an entity with separate legal personality and its members: does item (1) adequately reflect this? Similar points can be made about items (3), (5) and (6). In relation to item (3), *Major v Brodie*[103] suggests that in some cases, both the separate entity and its members carry on the relevant business. It is not an 'either or' question. Similarly, as was clear in both *Major v Brodie*[104] and *Oxnard v Rahn*,[105] there can be cases where the debts of the separate entity are also the debts of its members (who may be liable to the entity's creditors). In relation to item (6), the Court of Appeal in *Memec* not only said that partners in a Scottish partnership have an 'interest' in its underlying assets but also recognised that those assets are beneficially owned by the partnership entity. It is not clear whether item (6) reflects this possibility, which is likely to arise in the many jurisdictions whose concept of partnership entails separate legal personality.

Overall the list seems too heavily influenced by the English common law conception of partnership, where there is no separate legal personality, and the partners alone carry on the business and own its assets. This seems too restrictive for a list intended to help classify non-UK entities. These are unlikely to align easily with such English common law preconceptions. A good example of this is the SNC in *Dreyfus*.[106] According to HMRC's revised thinking (*see* section 2.10.5), such an entity should be treated as 'transparent' for UK tax purposes because the expert evidence was defective and the SNC members were in fact entitled to its profits as they arose: *see* list item (4). Assuming this is correct, a SNC remains an entity formed by registration which is distinct from its members; it rather than its members carries on its business and beneficially owns its assets; and it is responsible for its business debts even though its members can be liable for them concurrently. Hence only one item on the list (admittedly a stronger factor) clearly points towards the transparency of a SNC.[107]

The list does not include other factors which might indicate the existence of a body corporate (and hence opacity), e.g., limited liability or whether the entity continues in existence regardless of changes in its membership ('perpetual succession'). Item 2 focuses on whether the entity has share capital, but there is no mention

102. The list is also discussed in Avery Jones: Partnerships *supra* [2002] British Tax Review 375 at 419-422 where the authors regard the HMRC criteria as not working very well when applied to civil law partnerships, especially those with legal capacity but lacking legal personality.
103. [1998] STC 491.
104. [1998] STC 491.
105. [1998] 3 All ER 19.
106. 14 TC 560.
107. As discussed in section 2.9.5, item (4) is also particularly important in distinguishing a 'body corporate' from a 'partnership', even though the distinction which it draws is largely semantic.

of the freedom to transfer that share capital.[108] The list therefore seems to be a non-exhaustive set of pointers to assist a holistic enquiry. There is also limited guidance on how these pointers should be weighted.

2.13.3 HMRC List of Entities Considered

HMRC have also published[109] a list of entities whose status as transparent or opaque they have considered, but only when reviewing the UK *income* tax treatment of members of such entities.[110] Again this list does not consider whether entities are bodies corporate or partnerships. Nor is any detail provided about the precise circumstances in which such entities were considered and the evidence used to reach the determination. The list should refer, in each case, to the general factors which led to HMRC's conclusion. This would help to connect individual cases with HMRC's preferred entity classification criteria. The equivalent Dutch list (*see* section 7.3.3) is much more helpful in this regard.

Hence this HMRC list should be treated with caution. Some of the determinations are quite old. It does not cover all situations which HMRC have considered. A notable omission is a 'Guernsey LP Inc', which HMRC have ruled (in 2010) to be 'transparent' for the purposes of taxing its UK-resident members. This entity (and the equivalent created under the Incorporated Limited Partnerships (Jersey) Law 2011) has been used in investment fund structures. It is a Guernsey LP where the general partner can irrevocably elect to treat it as a legal person under Guernsey law, which makes clear that it is not just a legal person but also a 'body corporate'. It also continues in existence, even if there is a change of partners, so there is perpetual succession. These features differentiate it from a Scottish partnership. HMRC's ruling sheds no light on the relationship between member and entity, despite legal personality and perpetual succession. It is believed that the ruling relies on local law giving a limited partner a right to a share of entity profits, whether or not distributed. If so, it is unclear how this entity is a 'body corporate', given the vested entitlement of members to underlying profits of the entity.

A recent addition is another much-used investment fund vehicle, the Luxembourg 'société en commandite spéciale' or SCSp, which is regarded as 'transparent'.

Not surprisingly, the list regards a silent partnership as opaque. Likewise, a US limited liability company (LLC): hence the *Anson* litigation discussed in section 2.14. HMRC seem readier to concede transparency in relation to civil law 'partnership' entities, such as the SNC and the Groupement d'Intérêt Economique, which have a

108. By contrast, this can be a relevant factor for the Dutch entity classification rules, just as it was under the pre-1997 US Federal entity classification rules. The latter also emphasised 'continuity of life' (i.e., perpetual succession) and limited liability: *see* Chapter 7.
109. In the International Manual at INTM180030 (accessed 24 May 2022).
110. Therefore, these entities have only been considered in relation to outbound investment from the UK, and not when taxing capital gains from such investments. Unless a non-UK entity is specifically treated as 'opaque' for UK capital gains taxation (e.g., if it is a trust which is not a 'bare trust' – *see* section 4.3 – or if it is a 'unit trust' – *see* section 4.3.6), it should be treated as transparent for UK tax on capital gains, if it is treated as transparent on the HMRC list.

fuller legal personality than Scottish partnerships. The HMRC approach is the same in relation to most US partnerships, LPs and limited liability limited partnerships (LLLPs). These almost always have legal personality which is fuller than that of a Scottish partnership. By contrast, HMRC regard a Jersey LLP (which also has separate personality and carries on the partnership business) as opaque. This is presumably the determination which led to an unsuccessful administrative law challenge by the taxpayer in *R v IRC ex parte Bishopp*.[111] The judge in that case did not rule on the UK tax classification of the entity, even though he heard argument on the point.[112]

2.13.4 Stamp Duty Lists

There is a separate list of entities in paragraph 6.124 of the old 2001 Stamp Office Manual.[113] HMRC regard these entities not just as opaque but as 'bodies corporate' for the purposes of stamp duty group relief (*see* section 5.5.3) under section 42 Finance Act 1930. 'Body corporate' status of transferor and transferee (and of certain related parties) is a prerequisite for such relief. The list contains entities which are also regarded as 'opaque' on the list at INTM180030, such as the German KGaA and the US LLC. The KGaA is an entity with features of both a body corporate and a partnership, from a UK perspective. There is no UK analogue. The entry on the Stamp Office list for Saudi Arabia states that 'A company organised pursuant to the laws of the Kingdom of Saudi Arabia has been accepted although it did not have perpetual succession.' No further explanation is provided.

An equivalent list now appears in the Stamp Taxes on Shares Manual at STSM042260.[114] It does not contain the earlier comment about a Saudi company. Nor is there any mention of the German KGaA, although similar entities such as a Luxembourg société en commandite par actions are treated as 'bodies corporate' for these purposes. Both a Liechtenstein anstalt and a stiftung (foundation) are regarded as 'bodies corporate'. Such entities are discussed further in section 4.1.2.

Although not included in either Stamp Tax list, HMRC have been known to treat a Delaware LP as a 'body corporate', and hence the parent company of a group, for stamp duty group relief purposes. This approach is very questionable. Even if a Delaware LP has legal personality and a change in its membership does not lead to it being dissolved, its members' interests (unlike those of shareholders) are insufficiently

111. [1999] STC 531.
112. Apparently, the UK tax authorities argued that a 'partnership' for UK tax purposes required: (i) putative partners with joint and several liability for the entity's business debts; (ii) multiple principals acting for the entity; and (iii) putative partners having an interest in both the assets and the profits of the entity. This thinking clings too closely to the English common law paradigm as does the UK tax authorities' response to the Law Commission. The latter's 2003 Report *supra* indicates that their proposals that all UK partnerships should have separate legal personality and that partners should simply be agents of this partnership entity were criticised by the UK tax authorities on the grounds that mutual agency of partners was the *precondition* for a partnership to be transparent for direct tax purposes.
113. Which has not been updated for some years.
114. STSM042260 – Stamp Taxes on Shares Manual – HMRC internal manual – GOV.UK (accessed 24 May 2022).

separate from the entity's underlying income, assets and business. That is so even if its members (like partners in a Scottish partnership) lack a proprietary interest in underlying assets. A Delaware LP should not be treated as a 'body corporate' for UK regulatory purposes either (e.g., when applying the definition of an 'open-ended investment company' in section 236 FSMA 2000).

2.14 *ANSON V IRC*

2.14.1 Introduction

The relevance of the HMRC lists needs to be reconsidered in the light of *Anson*.

The case involved an investment by Mr Anson, a UK-resident but non-UK-domiciled individual, in a Delaware LLC called Harbourvest, which carried on investment management business in the US, and in Massachusetts in particular.

The LLC did not elect (*see* Chapter 7) to be treated as a corporation for US Federal and state tax purposes. By default, it was therefore classified as a partnership for US tax purposes and not itself subject to US Federal or state income tax. Instead, its members were taxable at Federal and state level on LLC income allocated to them under the 1997 LLC Operating Agreement. They were taxed as partners on allocated income, whether or not distributed.

Because Mr Anson was entitled to claim the 'remittance basis' of UK income taxation, the UK only taxed his share of LLC income when he 'remitted' it to the UK, which he did. US tax on his allocated share of LLC income had been levied at an effective rate of 45%. He sought to credit this against his UK tax liability of 40% on the remitted income.

Credit for Federal income tax was claimed under the 1975 and (for later years) 2001 UK-US double tax treaties, as implemented in UK domestic law by section 788 ICTA 1988.[115] Credit for state income tax was not available under those treaties but was claimed as 'unilateral relief' under section 790 ICTA 1988.[116]

HMRC rejected all claims for credit on the basis that the sums remitted by Mr Anson were not the same income on which he had been taxed in the US. They were effectively dividends from a tax-opaque LLC and hence an income 'source' distinct from the underlying US profits of the LLC. An individual receiving such a dividend was not entitled to a UK credit for non-UK tax on the foreign profit pool which funded that dividend. HMRC's position reflected their long-held view (*see* section 2.13) that a LLC was 'opaque'.[117] HMRC's position created a substantial UK tax liability. On allocated US profits of 100, Mr Anson was liable for 45 of US Federal and state tax, leaving a post-tax amount of 55 to remit to the UK. At the prevailing UK rates, that sum was

115. *See* now sections 1-6 TIOPA.
116. *See* now sections 8-9 TIOPA.
117. By contrast, HMRC regard a Delaware LLP as 'transparent' for such purposes. Presumably, it was for this reason that Harbourvest subsequently converted into a Delaware LLP. The substantive differences between a Delaware LLC and a Delaware LLP are limited: *see* section 7.2.4.2. Hence both can often be used interchangeably in the US.

taxable at 40%. Without a UK foreign tax credit, there would be a further 22 of UK tax to pay in addition to 45 of US tax.[118]

Mr Anson appealed against the denial of a foreign tax credit on several grounds. The key ground of appeal for present purposes was that a foreign tax credit was available because the LLC was 'transparent'. For reasons of taxpayer anonymity, the First-Tier Tribunal (FTT) hearing was reported as *Swift v HMRC.*[119]

2.14.2 The First-Tier Tribunal

Detailed expert evidence of Delaware law was provided by both Mr Anson and HMRC. The Tribunal considered this and the 1997 LLC Operating Agreement. The Delaware law experts were asked questions based on the HMRC list discussed in section 2.13, which does not address whether members of an entity enjoy limited liability, whether they can freely transfer their interests or whether that entity exhibits 'perpetual succession'.

The Tribunal made key findings of fact, reflecting the expert evidence:

(1) The LLC was a legal entity brought into existence by executing a certificate of formation with the Delaware Secretary of State and entering into the 1997 LLC Operating Agreement. That agreement was between the LLC members only: the entity was not a party to it.
(2) The LLC itself carried on its business, and the business assets belonged beneficially to the LLC and not to its members. Under the Delaware Limited Liability Company Act ('the Delaware Act'), they had no interest in specific property of the LLC. Nor were they liable for the LLC's business debts for which it alone was liable.[120]
(3) In this particular case, 'the membership interest ... is not similar to share capital but something more similar to partnership capital of an English partnership, the transfer of which requires the consent of all the partners but the economic benefits can be transferred without consent and without the transferee becoming a partner (s. 31 of the Partnership Act 1890). Normally a share in a UK company is transferable and needs to be registered and if there are restrictions on transfer these are that the consent of the directors (not all the other shareholders) is required'.
(4) Crucially, members of this LLC had an interest in its profits as they arose. The profits of the LLC did not 'belong to the LLC in the first instance and then become the property of the members because there is no mechanism for any such change in ownership, analogous to the declaration of a dividend. It is true ... that the assets representing those profits do belong to the LLC until the distribution is actually made but we do not consider that this means that the

118. Ignoring Dollar: Sterling rate movements and possible timing differences.
119. [2010] UKFTT 88.
120. Hence the position of LLC members differed from that of partners in a Scottish general partnership or members of a French SNC.

> profits do not belong to the members: presumably the same is true for a Scots partnership. *Conceptually, profits and assets are different* [emphasis added] ... s18-503 of the [Delaware] Act ... does not contemplate that profits can belong to the LLC as they must always be allocated to the members'.

The FTT further considered Article IV of the LLC Operating Agreement which set out the allocation mechanism. Each LLC member had a capital account to which capital contributions and income and expense allocations were credited and from which distributions were deducted. Allocations were to be made in conformity with Subchapter K (partnerships) of the US Internal Revenue Code. Each year's book income and expense were to be allocated to members' capital accounts. After making tax adjustments, Mr Anson's share of that net allocated amount was income for US Federal and state tax purposes.

Article V of the LLC Operating Agreement required mandatory distribution of any excess on capital accounts within seventy-five days of the end of each calendar year, subject to cash being available and the need to create reserves or withhold amounts in respect of US tax. Given the effect of Article IV in creating member income entitlements, Article V had little direct relevance.

The FTT did not address whether the LLC had 'perpetual succession' or 'continuity of life'. In particular, it did not consider section 18-801 (Dissolution) of the Delaware Act. Whether the LLC had 'perpetual succession' seemed to depend on the LLC Operating Agreement, together with section 18-801. No evidence was produced in this regard.[121]

In the 1975 UK-US double tax treaty,[122] the key provision was Article 23(2)(a), which for present purposes read:

> (2) Subject to the provisions of the law of the United Kingdom regarding the allowance as a credit against United Kingdom tax of tax payable in a territory outside the United Kingdom (as it may be amended from time to time without changing the general principle hereof) –
>
> (a) United States tax payable under the laws of the United States and in accordance with the present Convention, whether directly or by deduction, on profits or income from sources within the United States (excluding in the case of a dividend, tax payable in respect of the profits out of which the dividend is paid) *shall be allowed as a credit against any United Kingdom tax computed by reference to the same profits or income by reference to which the United States tax is computed* [emphasis added].

Article 24(4) of the 2001 treaty[123] was worded very similarly. As for unilateral relief, section 790(4) ICTA 1988 provided:

121. For a fuller discussion of this point, *see* Montagu: '*Anson* and Entity Classification Revisited in Light of Brexit' *supra*, 466 at 478-487. In practice, a LLC would be expected to have 'perpetual succession'.
122. SI 1980/568.
123. SI 2002/2848.

> Credit for tax paid under the law of the territory outside the United Kingdom and computed by reference to income arising or any chargeable gain accruing in that territory *shall be allowed against any United Kingdom income tax or corporation tax computed by reference to that income or gain* [emphasis added].

Was Mr Anson's UK tax 'computed by reference to the same profits or income' by reference to which US tax was computed, or was he only taxable in the UK on the equivalent of a dividend? The FTT found for Mr Anson:

> [This LLC] stands somewhere between a Scots partnership and a UK company, having the partnership characteristics of the members being entitled to profits as they arise and owning an interest comparable to that of a partnership interest, and the corporate characteristics of carrying on its own business without liability on the members and there being some separation between Managing Members and other members falling short of the distinction between members and directors. Since we have to put it on one side of that dividing line, *we consider that it is on the partnership side particularly in relation to its income* [emphasis added].
>
> The factor we are mainly concerned with ... is whether the profits belong to the members as they arise. We have concluded that this is the effect of the LLC Operating Agreement and the [Delaware] Act. Accordingly [Mr Anson] is taxed on the same income in both countries and is entitled to double taxation relief. ...

Of particular interest is the comment which basically states that the LLC in question is a type of partnership. This should be contrasted with *Dreyfus,*[124] which was not cited in *Anson*. There SNC members, unlike LLC members, were directly liable to creditors for their debts. Yet the Court of Appeal ruled that it was not a partnership for UK tax purposes, largely because SNC members were *not* entitled to its profits as they arose.[125]

As discussed, the FTT never addressed whether the LLC had 'perpetual succession'. It has been argued that if it did, then the decision should have gone against the taxpayer because the LLC would have been properly characterised as a company.[126] This is doubtful. 'Partnerships' can take various forms and arise from different legal cultures. That plus the practicalities of operating partnerships as a business entity[127] may well mean that such entities exhibit 'perpetual succession'. This should not by itself lead to them being characterised as companies if, in particular, members are entitled to underlying profits as they arise.[128]

Under English partnership law, LPs exhibit a form of 'perpetual succession'. Section 6(2) of the Limited Partnerships Act 1907 states (in vivid Victorian prose) that

---

124. 14 TC 560.
125. A ruling with which the UK tax authorities now disagree: *see* section 2.10.5.
126. *See* Montagu; '*Anson* and Entity Classification Revisited in Light of Brexit' *supra*.
127. It is hard to imagine a large professional partnership being structured so that a change in membership, or the bankruptcy of a member, triggers a dissolution of the partnership. Even if it does so technically, this is most unlikely to have commercial significance: clients and third parties will deal, and intend to deal without interruption, with the partnership as it exists from time to time.
128. Under the old pre-1997 US Federal entity classification rules, 'continuity of life' (i.e., perpetual succession) was only one of four equally weighted corporate characteristics. Presumably for practical reasons, it alone was never conclusive when deciding if an entity was a partnership or a corporation for US tax purposes. *See also* section 7.2.6.1 below.

'a limited partnership shall not be dissolved by the death or bankruptcy of a limited partner, and the lunacy of a limited partner shall not be a ground for dissolution of the partnership by the court unless the lunatic's share cannot be otherwise ascertained or realised'.

In paragraph 316 of the Law Commission *supra*, changes were recommended such that English law partnerships would be legal entities and would not (even in theory) dissolve automatically on a change of partners. There was no suggestion that these changes would make a partnership a body corporate.

Finally, a French SNC often exhibits 'perpetual succession', even though HMRC now regard it as 'analogous to a partnership' for UK tax purposes. Why should a LLC be treated differently?

2.14.3 The Upper Tribunal

HMRC appealed to the Upper Tribunal where Mann J. found against the taxpayer,[129] ruling that the FTT had incorrectly determined that Mr Anson had a proprietary entitlement to the LLC profits. He then ruled that the LLC was not transparent and its members had no meaningful interest in its profits.

Mann J. made the following comments in particular:

> Like Robert Walker J [in *Memec*], a proprietary right in the underlying assets seems to me to be a crucial factor in the inquiry, and Mr Anson had none. I find it difficult to envisage any case of transparency where there is no such right, but whether or not that is possible, the absence in this case is fatal to the taxpayer's case. LLC owns everything. ... The interest of the members is not comparable to the interests of Scottish partners because they do not have an interest in the assets of the LLC. They certainly do not have a direct interest (statute provides that) and in my view there is no case for saying they have an indirect interest either, in the sense in which Peter Gibson LJ [in *Memec*] held that Scottish partners have such an interest in the assets of their partnership.

2.14.4 The Court of Appeal

The Court of Appeal, like the Upper Tribunal, ruled in favour of HMRC. The sole reasoned judgment was given by Arden LJ (as she then was).[130]

Arden LJ made the following preliminary comment:

> I propose to use the term 'tax transparent', in relation to UK tax, to describe the income of a member of an entity which is to be regarded as having the same source for the purposes of UK tax law as that of the entity from which it is derived. For this purpose, an entity includes a partnership or a trust which does not have a separate legal personality.

129. [2011] STC 2126.
130. [2013] EWCA Civ 63.

Arden LJ then ruled that following *Memec* if the taxpayer is entitled to the profit of an entity because of some contractual arrangement, it must show that the contract is not itself the source of the profit, but only a mechanism to secure a right to a profit from another source, in order to establish tax transparency. This will usually mean showing a proprietary right to the underlying profits. It was accepted that the profits of an English partnership are those of its partners because the business is carried on by the partners as principals and agents for each other.[131] Arden LJ then made further comments about the need for a taxpayer to show a proprietary interest in order to demonstrate an entitlement to underlying profits of an entity as they arise:[132]

> For these reasons, in order for a member of an entity to show that he was entitled to profits from the moment that the profit arose he will have to show that he has an interest in the assets to the value of the profit. This will necessarily be a proprietary interest.
>
> A partner in an English partnership has an equitable interest in the partnership assets and thus he will be able to show that he has a proprietary interest to the extent of his profit and share in the partnership.
>
> Likewise an income beneficiary under an interest in possession trust will be able to show an equitable interest in the income in question.
>
> [Counsel for HMRC] submits that it is impossible for the profits of a business to belong to a person other than the person carrying on the business. I agree that it is difficult to think of examples where this would be the case, save perhaps in one case. That is the case of an agency company. ... But even in that example, the agency company may be little more than a nominee.
>
> In my judgment, it would be unusual but not impossible for an entity with a separate legal personality, such as a company, to be tax transparent for English law purposes. One example would be the Scottish partnership where the partnership is a separate legal entity and holds the assets of the business in common: this has been held by this court to be tax transparent. ...

The court agreed[133] with the Upper Tribunal that the FTT had ruled erroneously that Harbourvest's profits belonged to its members in a proprietary sense. In fact, they belonged to Harbourvest, and the members' right to have profits allocated to their capital accounts represented a transfer of an entitlement to the profits, after Harbourvest had taken the sums which it needed (e.g., to create reserves or fund US withholding tax payments). Harbourvest was not analogous to a partnership: it had separate legal personality and unqualified ownership of its assets. Its members had no interest in those assets. The court did not accept the FTT's distinction between an entitlement to profits (which need not be proprietary) and an entitlement to assets (which would necessarily be proprietary).

The automatic allocation provisions in the LLC Operating Agreement merely avoided the need for a managing members' resolution before allocating profit.[134]

131. Per Fox LJ in *Padmore v IRC* 62 TC 352.
132. [2013] EWCA Civ 63 at paragraphs 59-63.
133. [2013] EWCA Civ 63 at paragraphs 83-86.
134. The court declined to hear late taxpayer submissions regarding an Exchange of Notes relating to the 2001 UK-US treaty. This is discussed further in section 6.4.3.

2.14.5 The Supreme Court

The Supreme Court gave judgment in favour of the taxpayer in July 2015, in a single reasoned judgment of Lord Reed.[135] The Supreme Court had considered the nature of a Scottish partnership, with submissions from Scottish counsel.

Lord Reed noted the findings of the FTT regarding Articles IV and V of the LLC Operating Agreement.

He noted that Mann J. had stressed the need for LLC members to have a proprietary right in its underlying assets in order to claim a UK foreign tax credit because otherwise, they lacked an entitlement to the LLC's profits.

He then gave some support to the analogy drawn by the FTT between the interest of a LLC member and that of a partner in a Scottish partnership:[136]

> [The First-Tier Tribunal] ... based its conclusion that 'the profits belong as they arise to the members' not upon a confusion between profits and assets but upon the expert evidence as to the combined effect under Delaware law of sections 18-101(8) and 18-503 of the [Delaware] Act, which respectively defined a member's interest in an LLC as his share of profits and losses, and required the profits and losses to be allocated among the members in the manner provided in the LLC agreement, and article IV of the LLC agreement itself. ... *The natural reading of the [First-Tier Tribunal's] decision, in those circumstances, is that when it described the profits as belonging to the members it was referring to a right in personam rather than a right in rem* [emphasis added].
>
> It would also be consistent with the comparison which the [FTT] made between the LLC and a Scottish partnership. Although taxed in the same way as an English partnership ..., a Scottish partnership differs in possessing separate legal personality. The partners do not, therefore, have any direct proprietary interest in any of the partnership assets (unless they happen to hold assets as trustees for the partnership). ... What the partners do own is a share of the partnership. That share is an incorporeal moveable right. ... Those rights are broadly analogous to those of a member of the LLC under the [Delaware] Act, as found by the [FTT]. ... There are, of course, also some differences: in particular, the partners in a Scottish partnership, other than a limited partnership, have an unlimited liability for its debts, whereas the members of the LLC had no liability for its debts beyond their initial capital contributions, prior to their repayment. *Nevertheless, given the points of similarity, the comparison made by the [FTT] between the LLC and a Scottish partnership was understandable, and did not carry the implication [of a member's proprietary interest in partnership assets] which Mann J supposed* [emphasis added].

Lord Reed also queried the approach of the Court of Appeal. It was not clear that it had followed *Memec* when it focused on whether the taxpayer had a proprietary right to the profits of Harbourvest as they arose.[137] In *Memec*,[138] the Court of Appeal

135. [2015] STC 1777. Before becoming a member of the Supreme Court, Lord Reed was a senior Scottish judge and therefore especially well qualified to opine on Scottish partnerships.
136. In paragraph 38 of his judgment.
137. An old House of Lords case not discussed in *Anson* is *Drummond v Collins* 8 TC 525, which supports the analysis of both the FTT and the Supreme Court. In *Drummond*, minor children were merely discretionary income beneficiaries of a US trust and their guardian received sums from the trustees on their behalf for their education and maintenance. All the courts ruled that

'adopted ... an approach[139] to "transparency" which involved analysing the characteristics of the partnership agreement under the governing foreign law, comparing those characteristics with the characteristics of paradigm examples of arrangements which were transparent (such as English and Scottish partnerships) or opaque (such as UK companies), and determining whether in the light of that comparison ... the foreign partnership was relevantly similar to the transparent or opaque UK entities. That was the approach followed by the [FTT] in the present case'.

Overall Lord Reed expressed concern that the Court of Appeal (unlike the FTT) continued to confuse profits with assets. It also did not address the key question of whether the income taxed in one country was the same as the income taxed in another.[140]

Lord Reed finally addressed the taxpayer's argument that, based on Delaware law, the same profits were being taxed in both the UK and the US. *Memec*[141] was referred to. It was noted that the question in Memec was: did the presence of the 'silent partnership' mean that the UK taxpayer could be treated as receiving a share of the dividends paid by the German subsidiaries to the German subholding company? If so, a UK foreign tax credit would be available for trade tax on the profits of the German subsidiaries which were used to fund those dividends. This differed from the question in *Anson* about whether the same profits directly earned from the LLC's activities were being directly taxed in both the UK and the US.

---

these payments were income which was UK-taxable because its source was a 'foreign possession' (the US trust fund) and it had been remitted to the guardian in the UK. The House of Lords (in particular Lord Parker at pp. 539-540 and Lord Wrenbury at p. 541) made clear that income could be 'sourced' from a 'foreign possession', and taxable as such, even though the taxpayer (the guardian) did not have a proprietary right to the 'foreign possession' because the children were discretionary beneficiaries. As Lord Wrenbury put it at p. 541: 'It is, however, contended that the case is not within [Schedule D Case V] for that this is not a foreign possession. This argument ... is that property e.g. income derived from assets in another country, is not a foreign possession unless the person taxed owns the corpus of the foreign possession. *If this were true no life tenant or other person having a limited interest in property abroad would be assessable under [Schedule D Case V]. The test is not, I think, whether there is an absolute interest in a foreign possession, but whether there is such an interest in a foreign possession that the party assessed derives income from it* [emphasis added]. ... The income is annual profits arising to a person residing in the United Kingdom from property situate elsewhere than in the United Kingdom.'

138. [1998] STC 754.
139. *See* paragraph 45 of Lord Reed's judgment.
140. During the Supreme Court hearing, Mr Anson advanced his earlier argument that, in the light of the FTT's findings of fact and as a matter of UK tax law, he was liable to UK tax on his allocated share of the LLC's underlying trading profits, which was the same income that had been taxed in the US. He also argued that, even if US tax was charged on the profits of Harbourvest and he was only liable to UK tax on distributions from those profits, nevertheless UK and US tax were in fact charged on 'the same profits or income' for the purposes of the 1975 and 2001 double tax treaties. The Supreme Court dismissed this argument. In particular, the taxpayer could not derive comfort from the fact that Article 23(2)(a), not (b), contained the words '(excluding in the case of a dividend, tax payable in respect of the profits out of which the dividend is paid)'. This new taxpayer argument had no bearing on the tax transparency of Harbourvest and is not considered further.
141. [1998] STC 754.

Lord Reed concluded that Mr Anson's UK tax liability was computed by reference to the same income as was taxed in the US. He was therefore entitled to a UK foreign tax credit for the US tax liability, at both Federal and state levels. Lord Reed stressed[142] that:

> [T]he rights of a member of the LLC were found to arise from the [Delaware] Act, combined with the LLC Agreement. ... that agreement was not a contract between the LLC and its members: the LLC was not a party to it, but was brought into being by it, on the terms set out in it and in the provisions of the [Delaware] Act. It was thus the constitutive document of the LLC. It was against that background that the [FTT] made findings which contradict the premise that the profits belong to the LLC in the first instance and are then transferred by it to the members. Their conclusion, on the contrary, was that, under the law of Delaware, the members automatically became entitled to their share of the profits generated by the business carried on by the LLC as they arose prior to, and independently of, any subsequent distribution.

Those FTT findings were findings of fact which were fully justified by the evidence of Delaware law. Furthermore, the FTT had not made the error of concluding that the LLC members' profit entitlement was a proprietary right. Hence its findings in favour of the taxpayer were not open to challenge, and a full UK foreign tax credit was available.

2.14.6 HMRC Response to *Anson*

The HMRC response to the Supreme Court decision in *Anson* has been guarded, although it is understood that HMRC have major reservations about the accuracy of the FTT findings regarding the nature of a member's interest in a Delaware LLC. HMRC's main published statement on *Anson* was on 25 September 2015, in Revenue and Customs Brief 15 (2015). The key comments were as follows:

> Lord Reed delivered the unanimous judgment of the court and he made clear that he relied on the facts found by the FTT, in particular those regarding the rights of Mr Anson that arose from the Delaware LLC Act and LLC agreement.
>
> The FTT made findings that the profits of the LLC did not belong to the LLC in the first instance but the members became automatically entitled to their share of the profits as the profits arose and before any distribution. The FTT also found that the interest of a member in the LLC was not similar to share capital.
>
> HMRC has after careful consideration concluded that the decision is specific to the facts found in the case. This means that where US LLCs have been treated as companies within a group structure HMRC will continue to treat the US LLCs as companies, and where a US LLC has itself been treated as carrying on a trade or business, HMRC will continue to treat the LLC as carrying on a trade or business.
>
> HMRC also proposes to continue its existing approach to determining whether a US LLC should be regarded as issuing share capital. Individuals claiming double tax relief and relying on the *Anson v HMRC* decision will be considered on a case by case basis.

142. *See* paragraph 119 of the judgment.

HMRC correctly note that, like any other non-UK entity classification case, *Anson* turned on findings of fact regarding relevant non-UK law. US LLCs are a very flexible vehicle, and so much will depend on the governing agreement of a particular LLC, together with the LLC law of the state in which it is formed. Almost all US states have such a law: *see* section 7.2.4.2.

It cannot therefore be said that, on the basis of *Anson*, all LLCs are 'transparent' for the purposes of taxing their income in the UK. HMRC's commentary on the UK-US treaty[143] states that, at least for foreign tax credit purposes, LLCs 'should generally be regarded as taxable entities and not as fiscally transparent'. LLCs have been extensively used in cross-border corporate structures (e.g., 'tower' group financing structures) on the basis that they are companies and that their members' interests are 'ordinary share capital' for UK tax purposes. HMRC are clearly not minded to disturb such arrangements. Taxpayers requiring 'opacity' may not want to rely solely on the September 2015 statement, which is insufficiently case-specific to be clearly binding on HMRC. Instead, relevant LLC documentation will need to ensure that, under the law of the relevant state, LLC members have no entitlement to profits as they arise but only to distributions as and when the LLC chooses to distribute.[144]

If a LLC is to be respected as a company within a tax group for UK tax purposes, members' interests will need to be treated as 'ordinary share capital'. Taxpayers will need to review the structure of LLC members' interests, given the finding in *Anson* that members' interests in Harbourvest were not akin to share capital.

Revenue & Customs Brief 87/09[145] gave guidance (now archived) on when a member's interest in a company amounts to 'ordinary share capital'. The following comments related to Delaware LLCs:

> Section 18-702c of the Delaware Limited Liability Act provides that: 'Unless otherwise provided in a limited liability company agreement, a member's interest in a limited liability company may be evidenced by a certificate of limited liability company interest issued by the limited liability company.'
>
> If a DLLC issues 'shares' in this way *and other factors relating to the company suggest that it has share capital* [emphasis added] then we will accept that these 'shares' may be regarded as 'ordinary share capital'. ...

143. Section DT19853 of the Double Taxation Relief Manual (accessed 27 May 2022).
144. This is likely to require removal of any language in the LLC Agreement that automatically allocates income and expense to members' capital accounts. Instead, members' interests should take a form similar to paid-in share capital and it should be clear that the entitlement to underlying profits lies with the LLC itself. Confirmation from local counsel will be needed that such modifications are effective under the relevant local law. US tax advice will also be required if the LLC is being taxed as a partnership in the US, not least because the capital account provisions in the LLC Agreement are typically designed to satisfy Subchapter K (partnerships) of the Internal Revenue Code.
145. Later set out in Appendix 11 of the Capital Gains Manual (now archived). *See* now Company Taxation Manual CTM00516 (accessed 27 May 2022), which simply states that a LLC organised under the law of a US state may issue transferable interests akin to share capital but they may not be evidenced by a certificate of interest. The lack of a certificate does not prevent members' interests being 'ordinary share capital' 'provided (as would be expected to be the case) that the interests are clearly defined and recognisable as equity (ownership) interests in the entity'. *See also* the discussion of a 'share' in section 2.10.5.

> It should be noted that not all DLLCs issue share certificates but they may still have 'ordinary share capital'. Regard must be had to the particular terms of the agreement by which the LLC has been created. ...
>
> Other States within the United States of America have comparable legislation to Delaware. Where it can be shown that a particular State has legislation analogous to the Delaware legislation with which we are familiar, HMRC would expect to be able to provide advice in line with that for DLLCs.

This guidance made clear that whether a Delaware LLC member's interest amounts to 'ordinary share capital' will depend on the nature of those interests under Delaware law. Issuing certificates of LLC interest may help to indicate that LLC members' interests are 'ordinary share capital'. However, those interests will also need to represent a fractional interest in a fund of entity 'capital' which is not freely repayable to members.

Chapter 3

The Law Following *Anson*

3.1 THE RADICALISM OF *ANSON*

In *Anson*, the most senior UK domestic court has addressed a question of 'tax transparency', in relation to a non-UK entity with legal personality. The decision shows a willingness to break away from a rather narrow common law perspective in addressing such questions, echoing *Ryall v DuBois*.[146] It is also consistent with *Oxnard v Rahn*[147] and *Von Hellfeld v Rechnitzer*,[148] although none of these cases was cited. The UK corporation tax legislation applies to entities formed in other jurisdictions which are nevertheless UK-resident or have another relevant UK tax nexus. In deciding whether non-UK entities are subject to UK corporation tax, one needs to bear in mind that the nature of a 'body corporate' and a 'partnership', and the method of forming them, will often differ from the UK.[149]

The radicalism of *Anson* is both important and overlooked. For example, the observation has been made that 'Where an overseas entity has separate legal personality, as does an LLC, and under local law carries on the business itself, the starting point must be that it is not a partnership, as it is not the partners who are carrying on the business. And so it is a company. There is nothing in *Anson* to displace this

146. 16 TC 431.
147. [1998] 3 All ER 19.
148. [1914] 1 Ch 748.
149. *See* Avery Jones: Partnerships *supra* [2002] British Tax Review 375. The authors conclude that, because of key differences between common law and civil law concepts of agency (notably when an agent can make an undisclosed principal liable to a third party dealing with that agent), civil law partnerships have to be formed differently to achieve equivalent legal outcomes to the common law. This explains the prevalence of partnership entities with legal personality such as the French SNC. For further discussion of these agency issues, *see* Zweigert & Koetz (translated by Tony Weir): 'An Introduction to Comparative Law'. 3rd edition, Clarendon Press, published 1998, reprinted 2011 at 431-441.

view'.[150] While one can agree on the starting point, what follows is hard to square with *Anson*, where the FTT decided that the LLC itself carried on the business. It is also hard to reconcile with HMRC's view that the SNC in *Dreyfus* was 'analogous to a partnership'. It also fails to shed light on what is meant by the partners 'carrying on the entity's business'. In relation to non-UK entities, this concept cannot always be tied to the English law mutual agency paradigm.

3.2 ESCAPING THE ENGLISH PARTNERSHIP PARADIGM

'Transparency' was recognised in *Anson* for UK foreign tax credit purposes, even though the taxpayer was a member of a separate non-UK legal person created by a statutory registration process, owning its assets beneficially, incurring rights and liabilities as such; and itself (not its members) carrying on its business and being liable for its debts. In short, an entity which, from a UK perspective, looks more like a 'body corporate' than does a Scottish partnership. Much turned on evidential findings of Delaware law. Nevertheless, *Anson* shakes off the shackles of tying 'transparency' to whether the taxpayer had a formal proprietary interest in the underlying income and assets of the entity. This was the approach of the Upper Tribunal and the Court of Appeal in *Anson*. It was also the approach of the High Court in *Memec*.[151] Those courts were too wedded to the English law analysis of a partnership as merely an aggregation of members (the 'partners') based on mutual agency[152] and the law of trusts. This analysis is not even universal in common law countries, e.g., US states such as Delaware where partnerships routinely have legal personality. It is very much at odds with the formal partnership concept in most civil law countries, not least because of differences in the law of agency.[153] This judicial mindset also explains some of the problems when analysing Scottish partnerships.[154]

3.3 UNANSWERED QUESTIONS

While the Supreme Court in *Anson* broke new ground, to what extent is less clear. Much was made by the FTT and the Supreme Court of the automatic allocation of income and expense of the LLC to its members under its governing agreement. This underpinned the members' contractual entitlement to profits as they arose. Crucially,

150. *See* Philip Harle and Rupert Shiers: 'Analysis: Anson, Transparency and Brief 15/2015' (16 October 2015) Tax Journal, Issue 1281, at 9.
151. [1996] STC 1336.
152. *See* section 5 of the 1890 Act.
153. *See* Avery Jones: Partnerships *supra* [2002] British Tax Review 375.
154. There is a school of thought, that, when applying FSMA 2000, Scottish LPs are a form of 'company' because of their separate legal personality. However, section 4(2) of the 1890 Act makes clear that a Scottish partnership's separate legal personality does not stop it being a partnership. FSMA 2000 simply defines a 'body corporate' in section 417(1) as including a non-UK body corporate. A partnership is not included, not least because section 417(1) contains a separate definition of 'partnership' which includes a non-UK partnership.

it created a much closer relationship, between members and the LLC's underlying business, than that enjoyed by a shareholder in a company.

When considering the impact of *Anson*, it is important to remember that the Supreme Court only answered the narrow question of whether the taxpayer was taxable in the UK on the 'same income' which had borne tax in the US. If so, a UK foreign tax credit was available. It did not definitively comment on whether the LLC was a 'partnership' for UK tax purposes, but seemed sympathetic to the FTT's comments that on balance it was a form of partnership. Had it been required to do so, the Supreme Court would probably have regarded the LLC in *Anson* as a form of LP. The alternative would have been to treat it as a 'body corporate' which was nevertheless 'transparent' for certain UK tax purposes. This alternative would ignore the fact that there is no precise UK equivalent of a LLC. It would also be highly unusual without legislation requiring this outcome, and specifying precisely what it entails. A domestic body corporate would never be 'transparent' for UK tax purposes absent deeming rules to the contrary (notably those regarding a UK LLP, which treat it as a partnership for some, but not all UK tax purposes).[155]

Treating a LLC structured like Harbourvest as a LP would lead to a sensible outcome if that LLC carried on a trade in the UK, as well as having UK-resident members. In that case, the UK trading income of the LLC would only be taxable at the level of all members, as partners, together with any non-UK income of the LLC allocable to its UK-resident members. Taxation at member level would be governed by the detailed UK rules for taxing partners on their income and capital gains. By contrast, if the LLC were treated as a body corporate (not a partnership) but 'transparent' in relation to its UK-resident members following *Anson*, the outcome would be very odd if the LLC also carried on a trade through a UK 'permanent establishment'. The LLC would be subject to corporation tax in its own right, as a 'company', on its UK trading income. Yet that income would also be automatically allocated to its members as per the LLC agreement and taxable in their hands because the LLC was 'transparent'. What rules would govern the details of this allocation if the special UK rules for taxing income and gains of partnerships did not apply? Even if this allocation could be achieved, double taxation would be a risk. Corporation tax is a primary liability of the taxable entity. It is not a representative charge on behalf of its members, who could not set any corporation tax liability of the LLC against their own liability on both its distributed and undistributed income. The corporation tax definition of 'income' also differs from that

155. Interestingly, the 2009 EU Mergers Tax Directive (Directive 2009/133/EC) envisages that some 'companies' (as listed in that Directive) *can* be 'transparent' for the purposes of the Directive, which (in Articles 4 and 8(3)) restricts tax relief where transactions involve 'transparent' companies. Those restrictions do not impose a 'pass-through' tax regime in the *same* jurisdiction on both the entity and its members in respect of its underlying income and gains. Rather, the Directive is only addressing the situation where a 'company' is regarded as a corporate taxpayer in one Member State but as 'transparent' in another Member State 'on the basis of [the latter] Member State's assessment of the legal characteristics of that company arising from the law under which it is constituted'. This would be true, for example, of an 'open' Dutch CV with members resident in France. The CV would be taxable as a company in the Netherlands (*see* section 7.3.2) but treated as a partnership in France. Similar words are used in Article 4(2) of the 2011 Parent-Subsidiary Directive (Directive 2011/96/EU).

for income tax, e.g., when taxing debt, derivative contracts and intangible fixed assets. Hence, would tax be chargeable at both entity level (corporation tax) and member level (income tax) on income computed on different bases?[156] What this illustrates is that a non-UK business entity which is 'transparent' when taxing its UK-resident members also needs to be categorised, for corporation tax purposes, under section 1121 CTA 2010 because it may acquire a UK tax presence itself. The main 'transparent' entity contemplated in section 1121 is a 'partnership', in order to exclude it from corporation tax.

3.4 ONGOING PRACTICAL PROBLEMS

Anson marks a willingness to look beyond English domestic law paradigms when classifying non-UK entities. However, UK courts will wish to retain the last word. Otherwise, the UK will have lost control of the boundaries of its own tax system. Without reform imposing more prescriptive rules, the tax classification of non-UK entities will continue to involve asking detailed questions about the entity's structure compared to UK entities. Many of these questions may be meaningful and significant from a UK legal standpoint (e.g., is an entity member entitled to profits as they arise?; does the entity have legal personality?) but may matter much less from the standpoint of the relevant non-UK legal system, which may well approach such questions differently.

Without such reform, classifying non-UK entities is therefore likely to remain expensive, time-consuming and uncertain for both taxpayers and HMRC, requiring a deeper understanding of the legal system which gave birth to the entity. HMRC have limited resources to devote to this area,[157] and entity classification questions will almost certainly require evidence from experts on the relevant foreign law. Experts often disagree on material issues. Furthermore, the key questions which the UK regards as important may lack meaning, or have an entirely different meaning, from the standpoint of the relevant non-UK legal system. As already mentioned, German and Swiss law consider that an entity can lack legal personality and yet have full legal capacity, whereas English law sees legal personality and full capacity as two sides of the same coin. Such nuances complicate the answers provided by local law experts.

156. It is therefore very doubtful whether *Anson* gives birth to the concept of a 'transparent body corporate' for UK tax purposes although it has been suggested otherwise: *see* Charles Yorke: 'Anson: Entity Classification Revisited' (8 July 2015) Tax Journal. There seem to be similar suggestions in Chapter 6 'An International Perspective'. of Crossley and Baldwin: Taxation of Partnerships and LLPs. Thomson Reuters/Sweet & Maxwell 2021 (hereinafter 'Crossley and Baldwin'). The 'transparent body corporate' idea is especially hard to reconcile with the UK legislation taxing capital gains. With specific and detailed exceptions for 'bare trusts' (*see* section 4.3.2) and partnerships/UK LLPs (*see* Appendix A), this legislation treats all entities (including trusts) as 'opaque'. Where 'transparency' is permitted, it has a precise, and usually fairly radical meaning: *see* section 4.3.2 and Appendix A. There is no such clarity about what 'transparency' would entail if applied to a body corporate, which strongly suggests that it is 'opaque'.

157. HMRC give rulings on transparency and entity classification issues but this is likely to be a slow process. It will involve the taxpayer providing HMRC with all necessary information (including evidence of relevant non-UK law) as well as detailed supporting analysis.

3.5 POST-*ANSON* FLEXIBILITY

Anson further increases the divide between how the UK classifies domestic and non-domestic entities for tax purposes. Entities formed under UK domestic law are classified quite prescriptively. Taxpayers have little or no scope to change that classification. In particular, companies incorporated in the UK (and, in particular, under Companies Act 2006) are taxable entities as such (leaving aside the special rules applying to UK LLPs and EEIGs). Could a UK private limited company, with articles of association mirroring the allocation provisions in *Anson*, successfully claim that it was not subject to UK corporation tax and that each of its shareholders was taxable on a pro rata share of its underlying profits, whether or not distributed? This seems very doubtful. Were a court to accept such an argument, the UK corporation tax base would be radically affected.

The UK entity classification approach is more flexible and fact-sensitive regarding non-UK entities. There the UK's 'resemblance' approach is less prescriptive, works by analogy from UK paradigms and is influenced by the precise UK tax rules which are being applied. *Anson* increases this flexibility. Indeed, it gives a taxpayer greater control over whether an entity is 'transparent' for UK tax purposes, provided that its constitution is drafted appropriately and is valid under the relevant governing law. This extra flexibility further advantages those taxpayers with the advisory resources and sophistication to exploit it. It may make it more attractive to conduct UK operations through a UK 'permanent establishment' of an entity formed outside the UK, rather than through a UK entity whose tax classification can be manipulated less easily.

There must, however, be limits to this flexibility even in relation to non-UK entities. Otherwise, the UK will have lost control of the boundaries of its tax system. In particular, if the evidence shows that a non-UK entity is not just a separate legal person but has a legal structure and status in the relevant jurisdiction equivalent to a 'body corporate' in English law, then that entity should be regarded as a 'body corporate' for UK tax purposes, even if its constitution purports to give members rights to underlying entity profits as they arise. A good example of such entities would be those US entities whose names include the suffix 'Inc.' or 'Corp'. Here there is a clear intention to create not just a separate legal person but also the sharp demarcation between the rights of the entity and the rights of its members which distinguishes a 'body corporate'.[158]

3.6 EU LAW ISSUES?

The post-*Anson* approach to classifying non-UK entities may raise issues under EU law. Despite the UK having left the EU, these are discussed in section 6.7.6.5.

158. Delaware law, like that of most US states, allows the creation of such incorporated entities, as well as partnerships and LLCs. The LLC alternative is, as noted in *Anson*, a hybrid entity sitting somewhere between a classic general partnership and a 'body corporate'. The 'body corporate'-versus-'partnership' distinction in English law has historically been more binary, although now modified somewhat by introducing UK LLPs.

3.7 ONGOING STATUS OF HMRC TRANSPARENCY GUIDANCE

In the wake of *Memec*, HMRC published the list discussed in section 2.13. The limitations of that list have already been discussed, but post-*Anson*, it needs to be treated with extra caution. It is not clear that Harbourvest would have been 'transparent' on the basis of the HMRC criteria. While HMRC accord particular significance to an entity's profits accruing to members as they arise (as in *Anson*), Harbourvest LLC was also a separate legal person which owned assets, incurred liabilities and carried on business on its own behalf, not that of its members. Under the listed criteria, most factors therefore pointed towards non-transparency. Hence, the list seems too restrictive following *Anson*. At the very least, item (iv) in the HMRC list seems to have acquired much greater significance.[159]

3.8 IS *MEMEC* CORRECT?

Is *Memec*[160] good law following *Anson*? The Supreme Court did not overrule *Memec*, in which a somewhat different question of 'transparency' was considered in relation to the UK foreign tax credit rules.

In *Memec*, the Court of Appeal focused on whether the 'silent partner' was in fact carrying on a 'business in common' with the other partner. The apparent lack of such a 'business in common' precluded the transparency normally associated with a partnership. Hence, no UK foreign tax credit was available. The Court of Appeal seems to have given little weight to the fact that a 'silent partnership' is one mechanism whereby German law achieves an outcome similar to a LP registered under the Limited Partnerships Act 1907. Such LPs are common collective investment vehicles. The limited partners are typically passive investors (e.g., tax-exempt pension funds) which, for non-tax reasons, often provide partnership capital by way of profit-linked, subordinated debt. Hence, their position resembles a silent partner. It is accepted that the classic UK LP involves a 'business in common' between the limited and general partners, for the purposes of section 1(1) of the 1890 Act. This is so even though the limited partner will necessarily play a very passive role and not engage in partnership management.

Therefore, it is harder to accept post-*Anson* that the Court of Appeal decision was correct. The silent partner's interest may be 'just a contractual one', but then so is the interest of a limited partner in a Scottish LP registered under the 1907 Act. The partnership's separate legal personality denies the limited partner a proprietary interest in partnership assets, but it is still a partner in the business, although passive and barred from taking part in management if its liability is to remain limited.

Under German law, the 'silent partner' can behave as a partner in relation to the other partner who carries on the business, by sharing profits and absorbing a share of any losses, without becoming directly liable to third parties for obligations of the

159. Although HMRC's disagreement with *Anson* is well known.
160. [1996] STC 1336 and [1998] STC 754.

partnership. This is because the identity of the silent partner is typically not disclosed to third parties. Furthermore, under the German law of agency, the other partner would have to act 'in the name of' the silent partner when dealing with third parties in order to make the silent partner liable to them.[161] It would be unusual for the other partner to do that.

By contrast, under English law, all partners are each other's agents when acting in the course of partnership business. Hence, they can bind each other in relation to third parties. Therefore a partner who is an undisclosed principal can become liable to a third party dealing with the partnership, through the agency of another partner. Without the 1907 Act registration procedure which limits partner liability, an undisclosed limited partner would automatically have unlimited liability, via the general partner, to third parties dealing with the LP. Registration limits the limited partner's liability to those third parties, provided that it does not take part in managing the partnership business.[162] Therefore, English and German law limit the liability of a limited/silent partner in different ways, because of important differences in their underlying approach to the law of agency. The German approach is neater and simpler. However, these non-tax differences should not obscure for tax purposes the strong similarities between the role of the 'silent partner' on the one hand, and the limited partner on the other, especially if the limited partner has no proprietary interest in partnership assets because the LP is formed under Scottish law.

In response, HMRC can point to section 2(3)(d) of the 1890 Act. This presumes rebuttably that 'the advance of money by way of loan to a person engaged or about to engage in any business on a contract with that person that the lender shall receive a rate of interest varying with the profits, or shall receive a share of the profits arising from carrying on the business, does not of itself make the lender a partner with the person or persons carrying on the business or liable as such ...'.

An example of such a profit-related loan arrangement falling short of partnership is a so-called theatre angel. This is someone who provides financial backing for a theatre production by way of a limited-recourse loan carrying a right to a share of any profit from the production. HMRC practice is to treat such arrangements simply as lending. The profit over and above any return of investment is taxed as an 'annual payment'.[163] While this example is interesting, it is not conclusive when reviewing *Memec*, especially given the widespread use of profit-linked subordinated loans to fund partner capital in a 1907 Act LP. Furthermore, as discussed already, German law also distinguishes between a profit-linked loan and a 'silent partnership'.

One can even query why some 'theatre angel' arrangements are not treated as a partnership interest, as in *Pooley v Driver*.[164] If they were, registration under the 1907

161. Civil law countries such as Germany apply the law of agency in a way which makes it harder than under the common law for an undisclosed principal to become liable to third parties via an agent. A 'silent partner' is a good example of such an undisclosed principal. For further discussion, *see* Zweigert and Koetz, translated by Weir *supra*, 431-441.
162. Section 6(1) of the 1907 Act.
163. *See* section 683 ITTOIA 2005. For further guidance, *see* BIM66601 in the HMRC Business Income Manual (accessed 28 May 2022).
164. (1877) 5 Ch 458.

Act would be needed to limit the liability of the 'angel'. This would be cumbersome. This may explain why in practice, HMRC are willing to tackle the matter in a simpler way, at least for tax purposes.

In *Memec*, the Court of Appeal judges apparently emphasised that the silent partner only received its profit share, after the German company had taken a decision to pay out profits. There was no automatic entitlement to be *paid* such profits. This seems little different from a standard limitation on the rights of partners in an English partnership to receive cash 'drawings' on account of partnership profits. It should not detract from the underlying entitlement to a share of accruing profit, even if that profit cannot immediately be paid out in cash. Furthermore, *Drummond v Collins*[165] provides authority that income received by a person does not necessarily lose its underlying 'source' simply because a third party decides to allocate and pay that income to that person.

Following *Anson*, the conclusion in *Memec* on 'transparency' therefore seems too restrictive. This still leaves a difficult borderline. If a member of an entity can be taxed on the basis that it is 'transparent' even though the member has no proprietary interest in its assets and income, where does one draw the line? The member's interest is merely contractual. Yet so is the interest of a shareholder in a company; of a lender to an entity under a profit-linked loan; or of a bank counterparty under a 'total return swap'. These last three examples of contractual rights would not require their holder to be taxed as if the relevant entity were 'transparent'. Yet what (in substance) differentiates these three contractual entitlements from those of a member of an entity (e.g., a French SNC or a Delaware LLC) who is taxable on the basis that the entity is 'transparent'? The lender or swap counterparty may not be a subordinated creditor, which is important. That aside, the distinction to be drawn is the elusive one between a person who merely contracts with an entity versus someone whose rights in that entity mean that it is more deeply involved in its activities. That distinction will be affected by how those entitlements are drafted and structured, as is clear from the FTT ruling in *Anson*.

3.9 FINAL REMARKS

The UK rules for classifying entities as 'companies' or 'partnerships' are therefore a mixture of specific rules regarding some entity types (e.g., UK LLPs and 'unit trusts'), supplemented by judge-made rules in relation to other entities, especially non-UK entities, where a fact-driven 'resemblance' approach applies. The judge-made rules are often uncertain, very fact-dependent and can be cumbersome to operate.

There is less classification flexibility regarding entities formed under UK law, although (because of UK LLPs) a taxpayer can now choose a form of UK-incorporated

165. 8 TC 525. *Drummond v Collins* was cited in *Memec* but only mentioned in passing in the Court of Appeal's judgment. In *Drummond v Collins*, non-UK trustees of a non-UK trust exercised their discretion to pay underlying trust income from non-UK sources to UK-resident discretionary beneficiaries.

business entity which is 'transparent' for most tax purposes but which differs little from a private limited company. Is giving taxpayers such an easy choice good tax policy?

The courts have tried to limit the 'unincorporated association' concept in order to minimise the risk of imposing corporation tax on unincorporated entities. This is a sensible albeit rough-and-ready approach, but HMRC disagree.

Turning to non-UK entities, the courts, HMRC and taxpayers struggle, when pigeon-holing the wide variety of such entities, based on very different legal cultures and conceptual frameworks. Entities which are clearly and explicitly incorporated outside the UK can and should be classified as companies for UK tax purposes. However, other types of entity cannot be classified so easily and have features placing them somewhere between the English law concepts of a 'body corporate' and a 'partnership' lacking legal personality. UK law lacks a more nuanced range of business entities (ignoring Scottish partnerships and the 'transparent' body corporate known as the UK LLP). Hence much of the limited UK tax litigation has focused on this intermediate category of non-UK entity. It has so far not produced coherent classification criteria, nor a clear order of priority for applying them. The list of criteria produced over twenty years ago by HMRC was problematic in the first place and is now looking out-of-date. In any case it has no binding force.

Anson has cleared some undergrowth but has left important questions unanswered, not least because the Supreme Court was keen to confine itself to those issues needed to resolve the case. Adversarial litigation is not a good way to develop the UK entity classification rules. At least *Anson* suggests that, when considering non-UK entities in particular, the main defining feature of a 'partnership' is that members of the entity should be entitled to its underlying profits as they arise and that this can occur even if the entity has what the UK regards as legal personality. Such thinking is welcome even if it gives too much scope to well-informed taxpayers to pick their preferred UK tax treatment for non-UK entities. *Anson* also widens the gulf between the UK's approach to classifying UK versus non-UK entities. While this is not dissimilar to the Dutch approach (*see* section 7.3), it is very different to the US approach (*see* section 7.2).

Clear and effective entity classification criteria, which do not give taxpayers too much scope to choose their tax treatment, are essential to demarcate and protect the UK tax base. Those criteria determine the entities and arrangements which are not regarded as 'companies' for UK tax purposes. Such entities or arrangements are potentially 'transparent' (in particular, taxable only at the level of their members) for UK tax purposes. What 'transparency' means precisely will be explored in later chapters, especially in relation to trusts, which are considered next.

CHAPTER 4

Defining Trusts and Deciding When They Are 'Transparent' for UK Tax Purposes

4.1 INTRODUCTION

The trust is often regarded as a distinctive creation of the common law (and particularly of the English courts of equity), although some civil law jurisdictions have adopted trust-like concepts.[166] Trusts have long been a flexible tool for asset management and tax planning. UK tax legislation therefore has extensive rules regarding the taxation of trusts themselves; of those who set them up or fund them in any way; and of those with an interest in them. This chapter discusses the extent to which UK tax rules treat those interested in the trust as entitled to its underlying income and gains as they arise to the trustees, i.e., treat it as 'transparent'. The overall picture is complex and there is much room for improvement.

4.1.1 Identifying Trusts

What should be treated as a trust for UK tax purposes? While the tax difference between companies and partnerships has attracted a lot of analysis, the same is less true of the difference between trusts and other entities (e.g., companies), even though this can have major tax repercussions for the entity and those interested in it. One such repercussion is Inheritance Tax (IHT). This applies to trusts (or, more precisely,

166. France has created the concept of the 'fiducie'. Quebec, whose property law derives from the French civil law tradition, based on Roman law, enacted in 1994 a law of trusts or 'fiducie': *see* Marilyn Piccini Roy: 'Usufruct in Quebec' (2017) Trusts & Trustees, Volume 24, Issue 1, 17. The trust is a recognised concept in both Scotland and South Africa which have 'mixed' legal systems blending common law concepts with civil law concepts. In Scottish law, the trust has been recognised since the seventeenth century and is a judge-made concept (unlike Quebec). In South Africa, the courts began to develop the trust concept in the nineteenth century.

'settlements', a concept which includes but is not confined to trusts). However, it does not usually apply to companies.

Typically, a trust is not an entity or person at all under English law (unlike a body corporate or a Scottish partnership). Rather, it is a special relationship between the person or persons providing the assets subject to the trust (the 'settlor(s)'); the persons who benefit from those assets and income in one way or another (the 'beneficiaries');[167] and the person(s) who own the assets provided by the settlor but are obligated to administer them for the beneficiaries. The latter are the 'trustee(s)'. The trustee is simply an existing legal person acting in a particular capacity for the benefit of others. Setting up a trust therefore does not create a new legal entity[168] but does create an arrangement imposing particular obligations on the trustee(s) and, in some cases, on third parties dealing with trust assets. It is those third-party obligations (e.g., under asset 'tracing' claims) which have led beneficial interests in trusts to be seen as a form of property right (at least in common law jurisdictions), although the proprietary nature of a beneficial interest in a trust is heavily debated.[169] Trustees may be natural persons or non-natural persons (typically, bodies corporate, often purpose-formed). Trustees are often professional trustees remunerated as such. Under English law, the settlor may declare itself the trustee.[170]

The Recognition of Trusts Act 1987 gives effect in UK law to the Convention on the Law Applicable to Trusts and on their Recognition. Article 2 of that Convention[171] (scheduled to the 1987 Act) contains a useful description of a trust:
A trust has the following characteristics:

(a) the assets constitute a separate fund and are not a part of the trustee's own estate;
(b) title to the trust assets stands in the name of the trustee or in the name of another person on behalf of the trustee;
(c) the trustee has the power and the duty, in respect of which he is accountable, to manage, employ or dispose of the assets in accordance with the terms of the trust and the special duties imposed upon him by law.

---

167. Of course, in some situations, a trust may be set up to fulfil a specified purpose (notably, charity) rather than with specified beneficiaries.
168. In one limited sense, a trust always has an entity-like quality: if a trustee is replaced, this does not end the trust. Once constituted, it has, in US parlance, 'continuity of life', even if the identity of the trustee(s) changes over time.
169. *See Akers and others v Samba Financial Group* [2017] UKSC 6 in paragraph 35, where Lord Mance notes how courts in civil law jurisdictions (in particular, Scotland and Italy) have developed a separate concept of 'patrimony' to explain how property which English law would regard as held by a trustee can be protected from claims by a trustee's personal creditors. This 'patrimony' concept is not perceived by those jurisdictions as a new kind of property right.
170. This may not always be possible under the French 'fiducie' concept, which may require a founding contract between the settlor and a separate trustee.
171. As noted by Lord Sumption and Lord Collins in *Akers and others v Samba Financial Group* [2017] UKSC 6 (*see* paragraphs 91-92 and 99-101), the main purpose of that Convention is to ensure that the main features of a trust are recognised by parties to the Convention (in particular, civil law jurisdictions) which would not otherwise recognise a trust. Currently, only twelve states are parties to the Convention (notably, Italy, Liechtenstein, Luxembourg, Monaco, San Marino and Switzerland).

The reservation by the settlor of certain rights and powers and the fact that the trustee may himself have rights as a beneficiary are not necessarily[172] inconsistent with the existence of a trust.

This definition is designed to cover the trust concept in both common and civil law jurisdictions. Hence there is no reference to the common law concepts of 'legal' and 'equitable' ownership, which are alien to the trust concept in civil law jurisdictions and in those with a 'mixed' common and civil law heritage.

In *Investec Trust (Guernsey) Ltd and another v Glenalla Properties Ltd and others*[173] [2018] UKPC 7, [2018] 4 All ER 738, the Privy Council discussed the nature of a trust under English law. The majority[174] reiterated that a trust is not a legal person and that a trustee assumes liabilities as such personally and without limit. Hence unless the trustee explicitly incurs obligations 'as trustee only', its liabilities can be enforced against both trust and personal assets. However, a creditor has no direct access to the trust assets to enforce an obligation of the trustee, although the creditor can take a fixed charge over trust assets. The trustee has a right of indemnity from the trust estate, enforceable by equitable lien. A creditor of the trustee can be subrogated to this right of indemnity, but this may prove worthless, e.g., if the trustee is in breach of trust. The majority also alluded to the rather different approach of US trust law, where the trust is increasingly regarded as a legal person, with the trustee acting as its agent. This relieves the trustee of personal liability for trust obligations while giving trust creditors a direct claim against trust assets. In his dissent, Lord Mance developed this last point,[175] noting the Delaware statutory trust which is discussed below.

4.1.2 *Trusts v Companies and Foundations*

A trustee which is a 'company' for UK corporation tax purposes (e.g., a body corporate acting as trustee) cannot be subject to that tax in its capacity as trustee. Section 6(1) CTA 2009 states that 'A company is not chargeable to corporation tax on profits which accrue to it in a fiduciary or representative capacity except as respects its own beneficial interest (if any) in the profits'. Hence, corporation tax will not apply to the income and gains of a UK-resident corporate trustee from the assets which it holds on trust.[176] Any fees which it earns for acting as trustee are earned beneficially and so are subject to corporation tax.

172. There may be cases (discussed later) where the reservation of powers by the settlor is so extensive that the alleged trust is an illusion.
173. This non-tax case focused on the trust law of Guernsey and Jersey.
174. [2018] 4 All ER 738 at 756-760.
175. [2018] 4 All ER 738 at 797-798.
176. With the partial exception of unit trusts (*see* section 4.3.6), trusts which carry on an active trade or business are not automatically treated as 'companies' for corporation tax purposes. This differs from the US approach: *see* section 7.2. Recently, the Upper Tribunal in *BCMCayman LP, Bluecrest Capital Management Cayman Limited v HMRC* [2022] STC 1586, considered section 6 CTA 2009 where the corporate general partner of a Cayman limited partnership (which lacked legal personality) joined an English limited partnership, which carried on a UK trade. The

The words 'fiduciary or representative capacity' in section 6(1) should be limited to cases where the company is clearly acting as a trustee or nominee, as those concepts would be understood under English law. This is not limited to a trustee under an express trust. It could also include a company treated as a 'constructive trustee' under various equitable doctrines imposing constructive trusteeship as a remedy.

However, section 6(1) should not apply simply because the constitution of a body corporate requires it to pursue specific objects or to confer specified benefits on its members in a manner falling short of express trusteeship. This is so even if those objects could have been pursued via a purpose trust rather than by setting up a body corporate with specified objects. A good UK example is a company limited by guarantee formed to pursue charitable objects. Typically, its memorandum and articles of association require its income and assets to be applied solely for charitable purposes. No trust applies to the income and assets of such a company, even if the same goals could have been pursued by setting up a charitable trust instead. As the High Court

---

Upper Tribunal had decided that the corporate general partner joined the English partnership but the other Cayman partners did not. This aspect of the decision was discussed in section 2.9.6.

However, would the corporate general partner derive trading income from the English partnership 'in a fiduciary or representative capacity', i.e., on behalf of the other Cayman partners? If so, it argued that it was not subject to UK corporation tax on that income because of section 6 CTA 2009.

The Upper Tribunal ruled that despite section 6, the UK tax rules for computing and allocating partnership income (in Part 17 CTA 2009 where corporate partners are concerned) stood apart. Therefore, section 6 did not apply to the corporate general partner's share of trading income from the English partnership. That income share was subject to corporation tax, even if it was mainly derived on behalf of the other Cayman partners, and would have to be accounted for to them.

This is a very questionable reading of CTA 2009. Part 17 CTA 2009 does not impose a corporation tax charge, whereas Part 2 (of which section 6 is a key part) determines when corporation tax is charged. The conclusion is also hard to defend in policy terms. If the corporate general partner carried on the underlying UK trade as a sole trader, section 6 would remove the corporation tax charge on it to the extent it derived trading income for the other Cayman partners. The way in which section 6 applies should not depend on whether the taxpayer is a sole trader rather than, say, a partner with a 99% share in a trading partnership.

The Upper Tribunal decision, if correct, can lead to avoidance if UK-source income is derived via a partnership, rather than directly. Suppose the corporate trustee of a discretionary and accumulation trust is a UK sole trader. Section 6 will prevent it being subject to UK corporation tax because it acts as a fiduciary. Instead, it will be subject to UK income tax on trading income at higher rates under the rules discussed in section 4.3.5. These higher rates discourage tax-advantaged income roll-up in the trust. If the Upper Tribunal is correct, then those higher rates are avoided, and rolled-up trust income is only subject to the lower corporation tax rate, if the corporate trustee conducts the UK trade as a partner with a 99% partnership share, rather than as a sole trader.

Furthermore, if the Upper Tribunal is correct, there is a double taxation risk. There is no mechanism to give a credit for corporation tax payable by the trustee to discretionary beneficiaries who receive income from the trust. In particular, the 'tax pool' mechanism discussed in section 4.3.5 does not readily accommodate corporation tax at trustee level.

The facts of *Bluecrest* predate a 2018 change to Part 17 CTA 2009. Section 1258A CTA 2009 now provides that if a partner is trustee for a corporate 'beneficiary' who is 'absolutely entitled' to the partner's profit share then that beneficiary is treated as a partner for tax purposes if it is 'chargeable to tax' on those profits. There is an equivalent income tax rule in section 848A ITTOIA. These changes could make a difference in a future case, even if one accepts the Upper Tribunal's reasoning in *Bluecrest.*

made clear,[177] this kind of limited company does not hold its assets on trust, notwithstanding the charitable purposes in its constitution. It holds those assets beneficially for the purposes of the company winding-up legislation (in particular, so as to meet creditor claims). It should also be regarded as owning those assets beneficially for the purposes of section 6(1) CTA 2009.[178] Unlike a charitable trust, it will therefore be subject to corporation tax, although no doubt entitled to claim various charitable tax exemptions.

Hence a charitable company limited by guarantee should not be regarded as a trust for UK corporation tax purposes, although the distinction between such a company and a trust is clearly quite fine. Similarly, care is needed before treating as 'trusts' entities formed in jurisdictions which lack the trust concept but which seek to achieve broadly equivalent outcomes via the entity's constitution. This may include Anstalten and Stiftungen which are widely used for estate and tax planning in some civil law countries. Such entities may in fact be more properly regarded as 'bodies corporate', subject to a careful review of the entity's constitution, and the nature of a member's interest, under its governing law.

Such a review was carried out in the Canadian tax case of *Her Majesty the Queen v Peter Sommerer.*[179] An Austrian private foundation ('Privatstiftung') had been set up by an Austrian-resident founder. One of the potential beneficiaries of the foundation was Canadian-resident. The Canadian tax authorities sought to impute to that beneficiary capital gains realised on share disposals by the foundation. Both the Court of First Instance and the appeal court found for the taxpayer, mainly on grounds which applied even if the arrangements were a trust for Canadian legal and tax purposes. However,

177. In *Liverpool and District Hospital for the Diseases of the Heart v Attorney-General* [1981] 1 All ER 994.
178. A confusing case in this regard is *Von Ernst & Cie SA and others v IRC* [1980] STC 111. The issue was whether a discretionary trust fell outside the charge to Capital Transfer Tax (now Inheritance Tax – *see* section 5.3) because government bonds which it held were 'excluded property'. That depended on the status of one of the discretionary beneficiaries which was a UK charitable company. In particular (*see* Buckley LJ at [1980] STC 111 at 121d) was the charitable company a 'known person *for whose benefit* [emphasis added] the settled property or income from it had been or might be applied or who might become *beneficially entitled* [emphasis added] to an interest in possession in it'? Buckley LJ (with whom Templeman LJ concurred) said, at [1980] STC 111 at 122b-c, that '… a corporation which is by its constitution debarred from using or acquiring assets for the purposes of making or obtaining any profit for itself or its corporators, and which serves the purpose only of machinery for carrying on exclusively charitable activities, is not an object for whose *benefit* settled property or income from it can be applied or which might become *beneficially* entitled to an interest in possession in settled property within the meaning of [the statutory language]. … I think one must look at the character of such a body to see whether it, rather than the purposes which it exists to serve, is capable of benefiting within the meaning of the [statute] and … it is not capable of doing so. It is a mere conduit pipe, just as in my view the trustees of an unincorporated charity are'. In the *Liverpool District Hospital* case, Slade J distinguished *Von Ernst* as a decision on particular statutory words, 'and not on the broader basis that a corporate charity is, ex hypothesi, in the position of a trustee of its funds': *see* [1981] 1 All ER 994 at 1006c. His comments are consistent with the wider UK tax law on 'beneficial ownership', which occasionally provides that 'beneficial ownership' is lacking even though property is not strictly held on trust, e.g., the property of a company in liquidation, as discussed in *Ayerst v C&K (Construction) Ltd* [1975] 2 All ER 537.
179. 2012 FCA 207, on appeal from 2011 TCC 212.

detailed evidence of the relevant Austrian law was considered. The lower court ruled that the foundation was a corporation which, on the facts, was holding its property on trust for the beneficiaries, even though the judge did not regard the foundation as automatically a trust. The Canadian appeal court did not need to reach a final decision on this point but doubted the correctness of the lower court's decision. In effect, it reached a conclusion similar to that in *Liverpool and District Hospital for the Diseases of the Heart v Attorney-General.*[180] Although the foundation could replicate many of the effects of a trust, it had the same right as a corporation to deal with its own property. There was nothing in Austrian law (which did not recognise the trust concept) nor in the founding documents to suggest that the foundation was holding its property other than beneficially, even though (like any corporation) it had purposes. The foundation's beneficiaries were like the members of a company: their rights were 'only an inchoate right to receive distributions of corporate property from time to time at the discretion of the board of directors, and to share in the distribution of the corporate property upon its dissolution'.[181]

Unsurprisingly, there has been confusion about the correct UK analysis of a Liechtenstein foundation or 'Stiftung': *see* Part 98.9 of James Kessler QC: 'Taxation of

180. [1981] 1 All ER 994.
181. This is not a perfect analogy because foundations do not have members in the same way as companies. The court also reached its conclusion even though the founder had the right to revoke the foundation. In such a case, where beneficiaries only have the discretionary entitlements described in *Sommerer,* one may ask whether the founder (rather than the foundation) beneficially owns its assets. The UK courts have reached such a conclusion in relation to trusts where the alleged settlor retains a very high degree of control: *see JSC Mezhdunarodniy Promyshlenniy Bank, State Corporation 'Deposit Insurance Agency' v Sergei Viktorovich Pugachev and others* [2017] EWHC 2426 (Ch). The beneficiaries of a foundation (unlike the beneficiaries of a trust) usually have little or no right to hold those running the foundation to account: *see* Philip Baker: 'Beneficiaries of Trusts and Foundations' (June 2007) Gray's Inn Tax Chambers Review, Volume VI, Issue 2. Foundations therefore seem to be a civil law construct where the entity deliberately has no members and where the hand of the founder is intended to govern extensively the foundation and its assets. One commentator has described a foundation as a legal person which is not a corporation, which has no members but is a separate patrimony dedicated to a purpose: George Gretton: 'Trusts Without Equity' (2000) International and Comparative Law Quarterly, Volume 49, 599 at 616. For similar remarks regarding foundations under German law, *see* Dr Bernd Noll: 'Foundation and Trust in Succession Planning'. Cross-Border Investments with Germany: Tax, Legal and Accounting – Essays in Honour of Detlev J. Piltz: ed. Flick Gocke Schaumburg. Verlag Dr Otto Schmidt AG 2014, at p. 354. English law, by contrast, regards a trust as an inchoate gift-over-time by the settlor. Hence it gives greater weight to beneficiaries' rights, even in a discretionary trust. Another unusual structure for holding UK property but governed by Luxembourg law (the Grossherzogliches Fideicommis or Grand Ducal Estate) was also considered not to be a trust, in a recent UK divorce case: *see* Richard Frimston and Paolo Panico: 'When is a Trust not a Trust? Continental Property Arrangements and English Real Estate' (2019) Trust Quarterly Review, Volume 17, Issue 2, at 25-30.

In Interpretative Decision 2 of 2008 https://www.ato.gov.au/law/view/document?locid=aid/aid20082 (accessed November 2020), the Australian Taxation Office ruled that a Dutch foundation or 'stichting', with legal personality under Dutch law, was nevertheless a trust for Australian tax purposes when acting as a pension fund. The limited analysis is not easy to reconcile with *Sommerer*: in particular, the Decision states that because the foundation's bylaws give it 'a personal obligation to deal with the trust [sic.] property for the benefit of the beneficiaries', it therefore has 'an equitable obligation to deal with the property for the benefit of the beneficiaries'. This imposes a common law mindset on a civil law construct.

Non-Residents and Foreign Domiciliaries 2019-20' 18th edition. In brief, HMRC have been known to treat them as trusts, a view now shared by that commentator. However, it is more accurate, and more faithful to their civil law roots, to characterise them as bodies corporate, like the foundation in *Sommerer,* even though they have a specified purpose and beneficiaries. They may nevertheless be 'settled property' for inheritance tax purposes because of the breadth of section 43(2) Inheritance Tax Act 1986: *see* section 5.3.2. They may also fall within the wide definition of 'settlement' used in specific income tax and capital gains tax situations. That definition is discussed in section 4.2 and covers some 'arrangements' which may well not be trusts.[182]

Similar comments can be made about the Liechtenstein establishment or 'Anstalt'. The author agrees with HMRC that an 'Anstalt' should be regarded as a company, although they have been known to treat it as a trust in the (rare) case where it is not carrying on a business activity and there are no 'founder's rights' over the 'Anstalt'.[183]

4.1.3 Trusts as Separate Legal Persons?

A trust is not a separate legal person under English law, but a special relationship between settlor, trustee and beneficiaries. However, this may not be true in other jurisdictions which recognise the trust concept. For UK tax purposes, a separate non-UK entity calling itself a trust may therefore be treated as such depending on its structure under its governing law. For example, Delaware law allows the creation of a statutory trust.[184] This is a separate legal person distinct from its beneficiaries. Unless otherwise provided in its governing instrument, its beneficiaries have no interest in specific trust assets but, instead, have undivided beneficial interests in the statutory trust. Those interests are freely transferable unless otherwise provided. A statutory trust can sue and be sued in its own name, and can execute documents in its own name via an agent. It has a perpetual existence unless otherwise provided. In particular, it

182. *See* Kessler QC *supra,* at 98.9.5. *See also* Felicity Cullen 'Private Foundations: An Aspect of the Remittance Basis' (November 2008) Gray's Inn Tax Chambers Review, Volume VIII, Issue 1, who notes uncertainty about whether a foundation is a company or a trust for UK tax purposes. She also notes that a foundation can be both a 'company' and a 'settlement' for the purposes of UK taxation of chargeable gains, if the wide definition of 'settlement' applies. Hence UK-taxpaying beneficiaries may be taxable on the foundation's underlying gains, either under the non-UK-resident 'close company' attribution rules (if those beneficiaries have enforceable rights making them 'participators' within section 454 CTA 2010) or when they receive 'capital payments' from the foundation. This could trigger double taxation. For the purposes of stamp duty group relief, HMRC treat a Liechtenstein Stiftung and an Anstalt as a 'body corporate': *see* STSM042260 (accessed 8 June 2022).
183. Founder's rights give the founder of the Anstalt a transferable right to decide who the beneficiaries are from time to time, which seems inconsistent with the arrangement being a trust: *see* the discussion at 98.10 of Kessler QC *supra*. The author has in the past seen statements by advisers that an Anstalt or Stiftung is a trust, not a body corporate, because it can be created by a single individual and does not involve the coming together of at least two persons to form a body different from themselves. This seems at odds with *Sommerer* and overlooks the fact that under UK company law, a private limited company can have a single member.
184. Under the Delaware Statutory Trust Act 12 Del. C. 3801 et seq.

may not be terminated by a beneficial owner nor by the dissolution, termination or bankruptcy of a beneficial owner.

If beneficiaries have an undivided beneficial interest in all the underlying assets of the Delaware statutory trust, and that interest is enforceable against that entity, then it should be recognised as a trust for UK tax purposes. The fact that it enjoys a separate legal personality should make no difference.[185] Some advisers have suggested that a Delaware statutory trust is a body corporate. This seems incorrect if beneficial interest holders have an undivided beneficial interest in the underlying trust assets.[186] A body corporate is a legal person which owns its assets beneficially and conducts its business itself, while members merely have proprietary claims against that person and no interest in its underlying assets or business.

4.2 OVERVIEW OF UK TAX 'TRANSPARENCY' OF TRUSTS

When taxing the income and gains of trusts (or their beneficiaries), the UK does not automatically treat beneficiaries as owning the underlying trust income and assets. Rather, the trustees are usually treated as owning them and are taxable accordingly, even though non-discretionary beneficiaries may be seen as having a proprietary interest in the trust fund. Taxing the trustees is consistent with the idea that a trustee is not simply an agent of the beneficiaries.

Furthermore, trust income and gains will often be attributed to the settlor under rules which cut across the basic rules for taxing trust income and gains. There are in particular the 'settlement' rules. These not only attribute to the settlor income and gains of trusts in the strict sense of the word. 'Settlement' also includes[187] 'any disposition, trust, covenant, agreement, arrangement or transfer of assets', provided that an 'element of bounty' is involved. In short, genuinely commercial arrangements are not caught,[188] but difficult borderline situations can arise.

185. There is some similarity with Scottish partnerships where the partnership has legal personality even though the partners are regarded as carrying on the partnership business.
186. In *Investec Trust (Guernsey) Ltd and another v Glenalla Properties Ltd and others* [2018] 4 All ER 738 at 798, Lord Mance discussed Delaware statutory trusts and did not suggest that they are not trusts. Unlike an English law trust, the Delaware trust's assets can be accessed directly by creditors of the trust, while trustee liability is more effectively limited to the trust fund. The trustee is effectively an asset administrator. The trust's legal personality ring-fences trust assets so as to protect creditors, but does not stop it being a trust. In the same way, one can argue that a Delaware LLC of the *Anson* type is not a body corporate even though its legal personality helps to protect its creditors. For a wider discussion of how a trust can be a legal person, or at least have a separate existence, *see* A.M. Honoré: 'Obstacles to the Reception of Trust Law? The Examples of South Africa and Scotland'. Aequitas and Equity: Equity in Civil Law and Mixed Jurisdictions: ed. A.M. Rabello. Hebrew University of Jerusalem 1997, at 812-814 (hereinafter 'Honoré').
187. Section 620(1) ITTOIA. Section 1123(3) CTA 2010 indicates that a 'settlement' can exist for these purposes where property is vested in or managed by a person who is not a trustee strictly speaking.
188. *See IRC v Leiner* 41 TC 585, *Bulmer v IRC* 44 TC 1 and *IRC v Levy* [1982] STC 442. *See also IRC v Plummer* [1979] STC 793 although this decision was later reversed on other grounds in *Moodie v IRC* [1993] STC 188.

As discussed in section 1.2, the 'settlement' rules should be seen as anti-deferral rules rather than a form of tax 'transparency', not least because they give rise to a partial and asymmetrical 'look through'. In particular, income and gains[189] are usually attributed to a particular UK taxpayer but not any losses from the same underlying activities. In this respect, they differ from the US 'grantor trust' rules (*see* section 7.2.2) which apply to certain trusts as if their income and assets belonged to the 'grantor' (i.e., 'settlor').

4.3 'BARE TRUSTS'

This is the first category of trusts to consider when analysing the extent to which trusts are 'transparent' for UK income tax and capital gains tax purposes.

4.3.1 Bare Trusts and Income Tax

For income tax purposes, a 'bare trust' is not defined as such.[190] However, it is taken to mean a trust where the beneficiaries have vested *concurrent* interests in the trust income *and* capital. A trust with *successive* beneficial interests (e.g., a trust with a vested life interest followed by a remainder) cannot be a 'bare trust', nor can a discretionary or accumulation trust, nor any other trust where beneficial entitlements are contingent.

Where there is such a 'bare trust', HMRC in practice ignore the trustee(s), who are not expected to file tax returns and account for tax on trust income (although they can choose to do so). Those compliance duties fall to the beneficiaries, according to their proportionate interests in the trust. Hence such a 'bare trust' is income tax-'transparent', with beneficiaries being taxed as if each owned directly a pro rata share of the underlying trust income and assets. The trustees are effectively ignored, although, strictly, they should file a tax return in respect of any otherwise untaxed trust income.

4.3.2 Section 60 TCGA

4.3.2.1 The 'Transparency' Rule

For capital gains tax, the 'transparency' of 'bare trusts' is explicitly provided for in section 60 TCGA:

189. Before this legislation was rewritten in 2005, it imposed a stand-alone income tax charge under the old Schedule D Case VI. It now sits in Part 5 (Miscellaneous Income) ITTOIA but purports (*see*, e.g., section 624(1) ITTOIA) to tax directly the underlying income from that 'settlement', whatever its particular source(s).
190. However, for the purposes of Part 9 ITA, which deals with the income taxation of 'settlements' (*see* section 4.3.5), 'settled property' does not include (*see* section 466(2) ITA) property held by a person as nominee for another person; or as trustee for another person who is absolutely entitled as against the trustee; or who would be so absolutely entitled if that other person was not an infant or otherwise lacking legal capacity. This language closely resembles section 60 TCGA, the 'bare trust' rule for capital gains tax purposes: *see* section 4.3.2.

(1) In relation to property held by a person as nominee for another person or as trustee for another person *absolutely entitled* as against the trustee, or for any person who would be so entitled but for being an infant or other person under disability (or for two or more persons who are or would be jointly so entitled), *this Act shall apply as if the property were vested in, and the acts of the nominee or trustee in relation to the property were the acts of, the person or persons for whom he is the nominee or trustee (acquisitions from or disposals to him by that person or persons being disregarded accordingly)* [emphasis added]

(2) It is hereby declared that references in this Act to any property held by a person as trustee for another person absolutely entitled as against the trustee are references to a case where that other person has the exclusive right, subject only to satisfying any outstanding charge, lien or other right of the trustees to resort to the property for payment of duty, taxes, costs or other outgoings, to direct how that property shall be dealt with.

To fall within section 60, interests of beneficiaries must be fully vested, not contingent. They must also be of the same quality, if not quantity. So section 60 will cover a trust for A, B and C holding vested concurrent interests of 40%, 35% and 25% in the trust property. Their interests may differ in quantum, but they are qualitatively the same because they are fully vested *concurrent* interests. If they were vested *successive* beneficial interests (e.g., an interest for life with remainder), then section 60 would not apply.[191] In section 60(1), the word 'jointly' is not limited to the co-ownership concept of 'joint tenancy' under English property law. It covers other forms of co-ownership, so long as the interests are concurrent and fully vested.[192]

If the trust property consists of land or (possibly) a controlling shareholding in a private company or mortgage debts,[193] and there are several vested concurrent beneficial interests in that property, then a holder of one of those interests may not be 'absolutely entitled' as against the trustee(s) for section 60 purposes. This is because the trust property cannot be subdivided without being sold in its entirety. This point was first raised in *Stephenson v Barclays Bank Trust Co Ltd*[194] and was developed in *Crowe v Appleby.*[195] In that case, freehold land was held on trust for sale, initially for several concurrent life interest holders. Some but not all of those life interests came to an end. Goff J ruled that those holding fully vested reversionary interests in those parts of the trust property where the life interests had ended were not 'absolutely entitled' as against the trustee under what is now section 60, despite their own interests being fully vested. So long as *all* the life interests had not come to an end, those reversionary holders were not able to 'direct how that property shall be dealt with' for section 60(2) purposes because they only had part-shares in a single non-fungible asset. They could not call for immediate transfer of their respective shares in that asset nor interfere with the trustees' discretion to postpone sale. This would remain the case unless and until the trustee sold the land (e.g., at the direction of all the reversionary beneficiaries after

191. *Stephenson v Barclays Bank Trust Co Ltd* [1975] STC 151.
192. *Kidson v MacDonald* [1974] STC 54.
193. HMRC regard the same principle as applying where the trust property consists of a single work of art such as an old master: *see* CG37560 in the Capital Gains Manual (accessed 9 June 2022).
194. [1975] STC 151 at 164.
195. [1975] 3 All ER 529. Goff J's decision was affirmed by the Court of Appeal on other grounds in *Pexton v Bell and another, Crowe v Appleby* [1976] STC 301.

all the life interests had ended). At that point, they could call for their shares of the sales proceeds. Only then would their interests in the trust fall within section 60.[196] In *Crowe*, this had an important impact on the capital gains tax treatment of the sale of the land, all of which remained, until sale, 'settled property' within a single trust which was a separate taxable entity in its own right, unlike a trust falling within section 60.[197]

Section 60 applies to vested concurrent interests even if held by minors or persons under some legal disability. However, it will not apply where the interest of a person is expressly defined under the trust as contingent on reaching majority. This can lead to fine questions of interpretation.[198] The language in section 60(2) regarding charges and liens is to be read fairly restrictively. In particular, where there is a beneficial interest in the trust property (such as an annuity), which ranks prior to the beneficial interests purporting to be within section 60, that prior interest will not be a 'charge' within section 60(2). Hence it will give rise to successive interests and section 60 TCGA 1992 will not apply.[199]

A person can be 'absolutely entitled as against a trustee' for section 60 purposes even if that person is not itself a 'beneficial owner' of the relevant interest in the trust, e.g., where A, B and C co-own the shares of a company equally via a trust and C is itself the trustee of a second trust for D for life with a remainder to E.[200]

Scotland has its own law of trusts which differs from English trust law. This is discussed further in section 4.3.3.2. In particular, Scottish trust law recognises a form of trust called a 'trust for administration' which can be revoked in the settlor's (or, to use the correct Scottish term, the truster's) own favour. A 'trust for administration' can fall within section 60 TCGA, even though it might appear to create successive interests in the trust property. It can be difficult to identify whether a trust is in fact a 'trust for administration'.[201]

4.3.2.2 Pooled Property

So long as beneficial interests are fully vested, it does not matter that they are interests in what were previously separate items of property but which have since been pooled by the beneficiaries via a trust. Section 60 can still apply to that pooled property, as demonstrated by *Booth v Ellard*.[202] In that case, shareholders in a private company transferred their shares to trustees to hold them under what was in effect a shareholders' agreement. This arrangement aimed to ward off a possible takeover bid. The trustees could therefore vote all the shares held in trust in accordance with a majority

196. HMRC consider that this principle does not apply to land in Northern Ireland where the Law of Property Act 1925 does not apply so as to impose a trust for sale in the case of joint ownership of land. Hence a beneficiary of an Irish trust can call upon the trustees to transfer an undivided share in real property. Scotland is different again: *see* CG37530-1 and CG37543 in the Capital Gains Manual (accessed 8 June 2022).
197. *See* section 4.3.4.
198. *Tomlinson v Glyn's Executor and Trustee Company* [1970] STC 381.
199. *Stephenson v Barclays Bank Trust Co Ltd* [1975] STC 151, although *see also* section 4.3.2.4.
200. *See Hoare Trustees v Gardner* [1978] STC 89.
201. *See* CG34430 in HMRC Capital Gains Manual (accessed 8 June 2022).
202. [1978] STC 487 upheld at [1980] STC 555.

vote of the beneficiaries: unanimity was not required. Each shareholder put a number of shares into trust in return for a pro rata beneficial share of the total number of shares in trust which reflected the number of shares which that shareholder had contributed. The shareholder was entitled to the return of the same number of shares contributed, when the arrangements were unwound. The High Court and the Court of Appeal concluded that section 60 applied to the trust. Hence there was no disposal for tax purposes when shares were put into trust even though the shareholder was giving up individual ownership of a number of separate shares in return for an equivalent co-ownership interest in a larger block of shares which were subject to various restrictions, e.g., on voting. In the Court of Appeal, Buckley LJ stated:[203]

> Can it, then, be argued successfully that in the present case all the several settlors did in fact make a chargeable disposal of their shares because under [section 60] all the shares which are subject to the trust are to be treated as vested in the settlors collectively, whereas before the inception of the trust they were vested in them severally? I think not. The effect of the trust was to subject all the trust shares to powers and discretions conferred on the trustees for what was conceived to be the collective benefit of the settlors but, subject to those powers and discretions which the settlors collectively could override, *the measure of the beneficial interests of the settlors remained unaffected by the trust. There was no transfer of any beneficial interest from any one of them to any other* [emphasis added].

Oliver LJ added:[204]

> *[The beneficiaries'] interests in the mass precisely reflect the individual interests which they had before the [trust] deed was entered into* [emphasis added]. ... This was no more than a shareholders' voting agreement carried out through the medium of a trust, and it would seem capricious and unreasonable to tax these shareholders on a wholly illusory gain simply because of the technical machinery which they chose to adopt to effect an end which involved no quantitative alteration in their separate and individual beneficial entitlements.

The private company shares placed in trust in *Booth v Ellard* may have been fungible. There was no such fungibility in *Jenkins v Brown*[205] where section 60 was held to apply where family members used a trust to pool different pieces of farmland. As in *Booth v Ellard*, beneficial interests in the trust were calculated as a proportionate share of the aggregate value of the various items of property subjected to the trust. Each share corresponded to the relative value of what each participant had put in. In *Jenkins v Brown*, the judge ruled that when a participant withdrew the same piece of land he had put in, there was no disposal for capital gains tax purposes. That participant was simply realising his proportionate interest in the overall pool. There was no question of any trust beneficiary disposing of a fractional interest in that land to another beneficiary when it was withdrawn. The logic of the judge's reasoning suggests that there would also have been no disposal if the participant had taken back another piece of

203. [1980] STC 555 at 560.
204. [1980] STC 555 at 562.
205. [1989] STC 577.

land equal in value to what he had put in.[206] The judge was applying *Booth v Ellard* to non-fungible property but in doing so, he stressed that:[207]

> What the judgment of Buckley LJ [in *Booth v* Ellard] is not based on, in my view, is an analysis of the particular subject-matter of the trust ... The test that he applied was the measure of the beneficial interests of the settlors remaining unaffected [by putting property into the trust].

He continued:[208]

> [T]he basis of the reasoning of the Court of Appeal in *Booth v Ellard* [is] that one looks at the mass and not at the individual case in transactions such as the present, where property was put into a pool, and where that result is reached (that the interests in the mass precisely reflect the individual interests before the [trust] deed was entered into) there is for capital gains tax purposes no disposal.

HMRC note[209] that because of section 43 TCGA 1992, the base cost of a participant in the pool on an eventual disposal of the asset taken out of the pool should be the original cost of the first asset contributed to the pool by that participant.

The courts have therefore steered away from a theoretical 'transparency' interpretation of section 60 which would treat beneficiaries with vested concurrent interests in a trust of pooled property as if each had part-disposed of the property which it put into the trust, in return for a fractional interest in every other trust asset contributed by other beneficiaries.[210] The same 'no disposal' approach applies in reverse when property is taken out of that trust. In both situations, it is key that the beneficiary's proportionate interest in the trust should reflect the value of what that beneficiary contributed, relative to the value of the other trust assets when the beneficiary made its contribution.

---

206. In particular, at [1989] STC 577 at 588, he said: 'Again, on questions of value advice had been taken and it is not disputed but that the property that was distributed out to the various people with absolute interests [in the trust] ... accurately reflected their proportional entitlements [under the trust]. *It was a coincidence that they took out what they had originally put in* [emphasis added]. That happened because the values inter se of the several properties had not altered enough to make a difference and it was therefore possible to undo what had been done [when the trust was set up] without altering the proportions in which the beneficiaries were entitled.' *See also* in this regard Glen Loutzenhiser: 'Tiley's Revenue Law'. 10th edition, at 713-714.
207. [1989] STC 577 at 594.
208. [1989] STC 577 at 595.
209. At CG34380 of the Capital Gains Manual (accessed 8 June 2020).
210. This pragmatic approach avoids taxpayers being chargeable to tax on technical disposals of fractional interests in pooled assets when they contribute to or exit the section 60 trust. This is important because they are unlikely to have realised any cash on such a disposal with which to pay tax. This approach differs from that taken by HMRC to partnerships in Statement of Practice D12 (and in particular paragraphs 3 and 5 of SP D12) which interprets sections 59 and 59A TCGA. This divergence is odd because sections 59 and 59A (coupled with SP D12) impose on partnerships and UK LLPs a look-through approach which is similar to section 60 TCGA, although the statutory wording is less explicit. As SP D12 says, each partner/member of a limited liability partnership 'has ... to be regarded ... as owning a fractional share of each of the partnership assets and not an interest in the partnership itself'. Sections 59 and 59A are discussed further in Appendix A.

This approach has a number of consequences. If another person subsequently contributes chargeable assets (which could include non-sterling currencies) to the pool in return for becoming a beneficiary, then there should be no disposal by any party provided that the new beneficiary's proportionate interest in the pool reflects the relative value of its contribution to the expanded pool.

If that person instead contributes sterling cash to the pool in return for becoming a beneficiary, then because sterling is not a chargeable asset,[211] the logic of *Booth v Ellard* and *Jenkins v Brown* should not apply. In that case, there would be disposals to that contributor, by the other pool participants, of fractional interests in any other chargeable assets within the pool. Otherwise, there would be a risk of tax avoidance if a beneficiary who had contributed a chargeable asset to the pool could later withdraw a non-chargeable asset (sterling cash) in lieu of its contribution and thereby avoid tax altogether in respect of what it had contributed.

When non-fungible assets are pooled, the relative values of assets may change within the pool without, apparently, triggering a chargeable gain or an allowable loss on a withdrawal of property. Suppose A contributes Blackacre, B contributes Whiteacre and C contributes Greenacre, and at that time, each plot of land was worth 30. Each of A, B and C therefore acquires a one-third interest in the trust. Suppose the value of Greenacre then doubles while that of Blackacre and Whiteacre remains unchanged. Hence the value of the trust assets is now 120. C now wishes to have returned to him his one-third interest in the trust, which is now worth 40, not 120. That is not a taxable event because his 'interest in the mass' is equated with both the asset he put in and the asset(s) he gets out. Effectively he is treated as getting back the asset he originally put in, which happens to have gone up in value by one-third (10/30). The same applies to A and B even though their beneficial shares will have each grown by 10, purely because of the doubling in value of Greenacre, which was not contributed by either of them but by C.

Jenkins v Brown may give further scope for avoidance. Suppose A and B pool in a trust two pieces of land of equal value where A's base cost in the land A contributes is much higher than B's in the land that B contributes. B had wished to dispose of that land but was deterred from doing so by the size of the potential gain, given B's low base cost. However, A could subsequently withdraw from the pool and dispose of the land contributed by B but with the benefit of the much higher base cost in the land which A put into the pool. B will remain the beneficial owner of the unsold land contributed by A. Of course, B will have the same base cost in that land as in the land which B actually put into the pool (and which has now been withdrawn by A). There is therefore scope for 'shifting' base costs within a 'bare trust' to achieve a tax saving.

One final point is that *Booth v Ellard* and *Jenkins v Brown* made no mention of *Crowe v Appleby*.[212] Presumably, this was because all beneficiaries had fully vested concurrent interests so that they could withdraw assets from the pool relatively easily and could 'direct how that property shall be dealt with', for section 60 purposes. That was not the case in *Crowe*.

211. Section 21(1)(b) TCGA.
212. [1975] 3 All ER 529.

4.3.2.3 *Section 248A-E TCGA*

In 2010, section 248A-E TCGA were enacted.[213] These sit alongside *Jenkins v Brown.* They apply[214] where a person (the 'landowner') co-owns land with another person ('the co-owner'), but then disposes of an interest in that land for consideration which is or includes an interest in other land held jointly by the landowner and the co-owner. The legislation seems to relate only to UK land. Section 248B(1) and (2) gives the landowner capital gains tax deferral relief in respect of the interest which it disposes of. The extent of that deferral will depend in part on whether the amount or value of the consideration for the relinquished interest in land is less than, the same as or greater than the market value of that interest.[215]

These rules do not apply in respect of land which is eligible for relief from capital gains tax as a private residence.[216] Instead, section 248E provides relief on disposing of joint interests in a private residence.[217]

Section 248A and E are being amended to ensure they extend to transactions involving land held through a UK LLP or a Scottish partnership.

Section 248A-E only applies where there is a disposal by the landowner in the first place. *Jenkins v Brown* provides that there is no disposal if a beneficiary under a section 60 TCGA trust simply withdraws from the pool of trust assets an amount which corresponds to the percentage of the pool which it provided in the first place. Similarly, putting those assets into the trust in the first place, in return for a proportionate beneficial interest in other jointly held assets, should not result in a disposal.

4.3.2.4 *Flexible Scope of Section 60*

The relative flexibility of section 60 TCGA and the courts' willingness to apply its transparency rationale pragmatically (so as to avoid technical tax charges) is further illustrated by *AndersUtkilens Rederi A/S v O/Y Lovisa Stevedoring Co A/B and Keller Bryant Transport Co Ltd.*[218] *Anders* arose from a court order underpinning a litigation settlement, which required the defendant to sell its premises and certain other assets and to divide the proceeds with the plaintiff. The question arose whether that order created a trust over the property to be sold and thereby triggered a disposal for corporation tax on chargeable gains when that property was put into trust. Any such tax was potentially deductible, under the settlement, from the amounts to be shared between plaintiff and defendant. Goulding J ruled that because an order for specific performance would have been given in support of the court order, an immediate

---

213. Replacing Extra-Statutory Concession D26.
214. Section 248A TCGA.
215. *See* paragraphs CG73000 et seq. of the Capital Gains Manual and in particular the worked examples at CG73008 (accessed 9 June 2020). Not all situations will qualify for a full deferral of tax.
216. Section 248A(6) and section 248C TCGA.
217. Section 248D also deals with the (now historic) case where EU 'milk quota' is associated with the relevant land.
218. [1985] STC 301. Goulding J was the High Court judge in *Booth v Ellard* [1978] STC 487.

constructive trust was created over the premises and other assets. It was, however, a trust within section 60 TCGA, and the beneficiaries were the plaintiff and the defendant.

He commented in particular:[219]

> Counsel for the plaintiff seeks to distinguish the present case [from *Booth v Ellard*] because the defendant alone [in the present case] was entitled to the income (if any) arising from the property before the sale. Thus, he says the trust provided for successive interests, and the interests as co-owners of the plaintiff and defendant only became similar when the property was sold. However, that distinction has to be evaluated in the light of the parties' express and immediate duty to one another to obtain an early sale of the property, and in that context it seems to me altogether too technical and refined to exclude the application of [section 60 TCGA]. Like Oliver LJ in *Booth v Ellard,* I am happy to reach a conclusion that seems to me to accord with common sense and commercial reality.
>
> From and after making the compromise, the plaintiff and the defendant are accordingly to be treated as co-owners of the property under [section 60]. It follows, I think, first, that the compromise effected a part-disposal of the property by the defendant to the plaintiff within the scope of [section 60 TCGA], and second, that each of the parties subsequently made a disposal of its own interest to the final purchaser. The incidence of taxation must be ascertained accordingly.

The UK tax authorities declined to be joined as parties. This was strange, not least because the beneficial interests under the trust were drafted not as fixed pro rata shares of the trust property but as vested interests which varied in quantum under a financial 'waterfall'. The parties' percentage interests in the 'net sales proceeds' of the property could vary, depending on how much was realised. If those proceeds did not exceed £ 105,000, then the plaintiff was entitled to 100%. Nevertheless, these variable beneficial interests under the trust were implicitly recognised by Goulding J as vested and concurrent, even though there were circumstances in which the defendant's beneficial interest would have no economic value. A similar approach to defining beneficial interests has been adopted in receivables trusts for segregating cash flows in securitisation transactions. These seem to have been accepted as falling within section 60 TCGA, on the basis of *Anders.*

Goulding J's pragmatic dismissal of the argument that there were successive interests is interesting, especially given the decision in *Stephenson v Barclays Bank Trust Co Ltd*[220] on whether a prior beneficial interest (in that case, an annuity) could be a 'charge' within section 60(2).

Section 60 therefore imposes for capital gains tax purposes a rather radical form of transparency by disregarding the trust entirely and treating the beneficiaries as the co-owners of the trust property.[221] The courts have applied it quite flexibly and commercially, in order to minimise purely technical tax charges to which section 60 might otherwise give rise. However, there are limits. In particular, where there are vested concurrent beneficial interests under a section 60 trust, that does not permit any

219. [1985] STC 301 at 307.
220. [1975] STC 151.
221. *See* Fox J (as he then was) in *Harthan v Mason* [1980] STC 94 at 97, a case involving co-ownership of land on trust for sale.

beneficiary to claim sole entitlement to any particular asset of the trust. Rather each beneficiary has a fractional co-ownership interest in each and every trust asset.[222]

This radical form of transparency also has drawbacks. Chargeable gains (whether distributed or not) and allowable losses on any disposal of underlying trust assets will accrue pro rata to each and every beneficiary. A disposal may also arise where beneficiaries' fractional interests in trust assets are varied, even if no underlying asset is disposed of, e.g., where a beneficiary sells part of its beneficial interest to a third party. Hence, the radical approach of section 60 can give beneficiaries the compliance burden of tracking over time, and allocating base cost to their fractional interests in a pool of underlying trust assets which may change. They may also risk unfunded tax liabilities if the trustees sell an underlying trust asset but do not distribute the sale proceeds.

4.3.3 Trusts with a Vested Interest in Possession: Income Tax

Where the beneficial interests in a trust consist only of a vested interest in income, followed by an interest in remainder, there is a notable divergence between the income tax rules and the capital gains tax rules. The latter are discussed in section 4.3.4. The income tax rules offer a degree of 'tax transparency' for the holder of the interest in income. This form of 'transparency' differs from, and is less radical than, that discussed in section 4.3.2 in relation to 'bare trusts'.

4.3.3.1 The Rule in *Baker v Archer-Shee*

A succinct summary of the income tax position in relation to life interest trusts with a vested income beneficiary was provided by Vinelott J. in *IRC v Berrill*:[223]

> Under English law a beneficiary entitled to the income of trust property under a trust instrument which contains no power of accumulation is entitled to the income of each asset comprised in the trust property; *each asset constitutes a separate source of income* [emphasis added]. In *Baker* … .*v Archer-Shee* [1927] AC 844 at 866 …, Lord Wrenbury, describing the life interest of Lady Archer-Shee under a will governed by the law of New York (on the assumption, afterwards shown to be incorrect, that the law of New York was the same in this respect as the law of England), said:
>
>> 'It is, I think, if the law of America is the same as our law, an equitable right in possession to receive during her life the proceeds of the shares and stocks of which she is tenant for life. *Her right is not to a balance sum, but to the dividends subject to the deductions as above mentioned* [emphasis added]. Her right under the will is "property" from which income is derived.'
>>
>> The principle applies when the beneficiary is entitled to the income of trust property subject to an annuity (see *Nelson v Adamson* … [1941] 2 All ER 44 … .) or subject to a charge for administrative expenses or the trustees'

222. Subject to the treatment of 'pooled assets' in *Booth v Ellard* and *Jenkins v Brown*.
223. [1981] STC 784 at 797.

> remuneration, although, of course, a deduction can be made of the amount of the annuity and of the expenses and remuneration in ascertaining the beneficiary's total income. If on the other hand, a beneficiary has no right to receive income but is paid income (or a sum which for tax purposes falls to be treated as income) in the exercise of a discretion, the exercise of the discretion constitutes a new source of income (see *Cunard's Trustees v Inland Revenue Commissioners* .... 27 TC 122 at 132, per Lord Greene MR).

However, in order to understand the position better, one needs first to understand the basis on which income tax is charged *on the trustees* of a trust which is not a 'bare trust' but where there is a vested beneficial interest in trust income. That income can be charged at the basic rate of income tax (or, in the case of dividends, at the 'dividend ordinary rate') on any person 'receiving or entitled' to that income.[224] A beneficiary with a vested interest in the trust income can be charged as a person beneficially 'entitled' to that income. However, a trustee can also be charged on that trust income as a person 'receiving' or 'entitled' in law to it. This charge on the trustees is a 'representative' charge only. It can be disapplied if and to the extent that a beneficiary with a vested interest in the same income would not have been taxable in the UK. The consequence is an element of tax transparency: one must look through the trustee to the identity of the beneficiary, in order to determine whether and how the trustee is taxable.

This 'receiving or entitled' language was considered by the House of Lords in *Williams v Singer; Pool v Royal Exchange Assurance*,[225] where an assessment was

224. *See* section 8 (trading income), section 271 (property business income), section 371 (interest), section 385 (dividends and other distributions), section 404 (non-UK dividends) and section 581 (royalties) ITTOIA. These rules do not apply for corporation tax purposes: that tax is charged solely on any corporate beneficiary of the trust and not on the trustee. This is consistent with section 6(1) and 7 CTA 2009: *see* section 4.1.2. For the charge to tax at the basic rate, *see* section 11 ITA. For the dividend ordinary rate, *see* section 14 ITA. The meaning of 'receiving or entitled' has recently been considered by the Court of Appeal in *Khan v HMRC* [2021] STC 954, which did not involve a trust and where the author considers that the taxpayer was treated harshly on the facts. In that case, Andrews LJ (in the sole reasoned judgment at p. 974) ruled that 'receiving' does not require any element of practical control over the income in question, while 'entitlement' simply means the right to the income with no further connotation of beneficial ownership. Andrews LJ also said (at p. 968) that *Williams v Singer* does not deal with the meaning of 'receiving or entitled' to income. The author disagrees. Later, Andrews LJ states (at p. 969) that at most, *Williams v Singer* 'supports the proposition that the legal title to income which falls to be distributed under a trust is insufficient to make the trustee liable to pay the tax instead of the beneficiary. The trustee is only liable to pay the tax if he receives the money'. While this comment was made with the facts of *Williams* in mind (including the mandate of the non-UK dividends), it should be treated with caution for reasons given in the main text, especially if there is UK-source trust income, a UK-resident trustee and a non-UK-resident beneficiary.

225. 7 TC 387. In this joint appeal, the first case related to an English law marriage settlement, with UK-resident trustees and non-UK-source income, mainly US dividends. The life interest holder was a daughter of the founder of the Singer sewing machine empire. She was non-UK-resident (living in France) and presumably non-UK-'domiciled'. The second case related to a trust with UK-resident trustees for the benefit of the non-UK-resident wife of the Swedish author, Axel Munthe. Both cases arose against a backdrop of rapidly rising UK and non-UK income taxation because of the First World War. The UK then only gave limited double taxation relief for non-UK income taxes, especially if that tax (notably, US withholding tax) arose outside the old

raised on a UK-resident trustee of a trust which owned US shares and whose sole vested income beneficiary was non-UK-resident and non-UK-domiciled. Furthermore, the trustees had mandated that the dividends on the US shares should be paid directly to the non-UK bank account of the beneficiary, so that no dividends were received in the UK. Viscount Cave (with whom Lords Atkinson and Shaw concurred) made the following comments:[226]

> In short, the intention of the [Income Tax] Acts appears to be that, where a beneficiary is in possession and control of the trust income and is sui juris, he is the person to be taxed, and that, while a trustee may in certain cases be charged with the tax, he is in all such cases to be treated as *charged on behalf or in respect of his beneficiaries, who will accordingly be entitled to any exemption or abatement which the Acts allow* [emphasis added]. Applying the above conclusions to the present Case, it follows, in my opinion, first that the ... trustees, who have directed the trust income to be paid to the beneficial tenants for life and themselves receive no part of it, are not assessable to tax in respect of such income; and secondly, that, even if they were so assessable, they would be assessable as trustees on behalf of the life tenants, who would accordingly be [exempt on the basis that they are neither domiciled nor resident in the UK].

Lord Wrenbury said:[227]

> These sections point to the conclusion that the person to be taxed is the beneficiary, not the trustee, and nonetheless because under certain circumstances the beneficiary is to be reached through the trustee. If the trustee is a foreign subject resident abroad but the beneficiary is in the United Kingdom, taxation will not be escaped and, if the trustee is a British subject resident in the United Kingdom but the beneficiary is a foreign subject resident abroad, taxation is not imposed by reason of those facts.

The court made clear that the charge on trustees in such cases was a representative charge and the conclusion would not have differed if there had been no dividend mandate,[228] because the underlying income had a non-UK-source and the vested income beneficiary was non-UK-resident. Taxing the trustee in this case would have amounted to an extraterritorial extension of the UK taxing jurisdiction. The trustees' decision to direct, by mandate, the trust income to the tenant for life simply confirmed that the trustees were not persons 'receiving or entitled' to the income anyway.

Dominions in which case only a deduction, not a credit, was available. Therefore, avoiding UK tax on non-UK-source income could significantly reduce double taxation. For more on the colourful background to *Williams v Singer, see* David Parrott and John F. Avery Jones: 'Seven Appeals and an Acquittal: The Singer Family and Their Tax Cases' [2008] British Tax Review 56 (hereinafter 'Seven Appeals'). The double taxation relief position only significantly improved with the UK-US tax treaty of 1945: *see* John F. Avery Jones 'The History of the United Kingdom's First Comprehensive Double Taxation Agreement' [2007] British Tax Review 211.

226. 7 TC 387 at 412.

227. 7 TC 387 at 414.

228. The House of Lords noted that even if the income was mandated, the trustees still had limited tax information-filing obligations under what became section 76 TMA, which was repealed in 2011. It appears that the trustees did in fact receive some of the non-UK-source trust income. However, the case did not deal with this, and it was not assessed to income tax, presumably because the income beneficiary was non-UK-resident: *see* Seven Appeals' *supra* at 90, fn 216.

The Court of Session in *Reid's Trustees v Inland Revenue Commissioners*[229] further considered this 'receiving or entitled' language. In that case, the trustees were UK-resident as were the beneficiaries and the trust income was UK-source. Lord President Clyde stated that:[230]

> [T]rustees, albeit only the representatives of ulterior beneficial interests, are assessable generally in respect of the trust income [on the basis that they are receiving or entitled to it]; but ... – just because they represent those beneficial interests – they may have a good answer to a particular assessment, as regards some share or part of the income assessed, on the ground that such share or part arises or accrues beneficially to a cestui que trust [i.e. a beneficiary] in whose hands it is not liable to Income Tax.

The situation in *Baker v Archer-Shee*[231] was the converse of *Williams v Singer.* While the underlying trust income was non-UK-source, it was the beneficiary with a vested life interest in trust income who was UK-resident. The trustees were non-UK-resident. The key question was whether the life interest holder was to be treated as entitled beneficially to the underlying income of the trust as it arose. Put another way, was the life interest holder entitled to income which could be characterised as dividends if the trust had invested in dividend-yielding shares? Alternatively, was the holder of the life interest merely entitled to require the trustees to administer the trust and its assets appropriately and to hand over a simple balance sum of indeterminate trust income to the life interest holder, after relevant trust expenses had been deducted? As discussed below, the House of Lords, by a bare majority, ruled that the life interest holder was entitled beneficially to the underlying income of the trust as it arose and not entitled merely to a simple balance sum.[232]

The background to *Baker* was an important change made on the eve of the First World War by David Lloyd George, the then Chancellor of the Exchequer, to the 'remittance' basis rules. These had hitherto enabled UK-residents to defer income tax on all non-UK-source income which fell within the old Schedule D Case V charge as being income from a 'foreign possession'. Income tax was payable only when such income was 'remitted' (in essence, repatriated) to the UK. Section 5 Finance Act 1914 denied many UK-residents the benefit of the 'remittance' basis where the non-UK-source income was from a 'foreign possession' but was, in particular, derived from

229. 14 TC 512. Aspects of *Reid's Trustees* have been questioned on the basis that Lords Clyde and Blackburn incorrectly said that the trustees were 'entitled' to the trust income, whereas Lord Morison correctly said that they merely 'received' it and were accordingly taxable: *see* John F. Avery Jones et al.: 'The Treatment of Trusts under the OECD Model Convention' (December 1989) European Taxation, 379 at 384 fn 39 (hereinafter 'Avery Jones: Trusts'). While Lord Morison's statement cannot be faulted, the trustees were also 'entitled' to the trust income (and Lord Morison suggests as much at 14 TC 530). Under English trust law, they would have been legal owners of that income and, in any case, under Scots trust law (which applied in *Reid's Trustees)* the trustees alone can own trust income and assets.
230. 14 TC 512 at 525.
231. 11 TC 749.
232. *See* the earlier citation in the main text from *IRC v Berrill* [1981] STC 784 at 797.

'stocks, shares or rents'. The 'remittance' basis was preserved if the non-UK-source income was derived from a 'foreign possession' other than 'stocks, shares or rents'.[233]

Under the then rules, the husband of Lady Archer-Shee was assessed to income tax in respect of her income from a New York trust in which she held a life interest and where the income was not all 'remitted' to the UK. The question was whether that life interest was a 'foreign possession' entitling the holder to the income of the underlying trust assets as it arose. If so, then if that underlying income was derived from 'stocks, shares or rents', the 'remittance basis' was unavailable.

The case was first heard by Rowlatt J in the High Court who, like the Special Commissioners, found against the taxpayer. He first analysed the nature of the life interest and concluded that:[234]

> What this lady enjoys is not the stocks, shares and rents or other property constituting the trust fund under the will; what she has is the right to call upon the trustees, and, if necessary, to compel the trustees, to administer this property during her life so as to give her the income arising therefrom according to the provisions of the trust. *Her interest is merely an equitable one, and it is not an interest in the specific stocks and shares constituting the trust fund at all. ... But the question is whether that is so for the purposes of income tax* [emphasis added].

Despite the trust law position, he decided that, for income tax purposes, Lady Archer-Shee was entitled to the underlying income of the trust, and therefore, the 'remittance' basis was unavailable to the extent that this income was derived from 'stocks, shares or rents'.[235] He was aware that his decision created complications, e.g., if there were two concurrent life interest holders, only one of whom was UK-resident, and the trust was invested in non-UK stocks and shares as well as other 'foreign possessions'. To what extent was the UK-resident life interest holder entitled to the income from the non-UK stocks and shares?

The Court of Appeal reversed Rowlatt J and ruled in favour of the taxpayer. In essence, they agreed with Rowlatt J's analysis of the life interest as a matter of trust law but thought that this dictated the income tax outcome. As Lord Hanworth MR put it:[236]

> [W]hat they [i.e. the trustees] remit is not what I will call the dividends in specie in their actual form. ... They do not remit the whole of the income from the profits, but they remit a sum which has lost its origin or parentage; it has lost the shape of dividends, share warrants, or the like, and is merely a sum of money which

233. *See* Case V Rule 2 of Schedule D as it then was. The 1914 changes to the 'remittance' basis were an anti-avoidance measure. Those changes and the wider evolution of the 'remittance' basis (pre-2008) are analysed in John F. Avery Jones CBE: 'Taxing Foreign Income from Pitt to the Tax Law Rewrite: The Decline of the Remittance Basis'. Studies in the History of Tax Law: ed. John Tiley, Hart 2004, 15. The distinction drawn in 1914 disappeared when section 19 Finance Act 1940 denied UK-domiciled persons the benefit of the 'remittance' basis save in respect of trading, pension and employment income.
234. [1927] 1 KB 109 at 116.
235. [1927] 1 KB 109 at 117. He relied on *Williams v Singer* 7 TC 387, which in his view was based on allowing the non-UK-resident income beneficiary to look through the UK trustees to the underlying non-UK income of the trust.
236. [1927] 1 KB 109 at 120.

> represents the balance after payment of the sums which would properly fall upon the trust.

Hence the income was derived from a 'foreign possession' but was not derived from any underlying 'stocks, shares or rents' belonging to the trustees. The Court of Appeal relied on the House of Lords' decision in the probate duty case of *Lord Sudeley v Attorney-General.*[237] In that case, an estate was still being administered under an English law will. The court held that a beneficiary's right to residue of that estate was simply a right situated in England to have the executors administer the estate properly. It was not a right to any underlying non-UK property (in particular, mortgages on New Zealand real property) within the estate assets.[238]

The Court of Appeal was reversed by a bare majority of the House of Lords. The main majority judgment was given by Lord Wrenbury. Its essence has already been set out in the earlier citation from *IRC v Berrill.*[239] Lords Atkinson and Carson gave supporting judgments (the latter, like Rowlatt J, seeming to argue that the non-UK trustees could effectively be ignored on the basis of *Williams v Singer*).[240] The result was that the 'remittance' basis was not available. There were indications that the judges (Lord Wrenbury in particular) were aware of the anti-avoidance purpose of the 1914 legislation and were reluctant to allow that purpose to be frustrated by interposing a trust between relevant assets and a UK-resident beneficiary.[241] Furthermore, all the judges ruled on the basis that New York trust law was the same as English trust law (no evidence having been provided of New York trust law).

There were two strong dissenting judgments. In particular, Viscount Sumner ruled that, under English law:

> Lady Archer-Shee ... does not for Income Tax purposes own and is not entitled to any of the stocks, shares, securities or real property that form part of the New York trust estate. These belong to the trustee company, to whom also the annual payments made in respect of them by way of rent, interest or dividends 'arise', 'accrue' and 'belong'. All that she has is a right, in the forum of the trustee and of the trust fund, to have the trust executed in her favour ... and this 'possession'

237. [1897] AC 21.
238. *Lord Sudeley v Attorney-General* did not in fact provide strong support for the Court of Appeal position. The estate in that case was not fully administered, so the residual assets net of liabilities were not fully ascertained. This differed from the fully constituted trust in *Baker v Archer-Shee.* Even if the estate had been fully administered, the relevant beneficiary was only entitled to a quarter of the entire residue, so until assets were appropriated to satisfy that quarter share, it was not known what assets it would contain. This point was made by Lords Shand and Davey at [1897] AC 11 at 20-22. It is not relevant to *Baker v Archer-Shee* where Lady Archer-Shee was the *sole* life interest holder in the entire fully constituted trust fund.
239. [1981] STC 784 at 797.
240. 7 TC 387.
241. In 'The Archer-Shee Cases (1927) Trusts, Transparency and Source'. Chapter 6. Landmark Cases in Revenue Law: eds John Snape and Dominic de Cogan. Hart 2019, 139 at 149, Malcolm Gammie QC notes that from a UK income tax perspective, a life interest in a UK trust renders the trust transparent because under English trust law, the income beneficiary has an immediate entitlement to trust income. One can therefore look at the underlying trust assets and income for the purposes of a tax assessment. That is also true where non-UK trust law is to the same effect. In such cases, the trust disappears as a separate 'source' of income for tax purposes.

> neither consists in the trust's investments or any of them, nor is situated here. It is 'foreign'.[242]

On that basis, the life interest holder was entitled to the 'remittance' basis because her income was derived from her interest in the non-UK trust and not from the underlying trust investments. That trust interest was a 'foreign possession' other than 'stocks, shares or rents'. The dissenters also noted the problem which Rowlatt J had already identified, if the majority were correct: how to apportion trust income derived in part from stocks, shares and rents if there were two concurrent life interests in the non-UK trust fund, only one of which was held by a UK-resident.

The further twists and turns of the *Archer-Shee* litigation are discussed in section 4.3.3.2.[243] Interestingly, a similar point had already been considered by the Privy Council in *Syme v Commissioner of Taxes.*[244] *Syme* was not cited in *Baker,* even though the judgment in *Syme* had been given by the then Lord Sumner.[245] In *Syme,* the taxpayer was a life interest holder in a trust where the trustees owned and ran certain active businesses. The question was whether the life interest holder was entitled, under the relevant tax rules, to a lower tax rate in respect of his share of this trust income on the basis that it was derived from 'personal exertion', even though the life interest holder did not conduct the relevant businesses. The Privy Council found in favour of the life interest holder. 'Income derived from personal exertion' covered this situation. There was an underlying active business in Victoria which generated the income and that active business was carried on by trustees for the benefit of the taxpayer and others. Furthermore, both the Australian trustees and the life interest holder were taxable in respect of the *same* income. As Lord Sumner expressed it:

> What was the produce of personal exertion in the trustees' hands till they part with it does not, in the instant of transfer, suffer a change, and become the produce of property and not of personal exertion, as it passes to the hands of the cestui que trust [i.e. the beneficiary].[246]

Syme does not appear to have been influenced by any anti-avoidance issues, and the court did not allude to the importance of the governing law of the trust. *Syme* has been followed in Canadian cases involving the taxation of life interest holders.[247]

242. 11 TC 749 at 771-772.
243. In the words of Dr John Avery Jones, this litigation 'must be the longest running dispute in the history of tax, requiring two hearings in the House of Lords, three in the Court of Appeal, and four each in the High Court and the Special Commissioners to determine whether the life tenant of a trust receiving underlying income from securities, stocks, shares or rent received the same type of income as the underlying income, which meant that the remittance basis no longer applied, or a different type of income, trust income, from which the remittance basis had not been taken away'.
244. [1914] AC 1013, an appeal from the Supreme Court of Victoria in Australia.
245. It was briefly cited and distinguished somewhat unconvincingly in the later *Archer-Shee* litigation: *see* section 4.3.3.2.
246. [1914] AC 1013 at 1021. He also dismissed as 'mere bookkeeping' the argument that the link between the underlying business and the beneficiary's income entitlement was broken because that entitlement was only to a net amount remaining after the trustees had set off losses and expenses from their various businesses: *see* [1914] AC 1013 at 1020.
247. *Gilhooly v Minister of National Revenue* [1945] Ex. C.R. 141 and *Kemp v Minister of National Revenue* [1947] Ex. C.R. 578. *See also* Avery Jones: Trusts *supra,* at p. 384 fns 44 and 45. *Syme* was distinguished by the Court of Session in *Fry (Surveyor of Taxes) v Shiel's Trustees* 6 TC 583.

4.3.3.2 The Later *Archer-Shee* Litigation and Its Implications

Undaunted, the Archer-Shees produced expert evidence of New York trust law. Initially, they sought to raise this in relation to the tax years which had already been the subject of litigation in *Baker*. However, a majority of the Court of Appeal[248] ruled against them on the basis that, following the House of Lords' decision in *Baker*, the nature of the interest in the New York trust was 'res judicata'.

They then raised this new argument again when assessed for later years. Initially, the Inland Revenue asserted 'res judicata' for those later years too. However, they then dropped this point and the appeal proceeded. A majority of the Court of Appeal[249] ruled that the nature of the life interest in a trust governed by New York law was not sufficiently different from the English law position so as to alter the outcome compared to *Baker*. However, the taxpayers then succeeded in their 1930 appeal to the House of Lords in *Garland v Archer-Shee*.[250] That court ruled that once the evidence of New York law was taken into account, the position was in fact as set out by Viscount Sumner in his dissent in *Baker v Archer-Shee*.[251] As Lord Tomlin put it:[252]

> The evidence upon American law ... contains statements to the effect that the whole estate ... in the trust funds is vested in the trustees and that the words of the trust give to [Lady Archer-Shee] merely the right to resort to a Court of equity to

In that case, the question was whether the beneficiaries were entitled to a reduced rate of income tax on 'earned income' from a trade held by trustees for their benefit. The UK Finance Act 1907 only conferred a reduced rate on income 'immediately derived by the individual from the carrying on or exercise by him of his profession, trade or vocation'. This test was more stringent than the test in the Australian legislation in *Syme* which simply required the income to be 'derived from personal exertion'. That exertion did not need to be the beneficiary's.

248. In *Archer-Shee v Baker (Inspector of Taxes)* 15 TC 1. That second case stemmed from the order of the House of Lords to the Special Commissioners to give effect to their decision in *Baker*, and in particular to identify which of the trust's investments were 'securities' or 'stocks, shares or rents' for the purposes of Schedule D Cases IV and V. Income from any such assets would not be eligible for the remittance basis. The Commissioners' breakdown of the trust's investments is at 15 TC 1 at 4-6.
249. In this respect, the Court of Appeal disagreed with Rowlatt J. Lawrence LJ said, at 15 TC 693 at 721-722, that American law was like English law: a life interest holder in a trust of personality (e.g., securities) had no legal or beneficial interest in the corpus of trust assets. Furthermore, any extra discretion of the trustee under American law regarding when and how to apply income for the benefit of the life interest holder was immaterial: 'The whole of the net income must ultimately be either paid over to or applied for the benefit of Lady Archer-Shee ... thus showing conclusively that she has a right of property in the income and not merely a personal right against the trustee. Further the trustee cannot unreasonably or indefinitely withhold the payment or application of the income. ...'
250. 15 TC 693 at 729.
251. 11 TC 749. In 'The Archer-Shee Cases' *supra*, Malcolm Gammie QC states that, in *Garland v Archer-Shee*, the taxpayer's case depended on showing that the trust changed the character of what Lady Archer-Shee received and that in particular she 'received the income not as a matter of entitlement pursuant to her interest under the trust but as a result of the trustee's decision to exercise some discretion to pay her the income'. This is not meant to suggest that under New York law, the trust was discretionary: Lady Archer-Shee retained a fully vested life interest in the trust fund. It means only that under a *Garland*-type trust, the life interest holder has the right to have income paid over to, or applied for its benefit, with the trustees having some discretion regarding the manner and time of doing so.
252. 15 TC 693 at 735-736.

> compel the trustees to discharge the task imposed upon them which was to apply the money which they receive as a net income from the trust to her use, that they have, within the limits of reasonable and conscientious behaviour, an absolute discretion as to the application of the income for her benefit, that if they decided to apply the money for her benefit instead of paying it over they must exercise the power to do so reasonably, and that she had no right to any specific dividends or interest at all.
>
> In the face of these statements, I think the finding of fact must necessarily be that, according to American law, [Lady Archer-Shee] has no property interest in the income arising from the securities, stocks and shares constituting the trust fund but has only a chose in action available against the trustees. ... the assessable income ... is income arising from a possession out of the United Kingdom other than stocks, shares or rents, viz., a chose in action available against the American trustees [and hence eligible for the 'remittance' basis].

Doubt has been expressed about the accuracy of the evidence in respect of New York law on which this finding was based.[253] That evidence[254] was that Lady Archer-Shee 'had no right to any specific dividends or interest at all' and that 'whilst ... the whole of the net income ... must ultimately be paid over to or be applied for the benefit of Lady Archer-Shee, the manner and times of doing so were within the discretion of the trustees subject to judicial supervision'. Nevertheless, the relevance of the governing law of the trust, and how it analyses a life interest in that trust, is now firmly established. In *Kelly v Rogers*,[255] there was evidence that under the law of New Jersey, which applied to the trust in that case, the income entitlement of the beneficiary in that case was to such a sum as was required for her maintenance: she had no right to the income of any specific stocks and shares but only the right to require the trustee to administer the trust reasonably.[256]

The extent to which the governing law of the trust determines the UK tax position is not unlimited. It will be key in deciding the nature of the beneficiary's interest, but it will then be a question for UK tax law whether that interest gives rise to income or capital receipts. In *Lawson v Rolfe*,[257] it was agreed that the taxpayer had a life interest in a trust governed by the law of California which entitled her to the proceeds of specific shares in US companies. Her entitlement was not just a *Garland* right to have the trustees administer the trust properly. The underlying companies issued bonus shares (or 'stock dividends') to which the taxpayer, as holder of the life interest, was entitled under the governing law of the trust. She was assessed to UK income tax on these 'stock

253. The findings of fact of the Special Commissioners regarding New York law are at 15 TC 693 at 696-699. Doubts about the expert evidence are raised in the article referred to at fn 233 above and, in particular, the citation from Scott on Trusts (4th edition) in footnote 150 of that article. *See also* Avery Jones: Trusts *supra* p. 384 at fn 46. In 'The Archer-Shee Cases' *supra*, Malcolm Gammie QC is more hesitant about whether the expert evidence was flawed: *see* fn 44 at p. 154 of that article.
254. 15 TC 693 at 732.
255. 19 TC 692.
256. The Court of Appeal in *Kelly v Rogers* also endorsed Lord President Clyde in the Court of Session in *Reid's Trustees v the Commissioners of Inland Revenue.*
257. [1970] 1 All ER 761.

dividends'. Foster J agreed with the taxpayer that the 'stock dividends' were in fact capital, not income, for UK tax purposes:[258]

> Under Californian law the nature of Mrs Lawson's interest is that she is entitled to the income of her share and to bonus shares of a certain nature. But the court must then consider whether those bonus shares when issued have the character of capital or income in accordance with the law of England. In English law it was decided ... that shares credited to a shareholder in respect of a bonus being distributed by the company as capital were not income in the hands of that shareholder.[259]

In *Inland Revenue v Clark's Trustees,*[260] the Court of Session, in an estate duty case, ruled that Scottish law differed from English law, as determined in *Baker v Archer-Shee.*[261] Lord President Normand stated:[262]

> [In *Baker v Archer-Shee*], Rowlatt J ... said 'What this lady enjoys is not the stocks, shares and rents or other property constituting the trust fund under the will; what she has is the right to call upon the trustees to administer this property during her life so as to give her the income arising therefrom according to the provisions of the trust. Her interest is merely an equitable one, and it is not an interest in specific stocks and shares constituting the trust fund.' In my opinion that is a very accurate description of the rights of a beneficiary enjoying a life rent under a Scottish trust deed, and ... it is a very good description of what was proved to be the law of the State of New York in the second *Archer-Shee* case.

In the same case, Lord Moncrieff said:

> In my view, the right of property in the estate of the trust is vested in the trustees to the exclusion of any competing property, and the right of the beneficiary, exactly as is here said to be the right of the beneficiary under the law of New York, is merely a right *in personam* against the trustees to enforce their performance of the trust. It is true that in the assertion of that right a beneficiary will in certain cases obtain the aid of the Court to enable him to use the names of the trustees, but it is only as representing the trustees in such a case that he can attach or assert any property right over the assets of the trust.

This statement reflects important differences between the Scottish and English law of trusts. One commentator has recently described the Scottish trust concept as follows:

> Equity is absent from Scots law and under Scots law, separate rights of ownership cannot exist concurrently in the same property. Comparable concepts of 'rights' are used in matters of ownership of property and trusts. ... In a Scottish trust, the trustees are absolute owners of the trust property, and so have a *real right* to that property, and to hold and defend title to it from third parties. The beneficiaries in

258. [1970] 1 All ER 761 at 767. This shows that what is income for trust law purposes may not be income for UK tax purposes.
259. Foster J also ruled that a series of 'stock dividends' over a significant period did not amount to a separate source of income.
260. 1939 Scots Law Times 2.
261. 11 TC 749.
262. 1939 Scots Law Times 5.

> turn then have a *personal right* against the trustees for implementation and fulfilment of their duties as trustees to the beneficiaries. This right of the beneficiaries is therefore enforceable against the trustees, not against the specific trust property. Scots law then applies a concept of 'dual patrimony' to deal with the separation of ownership of the trust property by the trustees, and the ownership of the trustees' own personal property ... [emphasis added].[263]

The Scottish position has now been altered for income tax purposes by statute, so as to align it with English law as per *Baker v Archer-Shee.*[264] HMRC have published[265] a list identifying which jurisdictions do and do not characterise a life interest in the same manner as in *Baker v Archer-Shee.* Most Commonwealth jurisdictions follow the English law approach in *Baker,* but others (e.g., India, Quebec, South Africa) apparently characterise a life interest as in *Garland v Archer-Shee.*[266] The same is true of certain states of the US, such as New York, although apparently most US states follow the approach in *Baker.*[267]

263. Fiona Clarke: 'One Island, Two Systems: The Divergence of Trust Law in Scotland v England and Wales' (2019) Trust Quarterly Review, Volume 17, Issue 2, 5-10. For discussion of 'dual patrimony', *see* Gretton: 'Trusts Without Equity' *supra,* at 599-620, where the author accepts that there is ongoing uncertainty about the nature of a Scottish trust. That uncertainty was also discussed by Lord Hope in *Re Lehman Brothers International (Europe) (a company)(in administration) and another* [2012] 3 All ER 1 at 7-9: 'There are significant differences between English and Scots law as to [the trust's] nature and origin. For example, the law of Scotland does not accept that a relationship in trust can arise in equity. It has a more limited basis. Its origin can be traced back to the law of mandate or commission, which is part of the law of obligations: Stair *Institutes of the Law of Scotland* (1693) I.12.17. Various attempts have been made to explain the basis for the concept. They have not been successful, as its nature is considered to be of too anomalous a character to admit of a precise definition. But it can at least be said that the duty that the trustee owes to the beneficiary is fiduciary in character ... .'
264. Section 464 ITA (formerly section 118 Finance Act 1993). The 1993 changes enabled the life renter of a Scottish trust, like the life tenant of an English trust, to benefit from the lower rate of tax applied from 1993 initially to dividend income and from 1996 to all savings income.
265. At TSEM10423 of the Trusts, Settlements and Estates Manual (accessed 10 June 2020).
266. 15 TC 693. Like Scotland, both Quebec and South Africa have legal systems with deep roots in civil law (pre-1789 French law and pre-1800 Roman-Dutch law) but have nevertheless developed their own concept of the trust. For a comparison of the Scottish and South African conceptions of trust, *see* Honoré *supra,* at 793-818. It is not surprising that a life interest in a South African trust falls within *Garland v Archer-Shee* because a South African trustee will typically be the sole owner of the trust property for the purposes of administering it, while a trust beneficiary will only have a 'ius in personam' against the trustee requiring it to enforce the trust: *see* François du Toit: 'The South African Trust in the Begriffshimmel? Language, Translation and Taxonomy'. Rabels Zeitschrift fűr ausländisches und internationales Privatrecht. Max-Planck Institute October 2015, at 852, and especially at fn 110. Quebec's statute-based trust law makes the property of a Quebec trust a separate patrimony in which none of the settlor, the trustee nor the beneficiary has a proprietary right. The trustee's role is therefore purely administrative. Hence, a Quebec trust seems similar to a civil law foundation: *see* section 4.1.2 and also Gretton: 'Trusts Without Equity' *supra,* at 616. The trust concept in civil law jurisdictions and those with a 'mixed' civil law and common law heritage is further discussed in Donovan W.M. Waters QC: 'The Concept Called "The Trust"' (March 1999) Bulletin of the International Bureau of Fiscal Documentation 118, especially at 118-122.
267. For the reasons discussed above, there are doubts about HMRC's position regarding the law of New York.

The fact that the trustees of a life interest trust are also required to pay an annuity from trust income does not prevent *Baker v Archer-Shee* from applying when the trust is governed by English law.[268]

The rule in *Baker v Archer-Shee* may treat the holder of a life interest as entitled for tax purposes to income sourced directly from underlying trust assets. To that extent, it is a form of income tax 'transparency'. However, it is a more qualified form of 'transparency' than that imposed by section 60 TCGA.[269] This is evident in relation to the treatment of trust expenses, where it is clear that the trust is not simply disregarded. Where the trustees legitimately incur trust expenses or pay tax which in either case is chargeable against trust income, then those expenses reduce the *amount* of the income entitlement of the life interest holder even if they do not alter the underlying *source(s)* of that entitlement for tax purposes. Those expenses are not treated as incurred by the life interest holder, who is regarded as entitled to the income of the trust after those expenses are deducted. This is clear from two decisions of the Court of Session.[270] In both, a life interest holder argued that trust income applied by the trustees in meeting trust expenses, after paying income tax on it, was nevertheless income to which that beneficiary was entitled. If correct, the beneficiary would have been entitled to recover tax paid by the trustees on the income which they had used to meet those expenses. The court rejected the argument of the life interest holder.[271] The latter's interest is no greater than the amount the beneficiary is entitled to receive net of expenses of the trustees. Hence, tax paid by the trustees on the slice of trust income used to meet those legitimate expenses is not recoverable by the beneficiary, although that tax may be at a lower rate (20%) than the beneficiary's marginal income tax rate. The (reduced) amount to which the beneficiary is entitled must be grossed up where relevant by any tax paid by the trustees in respect of that amount. This trustee-level tax may then be creditable/recoverable by the beneficiary.[272]

It is very doubtful that the rule in *Baker v Archer-Shee* enables a life interest holder to claim tax losses in respect of income-generating activity carried on by the trust. It merely identifies the source of a taxpayer's income. If the activity which potentially generates that income produces a loss (e.g., where the trust conducts a loss-making trade), the life interest holder cannot claim its share of that loss for the purposes of

268. *Nelson v Adamson* [1941] 2 All ER Annotated 44.
269. Or indeed the transparency which would have arisen if the New York trustees, like the UK trustees in *Williams v Singer* 7 TC 387, had simply mandated payment of the underlying investment income directly to Lady Archer-Shee.
270. *Murray v Commissioners of Inland Revenue* 11 TC 133 and *Macfarlane v Commissioners of Inland Revenue* 14 TC 532, which were decided, respectively, before and after the House of Lords' decision in *Baker v Archer-Shee.*
271. It noted that in *Baker v Archer-Shee,* the Crown had conceded that the life interest holder was not taxable on trust income applied by the New York trustees in duly meeting trust expenses. For a possible explanation of this concession, *see* Malcolm Gammie QC: 'The Archer-Shee Cases' *supra*, fn 41 at 152-153.
272. Chapter 8 Part 9 ITA now sets out the rules regarding the impact of trust expenses on the amount of the life interest holder's entitlement. These rules also apply if the holder is subject to corporation tax: *see* section 611 CTA 2010. For an example of how these rules work, *see* Example 18.6 in Anne Fairpo and David Salter: 'Revenue Law: Principles and Practice'. 37th edition, Bloomsbury Professional, at 558.

setting it against other income as 'sideways relief' because (unlike the trustees) it does not 'carry on' that trade, as required by sections 61(1) and 64(1)(a) ITA. This contrasts with the more comprehensive tax 'transparency' which applies to a trading partnership. A partner's income source is the underlying income of the partnership business. If the partnership trades at a loss, the partner is entitled to set its share of that loss against other income,[273] precisely because it is treated as carrying on the single partnership trade by being a member of the partnership. As Vinelott J expressed it in *MacKinlay v Arthur Young McLelland Moores & Co*:[274]

> What has to be ascertained is the profits of the firm and not of the individual partners. That is not, I think, stated anywhere in the Income Tax Acts but it follows necessarily from the fact that there is only one business and not a number of different businesses carried on by each of the partners.

The rule in *Baker v Archer-Shee* has been described as a rule of English trust law, not of English tax law.[275] This has several consequences. The first is that the governing law of the relevant trust dictates whether the source, for UK tax purposes, of the life interest holder's income is the life interest itself or the income-producing assets which underlie it. It is unsatisfactory, as a matter of tax policy, that the tax treatment of a life interest can be varied by setting up a trust with the 'right' governing law.[276] Yet, this can have important practical implications. For example, in the UK 'offshore fund' rules, it can be important to decide whether a UK-resident holds an interest in a 'transparent fund'.[277] If (as is typical) that fund is a non-UK trust, it cannot be a 'transparent fund' unless the governing law is consistent with English trust law as per *Baker v Archer-Shee.*[278] The governing law does not just include the terms of the particular trust. For example, Irish trust law usually follows *Baker v Archer-Shee*, but Irish unit trusts are also subject to section 11 Irish Unit Trust Act 1990. This treats undistributed income of

273. Sections 62, 64 and 65 ITA and subject to the general restrictions on 'sideways relief' (e.g., sections 66-70 ITA).
274. [1986] STC 491 at 504-505. These dicta were approved by the House of Lords on appeal in [1989] STC 898 at 901. While the method of assessing income tax on partners has changed since the 1980s, this does not affect the accuracy of this statement. Furthermore, as the House of Lords made clear, this statement applies whether the partnership is small or (as in *MacKinlay* itself) large, with many partners.
275. Hence the importance of the governing law of the trust.
276. Interestingly, the decision in *Syme* [1914] AC 1083, which was a forerunner of *Baker v Archer-Shee,* makes no reference to the importance of the governing law of the trust.
277. A UK-resident with an interest in a 'transparent fund' can avoid a number of disadvantages: *see* Regulation 29 Offshore Fund (Tax) Regulations 2009 SI 2009/3001.
278. *See* the definition of a 'transparent fund' in Regulation 11 Offshore Fund (Tax) Regulations 2009 SI 2009/3001. Regulation 11 is a rare example of UK tax legislation using the term 'transparent'. The same *Baker*-dependent approach applies in paragraph 8 Schedule 5AAA TCGA. Paragraph 8 enables an income tax-'transparent', 'UK property-rich' 'offshore collective investment vehicle' to elect to be treated as a partnership when taxing its non-UK-resident investors on chargeable gains from investing in UK real property. This election is targeted at trust-based investment funds, which would otherwise be treated as a company, and their unit holders as shareholders, under Schedule 5AAA. For more, *see* Sarah Squires: 'Finance Act 2019 Notes: Section 13 – Disposals by Non-UK Residents Etc – and Schedule 1, Paragraph 21: Schedule 5AAA to the Taxation of Chargeable Gains Act 1992 – UK Property Rich Collective Investment Vehicles, etc' [2019] British Tax Review 278 at 285-287.

the unit trust as an 'asset of the scheme', and not of the unit holders. This is presumably why HMRC regard an Irish unit trust as 'opaque', according to the list mentioned in section 2.13.3.

Second, even as a rule of trust law, *Baker v Archer-Shee* is not easy to understand. It contrasts the case where the life interest holder is entitled to underlying trust income as it arises (net of expenses) with the case where the life interest holder is simply entitled to have the trust fund properly administered and the aggregate net income paid over to it or applied for its benefit. Yet this is not a real distinction[279] because the second situation seems present in all life interest trusts. Unlike bare trusts, the life interest holder has no entitlement to any of the underlying capital of the trust fund. Surely *any* holder of a life interest is only entitled to have the trust fund properly administered and the aggregate income paid to it or applied for its benefit, whatever the governing law of the trust? The key distinction seems to be between cases where the trustees do and where they do not have the right to apply income for the benefit of the life interest holder (rather than paying it to that person directly). Yet, this seems an immaterial distinction, which is what the majority of the Court of Appeal decided in *Garland v Archer-Shee*. The author shares their opinion. Whether and how income is taxable should not depend on such a fine semantic distinction which can be easily manipulated.

The real question is whether all life interest holders should, despite trustees' rights and powers, be regarded as entitled to underlying trust income as it arises so that each trust asset is a separate source of income when taxing that life interest holder. That should be a question of UK tax policy with a uniform answer for all life interest holders. There is much to be said for subjecting all life interest holders to the rule in *Baker v Archer-Shee*, which ensures that the source of income does not change simply by interposing a life interest trust. On that basis, the House of Lords in *Garland v Archer-Shee* took a wrong turn when it reversed the Court of Appeal.

The extent of that wrong turn is illustrated by the impact of *Garland v Archer-Shee* in cases like *Williams v Singer* (*see* section 4.3.3.1). Suppose that non-UK-source income is received by UK-resident trustees of a trust with a non-UK-resident life interest holder. The trust's governing law does not treat the life interest holder as entitled to underlying trust income. Therefore, the effect of *Garland v Archer-Shee* seems to be that the trustees cannot avoid a 20% 'representative' UK tax charge even though the trust income is non-UK-source and the life interest holder is non-UK-resident. Because the life interest holder is not entitled to underlying income but only to a distribution of net trust income, the source of its income is its right to enforce the UK-resident trust and not the underlying income. Hence, the holder cannot argue that an income tax charge at trustee level would (as in *Williams v Singer*) impose UK tax on a non-UK-resident in respect of underlying non-UK-source income. If this is the effect of *Garland v Archer-Shee*, it further highlights its flaws. Minor differences in the trust's governing law about the nature of a life interest may mean that the UK tax charge on trustees can now have an extraterritorial effect, contrary to *Williams v Singer*. Furthermore, the life

279. It is not easy to explain this distinction to non-UK lawyers in order to obtain their advice on the nature of a life interest in a non-English law trust.

interest holder is worse off than a non-UK-resident discretionary beneficiary of a UK-resident trust which distributes non-UK-source income. That beneficiary can rely on ESC B18 (*see* section 4.3.5) to recover UK tax at trustee level on that income. The courts may in fact decline to apply *Garland v Archer-Shee* in this extraterritorial way. In *Kelly v Rogers* (*see* section 4.3.3.2), Romer LJ indicated (obiter at 19 TC 713) that if the income beneficiary had been non-UK-resident, then the UK-resident trustees would not have been taxable on the trust's non-UK-source income. In that case (which postdated both *Williams v Singer* and the *Archer-Shee* litigation), the trust's governing law meant that the UK-resident income beneficiary had no entitlement to specific underlying trust income.

Third, describing the rule in *Baker v Archer-Shee* as a rule of trust law means that it does not catch all underlying trust income for UK tax purposes. There are a number of items which constitute 'income' for tax purposes which are not 'income' under trust law. Such items are not income of a life interest holder under the rule in *Baker v Archer-Shee.* This makes some sense: the life interest holder would not be entitled to require the trustees to pay it these amounts because they are not 'income' under trust law. Therefore, it should not be taxed as if it is entitled to these amounts as they arise. However, because these items are 'income' for tax purposes, then to that extent the trust is not 'transparent'. Some such items may be taxed as income at the level of the trustee alone, under section 481 ITA (*see* section 4.3.5). Good[280] examples of amounts which are 'income' for tax purposes, but not for trust purposes, arise under the 'short lease premium' rules and the rules taxing accrued income on transfers of debt securities. The former[281] treat as income part of the premium paid for granting shorter leases even though any premium (unlike rent) is typically regarded for trust law purposes as a capital receipt. The accrued income rules[282] impose income tax on that element of the sale price of a debt security which represents accrued but unpaid interest. For trust law purposes, that 'cum div' element would simply be part of the security's capital value (unlike the interest received on an interest payment date).[283]

Fourth, HMRC practice sometimes mitigates the trust law aspect of *Baker v Archer-Shee.* In particular,[284] where the trustees of a life interest trust carry on a taxable trade which entitles them to claim capital (depreciation) allowances on the assets used in that trade, HMRC allow the life interest holder to claim the benefit of those capital allowances in computing its income from the trust. This helps ensure that the life

280. These examples are not exhaustive.
281. Chapter 4 Part 3 ITTOIA and Chapter 4 Part 4 CTA 2009.
282. Part 12 ITA. For corporation tax, an equivalent income charge is achieved via the 'loan relationships' rules in Parts 5 and 6 CTA 2009.
283. Accrued income profits on transferring debt securities will be taxed on the trustees at the special income tax rates discussed in section 4.3.5 (*see* sections 481-482 ITA) unless the trust is a section 60 TCGA-type trust. In that case, the trust is income tax transparent along section 60 lines (*see* section 666 ITA). Where a debt security is bought by trustees with accrued interest ('cum div'), the element of the purchase price representing accrued interest is offset against interest payable on the next interest payment date. The person entitled to that interest therefore gets tax relief. If *Baker v Archer-Shee* applies, that person will be the life interest holder who thereby gets tax relief for an amount which, under trust law principles, is part of the capital cost of the security.
284. *See* TSEM3772 in the Trusts Settlements and Estates Manual (accessed 11 June 2022).

interest holder's taxable income is no greater than that of the trustees. However, this approach is not easy to reconcile with the rule in *Baker v Archer-Shee.* Where that rule applies to a trading trust,[285] it simply treats underlying income (defined under trust law principles) as the source of the life interest holder's trust income. Trust income takes no account of capital allowances which are a stand-alone tax depreciation relief. They are not the same as commercial depreciation based on accounting principles, which may or may not be reflected in the trust law definition of income. Capital allowances are therefore not built into the concept of trading income, for tax or trust law purposes.[286]

Therefore overall, the rule in *Baker v Archer-Shee* offers a life interest holder a degree of income tax 'transparency'. The life interest holder should therefore be entitled to any special tax rates applicable to the underlying trust income. If that income has been subject at source to non-UK taxation, the life interest holder should be much better placed to claim double taxation relief, e.g., by way of credit. However, this form of 'transparency' is less complete than that applying to 'bare trusts'. The rule is also idiosyncratic, not least because when it applies is part-dictated by the governing law of the relevant trust. These idiosyncrasies have knock-on effects when applying double tax treaties, as discussed in section 6.7.5.

4.3.4 Trusts with a Vested Interest in Possession: Capital Gains Tax

For capital gains tax purposes, there is no equivalent of *Baker v Archer-Shee.* Where a trust does not fall within section 60 TCGA, then the trust property will be 'settled property' for capital gains tax purposes.[287] The trustees will be treated as a separate and

285. Can the rule in *Baker v Archer-Shee* even apply to a life interest in a trust which is carrying on a trade? This point arose (without being decided) in judicial review proceedings regarding retrospective tax legislation: *see R on the application of Robert Huitson v HMRC* [2010] EWHC 97 (Admin) and, in particular, paragraphs 52-53. In that case, *Baker v Archer-Shee* was being used as part of a tax avoidance scheme involving treaty protection for profits of an Isle of Man partnership in which a UK-resident invested via a life interest trust. The court was not referred to *Syme v Commissioner of Taxes* [1914] AC 1013, discussed in section 4.3.3.1. In *Syme,* the Privy Council did apply to a trading trust a principle equivalent to *Baker v Archer-Shee. Syme* is certainly very persuasive authority on the point. Hence the statement in Glen Loutzenhiser: 'Tiley's Revenue Law'. 10th edition, at p. 581, fn 3478, that an 'active trust' may not be subject to the rule in *Baker v Archer-Shee* is doubtful. HMRC's guidance seems consistent with *Syme*: *see* TSEM3771 in the Trusts Settlements and Estates Manual (accessed 11 June 2022).

286. Capital allowances are regulated by the Capital Allowances Act 2001. Under the HMRC practice described in the main text, if the life interest holder can claim the benefit of capital allowances, then presumably the trust income must be adjusted to exclude any commercial depreciation already reflected in it for trust law purposes. Otherwise, the life interest holder's taxable income would be reduced by both capital allowances and commercial depreciation. HMRC practice seems generous to the life interest holder in other respects. If capital allowances are claimed in respect of an asset used by trustees in a trade but that asset is later sold for more than its tax-written-down value, the excess over that value may be clawed back as income for tax purposes. That clawback, however, may not be income for trust law purposes. Trust law is likely to see the clawback as part of the disposal price of a capital asset of the trust. Because that amount is not trust income, the life interest holder should, in principle, not be taxed on it although it represents a clawback of excess reliefs used to reduce the life interest holder's taxable income from the trust.

287. Section 68 TCGA.

continuing person distinct from the persons who are trustees from time to time.[288] Where that notional separate person is UK-resident,[289] then it is potentially subject to capital gains tax at normal rates in its own right.[290]

Some 'interest in possession' trusts (because of the identity of the particular beneficiary) are eligible to pay tax on gains in respect of certain business assets owned by the trust at only 10% because of 'business asset disposal relief'.[291] Likewise, certain 'interest in possession' trusts can benefit from 'investors' relief' on disposing of shares.[292] This is a preferential 10% rate of capital gains tax when certain non-listed shareholdings are disposed of. Trusts with no interest in possession cannot benefit from either relief.

Therefore a trust outside section 60 TCGA is in principle 'opaque' for capital gains tax purposes, whether or not there is a vested interest in possession. This is true even if the trust is non-UK-resident under the rules in section 69 TCGA. A transfer of assets to the trust will therefore be an outright disposal of the entire property being settled, even if the settlor is a trustee and/or a beneficiary too.[293] Generally, a transfer of an asset from a UK-resident trust to a beneficiary will trigger a deemed disposal and reacquisition of that asset by the trustees at open market value.[294] If that results in a gain, the tax is a liability of the trust which cannot be sheltered with reliefs (e.g., losses) available to the beneficiary. If it results in a loss, there is limited scope[295] for the beneficiary to use those losses, provided they cannot be used by the trustees. In some cases, there may be scope for trustees to transfer a chargeable asset to a beneficiary without triggering gain if 'hold-over' relief is claimed. In that case, the beneficiary acquires the asset at the historic base cost of the trustees.[296]

This 'opaque' tax treatment can mean that the UK tax burden in respect of capital gains is higher if assets are held in a UK-resident trust than if they are held directly by the UK-taxpaying beneficiaries. While the tax system should not encourage the use of trusts to avoid tax, making it detrimental tax-wise to put assets into a trust seems a step

288. Section 69 TCGA.
289. Under section 69(2A)-(2E) TCGA. Rates of tax are currently 28% for capital gains in respect of, in particular, residential property and 20% in respect of almost all other capital gains. Because a UK-resident trust is now subject to capital gains tax at full marginal rates, the rules which used to attribute trust gains to a UK-resident settlor were abolished in 2008 for UK-resident trusts. This further reduces the effective 'transparency' of such trusts for capital gains tax purposes.
290. Unlike when section 60 TCGA applies.
291. *See* Chapter 3 Part V TCGA and in particular, section 169J TCGA. The relevant 'interest in possession' must not be for a fixed term.
292. *See* Chapter 5 Part V TCGA and in particular, section 169VH TCGA. Again, the relevant 'interest in possession' must not be for a fixed term.
293. Section 70 TCGA.
294. Section 71(1) TCGA. The beneficiary then acquires the asset at open market value.
295. Section 71(2) TCGA.
296. Chapter 4 Part 2 Finance Act 2005 creates a special elective tax regime for trusts for 'vulnerable beneficiaries'. This regime does not give rise to a fully 'transparent' trust for income tax and capital gains tax purposes. However, it permits the trustees' income and capital gains tax liabilities to be modified by reference to what the tax position would have been if the 'vulnerable beneficiary' had been directly entitled to the trust's income and gains. This is likely to lead to a reduced effective tax rate on the trust's income and gains.

too far, especially as a trust is above all a mechanism for protecting assets for its beneficiaries.

Because trusts outside section 60 TCGA 1992 are not 'transparent' for capital gains tax purposes, complex additional rules deal with the consequences, and in particular the avoidance possibilities, to which an 'opaque' trust gives rise. While space does not allow a detailed analysis, a good example are those rules which can attribute capital gains of non-UK-resident or dual-resident settlements to certain UK-resident settlors[297] or to beneficiaries[298] of such settlements. These rules limit the scope for deferring UK capital gains tax by allowing gains to roll up untaxed in 'opaque' trusts which are otherwise outside the UK tax charge.

There is relief from capital gains tax on a disposal of an interest in a trust falling outside section 60 TCGA.[299] This reflects the fact that the trust (if UK-resident) is itself a separate taxable person for capital gains tax. Therefore a further tax charge should not necessarily arise when disposing of a trust interest which reflects underlying gain already taxable at trust level. However, these tax-relieving rules on disposals of trust interests are disapplied routinely to limit avoidance.[300] That resurrects the risk of economic double taxation of trust capital gains: once at trust level and again at beneficiary level.

4.3.5 Trusts with No Vested Interest in Possession: Income Tax and Capital Gains Tax

Trusts with no vested interest in possession are outside section 60 TCGA. Therefore, they are not 'transparent' for capital gains tax purposes and are subject to the rules summarised in section 4.3.4.

The income taxation of such trusts in practice confers a degree of relief from income taxation on beneficiaries, to reflect income tax borne by the trustees. Thus, double taxation of income at the level of both the trustees and the beneficiary is avoided. Furthermore, the tax ultimately payable on that income can be managed so that it is roughly what would have been paid if the beneficiary had been entitled to the underlying trust assets directly. However, this mechanism for avoiding trust income being taxed twice is not really 'transparency', not least because beneficiaries are not currently taxable on underlying trust income, as it arises to the trustees and whether or not distributed.

297. Section 86 and Schedule 5 TCGA.
298. Sections 87-96 TCGA.
299. Section 76 TCGA.
300. *See* section 76(1A) and (1B) TCGA, section 76A and Schedule 4A TCGA and section 85 TCGA. Section 85 in particular disapplies the section 76 exemption when an interest in a non-UK-resident trust is disposed of. The rule assumes that the trust is not subject to UK capital gains tax. However, this is not necessarily true, especially if the trustee has direct or indirect holdings in UK real property.

The rule in *Baker v Archer-Shee* is inapplicable. Instead Part 9 ITA applies. Section 479 ITA charges income tax[301] at the 'dividend trust rate'[302] (on dividend income) or the 'trust rate'[303] (on other income of the trust) where 'accumulated or discretionary income arises to the trustees of a settlement'[304] which is not a charitable trust. This charge to tax on the trustees is not merely a representative charge. Hence, unlike the income tax charge on trustees of interest in possession trusts, its scope is not qualified by the tax status of any beneficiary.[305]

The income tax rates on trustees of this kind of trust are equal to the highest individual income tax rates. This discourages accumulation of income within the trust. This contrasts with the corporation tax treatment of a UK-resident company whose undistributed income is taxed at a fairly low rate (19%, rising to 25% from April 2023), which is significantly less than individual income tax rates. This encourages companies to retain income. A private investment company and a discretionary trust may not be radically dissimilar in the way they are structured. However, they will be subject to very different regimes and rates for taxing their income.

Section 480 ITA defines 'accumulated or discretionary income':

(1) Income is accumulated or discretionary income so far as –
 (a) it must be accumulated, or
 (b) it is payable at the discretion of the trustees or any other person,
 and it is not excluded by subsection (3).
(2) The cases covered by subsection 1(b) include cases where the trustees have, or any other person has, any discretion over one or more of the following matters –[306]
 (a) whether, or the extent to which, the income is to be accumulated,
 (b) the persons to whom the income is to be paid, and
 (c) how much of the income is to be paid to any person.
(3) Income is excluded for the purposes of subsection (1) so far as –
 (a) before being distributed, it is the income of any person other than the trustees,[307]
 (b) it is income from property within subsection (4), or
 (c) it is income from service charges which are paid in respect of dwellings in the United Kingdom and are held on trust.

301. This charge can in principle apply to relevant non-UK-resident trusts in respect of their UK-source income: *see IRC v Regent Trust Co Ltd (as Trustee of the Butt 1970 Settlement)* 53 TC 54. However, this will be subject to the limits on the UK income tax charge in respect of non-UK-residents in Chapter 1 Part 14 ITA (and in particular sections 811-812 ITA). These limits will usually apply provided there are *no* actual or contingent UK-resident beneficiaries of the trust.
302. Currently 39.35%: *see* section 9 ITA. This equals the highest rate of UK income tax on individuals in respect of dividends and other 'distributions'.
303. Currently 45%: *see* section 9 ITA. This equals the highest rate of UK income tax on individuals.
304. Section 466 ITA makes clear that property held in trust is within a 'settlement' unless, in essence, the trust could fall within section 60 TCGA (*see* section 466(3), (5) and (6) ITA).
305. *See* the first part of section 4.3.3.1.
306. Section 480(2) ITA illustrates the breadth of section 480(1) consistently with how the predecessor legislation was interpreted in *IRC v Berrill* [1981] STC 784.
307. This carves out underlying trust income to which a beneficiary is entitled under the rule in *Baker v Archer-Shee*.

(4) Property is within this subsection if it –
(a) is held for the purposes of a superannuation fund ...[relating to a non-UK undertaking] ... .but
(b) is not held as a member of a property investment LLP [a form of UK LLP primarily invested in real estate].

Section 480(1) indicates that 'accumulated or discretionary income' means income as defined under trust law, rather than tax law.[308]

However, section 481 ITA extends the tax charge at the dividend trust rate or the trust rate to items of taxable income[309] listed in section 482 ITA. This brings into charge at the higher trust rates certain items which would not be regarded as income for trust law purposes and therefore would not be taxed in the hands of a holder of a vested interest in possession under *Baker v Archer*-Shee: *see* section 4.3.3.2. To that extent, a gap in the rule in *Baker v Archer-Shee* is plugged indirectly, although these items may thereby be taxed at a rate in excess of any interest in possession holder's effective personal tax rate.

The section 481 charge does not apply to unit trusts (*see* section 4.3.6), nor to charitable trusts, nor to property held by superannuation funds for non-UK undertakings. It also does not apply to 'accumulated or discretionary income'[310] or what would be such income barring the exclusions in section 480(3)(a)[311] or (c).

The income tax charge at the trust rate or dividend trust rate can be reduced by certain expenses of the trustees.[312] Those expenses must be properly chargeable to income of the trust under general trust law, ignoring the express terms of the settlement.[313] Section 486 sets out the steps for grossing up the relevant expenses and

308. *See also* 29.2.3.2 in Glen Loutzenhiser: 'Tiley's Revenue Law'. 10th edition. In *Trustees of the PL Travers Will Trust v HMRC* [2014] SFTD 265, the First-Tier Tribunal (Tax) analysed the principles determining whether trust receipts are income or capital under trust law. It applied them to two categories of copyright royalty received by a trust. When deciding if an amount is income or capital under trust law, the key is the settlor's presumed intention about whether that amount should be available for the income or capital beneficiaries. This will depend on the facts. So a cash dividend paid on shares from accumulated profits, and not capitalised, should be trust income: *see Trustees of the Bessie Taube Discretionary Settlement Trust v HMRC* [2011] SFTD 153. It is irrelevant that the size of the dividend greatly devalues the shares (which form part of trust capital). By contrast, an amount can remain part of trust capital even if, as a corporate law matter, it is technically a distribution in specie, e.g., the receipt of new shares for old shares held by the trust on a company demerger: *see Sinclair v Lee* [1993] Ch 497.
309. These include 'accrued income profits' of trustees in respect of debt securities, and amounts realised under the 'offshore fund' rules or in respect of 'deeply discounted securities'. They also include certain distributions to trustees on a redemption or repurchase of a company's shares. The items in the last sentence are subject to the dividend trust rate, rather than the trust rate, of tax. The items listed do not include a balancing charge recapturing excess capital allowances. This would be taxed as income in the non-trust context, but for trust law purposes, it would probably be part of the disposal proceeds of a capital asset and hence not income: *see* section 4.3.3.2.
310. As defined in section 480 ITA and charged under section 479 ITA.
311. Hence the section 481 charge does not apply to income already taxable at the level of any life interest holder under *Baker v Archer-Shee.*
312. Chapter 4 Part 9 ITA.
313. Section 484(5) ITA. Therefore, relief for trustee expenses cannot be expanded by providing in the settlement for a broader class of expenses to be chargeable to trust income. This is consistent with the less explicit predecessor legislation: *see Carver v Duncan, Bosanquet v Allen*

setting them off against different types of income taxable at the trust rate or the dividend trust rate. Trust income offset by expenses in this way remains fully taxable in the hands of the trustees at the basic rate (currently 20%) or basic dividend tax rate (8.75%) because they are still 'receiving or entitled' to it.[314]

Relief from economic double taxation of the same income (at both trustee and beneficiary levels) stems from Chapter 7 Part 4 ITA (and especially sections 493-494). However, these rules *only* apply where an 'annual payment' is made by the trustees in the exercise of a discretion,[315] *when they are UK-resident*. Furthermore, that payment to the beneficiary must either be income of the beneficiary purely because of the fact of payment[316] or be treated as income of a settlor under the rules attributing to the settlor any 'settlement' income in fact paid to the settlor's minor children.

Where sections 493-4 ITA apply, the 'annual payment' made by the trustees is grossed up for income tax purposes at the special trust rate of 45%. The beneficiary is treated as having paid income tax equal to the amount of that grossing-up.[317] If that

---

[1985] STC 356, which also ruled that expenses whose object is to benefit both the income and capital beneficiaries must be charged to trust capital. Whether trust expenses are properly chargeable to income or capital of the trust was also considered in *In re Bennett, Jones v Bennett* [1896] 1 Ch 778 and *In re Sherry, Sherry v Sherry* [1913] 2 Ch 508 and, more recently, in *Revenue and Customs Commissioners v Trustees of the Peter Clay Discretionary Trust* [2009] STC 469. There the court accepted that if trustee and other professional fees can be properly apportioned between those attributable to dealing with the income of the trust and those attributable to dealing with trust capital (including income which the trustees have decided to accumulate), then the fees attributable purely to income can be charged to income and deducted under what is now section 484(5) ITA.

314. Section 484(4) ITA. The 'representative' charge on trustees' income is thereby reinstated where the higher rate charges in sections 479 and 481 ITA fall away.

315. Vinelott J in *IRC v Berrill* [1981] STC 784 at 798 stated (in relation to similar wording in the predecessor legislation) that the exercise of a discretion should be read broadly. It could therefore apply where a beneficiary's right to trust income becomes indefeasible because a power of accumulation or a power to divert income to some other beneficiary or purpose comes to an end, without the trustee exercising that power.

316. Therefore, the payment must amount to a *new* income source (and not an advance of trust capital) in the hands of the beneficiary because the trustees exercise a discretion. That would not be the case if the beneficiary were already entitled to the underlying income under the rule in *Baker v Archer-Shee.* Generally, there would be such new income if a discretion were exercised in favour of the beneficiary. There is considerable authority on whether such discretionary payments are income or capital in the hands of beneficiaries: for example, *Trustees of the Will of H.K. Brodie v IRC* 17 TC 432; *Lindus & Hortin v IRC* 17 TC 442; *Jackson's Trustees v IRC* 25 TC 13; *Cunard's Trustees v IRC* 27 TC 122. Such payments (even if made from trust capital) are likely to be income in the hands of the beneficiary if there is evidence of an intention to create an annuity or to ensure that the beneficiary maintains a specified level of income. However, such payments, even if recurrent, may still not be income, if made under a power to appoint capital: *see Stevenson v Wishart* [1986] STC 74 and [1987] STC 266. In that case, it was key that the beneficiary was the object of a separate power to appoint capital and was not just an income beneficiary, even though trust capital was being applied on a recurrent basis for an 'income' purpose (funding care home expenses). While such a distribution of capital will not attract income tax, it is very likely to trigger inheritance tax: *see* section 5.3. *See also* Avery Jones: Trusts *supra*, p. 388 at fn 83.

317. If the trust is caught by the 'settlement' rules in section 619 ITTOIA, things work differently. The recipient of the annual payment is then treated as having paid income tax on that amount at the additional rate of 45%. That deemed tax payment is fully creditable against the recipient's own tax liability on the annual payment but is not refundable: *see* section 685A ITTOIA. If the beneficiary receiving the income distribution from the trust is subject to UK

beneficiary has relevant reliefs and allowances, a refund may be obtained of the tax thereby treated as paid at source on this 'annual payment'. Any such refund corresponds to the tax paid by the trustees under sections 479 and 481 ITA. This is because much of that tax at trustee level is allocated to a 'tax pool'.[318] The pool's running total is matched against the amount by which 'annual payments' from the trust have been grossed up. If the running total equals or exceeds the amount of the gross-up, the trustees have no further obligation to account for tax equivalent to that which the beneficiary is treated as paying in respect of the 'annual payment'.

These complex rules are a form of relief from economic double taxation rather than outright 'transparency'. The beneficiary has no entitlement to underlying income of the trust. The 'source' of its income is instead the exercise of a discretion in its favour. Moreover, the income from that separate source does not 'mirror' the characteristics of the trust's underlying income. This is especially clear if the only income of the trustees consists of dividends. The trustees will be taxed at the 'dividend trust rate' of 39.35%, but any discretionary payment funded by those dividends will be grossed up and taxed at 45%. That payment by the trustees is a distinct income item which is not treated as a dividend, despite being funded by underlying dividend income.[319] It will probably arise after that underlying income arises to the trust. Because the 'dividend trust rate' is less than 45%, the trustees will have to make good the shortfall between 39.35% tax on their dividend income and the 45% tax treated as paid on the discretionary payment.[320] Alternatively, they will have to limit the latter payment so that the amount of the gross-up does not exceed tax at trust level on the underlying income.

The beneficiary, if non-UK-resident, will usually be unable to use a double taxation treaty to recover UK tax treated as paid in respect of the 'annual payment'. The UK has increasingly insisted, when negotiating treaties, that income from trusts and estates be excluded from the 'Other Income' Article.[321] This preserves UK taxing rights in relation to UK-resident trustees. However, as discussed below, the non-UK-resident beneficiary may be able to claim other reliefs from UK tax.

Section 111 TIOPA gives a UK-taxable beneficiary receiving discretionary income from UK-resident trustees the right to a UK foreign tax credit for creditable non-UK tax borne by those trustees. To this extent, the trust is 'looked through'. In order to trigger

corporation tax, section 610 CTA 2010 ignores that distribution for corporation tax purposes but the beneficiary cannot obtain a refund of tax treated as paid on it.

318. *See* sections 497 and 498 ITA. The 'tax pool' cannot include any UK tax cancelled out by the trustees claiming a credit for non-UK tax in respect of trust income.
319. Contrast the US tax treatment of a 'complex trust': *see* section 7.2.2.
320. *See* Example 18.5 on pp. 556-557 in Anne Fairpo and David Salter: 'Revenue Law: Principles and Practice'. 37th edition, Bloomsbury Professional.
321. *See*, for example, Article 22(1) of the UK-US treaty of 24 July 2001: SI 2002/2848. The Exchange of Notes states: 'It is understood that the purpose of the exclusion from the paragraph for income paid out of trusts or the estates of deceased persons in the course of administration is to allow a recipient of such income the relief that would have been available to him under the provisions of the [treaty] had he received the income direct instead of through the trust or estate.' This refers to the further rules and practices which HMRC has now adopted in this area and which are discussed in the main text. *See also* Statement of Practice 3/86.

this credit, the trustees must certify[322] to HMRC that the discretionary payment is made at least in part from income giving rise to creditable non-UK tax and from a specified source. That income must have arisen to the trustees not earlier than six years before the end of the UK tax year[323] in which the discretionary income payment is made.

Section 111 seems consistent with *Drummond v Collins* 8 TC 525. There it was decided that discretionary payments of income to UK-resident beneficiaries by the non-UK trustees of a foreign trust had as their 'source' the non-UK trust fund, even though the beneficiaries had no proprietary interest in it. Section 111 is limited to cases where the trustees are UK-resident, unlike *Drummond*. Where discretionary trustees are non-UK-resident, a UK-taxable beneficiary may be able to rely on *Drummond* to claim a credit (under sections 8 and 9 TIOPA) for non-UK tax on underlying trust income if it can show that its discretionary entitlement has been funded from the same taxed underlying income. In that case, the 'source' of the discretionary payment is the same as that of the underlying income. In practice, it may be hard to 'trace' a discretionary entitlement to particular taxed items of underlying trust income. However, ESC B18 may apply and is discussed next.

HMRC by concession allows 'transparent' income tax treatment of beneficiaries in trusts where there is no vested interest in possession.[324] This concession allows beneficiaries to 'look through' the trust for certain additional purposes and falls into two parts. The first applies to UK-resident trusts. Where a beneficiary of such a trust receives a discretionary payment within sections 493-494 ITA, the beneficiary may claim tax relief to the extent that the discretionary payment is made from underlying trust income which would have given rise to certain reliefs if it had been received directly by the beneficiary. The reliefs are those applying to certain tax-exempt UK government securities targeted at non-UK-residents;[325] double tax treaty relief; and any other relief which would have been available because the beneficiary is non-UK-resident. In short, the first part of ESC B18 is targeted at non-UK-resident beneficiaries of a UK-resident discretionary trust. It gives relief to the extent that the discretionary payment is made from income arising to the trustees within six years before the end of the UK tax year in which that payment is made.[326] The payment is treated as made

322. In practice, the trustees may not be willing to do this.
323. 6 April to the following 5 April.
324. Extra-Statutory Concession (ESC) B18 (and for UK estates in the course of administration, ESC A14). These Concessions are quite radical and should surely be put on a statutory basis, given the tax authorities' limited powers to grant ESCs under their tax management powers: *see* Lord Hoffmann in *R (on the application of Wilkinson) v Inland Revenue Commissioners* [2006] STC 270 at 276. A similar point applies to the concessions built into Statement of Practice D12, which is discussed in Appendix A.
325. So-called FOTRA Securities: *see* Chapter 6 Part 6 ITTOIA and sections 1279 and 1280 CTA 2009.
326. In a limited number of UK double tax treaties (notably, with Hong Kong, Panama and Spain), the first limb of ESC B18 has in effect been reflected in the 'Other Income' Article: *see* Brabazon *supra*, at p. 248. In the UK-Spain treaty, paragraph V of the Protocol also entitles a Spanish-resident beneficiary of a UK trust to a Spanish foreign tax credit for 'the effective income tax paid in the United Kingdom by the beneficiary as a consequence of the income distribution', after all relevant repayment claims (e.g., under the 'Other Income' Article) have been made. For a simplified example of how ESC B18 operates, *see* Naomi Wells, 'Staying Offshore' Taxation (17 January 2019) 12 at 13.

ratably out of all sources of trust income on a last-in-first-out basis. Hence ESC B18 contains 'tracing' rules. The trustees must be fully UK tax-compliant. The beneficiary must claim relief within five years and ten months from the end of the tax year in which it received the discretionary payment. This time limit, plus the six-year condition mentioned above, ensures that HMRC's obligation to give relief is not open-ended.

The second part of ESC B18 applies where a beneficiary (whether or not UK-resident) receives a payment from discretionary trustees which is not within sections 493-494 ITA (because non-UK-resident trustees exercise their discretion outside the UK). Where a non-UK-resident beneficiary receives a discretionary payment from trust income which would have been chargeable to UK tax if received directly by it, that beneficiary may claim by concession a UK personal tax allowance in respect of that income. However, it can only claim relief for UK tax in fact paid by the non-UK-resident trustees on that income (e.g., on UK-source rental income) from which the discretionary payment is sourced. Where the payment is sourced from interest on FOTRA Securities, the beneficiary can claim a UK tax exemption for the discretionary payment.

A UK-resident beneficiary receiving a discretionary payment from non-UK-resident trustees may claim credit for UK tax in fact paid by the trustees on income funding that payment, as it was from a UK-resident trust to which Chapter 7 Part 9 ITA applied.[327] The trustees must be fully UK tax-compliant, which will include paying UK tax on UK-source income (*see* fn 316). The beneficiary must claim relief within five years and ten months from the end of the tax year in which it receives the discretionary payment.

4.3.6 'Unit Trusts'

4.3.6.1 The Concept of a 'Unit Trust'

No discussion of how trusts are treated for UK tax purposes, and whether they are 'transparent', would be complete without considering 'unit trusts'. These are a trust-based form of collective investment vehicle which has been widely used in the UK, both for retail and non-retail investors and for all forms of investment. Since the late 1990s, UK 'unit trusts' have increasingly been displaced, as a retail collective investment vehicle, by UK 'open-ended investment companies'. However, in other areas, they have continued to flourish, notably in relation to investment in UK

327. No credit is given for any non-repayable UK tax treated as paid on income of the non-UK-resident trustees, where that tax would not be added to the 'tax pool' (*see* above in the main text) if the trustees had been UK-resident. The most obvious example of such non-repayable tax was the old UK 'tax credit' on UK-source dividend income, abolished in 2016. However, this non-repayable UK tax is also ignored when grossing up the beneficiary's discretionary income for the purposes of applying ESC B18. ESC B18 should also entitle the UK-resident beneficiary to a foreign tax credit for non-UK tax imposed on distributed trust income in the state of source (but not any third-country tax on the trustees): *see* Avery Jones: Trusts *supra*, at pp. 402 and 405.

commercial property, which often takes place via a Jersey property unit trust or JPUT.[328]

A 'unit trust scheme' is defined for tax purposes by reference to the UK's legislation regulating financial services. Section 237(1) FSMA 2000 provides that '… "unit trust scheme" means a collective investment scheme under which the property is held on trust for the participants, except that it does not include a contractual scheme'. The core concept of a 'collective investment scheme' ('CIS') is discussed below. 'Contractual schemes' are a relatively new form of regulated UK collective investment structure for non-retail investors. They are intended to be fully income tax transparent in the UK and are constituted either as contractual co-ownership schemes or (more rarely) as LPs formed under the Limited Partnerships Act 1907.[329] They are of limited significance to the present discussion.

CIS is mainly and broadly defined in section 235 FSMA:

> (1) In this Part, 'collective investment scheme' means *any arrangements with respect to property of any description, including money, the purpose or effect of which is to enable persons taking part in the arrangements (whether by becoming owners of the property or any part of it or otherwise) to participate in or receive profits or income arising from the acquisition, holding, management or disposal of the property or sums paid out of such profits or income* [emphasis added].
>
> (2) The arrangements must be such that the persons who are to participate ('participants') do not have day-to-day control over the management of the property, whether or not they have the right to be consulted or to give directions.
>
> (3) The arrangements must also have either or both of the following characteristics:

328. The attraction of a JPUT stems mainly from its 'semi-transparent' status for UK tax purposes. It has been treated as a non-UK-resident company, and hence 'opaque', for UK capital gains tax and SDLT purposes. Hence, interests in it could typically be sold by non-UK-resident investors without incurring SDLT or tax on capital gains (although this capital gains tax advantage largely ended in April 2019). However, a JPUT is typically 'transparent' for income tax purposes because it is formed under a governing law (e.g., Jersey) which is consistent with English law as per *Baker v Archer-Shee.* Income tax 'transparency' enables JPUT investors to claim capital allowances when computing their share of the underlying net rental income from the UK property. If the JPUT is 'transparent' for income tax purposes, as per *Baker v Archer-Shee,* paragraph 8 Schedule 5AAA TCGA allows all unit holders to elect irrevocably to treat it as a 'transparent' partnership (within section 59 TCGA) for the purposes of UK tax on capital gains. If the unit holders are non-UK-resident tax-exempts, this election can ensure that any gain on disposing of the UK property interest held by the JPUT is not taxable, which since April 2019 may not be the case otherwise. If this election is made, a sale of a JPUT interest will also be treated as a sale of the underlying property so that a purchaser of the JPUT interest will get a 'stepped-up' base cost in that property for the purposes of UK tax on chargeable gains. This would not be the case if it were held by a non-UK-resident company, which cannot elect for partnership treatment. The main text further discusses the UK tax treatment of 'unit trusts'. The UK tax benefits of a JPUT will not be available unless it is a 'collective investment scheme' (*see* the main text) for UK regulatory purposes. This will not be the case if there is only one unit holder and may not be the case if the manager of the JPUT is a company affiliated with the trust's unit holders: *see* fn 333.
329. 'Contractual schemes' enabled the UK to offer a non-trust-based tax transparent collective investment vehicle which could compete with the Luxembourg 'fonds commun de placements' or FCP.

(a) the contributions of the participants and the profits or income out of which payments are to be made to them are pooled;
(b) the property is managed as a whole by or on behalf of the operator of the scheme.

(4) If arrangements provide for such pooling as is mentioned in subsection (3)(a) in relation to separate parts of the property, the arrangements are not to be regarded as constituting a single collective investment scheme unless the participants are entitled to exchange rights in one part for rights in another.
(5) The Treasury may by order provide that arrangements do not amount to a collective investment scheme:
(a) in specified circumstances; or
(b) if the arrangements fall within a specified category of arrangement.

This wide definition underpins the UK regulation of the marketing and managing of all types of collective investment vehicle.[330] It has been borrowed for tax purposes. It catches all kinds of 'arrangement', which will include certain trusts but much else besides.[331] 'Arrangements' need not be legally enforceable.

The CIS definition is somewhat unclear. This is problematic because there are serious criminal and other consequences if a person is not properly regulated to run a CIS. Therefore, under section 235(5) FSMA, regulations[332] expressly carve out of that definition a number of structures. The list of carve-outs is eclectic,[333] but its impact is limited for tax purposes. Therefore, the main definition in section 235(1)-(4) remains of primary importance. Hence any trust-based structure for collective investment is likely to be a CIS and hence a 'unit trust scheme'.[334]

330. *See* in particular section 19 FSMA.
331. Section 235(1) FSMA makes clear that participants in a CIS need not own the underlying CIS property, e.g., if the CIS were an open-ended investment company, rather than a trust.
332. Financial Services and Markets Act 2000 (Collective Investment Schemes) Order 2001 (SI 2001/1062) ('the 2001 Order').
333. Paragraph 4 of the 2001 Order provides that 'arrangements do not amount to a collective investment scheme if they are operated otherwise than by way of business'. Paragraph 8 carves out certain employee share schemes. Paragraph 10 states that 'arrangements do not amount to a collective investment scheme if each of the participants is a body corporate in the same group as the operator [of the arrangements]'. Paragraph 21 provides that:

> (1) Subject to subparagraph (2), no body incorporated under the law of, or any part of, the United Kingdom relating to building societies or registered societies or registered under any such law relating to friendly societies, and *no other body corporate other than an open-ended investment company, amounts to a collective investment scheme* [emphasis added].
> (2) Subparagraph (1) does not apply to any body incorporated as a limited liability partnership.

334. The Supreme Court in *The Financial Conduct Authority v Asset LI Inc and others* [2016] 3 All ER 93 confirmed the breadth and fact-sensitivity of section 235 FSMA. Lord Sumption distinguished between: (i) cases where the investor retains entire control of the relevant property but employs an investment professional to advise on exploiting that property; and (ii) cases where that investor and other investors surrender control over their property to the scheme operator so that it can be either pooled or managed in common, in return for a share of the profits generated by the collective fund. Only (ii) is a CIS but this can apply even where investors retain legal and/or beneficial ownership of the property (e.g., if the property is co-owned under a trust).

Regulations enacted[335] purely for tax purposes ensure that certain structures which are potentially trust-based are not taxed as 'unit trust schemes'. These regulations have no bearing on the regulatory status of these structures. The most important structure covered by these regulations, for both income tax and capital gains tax purposes, is a unit trust scheme which is a 'limited partnership scheme'.

The regulations provide[336] that 'A unit trust scheme is a limited partnership scheme when the scheme property is *held on trust* [emphasis added] for the general partners and the limited partners in a limited partnership.' This means a LP formed under the Limited Partnerships Act 1907. Hence this carve-out should be irrelevant where a LP has legal personality enabling it to own assets beneficially. Such structures should not involve any trust over scheme property, so the question of 'unit trust' status should not arise.[337] Scottish limited partnerships have separate legal personality enabling them to own assets beneficially. Therefore, unlike English limited partnerships, they should not need to rely on the 1988 Regulations to avoid being classified as 'unit trust schemes' for capital gains tax and income tax purposes.[338]

4.3.6.2 Tax Treatment of Unit Trusts

4.3.6.2.1 Authorised Unit Trusts

If a trust is a unit trust scheme for tax purposes, then the next question is whether it is an 'authorised unit trust scheme'. This (*see* section 237(3) FSMA) is 'a unit trust scheme which is authorised for the purposes of [FSMA] by an authorisation order in force under section 243 [FSMA]'. Authorisations are in essence only granted where the UK regulatory authorities are satisfied that the unit trust can properly be marketed to the public and, in particular, to retail investors.

Section 617 CTA 2010 then provides:

> (1) In respect of income arising to the trustees of an authorised unit trust, and for the purposes of the provisions relating to relief for capital expenditure, the Tax Acts have effect as if:
> (a) the trustees were a UK resident company; and
> (b) the rights of the unit holders were shares in the company.

335. Capital Gains Tax (Definition of Unit Trust Scheme) Regulations 1988: SI 1988/266 as amended. Income Tax (Definition of Unit Trust Scheme) Regulations 1988: SI 1988/267 as amended. Capital Gains Tax (Pension Funds Pooling Schemes) Regulations 1996: SI 1996/1583 as amended. Income Tax (Pension Funds Pooling Schemes) Regulations 1996: SI 1996/1585 as amended.
336. Paragraph 4 of the Capital Gains Tax (Definition of Unit Trust Scheme) Regulations 1988 and paragraph 8 of the Income Tax (Definition of Unit Trust Scheme) Regulations 1988.
337. Of course, the relevant partnership, even if not trust-based, could still be a 'collective investment scheme' for UK regulatory purposes, e.g., a partnership-based collective investment vehicle.
338. *See* 2 for a discussion of Scottish partnerships. Questions remain whether a non-UK LP lacking legal personality can be a 'unit trust scheme'. For example, section 20 Limited Partnerships (Guernsey) Law 1995 suggests that a Guernsey LP's property is 'held by the general partners jointly on trust as an asset of the partnership'.

(2) References in the Corporation Tax Acts to a body corporate are to be read in accordance with subsection (1)

Hence the income profits of an authorised unit trust are subject to corporation tax.[339] Section 618 CTA 2010 applies a special rate of corporation tax to an authorised unit trust, equal to the basic rate of income tax for the corresponding tax year (currently 20%).[340]

However, dividend income of the authorised unit trust will typically be exempt from corporation tax because of the general corporation tax exemption for such income.[341] Interest income will be taxable, but there is scope for the unit trust to be treated as paying interest distributions[342] which are deductible by it (and taxed as interest in the hands of unit holders).

An 'authorised unit trust' is also treated as a UK-resident company for capital gains tax purposes,[343] and its unit holders are treated as shareholders. However, section 100(1) TCGA provides that the capital gains of an 'authorised unit trust' are not subject to capital gains tax. This helps to ensure that an 'authorised unit trust' normally incurs no UK tax itself, provided that its activity does not amount to trading.[344] Unit holders are taxed on the income of the trust as it arises in a number of different ways.[345] In brief, the income of the trust is treated in every period of account as distributed to unit holders in a form which is either interest or dividends for UK tax purposes. There is therefore no scope for deferring investor taxation on the income of the unit trust, even if it is retained or reinvested by the trust.

Therefore, overall, an authorised unit trust is not 'transparent' for the purposes of income tax or capital gains tax. The source of the unit holder's income and gains is its rights as a unit holder against the trustees. The trust is not 'looked through' so as to treat unit holders as entitled to the underlying income, gains and assets of the trust. Therefore, unit holders typically do not pay tax on capital gains unless and until they dispose of their units at a gain. There is no unit holder entitlement to losses of the

339. Unlike its capital gains: *see* fn 343.
340. The normal 'mainstream' rate of corporation tax is 19% but will rise to 25% from April 2023.
341. *See* Part 9A CTA 2009.
342. *See* Regulations 18-21 Authorised Investment Funds (Tax) Regulations 2006: SI 2006/964, as amended ('The 2006 Regulations').
343. Section 99(1) TCGA. This makes clear that its capital gains are only chargeable to capital gains tax, not to corporation tax on capital gains. The authorised unit trust therefore cannot access certain reliefs (e.g., group relief) from corporation tax on capital gains.
344. The full details of the taxation of authorised unit trusts and their unit holders are beyond the scope of this work, as is a discussion of the concept of 'trading'. The rules for taxing the trust's income and that of its unit holders are in the 2006 Regulations, which contain a very similar regime for UK 'open-ended investment companies' and their shareholders.
345. *See* the 2006 Regulations. Section 99B TCGA ensures that unit holders get increased capital gains tax base cost in their units where those units are accumulation units. A holder of 'accumulation' units is *treated* at least annually as receiving a distribution for tax purposes but receives no matching cash payment because the corresponding income is reinvested by the unit trust. The section 99B addition to base cost in those units reflects the income retained and reinvested by the trust but which is still treated as distributed to the unit holder for tax purposes.

trust.[346] Overall, unit holders avoid the compliance complications to which full transparency of the trust could give rise, not least the need to identify and trace fractional interests in the underlying assets of the trust. The composition of those assets is likely to change, as is the identity of unit holders.[347]

However, the tax treatment of an authorised unit trust ensures that there should normally be little or no tax at the level of the unit trust itself. This makes the trust viable as a collective investment vehicle: interposing it must not create significant extra tax compared to direct investment by unit holders in the trust's underlying investments. The trust is treated as making periodic distributions of its income (whether or not it does so in fact) which ensures timely taxation of trust income at unit holder level. Furthermore, the tax regime for authorised unit trusts allows some income distributions of the trust to be treated if they were payments of (deductible) interest[348] or of dividends. Therefore, unit holders can be treated, for UK tax purposes, as receiving different forms of income which to some extent reflect the investment base and underlying income sources of the trust, even though that unit trust is regarded as an 'opaque' company for tax purposes. Therefore the income tax result (but not the capital gains tax result) for unit holders has similarities with full 'transparency'.[349]

4.3.6.2.2 Unauthorised Unit Trusts

Unit trusts which are not 'authorised' are known as 'unauthorised unit trusts'. They are not automatically regarded as UK-resident, although they can be.[350] Section 99 TCGA will (with an exception mentioned below) treat any unauthorised unit trust as a company, and its unit holders as shareholders, for the purposes of UK capital gains tax (not corporation tax). Hence it will not be 'transparent' for those purposes, in the same way as an 'authorised' unit trust. Unit holders thereby avoid the compliance complications to which full transparency of the trust could give rise.[351]

---

346. A similar approach for capital gains tax (*see* section 103D TCGA) applies to contractual co-ownership schemes. These are income tax-'transparent', but non-trust-based UK collective investment schemes regulated under section 235A FSMA. *See also* fn 329. Section 103D also applies to those non-UK funds ('offshore funds') which are income tax-'transparent' under the rule in *Baker v Archer-Shee*, e.g., Luxembourg 'fonds commun de placements'. Units in such schemes or funds are usually *not* treated as shares in a company for capital gains tax purposes, but they *are* treated as separate assets from the underlying assets of the fund.
347. By contrast, *see* the earlier discussion of section 60 TCGA at section 4.3.2.
348. Provided that the unit trust's investments comprise specified levels of debt instruments and related derivatives: *see* the 2006 Regulations, and especially Regulations 18-21.
349. This analogy can only be taken so far. If underlying income of the authorised unit trust has suffered non-UK withholding tax, the trust itself will probably be unable to claim an effective foreign tax credit for that non-UK tax. Moreover, because the unit holder is *not* entitled to that underlying income, it cannot claim a UK foreign tax credit either. There is no equivalent for authorised unit trusts of section 111 TIOPA or ESC B18: *see* section 4.3.5 above.
350. Whether such a unit trust is UK-resident will depend on whether it is 'centrally managed and controlled' in the UK.
351. *See* the discussion of trusts within section 60 TCGA at 4.3.2. If the unauthorised unit trust is non-UK-resident and is treated as a company under section 99 TCGA, some UK-resident unit holders may sometimes be taxable by attribution on its undistributed gains: *see* the anti-avoidance rules in sections 3-3G TCGA.

The exception mentioned above is if the trust is an 'offshore fund' which is treated as income tax-'transparent' under the rule in *Baker v Archer-Shee*.[352] This will often be the case with non-UK-resident unit trusts, such as JPUTs. That kind of trust is not treated as a company and unit holders' interests in it are not usually treated as shares. Those interests are, however, treated for capital gains tax purposes as separate assets from the underlying trust assets.[353]

For UK income tax purposes, if a non-UK-resident unauthorised unit trust has a governing law which follows *Baker v Archer-Shee*, the unit holder is typically subject to tax-'transparent' treatment consistent with *Baker v Archer-Shee*. This may lead to UK tax on the unit holder's share of both undistributed and distributed income.[354] However, it may also be easier for the unit holder to claim double taxation relief, such as a credit for any non-UK income tax borne by the trustee. The unit holder may also be able to rely on more favourable rules for computing its income from the trust.[355]

If an unauthorised unit trust is UK-resident, the Unauthorised Unit Trusts (Tax) Regulations 2013 ('the 2013 Regulations') govern.[356] They create a category of 'exempt unauthorised unit trusts', whose trustees are UK-resident in the relevant period of account; whose unit holders throughout that period are 'eligible investors' and which is approved by HMRC[357] as an 'exempt unauthorised unit trust'. 'Eligible investors' are essentially those exempt from capital gains tax or corporation tax on a disposal of their units (other than because of non-UK-residence), e.g., charities, UK-approved pension funds and entities enjoying sovereign immunity (including some 'sovereign wealth' funds). Hence the 'exempt unauthorised unit trust' is targeted at tax-exempt unit holders. Its capital gains are not subject to UK tax.[358] Income of such a trust is treated as that of the trustees, not the unit holder and is chargeable at the basic rate (currently 20%).[359] Likewise, only the trustees can claim tax relief for capital expenditure.[360] The rules discussed at section 4.3.5 for taxing discretionary payments by UK-resident trustees do not apply to an 'exempt unauthorised unit trust'.

Unit holders of an 'exempt unauthorised unit trust' are treated as receiving from it taxable income if an amount is shown in the trust's accounts as income available for payment to them or for investment.[361] Those deemed income payments to unit holders

352. *See* section 99(1A) TCGA.
353. Section 103D TCGA. *See also* fn 346. Because this kind of non-UK-resident trust is not deemed to be a company, unit holders should not be taxable under sections 3-3G TCGA on its undistributed gains: *see* fn 351.
354. The unit holder will get an addition to its UK base cost in its units for capital gains tax purposes where it is taxed on undistributed income which is reinvested by the trustees: *see* section 103D(4) TCGA.
355. *See* the summary of the UK tax treatment of a JPUT in section 4.3.6.1 and fn 328. A JPUT is a well-known type of non-UK-resident unauthorised unit trust.
356. SI 2013/2819, as amended. The previous rules applying to UK-resident unauthorised unit trusts were mainly in sections 504-506 ITA. They were perceived to foster avoidance and were repealed.
357. *See* Regulations 4-9 of the 2013 Regulations for the approval process.
358. Regulation 10 of the 2013 Regulations.
359. Regulation 12(1) of the 2013 Regulations.
360. Regulation 13 of the 2013 Regulations.
361. Regulations 15 and 16 of the 2013 Regulations.

can be deducted from the net income of the trustees.[362] Hence although unit holders cannot 'look through' to the underlying income source, the rules minimise any income tax liability at the level of the trustees. That liability is shifted to the unit holders, who are of course tax-exempts.

Any UK-resident unauthorised unit trust which is not an 'exempt unauthorised unit trust' is a 'non-exempt unauthorised unit trust'. It is treated as a UK-resident company for tax purposes, and its unit holders are treated as shareholders.[363] Hence unit holders cannot 'look through' to the trust's underlying income source. There is a tax charge (19% rising to 25% in April 2023) at trust level, plus a potential income tax charge at unit holder level, because the trust is within the corporation tax regime. There is no scope for a unit holder to recover or credit the tax charge at trust level.

4.3.7 Trusts: Conclusion

There has been relatively little focus on how to define a trust for UK tax purposes, especially when dealing with non-UK asset protection vehicles (notably, foundations) which have similar effects but which are based on non-common law legal traditions. The debate is further complicated by the UK direct tax and inheritance tax concept of 'settlement' which can cover arrangements (including foundations) which are not a trust in an English common law sense. The limited case law manages to establish a borderline between a trust and a body corporate, although much will turn on the relevant facts, including the effect of the arrangements under relevant non-UK tax law. It is easier to draw that line where beneficiaries have vested interests allowing them to dictate how underlying assets are used, unlike the members of a company. Otherwise, the borderline can be very fine. What is the difference between a foundation (which appears to be a separate legal entity with no members and whose beneficiaries have very few rights) and a discretionary and accumulation trust (which may or may not be a separate legal entity, which has no members and whose discretionary beneficiaries have greater, but still very diffuse rights)?

The borderline between a trust and a body corporate is nevertheless very important. Under UK tax law, a body corporate is not 'transparent', and its members will be subject to tax on their income and gains from that entity, usually with no offset for entity level tax. The position in relation to trusts is less simple, and sometimes gives rise to a 'transparent' approach. In addition, trusts are often subject to UK inheritance tax but this is much rarer in relation to a body corporate.[364]

It would make sense to redraw the borderline between 'settlements' and other entities (notably, bodies corporate and partnerships) for UK tax purposes. The current borderline is too flimsy and too formalistic, which is a gift to tax planning. It would be better to distinguish between arrangements whose primary purpose is the conduct of business and those whose primary purpose is the protection and distribution of assets

---

362. Regulation 18 of the 2013 Regulations.
363. Regulation 28 of the 2013 Regulations which also provides that such a unit trust is a 'body corporate' for corporation tax purposes. This may be relevant for grouping purposes.
364. *See* section 5.3.

(even if investment of assets is an ancillary activity). The 'settlement' label should be reserved for the latter, and their precise legal form (trust, foundation, limited company) should be immaterial.[365]

The trust concept is malleable. At one end of the spectrum, it covers simple arrangements for concurrent co-ownership, often with a fairly fixed class of assets and beneficiaries. On the other end, it covers complex arrangements under which beneficiaries have a diffuse nexus with the trust property, settlor control is extensive and the role of the trustees is more wide-ranging.[366] Discretionary and/or accumulation trusts are such arrangements. Yet again, the 'unit trust' is an example of complex co-ownership arrangements where trustees often oversee active management of a shifting and varied asset portfolio, while the class of beneficiaries is broad and fluctuating. In the case of 'unit trusts', holders of beneficial interests have a much clearer nexus with trust property than in a discretionary trust.

The variety of trusts militates against a single approach to their tax 'transparency'. Therefore, the current rules often do not regard full 'transparency' as appropriate, especially in relation to income taxation of discretionary and accumulation trusts. Furthermore apart from section 60 trusts, the UK treats trusts as separate taxable persons from their beneficiaries when taxing capital gains.[367]

Even when tax 'transparency' is appropriate, it means different things in different scenarios.[368] Such differences may be hard to justify, not least the oddities regarding *Baker v Archer-Shee*. Generally, UK law on when and how trusts are 'transparent' has evolved in a fairly ad hoc way.

Treating a trust as 'transparent' can create as many problems as it solves for beneficiaries.[369] It avoids taxation both at trust level and at the level of those with an interest in the trust.[370] It may also give those interest holders easier access to relief for source-based tax (notably, foreign tax) on underlying trust income and gains. It may even give those interest holders access to trust losses (e.g., under section 60 TCGA).

---

365. The suggested distinction has much in common with the definition of a 'trust' for US Federal tax purposes, which focuses on whether an arrangement aims to vest in a third party responsibility for protecting property for beneficiaries, who cannot share in the discharge of that responsibility. Those beneficiaries are therefore not associates in a joint enterprise for the conduct of business for profit. Under the US definition, a foundation can therefore be a 'trust': *see* Ismael Hajjar, Midya Omar and Suzanne Reisman: 'DIFC and ADGM Foundation Laws: A UAE/US Perspective' (2019) Trust Quarterly Review, Volume 17, Issue 2, 31 at 34-35. *See also* section 7.2.2 below.
366. Not only must they administer the trust property but they must also make sensitive decisions about who is to benefit, and how.
367. Section 69 TCGA provides that 'the trustees of a settlement shall, unless the context otherwise requires, together be treated as if they were a single person (distinct from the persons who are trustees of the settlement from time to time)'. This departs from the normal UK approach of seeing a trust, not as an entity but as a relationship between trustees and beneficiaries.
368. The 'look through' imposed by section 60 TCGA is much more radical (the trust is effectively disregarded) than transparency under *Baker v Archer-Shee*, where the trust is not disregarded and the rule is limited to determining the tax 'source' of the income of a beneficiary with a vested income entitlement.
369. UK tax law does not allow a beneficiary of a trust to elect to be taxed personally as if the trust were 'transparent'. Generally, the UK does not allow 'transparent' tax treatment to be elective.
370. Thereby simplifying compliance and avoiding any risk of taxing trust income and gains twice.

However, it may also mean that beneficiaries will be currently taxed on undistributed income and gains of the trust, without receiving cash from the trustees to pay that tax.[371] Furthermore, having an interest in a fully 'transparent' trust gives the beneficiary compliance headaches. It must track over time its proportionate interest in each underlying asset and income source of that trust. Those headaches worsen if the trust's beneficiaries, its income and assets change regularly.[372]

The courts are alive to the pitfalls of 'transparency', even where it is in principle appropriate. When applying section 60 TCGA,[373] *Booth v Ellard* and *Jenkins v Brown*[374] steered away from a purist approach to 'transparency'. This avoided unfunded tax charges[375] on pooling and unpooling assets, where there was no change in each participant's proportionate economic interest in the asset pool.

Of course where a non-'transparency' approach is more appropriate,[376] other issues arise. In particular, are the income and gains of the trust taxable at the level of both the trustees and the beneficiaries? If there is underlying tax at source on trust income and capital gains, what relief can be given for that tax to beneficiaries? There is no simple answer. As discussed, an imperfect relief from double UK taxation of trust income has been provided to beneficiaries of UK-resident discretionary and accumulation trusts. That relief has developed into a modified 'transparent' approach by concession.[377] In relation to capital gains of trusts,[378] the policy response has been much more limited.[379] Capital gains of a UK-resident trust may well be double taxed, at both trustee and beneficiary levels. Beneficiaries have very little access to the capital losses of UK trusts.[380]

For 'authorised' and 'exempt unauthorised' unit trusts, which are collective investment vehicles, practical solutions other than full 'transparency' have been adopted but with a similar economic outcome. These ensure little or no 'sticking' tax on income and gain at unit trust level.[381] By contrast, the 'non-exempt unauthorised unit

371. This would be especially unsatisfactory for discretionary beneficiaries.
372. This situation could well arise in respect of an actively managed unit trust. Hence treating unit holders' interests as a separate asset for capital gains tax purposes, under sections 99 and 103D TCGA, avoids unit holders having to track fractional interests in underlying trust assets. While this makes the unit trust 'opaque' for capital gains tax, locating it offshore or claiming a relevant exemption (e.g., under section 100(1) TCGA) should avoid capital gains tax at trust level.
373. Which requires a transparency approach to certain trusts.
374. [1980] STC 555 and [1989] STC 577.
375. Potentially caused by fractional interests in pooled assets being swapped between beneficiaries of the section 60 trust, when they pooled and unpooled those assets.
376. If a discretionary beneficiary is only subject to tax on income in fact distributed to it, that avoids it being taxed on underlying undistributed income. This is clearly appropriate.
377. That concessionary relief can apply to both UK-resident and non-UK-resident trusts.
378. Other than trusts within section 60 TCGA 1992.
379. Practically, it is easier to avoid double taxation of capital gains in the first place by locating the residence of the trust in a tax haven. Then one needs to be concerned only with tax on any UK-taxpaying beneficiaries or the settlor, and with (any) tax at source on capital gains of the trust (e.g., real estate gains).
380. For a useful summary, *see* Davies: 'Principles of Tax Law'. Geoffrey Morse, David Williams and Sandra Eden. 8th edition (2016), Sweet & Maxwell, at 279-286.
381. Avoiding two layers of taxation (one at vehicle level and another at the level of the investors) is crucial if a collective investment vehicle is to be viable.

trust' (*see* section 4.3.6.2.2) is taxed as a UK-resident company, meaning taxation at both entity and investor levels.

The unit trust rules can go further than merely avoiding entity level taxation. If the governing law of a non-UK-resident unit trust follows the rule in *Baker v Archer-Shee*, income tax is avoided at unit trust level *and* beneficiaries may obtain other tax benefits, e.g., a more favourable basis of income computation or effective relief for tax at source on underlying trust income. The beneficiaries will, however, be taxable on their share of income, even if undistributed. The UK 'authorised unit trust' regime removes entity level taxation in practice and also enables some distributions of trust income to be taxed as if they were payments of interest or dividends. Therefore, UK-taxpaying unit holders can be taxed largely as if they were entitled to the trust's underlying income, which can be beneficial (e.g., by accessing lower tax rates on dividends). At the same time, they avoid the compliance headaches of a truly 'transparent' structure.

Whether, when and how to treat an entity/arrangement as 'transparent' is a tax policy question not confined to trusts. Similar questions arise in relation to companies. For companies, the policy adopted has been more uniform and different. A company is usually regarded as a taxable entity in its own right.[382] The question is then what relief to give its members for entity level taxation when they derive dividends or capital gains from their holdings in the company. A discussion of the general UK taxation of dividend income is beyond the scope of this work.[383] However, any relief to company members for entity level taxation typically falls well short of what it would be if that entity were 'transparent'.

Despite some similarities between trusts and companies, there is no reason why trusts should always be subject to tax both at entity level and at the level of the beneficiaries. Where trusts are 'transparent', there is ultimately one level of tax only, at beneficiary level. However, there are many cases where that is not so. The non-tax justification for trusts is that they offer sophisticated asset protection, which can also reconcile over time conflicting claims on that wealth. In principle, a beneficiary of a trust should not be taxed, directly or indirectly, more heavily than if that person had invested directly in the trust assets. This could be achieved without invariably treating trusts as fully 'transparent' for tax purposes.

The current UK rules for taxing income and, in particular, capital gains of trusts do not achieve tax neutrality between direct investment and investment via a trust, especially when the trustees are UK-resident. This greatly assists the 'offshore trusts' industry, in jurisdictions such as Jersey and Guernsey. At the very least, the UK should change its rules on income or capital distributions so that beneficiaries who are taxed

382. For philosophical reasons that are contested: *see* Glen Loutzenhiser: 'Tiley's Revenue Law'. 10th edition, at 59.4.2.
383. Since introducing corporation tax in 1965, the UK at first adopted a 'classical' system where dividends were separately taxed with little or no relief to members for entity level taxation. It later give some relief to members for entity level taxation via 'partial imputation'. This was found to contravene EU law. Corporate members now enjoy a broad exemption in respect of their dividend income, while non-corporate members are fully taxed on dividend income with limited relief (mainly via a lower tax rate) for entity level taxation.

on those distributions can more effectively 'trace' them to underlying income and capital gains of the trust, thereby benefiting from any preferential tax rates on those items. They could also then benefit from relief for non-UK tax on the underlying source as well as any UK tax already collected at trustee level. This change of approach would need safeguards to prevent taxpayer 'cherry-picking' among items of income and gain. It would build on the approach of ESC B13 in relation to income tax, and section 87 TCGA in relation to distributions of capital gain from non-UK-resident trusts. It goes beyond the narrow rule in *Baker v Archer-Shee* by offering a measure of 'transparency' to all beneficiaries without taxing them on undistributed income or gain, and without automatically giving them a heavy compliance burden.[384] It does not address the problems of IHT on 'settlements' which are discussed in section 5.3.

384. For how this is achieved in the US, Australia and New Zealand, *see* Brabazon *supra*, at pp. 58-61 and Appendix (at pp. 293-345). To prevent a trust being used to defer tax on income and gain prior to distribution, interim taxation could be imposed at trustee level if the trustees were UK-resident (with a credit or refund for that tax against any tax on distributions to beneficiaries). If the trustees were not UK-resident, a sliding scale of UK tax rates on beneficiaries could be used to encourage earlier distributions (cf. section 91 TCGA). In any case, the settlor may already be subject to UK tax on undistributed trust income and gain under 'settlement' or other anti-deferral rules. HMRC launched a consultation on all aspects of the UK taxation of trusts on 7 November 2018: *see* 'The Taxation of Trusts: A Review' (publishing.service.gov.uk) (accessed 12 June 2020). So far, this has not led to any changes although a Summary of Responses was published in March 2021 https://assets.publishing.service.gov.uk/government/uploads/system/uploads/attachment_data/file/972107/The_taxation_of_trusts_a_review_-_summary_of_responses.pdf (accessed 1 April 2021).

CHAPTER 5

The Wider Concept of 'Tax Transparency' and Its Meaning in Other Areas of UK Tax Law

5.1 INTRODUCTION

This work has so far touched on the concept of 'tax transparency' as it relates in particular to taxing income and capital gains. This chapter discusses further aspects of the 'transparency' concept. It considers, in particular, what this means in relation to IHT, VAT and stamp duty land tax (SDLT). To begin, it is useful to consider attempts at international level to define 'tax transparency'. These help to show how this concept contains a number of different but related ideas.

5.2 THE BEPS DEFINITION OF 'TAX TRANSPARENCY' AND RELATED ISSUES

As part of the Organisation for Economic Co-operation and Development's (OECD's) 2015 conclusions regarding BEPS ('Base Erosion and Profit Shifting'), document[385] entitled 'Neutralising the Effects of Hybrid Mismatch Arrangements' was published. Part II of that document (and in particular, Chapter 14) recommended changes to Article 1 of the OECD Model Double Taxation Convention ('the OECD Model') regarding 'transparent entities' and, in particular, a new Article 1(2):[386]

385. OECD (2015), Neutralising the Effects of Hybrid Mismatch Arrangements, Action 2 – 2015 Final Report, OECD/G20 Base Erosion and Profit Shifting Project, OECD Publishing, Paris http://dx.doi.org/10.1787/9789264241138-en (accessed 14 June 2022).

386. For an extensive discussion of Article 1(2), *see* Austry Nikolakakis et al.: 'Some Reflections on the Proposed Revisions to the OECD Model and Commentaries and on the Multilateral

> For the purposes of this Convention, income derived by or through an entity or arrangement that is treated as *wholly or partly fiscally transparent* [emphasis added] under the tax law of either Contracting State shall be considered to be income of a resident of a Contracting State but only to the extent that the income is treated, for purposes of taxation by that State, as the income of a resident of that State.

Article 1(2) of the 2017 version of the OECD Model[387] now incorporates that wording as does, in essence, Article 3(1) of the OECD Multilateral Instrument to implement tax treaty-related measures to prevent Base Erosion and Profit Shifting (the MLI). The MLI[388] was first signed on 24 November 2016.[389]

Article 1(2) (which is discussed further in section 6.1) attempts to ensure that a double taxation treaty does not give rise to double taxation or unintended double non-taxation of income which flows cross-border via an intermediate entity, simply because the parties to the treaty characterise that entity differently. It is accompanied by revisions to the Commentary on Article 1 of the OECD Model. Paragraphs 9 and 10 of the Commentary on Article 1 now read:

> 9. The concept of 'fiscally transparent' ... refers to situations where, under the domestic law of a Contracting State, the income (or part thereof) of the entity or arrangement is not taxed at the level of the entity or the arrangement but at the level of the persons who have an interest in that entity or arrangement. This will normally be the case where the amount of tax payable on a share of the income of an entity or arrangement is determined separately in relation to the personal characteristics of the person who is entitled to that share so that the tax will depend on whether that person is taxable or not, on the other income that the person has, on the personal allowances to which the person is entitled and on the tax rate applicable to that person; also, the character and source, as well as the timing of the realisation, of the income for tax purposes will not be affected by the fact that it has been earned through the entity or arrangement. The fact that the income is computed at the level of the entity or arrangement before the share is allocated to the person will not affect that result. States wishing to clarify the definition of 'fiscally transparent' in their bilateral conventions are free to include a definition of that term based on the above explanations.

Instrument, with respect to Fiscally Transparent Entities' [2017] British Tax Review 295. This article is hereinafter referred to as 'Some Reflections'. Article 1(2) is also discussed in section 6.1.

387. http://www.oecd.org/ctp/model-tax-convention-on-income-and-on-capital-full-version-9a5b369e-en.htm (accessed 2 July 2020).
388. http://www.oecd.org/tax/treaties/multilateral-convention-to-implement-tax-treaty-related-measures-to-prevent-BEPS.pdf (accessed 2 July 2020).
389. The UK signed the MLI on 7 June 2017 and deposited with the OECD its instrument of ratification and final list of reservations and notifications (regarding the MLI's operative provisions) on 29 June 2018. The MLI entered into force in the UK on 1 October 2018, as a Schedule to the Double Taxation Relief (Base Erosion and Profit Shifting) Order 2018 SI 2018/630. It took effect in the UK for the purposes of UK treaties from 1 January 2019 (for withholding tax), from 1 April 2019 (for corporation tax) and from 6 April 2019 (for income tax and capital gains tax). However, the date when, and the extent to which, specific UK treaties are modified by the MLI also depends on when the relevant treaty partner deposits its instrument of ratification, acceptance and approval. It also depends on what that instrument says.

> 10. In the case of an entity or arrangement which is treated as partly fiscally transparent under the domestic law of one of the Contracting States, only part of the income of the entity or arrangement might be taxed at the level of the persons who have an interest in that entity or arrangement as described in [the previous paragraph] whilst the rest would remain taxable at the level of the entity or arrangement. This, for example, is how some trusts and limited liability partnerships are treated in some countries (i.e., in some countries, the part of the income derived through a trust that is distributed to beneficiaries is taxed in the hands of these beneficiaries whilst the part of that income that is accumulated is taxed in the hands of the trust or trustees; similarly, in some countries, income derived through a limited partnership is taxed in the hands of the general partner as regards that partner's share of that income but is considered to be the income of the limited partnership as regards the limited partners' share of the income[390]...).

This attempt to define 'tax transparency' is fairly limited.[391] Its focus is simply on whether or not underlying income of the entity or arrangement is taxed at the level of those with an interest in it on the same basis (and at the same time),[392] while retaining the same source and character, as if the holder of that interest had been directly entitled to the underlying income. There is no requirement that the holder of that interest must be entitled to claim any tax losses of the entity or arrangement. Equally, there is no requirement that under the relevant tax law, the holder of the interest must be treated as owning a share of the underlying assets of the entity or arrangement. These more radical interpretations of 'tax transparency'[393] are not mentioned.

A more radical approach to 'transparency' appears in the UK corporation tax legislation which implements the proposals in part I of the BEPS Action 2 Final Report

390. For example, this would be the Dutch position in relation to a so-called open CV: *see* section 7.3.2.
391. The authors of 'Some Reflections' indicate that paragraph 10 of the OECD Commentary on Article 1(2) is based on regulations on 'fiscal transparency' under section 894(c) US Internal Revenue Code. There is some debate, mentioned in 'Some Reflections', about whether the words 'entity *or arrangement*' [emphasis added] in Article 1(2) also cover structures which might fall short of being an 'entity', e.g., back-to-back loans. Interestingly, the OECD defines a 'fiscally transparent' entity more broadly in its December 2021 publication: 'Tax Challenges Arising from the Digitalisation of the Economy Global Anti-Base Erosion Model Rules (Pillar Two). Inclusive Framework on BEPS'. https://www.oecd.org/tax/beps/tax-challenges-arising -from-the-digitalisation-of-the-economy - global-anti-base-erosion-model-rules-pillar-two. htm. Article 10.2.2 states that an entity is 'fiscally transparent' in a jurisdiction which 'treats the income, expenditure, profit or loss of that [entity] *as if it were derived or incurred by the direct owner of that [entity] in proportion to its interest in that [entity]*' [emphasis added]. This wording edges closer to looking through the entity more fully.
392. The issue of the timing of the tax charge is obscured by the partial transparency example of the trust in paragraph 10 of the Commentary on Article 1(2). A contrast is drawn between income taxable at beneficiary level on *distribution* [emphasis added] versus income accumulated at trust level. Classically, if a trust is transparent, the beneficiary must be taxable on its share of underlying trust income as it arises to the trust whether or not it is distributed. Similar points are made in 'Some Reflections'. In fairness to paragraph 10, a more limited interpretation of 'transparency' could cover cases where a beneficiary (e.g., of a discretionary trust) is not taxed on undistributed trust income but any distribution to it is treated as paid directly from underlying trust income and gains (as under ESC B18 – *see* section 4.3.5).
393. *See*, for example, section 60 TCGA whereby beneficiaries of certain trusts are treated as co-owning the underlying trust assets and the trust is effectively disregarded: *see* section 4.3.2.

for combatting avoidance via hybrid mismatches. In particular, section 259BE TIOPA reads:

> (1) For the purposes of this Part, an entity is 'hybrid' if it meets conditions A and B.
> (2) Condition A is the entity is regarded as being a person for tax purposes under the law of any territory.
> (3) Condition B is that:
> *(a) some or all of the entity's income or profits are treated (or would be if there were any) for the purposes of a tax charged under the law of any territory, as the income or profits of a person or persons other than the person mentioned in subsection (2), or*
> *(b) under the law of a territory other than the one mentioned in subsection (2), the entity is not regarded as a distinct and separate person to an entity or entities that are distinct and separate persons under the law of the territory mentioned in that subsection* [emphasis added].

For these purposes, HMRC guidance (International Tax Manual INTM550630) considers that a 'person' will include a partnership.

Section 259BE(3)(b) TIOPA goes further than the OECD Commentary on Article 1(2). It envisages an 'entity' (undefined) being disregarded altogether for tax purposes. However, this is not the sole test of hybrid entity status for these purposes: section 259BE(3)(a) TIOPA operates independently and is more in line with the approach of Article 1(2) and the Commentary. Section 259BE(3)(a) seems broad enough to cover a situation where the entity's hybrid status arises solely because its income is treated as the income of another person under 'controlled foreign company' or equivalent income attribution legislation.[394] Such legislation is not usually seen as an example of 'tax transparency'.[395]

Further points can be made about 'tax transparency' in the light of Article 1(2) of the OECD Model.

First, 'tax transparency' is not a unitary concept in UK tax law. It is a catchphrase which covers a range of situations where, to varying degrees, the taxation of the holder of an interest in an entity is meant to reflect the tax result if that holder had been directly entitled to a share of the entity's underlying income and/or assets. The extent of this 'look through' treatment is dictated by the structure and policy of the relevant tax rules. Where income is being taxed, the rules do not need to impute ownership of underlying assets of the entity to the holder of an interest in it. All that is needed to

394. For this to be the case, the controlled foreign company, etc., legislation would probably have to attribute to that person the entity's actual income. It would not be enough if the relevant legislation (e.g., the UK controlled foreign company legislation – *see Bricom Holdings Ltd v IRC* [1997] STC 1179) only taxed that person on a special type of deemed income, measured by reference to but distinct from the entity's actual underlying income.

395. The authors of 'Some Reflections' consider that Article 1(2) of the OECD Model was probably not intended to cover cases where an entity's income was attributed to its members under controlled foreign company rules or equivalent anti-deferral regimes unless the relevant regime effectively disregards the entity altogether. This is probably rare. It is not the effect of the UK controlled foreign company legislation in Part 9A TIOPA. Nor is it the effect of the UK 'settlements' rules in Part 5 Chapter 5 ITTOIA and the 'transfer of assets abroad' rules in Part 13 Chapter 2 ITA. There is further discussion of this issue in section 6.1.

achieve 'look through' taxation is a rule treating the holder's income entitlement as having the same character and source, and arising at the same time, as the underlying income of the entity while respecting its separate existence. A good example is the rule in *Baker v Archer-Shee,* discussed in section 4.3.3. This kind of rule will probably not suffice if 'look through' tax treatment is required for transactions involving underlying assets of the entity (e.g., capital gains tax). It may also not suffice if the interest holder is to claim losses of the entity. Lastly, it will not be radical enough if the aim is to tax the holder of the interest as if the entity did not exist at all, e.g., if the holder wishes to claim a 'participation exemption' in respect of profits from a significant shareholding owned by a trust or partnership in which the holder has an interest.

Second, where income is being taxed, is it necessary, for an entity to be 'transparent', that the interest holder's income entitlement has *precisely* the same character and arises at *exactly* the same time as if the underlying income had been derived directly by that holder? If the interest holder's income entitlement is treated as having the same character and source as the underlying income of the entity, surely there is 'transparency' even if this entitlement requires a prior decision to allocate income (e.g., by the trustees of a discretionary trust)? That allocation decision may well be taken after the underlying income arose.[396]

Third, if 'transparency' leads to disregarding an entity, so that it becomes a tax 'nothing', this will need to be very clearly indicated. For example, can a UK 'group' relationship between two companies be traced via a partnership, e.g., for the purposes of corporation tax 'group relief'? This important question arises where one company is a partner in a partnership which in turn holds shares in the second company concerned. The situation is discussed further in Appendix A.

Arguing that tracing ownership through a partnership is possible because it is 'transparent' begs the question of what transparency means. Whether the partnership has legal personality or not, UK corporation tax rules do not clearly allow a corporate partner to demonstrate that it has the necessary 'beneficial ownership' of shares held by the partnership in the second company in order to be 'grouped'. Section 1258 CTA 2009 merely states that 'Unless otherwise indicated ... a firm[397] is not to be regarded for corporation tax purposes as an entity separate and distinct from the partners.' This does not mean that there is no partnership at all for tax purposes. Otherwise, the reference to a 'firm' would be redundant. Rather it states that for income and corporation tax purposes, the firm is only the aggregation of its partners. This is the classic English (but not Scottish) common law conception of partnership. Section 1258 therefore puts English and Scottish partnerships on an equal footing when computing their income for corporation tax purposes. However, the corporate partner wishing to establish a group relationship with another company via the partnership does not 'beneficially own' any specific partnership assets (including any shares of another company held by the partnership). It has only a contingent claim, in a solvent winding-up of the partnership, to a part-share in some or all of those assets net of the

396. *See* the discussion at section 4.3.5 of section 111 TIOPA and ESC B18.
397. Defined in section 1257 CTA 2009 as persons carrying on a trade or business in partnership.

firm's liabilities.[398] This was emphasised in *Bayonet Ventures LLP and another v HMRC* [2018] UKFTT 262 (TC), which considered section 863 ITTOIA. This treats a UK LLP carrying on business 'with a view to profit' as a partnership for income tax purposes, just as section 1273 CTA 2009 does for corporation tax. The judge pointed out that section 863 did not treat all the activities of the LLP as carried on directly by its members. Therefore, the LLP could not simply be ignored so as to treat a loan to it by a pension fund as being made directly to the LLP members. Section 863 merely assimilated the position of LLP members to that of partners in a common law partnership.

The judge continued:

> Property which belongs to a partnership, whether a limited liability partnership or a non-LLP, is no more the property of the individual partners than the property of a body corporate is the property of its shareholders. Such property might become the property of the members and/or shareholders upon winding up or dissolution once debts and liabilities have been paid, but until that time it is the property of the partnership (firm) or, as appropriate, the LLP, each of which are recognised in law as having a legal persona separate and distinct from the members of the partnership.

One can take issue with parts of this statement. However, the judge was correct that individual partners cannot contend, prior to partnership dissolution, that they own particular assets forming part of the partnership property.[399] Indeed, even in a solvent

398. There are rules enabling one company to establish its indirect 'beneficial ownership' of ordinary share capital in another company but only via one or more intermediate 'bodies corporate', not partnerships: *see* sections 1154-1157 CTA 2010. Despite being formed as a body corporate, a UK LLP is typically regarded under section 1273(1) CTA 2009 as a partnership for corporation tax purposes. Section 1273(2)(c) further specifies that for corporation tax purposes, 'references to a company [which will include a body corporate] do not include such a limited liability partnership'. Section 1121(1) CTA 2010 (*see* section 2.2) defines 'company' so as to include a 'body corporate' or an 'unincorporated association' but not a partnership. Hence a UK LLP carrying on a business 'with a view to profit' is not normally a 'body corporate' for the purposes of tracing share ownership through it under sections 1154-1157 CTA 2010.

399. The judge's thinking is supported by the Privy Council in *Hadlee v Commissioner of Inland Revenue* [1993] STC 294 at 297-298, which stressed that a partner 'does not have title to specific partnership property but has a beneficial interest in the entirety of the partnership assets. ... This beneficial interest ... is in the nature of a future interest taking effect in possession on ... the determination of the partnership. ... He has rights ... to share in *the surplus assets* [emphasis added] of the partnership on a dissolution'. *Hadlee* was a decision regarding New Zealand law which in this respect was treated as identical to English law. It was followed by the High Court in *Fengate Developments v Customs and Excise Commissioners* [2004] STC 772. In *Sandhu v Gill* [2006] 2 All ER 22 at 27-29, Neuberger LJ (as he then was) made statements to the same effect as *Hadlee* in a non-tax case. All these cases involved partnerships which did *not* have separate legal personality. Such personality makes it even harder to 'look through' a partnership. A much-cited decision is that of the Court of Appeal in *IRC v Gray* [1994] STC 360. This was a valuation case, for Capital Transfer Tax (now inheritance tax) purposes, where a key asset was the deceased's majority share in an English law farming partnership. Was this share to any extent 'land'? Hoffmann LJ (as he then was) stated (clearly *obiter)* at p. 377 that it was 'land'. In particular, he said 'As between themselves, partners are not entitled individually to exercise proprietary rights over any of the partnership assets. This is because they have subjected their proprietary interests to the terms of the partnership deed which provides that the assets shall be employed in the partnership business, and on dissolution realised for the purposes of paying debts and distributing any surplus. *As regards the outside*

dissolution, all they may end up owning is cash after assets have been liquidated and liabilities discharged. Hence the direct tax 'transparency' of a partnership does not mean that, as a strict legal matter, one can 'look through' it so as to trace a group relationship.

Strict legal analysis aside, the 'tracing' position in practice is more nuanced. The ability to trace corporate affiliation is therefore examined in greater detail in Appendix A.

There are other situations where the 'transparency' of an entity does not entail its total disregard for UK tax purposes, even though it is not taxable in its own right and may lack legal personality. While a partnership is 'transparent' for UK direct tax purposes, its existence will still be recognised when applying the 'remittance' rules whereby individuals not UK-domiciled for tax purposes can defer UK tax on non-UK income and gains.[400] If such an individual applies non-UK income and gains by investing in a non-UK partnership outside the UK, which then invests in a UK-situated asset, HMRC accept that the non-UK partnership acts as a buffer, although they may check whether the entity really is a partnership. The result is that the income and gains are not a taxable 'remittance' to the UK, whereas there would have been an immediate UK tax liability if the individual had used the income and gains to buy directly the underlying UK asset. The converse may also be true. Hence, investment in a UK-managed (and therefore UK-'situated') partnership is the acquisition of a UK asset both for the purposes of the 'remittance' rules and for IHT. This is the case whether or not the partnership's assets are situated in the UK.[401]

Before considering how UK taxes, other than taxes on income and gain, address 'transparency' issues, the reader is referred to Appendix B. This explores specific

---

world, however, the partnership deed is irrelevant [emphasis added]. The partners are collectively entitled to each and every asset of the partnership, in which each of them has an undivided share. It is this outside view which identifies the nature of the property falling to be valued for the purpose of capital transfer tax. … .' These comments are not a secure basis for treating a partnership as a simple co-ownership arrangement when deciding whether companies can trace share ownership through a partnership in order to form a group. Hoffmann LJ's dicta do not cover a partnership with separate legal personality. They also overstate the position in relation to an English law general partnership, where, in the 'outside world', a personal creditor of a partner (but not of the firm itself) cannot enforce a claim against partnership property, even though the partner has an interest in it. Section 23 of the 1890 Act limits that creditor to enforcing its claim against the partner's share (i.e., the contingent claim to surplus), and not the underlying partnership property. If partners were mere co-owners of the partnership assets, a personal creditor could presumably enforce directly against the partner's share of the underlying property. In a case involving estate duty (the predecessor of Capital Transfer Tax), Buckley J was much more guarded than Hoffmann LJ: see *Burdett-Coutts v IRC* [1960] 3 All ER 153 at 158.

400. *See* Part 14 Chapter A1 ITA. A partnership, unlike a 'close company', is not a 'relevant person' who can make remittances: section 809L and 809M ITA. If the partnership lacks legal personality, this does not seem to matter.

401. Schedule A1 Inheritance Tax Act 1984 now limits the use of non-UK 'close companies' and partnerships to shield UK residential property from IHT. However, it does not simply 'look through' to the UK assets. Rather, the interest in the company or partnership is not 'excluded property' for IHT where its value is attributable to UK residential property or (broadly) loans used to acquire such property: *see* Emma Chamberlain 'Finance (No. 2) Act 2017 Notes: Section 33 and Schedule 10 – Inheritance Tax on Overseas Property Representing UK Residential Property' [2017] British Tax Review at 594-605.

problems applying the 'transparency' concept, for corporation tax purposes, to partnership transactions involving certain financial assets and liabilities, as well as intangible assets.

5.3 INHERITANCE TAX AND 'TAX TRANSPARENCY'

Inheritance tax (IHT) is the UK tax on estates and gifts. It typically arises in respect of 'transfers of value' by individuals which are either gifts or transfers at an undervalue. The same value transfer may also give rise to capital gains tax, which is triggered by a 'disposal' of 'assets'. However, IHT, unlike capital gains tax, is not a tax on 'profit'.

It does not matter for IHT whether the transfer of value arises during the individual's lifetime or on death (e.g., under a will). However, there are significant exemptions for certain lifetime transfers occurring at least seven years before death[402] plus a generous exemption for transfers between spouses, whether on or before death.[403] IHT is typically a percentage of the value of the transfer, to the extent that it is not arm's length. Rates for taxable lifetime transfers by individuals are typically half those applying to transfers on death.[404] IHT is imposed primarily on the transferor rather than the transferee. Overall, it is a tax on the value of certain transactions.[405]

Situations can arise where transfers of value or other events triggering IHT do not amount to direct value transfers by an individual. These involve transactions via interposed entities or arrangements (notably, partnerships, companies and trusts). Should those transactions be taxed by 'looking through' to any individuals with an interest in, or other relevant connection with, the entity or arrangement? There is no single answer to this question and no necessary reason why the IHT answer should be the same as for UK tax on income or capital gains. Over time, the IHT answer has changed, especially as it relates to IHT and trusts. The net result is an increasingly penal IHT regime for trusts. They are now largely taxed on an 'opaque' basis, which has been heavily criticised.

5.3.1 Partnerships

Where transfers of value involve partnerships, HMRC 'look through', but do not disregard the partnership. To that extent, there is symmetry with the taxation of income and gains. The statutory basis for this approach is unclear but the practice seems well established.[406] Section 267A IHTA applies specifically to UK LLPs:[407]

402. Potentially Exempt Transfers or PETS: Section 3A Inheritance Tax Act 1984 (IHTA).
403. Section 18 IHTA.
404. Section 7 and Schedule I IHTA. The current maximum rate on transfers on death is 40%.
405. Certain jurisdictions (e.g., Ireland) tax the recipients of gifts in respect of the value *received*. This can be seen as a form of income taxation. This characterisation is not applicable to IHT because the tax falls primarily on the transferor. Furthermore, the IHT charge is not typically tied to the circumstances of the transferee, nor the amount received by the transferee.
406. *See* IHTM25094 of the HMRC Inheritance Tax Manual (accessed 2 August 2022), although HMRC also state in that guidance that an interest in a traditional partnership 'is a "chose in action" (the right to recover assets through an action), valued by reference to the net

For the purposes of this Act and any other enactments relating to inheritance tax:

(a) property to which a limited liability partnership is entitled, or which it occupies or uses, shall be treated as property to which its members are entitled, or which they occupy or use, *as partners,*
(b) any business carried on by a limited liability partnership shall be treated as carried on *in partnership* by its members,
(c) incorporation, change in membership or dissolution of a limited liability partnership shall be treated as formation, alteration or dissolution *of a partnership*, and
(d) any transfer of value made by or to a limited liability partnership shall be treated as made by or to its members *in partnership* (and not by or to the limited liability partnership as such) [emphasis added].

The wording does not disregard the LLP. It assimilates the IHT position of LLP members with that of partners in a true partnership. With that proviso, section 267A 'looks through' the LLP entity when subjecting its members to IHT on transactions involving LLP assets.[408] This approach contrasts with the IHT treatment of 'close companies' (*see* section 5.3.5) whose structure, operation and management may differ little in practice from a UK LLP.

One important exception to the IHT 'look through' approach in relation to partnerships and UK LLPs concerns 'business property relief'.[409] This applies, in particular, to an 'interest in a business'.[410] That includes a share in a partnership. Hence, for the purposes of this relief, the partnership share is treated as a distinct intangible asset, and not a collection of fractional entitlements to underlying partnership assets. This is sensible.

A partnership share is also treated as a separate intangible asset when determining the 'situs' of a partner's interest for IHT purposes. Non-UK 'situs' assets may be 'excluded property' for IHT purposes if the partner is not UK-'domiciled' for such

underlying assets of the business'. HMRC practice seems to originate from the simple fact that an English common law partnership lacks legal personality. This is not true of Scottish partnerships (as HMRC acknowledge) nor of many non-UK bodies which style themselves as 'partnerships'.

407. A UK LLP is a body corporate for non-tax purposes.

408. Inheritance Tax Manual IHTM25094 (accessed 2 August 2022) states that 'an interest in a LLP is deemed to be an interest in each and every asset of the partnership', whereas an interest in a traditional partnership is a 'chose in action' valued by reference to the net underlying business assets. There are quite close similarities with the IHT approach adopted for UK LLPs and that applying to them for capital gains tax in section 59A TCGA: *see* Appendix A. There is a lack of clarity (cf. SP D12 in relation to section 59A) about quantifying a member's share in LLP assets for IHT purposes. HMRC have also sometimes ignored the 'look through' effect of section 267A and argued that, whereas 'business property relief' would be available if shares in an unquoted trading company were held directly, it is not available where those shares are held by a UK LLP and a member of that LLP either dies or transfers a LLP interest. HMRC's stance (*see* IHTM25094 (accessed 2 August 2022)) is strange although it can be argued that 'business property relief' should apply anyway: *see* James Kessler and Oliver Marre: 'A Merry Dance' Taxation, (20 March 2014) at 8.

409. Sections 103-114 IHTA.

410. Section 105(1)(a) IHTA. There is a similar approach in section 227 IHTA, which deals with when IHT can be paid in instalments in relation to 'qualifying property'. Such property (*see* section 227(2)) includes 'business or an interest in a business'.

purposes. The basic private international law rule is that the principal place of the partnership's business determines the 'situs' of a partnership share. This seems to be the case for IHT even if a non-UK partnership owns UK assets. Schedule A1 IHTA (mentioned in section 5.2 and footnote 401) can override this where a non-UK partnership owns UK residential property.

5.3.2 Trusts/Settlements

Much IHT legislation relates to the taxation of trusts. A full analysis is beyond the scope of this work. The focus instead is on the degree to which the IHT rules 'look through' certain types of trust. The broad thrust of the rules since 2006 has been not to 'look through' trusts. This causes disadvantages when holding property through a trust rather than directly. These disadvantages are not easy to justify.

The special IHT rules regarding trusts only apply if an arrangement involves 'settled property'. This means property comprised in a 'settlement', as defined in section 43 IHTA. Not all trusts are 'settlements' for these purposes. Moreover, not all 'settlements' are trusts. Section 43(2)-(4) reads:

> (2) Settlement means any disposition or dispositions of property, whether effected by instrument, by parol or by operation of law, or partly in one way and partly in another, whereby the property is for the time being:
> (a) held in trust for persons in succession or for any person subject to a contingency or
> (b) held by trustees on trust to accumulate the whole or any part of the income of the property or with power to make payments out of that income at the discretion of the trustees or some other person, with or without power to accumulate surplus income; or
> (c) charged or burdened (otherwise than for full consideration in money or money's worth paid for his own use or benefit to the person making the disposition) with the payment of any annuity or other periodical payment payable for a life or any other limited or terminable period,
> *or would be so held or charged or burdened if the disposition or dispositions were regulated by the law of any part of the United Kingdom; or whereby, under the law of any other country, the administration of the property is for the time being governed by provisions equivalent in effect to those which would apply if the property were so held, charged or burdened* [emphasis added].
> (3) A lease of property which is for life or lives, or for a period ascertainable only by reference to a death, or which is terminable on, or at a date ascertainable only by reference to, a death, shall be treated as a settlement and the property as settled property, unless the lease was granted for full consideration in money or money's worth; and where a lease not granted at a rack rent is at any time to become a lease at an increased rent it shall be treated as terminable at that time.
> (4) In relation to Scotland, 'settlement' also includes:
> (a) an entail;
> (b) any deed by virtue of which an annuity is charged on, or on the rents of, any property (the property being treated as the property comprised in the settlement), and

(c) any deed creating or reserving a proper liferent of any property whether heritable or moveable (the property from time to time subject to the proper liferent being treated as the property comprised in the settlement);

and for the purposes of this subsection 'deed' includes any disposition, arrangement, contract, resolution, instrument or writing.

The special rules for Scotland in section 43(4) reflect the fact that Scottish law does not draw the same distinction as English law between legal and equitable ownership of property (*see* section 4.3.3.2). Given its roots in French law, Scottish law can give rise to non-trust-based arrangements for enjoying another's property for life which do not exist under English law, such as the (rare) 'proper liferent'. This appears to be[411] the Scottish equivalent of the civil law 'usufruct': namely, 'the right to enjoy property belonging to another, as if its owner, at the expense of preserving that property'.[412] Section 43(4) is confined to Scottish 'proper liferents' and does not extend to usufructs in general. Furthermore, section 43(4)(c) only makes a 'proper liferent' settled property for IHT purposes, but not for other tax purposes (e.g., capital gains tax).

Section 43(3) and, above all, the last lines of section 43(2) clarify that certain entities or property-holding arrangements which would not necessarily be trusts under English law can nevertheless be 'settlements' for IHT. This is especially important in relation to non-UK arrangements for holding property, such as Anstalten or Stiftungen. These are widely used for the purposes of wealth preservation and, as discussed in section 4.1.1, may well be characterised by English law as companies. They could

411. Can a civil law 'usufruct' be 'settled property' under the closing words of section 43(2) IHTA? HMRC regard a usufruct created under a civil law system other than Scotland as a 'settlement' because of the closing words of section 43(2). This view is challenged in James Kessler KC *supra* in section 98.15. It has also been argued that a usufruct of French immovable property cannot be a 'settlement' within those closing words for two reasons. First, the French law of immovable property would not recognise a trust over such property in France, and English private international law would respect French law as the 'lex situs'. Hence the first part of the words emphasised above in section 43(2) cannot apply. Second, because property subject to a usufruct is not centrally administered, the last part of those words is irrelevant: *see* the reference to 'the administration of the property'. For further details, *see* Peter Harris: 'French Usufructs and Section 43(2) IHTA 1984' (2018-2019) The Tax Planning Review, Volume 7, at 1. HMRC state, in their Capital Gains Manual at CG31301 and CG31305 (accessed 15 June 2022), that a French usufruct is 'broadly similar' to a Scottish liferent. The latter, if a 'proper liferent', is not 'settled property' for capital gains tax purposes, but section 63 TCGA treats the person entitled to possession on the death of the liferenter as acquiring the relevant assets at their then market value.

412. This is a translation of Article 587 of the French Civil Code: *see* James Kessler KC *supra* in section 98.15, p. 4535. Under French law, a usufruct is not a trust ('fiducie') but a 'démembrement' where the 'usufruitier' enjoys for a prescribed period the property of another, the 'nu propriétaire'. Each has duties to respect the interest of the other. For a further discussion of the UK tax treatment of Scottish liferents in particular and of usufructs in general *see* section 98.13 and 98.15 of James Kessler KC *supra*.

nevertheless be 'settlements' for IHT because of section 43(2).[413] They may also be 'close companies' for the purposes of the rules discussed in section 5.3.5.[414]

However, the IHT definition of 'settlement' does not catch 'bare trusts' where the only beneficial interests are vested and concurrent. So trusts within section 60 TCGA[415] should not be IHT 'settlements' and should therefore be 'looked through' for IHT purposes. For example, HMRC consider that this will be the case in relation to an absolute trust for a minor even though, under section 31 Trustee Act 1925, the trustees have certain discretions, during the minority, to apply trust income for that beneficiary or to accumulate it. Such an arrangement does not become a 'settlement' within section 43(2)(b) IHTA because, whether income is accumulated or not, it can only ever be applied for the benefit of that beneficiary.[416]

5.3.3 Settlements with a Qualifying Interest in Possession

Where arrangements are a 'settlement' for IHT purposes, a key initial question is whether there is a 'qualifying interest in possession' in the settled property. If so, then in limited cases, the holder of that 'interest in possession' will be treated, for IHT purposes, as beneficially owning the settled property underlying that interest. Section 49(1) IHTA states that:

> A person beneficially entitled to an interest in possession in settled property shall be treated for the purposes of this Act as beneficially entitled to the property in which the interest subsists.

Whether there is an 'interest in possession' requires a detailed review of the 'settlement' terms. This kind of interest is not fully defined by the legislation but has been defined by the courts as a 'present right to present enjoyment'.[417] This largely reflects a press release issued by the then Inland Revenue on 12 February 1976, which states that:

> [A]n interest in possession in settled property exists where the person having the interest has the immediate entitlement (subject to any prior claim by the trustees

413. In particular, the words 'governed by provisions equivalent *in effect*' [emphasis added] to a trust. It will be important to look closely at the nature of the relevant entity under its governing law: *see* the discussion of a Liechtenstein 'stiftung' in James Kessler KC *supra*, at 98.9.5., which that commentator regards as a 'settlement' for IHT purposes. The author agrees.
414. The IHT definition of 'settlement' is not restricted to arrangements with an 'element of bounty', unlike the 'settlement' legislation in Part 5 Chapter 5 ITTOIA attributing the income of certain 'settlements' to the settlor. Hence some commercial arrangements may be caught by the IHT 'settlement' provisions, although legislation has partly mitigated this: *see*, for example, the special regime for employee trusts in section 86 IHTA. It is unsatisfactory that technical IHT charges can potentially arise in respect of commercial arrangements.
415. *See* section 4.3.2 above.
416. *See* HMRC Inheritance Tax Manual IHTM16068 (accessed 18 June 2020).
417. *See* the majority of the House of Lords in *Pearson v IRC* [1980] 2 All ER 479. *Pearson* has been followed by the Scottish courts: *see Miller v IRC* [1987] STC 108 and, more recently, *Trustees of the Fairbairn or Douglas Trust v HMRC* [2007] STC (SCD) 338. Section 46 IHTA in fact defines an 'interest in possession' where IHT applies to Scotland. In particular, an interest under a 'proper liferent' (*see* section 5.3.2) is an 'interest in possession'.

> for expenses or other outgoings properly payable out of income) to any income produced by that property as the income arises; but ... a discretion or power ... which can be exercised after income arises so as to withhold it from that person negatives the existence of an interest in possession.[418] For this purpose a power to accumulate income is regarded as a power to withhold it, unless any accumulations must be held solely for the person having the interest or his personal representatives. On the other hand, the existence of a mere power of revocation or appointment, the exercise of which would determine the interest wholly or in part (but which, so long as it remains unexercised, does not affect the beneficiary's immediate entitlement to income) does not ... prevent the interest from being an interest in possession.[419]

A simple example of an 'interest in possession' is a vested life interest entitling the holder to settlement income. An 'interest in possession' exists even if the settlement gives rise to no income, but the holder is entitled to the use or enjoyment of settled property.[420] As the 1976 press release indicates, a trustee power to accumulate income from settled property may well prevent there being an 'interest in possession'. However, in HMRC's view, this is not the case (at least outside Scotland) where trustee powers are merely 'administrative', e.g., a power to use trust income to pay for advisers or for the upkeep and repair of trust property.[421]

An 'interest in possession' is 'qualifying' only if an individual is beneficially entitled to it[422] or (in limited circumstances) a company is beneficially entitled to it.[423]

Furthermore, if an individual becomes beneficially entitled to an 'interest in possession' after 21 March 2006, it will not be a 'qualifying interest in possession' unless it is an 'immediate post-death interest',[424] a 'disabled person's interest'[425] or a 'transitional serial interest'.[426] These concepts are complex.[427] Their overall effect is to

418. This was the situation in *Pearson,* according to the majority. Consequently, there was no 'interest in possession'. The same was true in *Re Trafford's Settlement Trusts, Moore & Osborne v IRC* [1984] STC 236, where there was a single current beneficiary of a discretionary trust of income, but the class of beneficiaries had not yet closed. Hence, the single current beneficiary could not claim an immediate entitlement to the income.
419. The minority in the House of Lords in *Pearson* regarded the situation as falling within this last sentence. The difference between the majority and minority analyses is slender.
420. *See* section 50(5) IHTA, as well as *Oakley and another (as personal representatives of Jossaume) v IRC* [2005] STC (SCD) 343, where a right to rent-free occupation of premises was an 'interest in possession' and not a lease.
421. *See* Inheritance Tax Manual IHTM16067 (accessed 18 June 2020). This view reflects the (fine) distinction drawn by the majority in *Pearson* between: (i) 'dispositive' powers under which trustees could divert the *net* income of the trust (e.g., by accumulating it for the benefit of other beneficiaries); and (ii) administrative powers which merely permitted trustees to deduct, from the *gross* income of the trust, expenses and taxes properly incurred in trust management or preserving the value of trust assets. *Miller v IRC* [1987] STC 108 was an example of an administrative power to use income to make good depreciation of trust assets. This did not prevent there being an 'interest in possession'.
422. Section 59(1)(a) IHTA.
423. Section 59(1)(b) and (2) IHTA.
424. Section 49A IHTA.
425. Section 89B IHTA.
426. Section 49B-E IHTA.
427. An 'immediate post-death interest' is one to which an individual becomes beneficially entitled under a will or intestacy on the death of the testator or intestate; the settled property is not within section 71A IHTA (trusts for bereaved minors); and the interest is not a 'disabled

limit the situations where holding an 'interest in possession' leads to the holder being treated as owning the underlying settled property.[428] In particular, it is now impossible to use a gift 'inter vivos' to set up a new trust with a 'qualifying interest in possession', unless it is for the benefit of a disabled person.[429] Hence much more settled property is subject to the very different, more onerous settled property regime discussed in section 5.3.4.

The fiction that the holder of a 'qualifying interest in possession' beneficially owns the underlying settled property has several IHT consequences. The disposal or termination (e.g., on death) of the 'qualifying interest in possession' is treated as if the holder had made a 'transfer of value' of the entire settled property in which that interest subsists or subsisted.[430] The settled property is aggregated for IHT purposes with the personal property of that holder. If this transfer of value of the settled property occurs on the death of the holder of the interest in possession, then the higher IHT rates on death apply. Nevertheless, no IHT is chargeable if the holder of the interest in possession itself becomes beneficially entitled to the underlying settled property or to a further interest in possession in it, or, in some cases, the settled property reverts to the settlor or is transferred to the holder's spouse, widow or widower. These exceptions from an IHT charge follow the logic of the holder of the interest in possession being treated as owning the underlying settled property. There is no IHT charge on the trust[431] itself, and any IHT charge largely reflects the personal IHT profile of the interest in possession holder. Hence, although there is not full 'transparency', the IHT regime where there is a 'qualifying interest in possession' aligns better with the IHT position where assets are owned directly, rather than via a settlement. Such alignment makes sense on the basis, familiar to English law, that the settlement is a form of gift-over-time to the beneficiaries.

In some cases, the statutory fiction is disapplied: if a person becomes entitled to an interest in possession because of a transaction for money or money's worth, the fiction that the interest holder owns the trust property is ignored when deciding if the giving of value for that interest is itself a 'transfer of value'.[432] This ensures that the actuarial value of the interest in possession is used to decide whether the person acquiring it has overpaid (and thereby made a 'transfer of value' to the extent of the overpayment). That actuarial value could well be less than the value of the underlying

person's interest' (within section 89B IHTA). A 'disabled person's interest' requires there to be a beneficiary who is a 'disabled person' (as defined). There are three different kinds of 'transitional serial interest'. In all three cases, the settlement must, *inter alia*, have commenced before 22 March 2006; it must not be a trust within section 71A IHTA (trusts for bereaved minors); and the interest must not be a 'disabled person's interest' (within section 89B IHTA).

428. *See* Glen Loutzenhiser: 'Tiley's Revenue Law'. 10th edition, at pp. 863-864 for some of the political background to these changes and, in particular, a belief by HMRC that 'flexible interest in possession' trusts were being used to create tax-efficient arrangements which were little different from discretionary trusts. The latter have never benefited from the less onerous 'interest in possession' regime.

429. This has important planning implications because only 'inter vivos' transfers of value can benefit from PET treatment.

430. Sections 51-52 IHTA.

431. Although the trustees can be secondarily liable for unpaid IHT.

432. Section 49(2) IHTA.

settled property, e.g., if there is a life interest measured by reference to the life of an old person.

Because the interest in possession holder can be treated as owning the underlying settled property, any 'reversionary interest' in that property is in principle 'excluded property', which is ignored for IHT purposes.[433] There are exceptions to that principle, e.g., where the reversionary interest has at *any* time been acquired for money or money's worth. These exceptions target avoidance based on the 'excluded property' status of a 'reversionary interest'.[434]

5.3.4 Settlements with No Qualifying Interest in Possession

If there is no 'qualifying interest in possession', a completely different IHT regime applies, and the settled property is referred to as 'relevant property'.[435] That regime is summarised below.[436] The summary assumes that the settlement's assets are not carved out of the 'relevant property' regime as 'excluded property', e.g., because the assets are non-UK-situated and the settlor is not treated as UK-domiciled for IHT purposes.

A transfer of assets by a settlor into a 'relevant property' settlement is likely to be subject to IHT at lifetime rates, taking into account the settlor's own 'cumulative total' of prior chargeable transfers.[437]

In addition, at each ten-year anniversary from when the trust was set up, IHT is charged at up to 6%[438] on the then market value of the 'relevant property' in the settlement.[439] The precise rate of tax depends on several variables. These include the then market value of the 'relevant property' plus the historic value of any 'related settlements' created by the settlor, certain other transfers of value by the settlor, as well as the historic value of any settlement property which is not 'relevant property', e.g., because there is a 'qualifying interest in possession' in that property. Therefore, the ten-year anniversary charge partly reflects the settlor's behaviour but takes no account of the fiscal circumstances of any beneficiary nor the nature of that beneficiary's interest (which may post-2006 be an 'interest in possession').

If assets were settled after the settlement was created or after the last ten-year anniversary, those assets are taxed by reference to the period for which they have been

433. Section 48(1) IHTA.
434. Defined in section 47 IHTA to include any vested or contingent 'future interest' under a 'settlement'. In Scotland, it includes 'an interest in the fee of property subject to a proper liferent'.
435. Section 58(1) IHTA.
436. Section 58(1) IHTA creates exceptions from the 'relevant property' taxation regime for specific types of settlement, e.g., charitable trusts, employee benefit trusts, certain pension schemes and 'decommissioning security settlements' (to secure legal obligations when oil fields are abandoned). Some of these exceptions relate to commercial arrangements which are otherwise 'settlements'.
437. In particular, that settlor transfer of value is usually not a PET.
438. The maximum 6% rate is the relevant IHT rate for transfers of value other than on death (currently 20%) multiplied by 0.3.
439. Sections 64 and 66 IHTA.

'relevant property'.[440] To determine this period, the relevant ten-year period[441] is split into three-month sub-periods.

Where assets are transferred out of the settlement, there is a separate IHT 'exit charge' of up to 6%.[442] A transfer out of a settlement can occur when it ends; when assets are distributed to a beneficiary or the latter otherwise becomes 'absolutely entitled' to an asset; when an asset becomes part of a trust regime (e.g., a charitable trust) outside the main 'relevant property' regime; or when a non-commercial transaction reduces the value of the settled property. Different computation rules apply depending on whether the transfer occurs before or after the first ten-year anniversary of the settlement.[443] The rate of charge is also linked to the period that the relevant assets have been in the 'relevant property' settlement since it was set up, or to the period since the last ten-year anniversary of the settlement's creation.

Overall, the 'relevant property' IHT regime takes no account of the circumstances of beneficiaries. It only takes limited account of the circumstances of the settlor. It does not treat beneficiaries as entitled to a share of the underlying 'relevant property', even if they have vested interests in it. Instead, it treats the settlement as an 'opaque' taxable entity. In addition to any IHT charge on creating the 'relevant property' settlement, this regime aims to tax the 'relevant property' once a generation (thirty years) at roughly the IHT rate for lifetime transfers of value (20%).[444] In aggregate, this tax is supposed to equate broadly to the IHT which would be collected on the death of an individual. Some have questioned whether thirty years (rather than national average age at death) is the right period on which to base the ten-year anniversary charge rate. The overall approach is very different from the IHT approach to bare trusts or to those with a 'qualifying interest in possession'. It is a significant deterrent to setting up trusts. While the 40% rate of IHT does not apply, even if beneficiaries of the settlement die while it is in existence, this, lower rate is more than offset by the non-availability of important exemptions which apply where a beneficiary holds property directly or via a non-'relevant property' settlement. In particular, the spouse exemption in section 18 IHTA does not operate in relation to a 'relevant property' settlement, nor is PET treatment applicable. 'Relevant property' settlements can still claim business property and agricultural property reliefs.

440. This applies in particular to income of the settlement which is accumulated so that it becomes part of the 'relevant property' from the date of accumulation.
441. The period up to the first ten-year anniversary or between such anniversaries.
442. Section 65 IHTA. This charge does not apply if the appointment of assets would be income for tax purposes in the hands of a UK-resident. It also does not apply to payments of costs and expenses in respect of 'relevant property'; nor where the transfer of assets occurs within three months of creating the settlement or within three months of a ten-year anniversary: *see* section 65(4) and (5) IHTA.
443. Sections 68-69 IHTA.
444. *See* HMRC Consultation Document dated 6 June 2014: 'Inheritance tax: A fairer way of calculating trust charges' at paragraphs 2.2 and 2.29. HMRC do not regard a settlor putting property into a discretionary trust (where it could remain undistributed for a long period) as equivalent, for IHT, to an outright gift by an individual, who has no further say in what happens to that trust property. While that may be true of discretionary trusts, the 'relevant property' regime also applies to many non-discretionary trusts with fully vested beneficial interests. Such trusts are closer to outright gifts.

The 2006 changes have therefore greatly expanded the scope of this 'opaque' IHT regime. For larger settlements in particular, this is more costly in actual tax terms, especially compared to what went before and compared to owning property directly.[445] It is also a complex and costly regime with which to comply. If the settlement is a UK-resident trust, its capital gains are also likely to be taxed on an 'opaque' basis, at top marginal rates of tax, as discussed in sections 4.3.4 and 4.3.5. It is strange that the tax rules should actively deter the use of settlements as a legitimate asset protection mechanism. Arrangements which are not 'settlements' (e.g., certain family investment company-based structures) may now offer a better method of asset protection without the burden of IHT and with no (or at least lower) tax on capital gains. This is an arbitrary outcome because a private investment company with different classes of shareholding may be little different, in substance, from a discretionary trust.

5.3.5 Inheritance Tax: Transfers of Value, Etc., Involving 'Close Companies'

While the IHT regime for 'relevant property' settlements limits the IHT-'transparency' of settlements for IHT, IHT may still be imposed by 'looking through' an intermediate entity which is a 'close company'.

Leaving aside 'relevant property' settlements, IHT mainly applies to transfers of value by individuals.[446] However, the charge is extended by Part IV IHTA to certain transactions involving 'close companies'. These are defined in CTA 2010, but need not be UK resident.[447]

445. For further discussion, *see* James Kessler KC: 'The Quest for Fair Inheritance Taxation of Trusts' at www.kessler.co.uk/about/Two lectures by James Kessler. The UK 'relevant property' regime is very unusual. This makes double taxation more likely, where settlements have a mix of UK and non-UK assets and/or beneficiaries. *See also* Emma Chamberlain: 'Reform of Inheritance Tax' [2020] British Tax Review 184 and especially at 198-199, although her proposals mainly focus on ending the ability of non-UK domiciliaries to set up trusts for UK-resident beneficiaries which are IHT-free (because they contain 'excluded property').
446. Sections 1 and 2(1) IHTA.
447. Section 102(1) IHTA. The definition of a 'close company' in Part 10 Chapter 2 CTA 2010 basically applies to a company which is under the 'control' of five or fewer economic 'participators' or of any number of economic 'participators' who are also 'directors': *see* section 439 CTA 2010. The very wide definition of 'control' in section 450 CTA 2010 catches many companies which are not obviously closely held. Some publicly listed and traded companies are not 'close': *see* section 446 CTA 2010. As the IHT meaning of 'close company' extends to non-UK-resident companies, and as the definition of 'settlement' (*see* section 5.3.2) is not limited to trusts, some non-UK entities (e.g., Stiftungen) may be both 'settlements' and 'close companies' for IHT. In part, this will depend on whether beneficiaries of such entities are 'participators' in a 'close company', which is often doubtful given their lack of enforceable rights – *see* section 454 CTA 2010. If an entity is both a 'settlement' and a 'close company', the IHT rules for 'close companies' operate very differently to those which apply to 'settled property' (*see* section 5.3.4). While the courts would no doubt prevent a direct double charge in relation to the same transaction, under both the 'settled property' and 'close company' rules, that is not the end of the story. Because different IHT rules apply to 'close companies' and 'relevant property' settlements, IHT charges may arise on different persons, at different times and in respect of different amounts.

Section 94 IHTA provides:

(1) Subject to the following provisions of [Part IV] of this Act, where a close company makes a transfer of value, tax shall be charged as if each individual to whom an amount is apportioned under this section had made a transfer of value of such amount as after deduction of tax (if any) would be equal to the amount so apportioned, less the amount (if any) by which the value of his estate is more than it would be but for the company's transfer; but for this purpose his estate shall be treated as not including any rights or interests in the company.

(2) For the purposes of subsection (1) above, the value transferred by the company's transfer of value shall be apportioned among the participators[448] according to their respective rights and interests in the company[449] immediately before the transfer, and any amount so apportioned to a close company shall be further apportioned among its participators, and so on; but
  (a) so much of that value as is attributable to any payment or transfer of assets to any person which falls to be taken into account in computing that person's profits or gains or losses for the purposes of income tax or corporation tax ... shall not be apportioned and
  (b) if any amount which would otherwise be apportioned to an individual who is domiciled outside the United Kingdom is attributable to the value of any property outside the United Kingdom, that amount shall not be apportioned.

(3) [The 'surrender' of certain reliefs (e.g. losses) by one company to another for corporation tax purposes is ignored in deciding whether there is a 'transfer of value' by the former company].

(4) Where the amount apportioned to a person under this section is 5 per cent or less of the value transferred by the company's transfer of value, then ... tax chargeable under subsection (1) above shall be left out of account in determining, with respect to any time after the company's transfer, what previous transfers of value he has made.

(5) [Provides for the limited IHT 'annual exemption' in respect of lifetime transfers to apply in respect of deemed transfers of value by an individual under section 94. Such a deemed transfer of value cannot be a PET].

Therefore section 94 apportions the 'transfer of value' by the 'close company' to certain persons (especially individuals) with an interest in it, who are then treated as having made an equivalent 'transfer of value'. If one of those persons is itself a 'close company', a further apportionment can be made among those holding relevant interests in that second 'close company', and so on. Section 94 does not cover ordinary corporate transactions which might otherwise trigger it. In particular, HMRC consider[450] that a dividend payment from subsidiary to parent is not a 'transfer of value' for section 94 purposes. Nor is a transfer of assets at an undervalue between a wholly owned subsidiary and its parent; or between two wholly owned subsidiaries. Any

448. 'Participator' is defined broadly as in section 454 CTA 2010 but omitting anyone who would be a 'participator' purely by being a 'loan creditor': *see* section 102(1) IHTA.
449. These are the rights and interests in the assets of the close company which could potentially be distributed to its 'participators': *see* section 102(2) IHTA.
450. Statement of Practice E15.

section 94 charge is a liability of the 'close company', although the 'participators' may be liable if the company fails to pay.[451]

Where rights attaching to the unquoted share or loan capital of a 'close company' are altered or extinguished, section 98 IHTA treats that as an IHT 'disposition' by the 'participators' holding the altered or extinguished rights. That disposition can give rise to a 'transfer of value'.[452] Section 98(3) specifically prevents this from being a PET. However, because it is a deemed disposition, not just a deemed transfer of value, all other IHT exemptions can be invoked in respect of it.[453]

Sections 99 and 100 IHTA adapt sections 94 and 98 IHTA where the 'participators' in the 'close company' include trustees of a 'settlement' for IHT purposes. Section 99 provides that if a transfer of value made by the company is apportioned to its trustee 'participators', then if there is a 'qualifying interest in possession' in the settled property, that interest shall terminate to the extent of that apportioned value. This may trigger IHT under section 52 IHTA. If there is no such 'interest in possession', then the trustee is treated as making a disposition reducing the value of the 'settled property' by the apportioned amount.

Section 100 applies where an alteration in the value of unquoted shares or loan capital of a 'close company' triggers a section 98 deemed disposition, and one of the affected 'participators' is a 'settlement' trustee. If there is a 'qualifying interest in possession'[454] in that 'settlement', it is treated[455] as ending to the extent that the alteration devalues any shares or loan capital which are attributable to that 'interest in possession'. Section 100 does not cover an alteration in the value of the company's shares or loan capital, when the 'participator' is a trustee of a settlement without a 'qualifying interest in possession'.

If the 'close company' itself holds an 'interest in possession' in a settlement, that company's 'participators' are generally treated as entitled to that interest.[456] This may subject them to the IHT 'settlements' regime where there is an 'interest in possession'. If those 'participators' also include the trustees of a 'settlement' in which another person holds a separate 'interest in possession', then the 'interest in possession' held by the company is further attributed via those trustees to the holder of that second 'interest in possession'.[457] Consequently, a transfer of value will occur on the death of that person or if the trustee participator's interest in the 'close company' is reduced other than for full value.[458]

451. Section 202 IHTA.
452. And hence give rise to IHT. Tax on chargeable gains may also arise because of 'value shifting', e.g., under section 29 TCGA.
453. *See* HMRC Inheritance Tax Manual IHTM04069 (accessed 18 June 2022).
454. If the individual only became beneficially entitled to the interest in possession after 21 March 2006, then it may not be 'qualifying': *see* fn 427.
455. This may trigger IHT under section 52 IHTA.
456. *See* section 101(1) IHTA and Statement of Practice E5. The latter is supported by *Powell-Cotton v IRC* [1992] STC 625. Generally, if the company became entitled to that interest in possession after 21 March 2006, section 101(1) only applies if the interest is an 'immediate post-death interest' or a 'transitional serial interest': *see* fn 427.
457. Section 101(2) IHTA.
458. *See* HMRC Inheritance Tax Manual IHTM04092 (accessed 19 June 2020), which also makes clear that if the participators in the company are trustees of a 'relevant property' settlement,

Part IV IHTA 1984 therefore contains 'look through' rules to prevent avoidance of IHT by individuals making 'transfers of value' indirectly via 'close companies'. It partly aligns the IHT position with what it would have been had the participators owned directly the company's assets. However, it stops well short of treating all transfers of value in respect of interests in a 'close company' as a deemed pro rata transfer of that company's underlying assets. In this and other respects, Part IV resembles the rules attributing capital gains of non-resident 'close companies' in sections 3-3G TCGA.[459] However, Part IV IHTA 1984 applies whether or not the transfer of value, etc., by a 'close company' is connected with arrangements to avoid tax. The IHT rules for taxing 'settlements' are less anti-avoidance rules than a flawed tax policy response to structures for protecting and preserving wealth where there is no direct beneficial ownership of that wealth by those standing to benefit.

As already mentioned, some entities may be both 'settlements' and 'close companies' for IHT purposes. In such cases, there is no clear guidance about which IHT regime takes precedence, and there is a clear risk of double taxation.

5.4 VAT AND 'TAX TRANSPARENCY'

5.4.1 Introduction

VAT is a tax on the provision of goods and services[460] rather than a tax on legal persons as such. The primary relevance of legal persons is to collect this transaction-focused tax. Therefore, the question arises less frequently how that tax should apply if a transaction is regarded as carried out, not by a particular entity but by those holding an interest in it.

Entities or arrangements which are often regarded as 'look through' for other tax purposes can nevertheless be 'opaque' for VAT. This applies in particular to partnerships and trusts.

5.4.2 Partnerships: General

A partnership is not typically 'looked through' for VAT purposes. Rather, it is an entity distinct from its underlying assets and partners. In *Staatssecretaris van Financien v Heerma*,[461] the sole economic activity of a Dutch farmer was renting a cattle shed to a Dutch partnership of which he and his wife were partners. The Court of Justice of the European Union (CJEU) regarded this as a supply for VAT purposes between two separate taxable persons, even though the purported lessor was dealing with a

then the participators' share of the interest in possession held by the company is treated as comprised in the 'relevant property' settlement.

459. Indeed, the same facts may trigger both an apportionment for IHT purposes under Part IV IHTA and an apportionment of chargeable gains from a 'close company' under sections 3-3G TCGA.
460. Technically, it applies to 'supplies' of goods and services (as defined) as well as to the 'importation' of goods.
461. Case C23-98 [2001] STC 1437.

partnership of which he was a partner. For VAT purposes, there was 'economic activity' (because rent was being charged) and the partner was acting 'independently' in relation to the partnership, not least because he was acting 'in his own name, on his own behalf and under his own responsibility'. The fact that the Dutch partnership lacked legal personality under Dutch law was irrelevant. That partnership was still a taxable person for VAT because it still had the 'de facto independence of companies', enabling it to enter into the lease.[462]

The fact that one does not 'look through' partnerships for VAT purposes is particularly clear regarding the VAT treatment of: (i) the admission of a new partner in return for a capital contribution and (ii) the transfer of a partnership share. (i) was considered by the CJEU in *KapHag Renditefonds 35 Spreecenter Berlin-Hellersdorf 3. Tranche GbR v Finanzamt Charlottenburg.*[463] It ruled that there was no 'supply' for VAT purposes by a German real estate investment partnership (a Gesellschaft des bürgerlichen Rechts) when a new partner was admitted to the partnership in return for a capital contribution. In particular, there was no supply by the partnership to the new partner of a fractional interest in the underlying assets of the partnership.[464] The CJEU analysis did not turn on the non-tax nature of the partnership, e.g., whether it had legal personality, although the Advocate-General seems to have assumed that it did. HMRC Business Brief 21/2004[465] points out that VAT may arise in such cases if goods or services are contributed *by* the new partner to the partnership in return for being admitted. The partnership may be able to recover some or all of this VAT. However, any such tax charge[466] (on the market value of contributed goods and services) is effectively a clawback of 'input VAT' previously reclaimed by the new partner in respect of those goods or services. Admission to the partnership remains a non-'supply' *by* the partnership for VAT purposes. The new partner acquires an ownership interest in the business entity, which is not analysed as a bundle of fractional interests in the entity's underlying assets.

HMRC similarly consider, based in part on *Kretztechnik AG v Finanzamt Linz,*[467] that a transfer of a partnership interest is a transfer of a chose in action which is a

462. A similar approach has been adopted by the CJEU in relation to 'freedom of establishment' and the UK capital gains tax exit charge on trusts: *see Trustees of the P Panayi Accumulation and Maintenance Settlements v HMRC* Case C-646/15 [2017] STC 2495. The court (at pp. 2517-2158) agreed with Advocate-General Kokott: 'that concept of "other legal persons" extends to an entity which, under national law, possesses rights and obligations that enable it to act in its own right within the legal order concerned, notwithstanding the absence of a particular legal form, and which is profit-making'. Despite lacking legal personality, the trust met this condition because it existed to generate profits from its assets and the trust and its trustees 'constitute an indivisible whole'.
463. Case C-442/01 [2005] STC 1500.
464. The partnership share is seen as an asset distinct from the underlying partnership assets, even though it derives its value from them. This is akin to the distinction between a share in a company and its underlying assets.
465. Dated 10 August 2004.
466. Under Articles 16 and 26 of Directive 2006/112.
467. Case C-465/03 [2005] STC 1118. The CJEU followed *KapHag*. Although *Heerma* was not cited, the Advocate-General stressed that the analysis did not turn on differences in legal characteristics between business entities (e.g., the presence or absence of legal personality).

distinct asset from the underlying assets of the partnership.[468] Again, VAT treats the partnership as an entity distinct from its underlying assets. Whether the transfer of that interest is a supply for VAT purposes depends on various factors discussed in HMRC Business Brief 30/2004.[469] None calls into question the distinction between the partnership interest and underlying partnership assets. If, rarely, the disposal of the partnership interest is a 'supply' (because the disponor carries on a business of dealing in such interests or it acquired the interest to exercise significant active influence over the partnership), it will typically be a VAT-exempt supply of a financial service.[470]

5.4.3 Partnerships: Section 45 VATA 1994 ('VATA')

Section 45 VATA is a special permissive rule regarding the VAT registration of partnerships. Section 45(1) provides:

> The registration under this Act of persons:
>
> (a) carrying on a business in partnership … .
>
> *may* [emphasis added] be in the name of the firm;[471] and no account shall be taken, in determining for any purposes of this Act whether goods or services are supplied to or by such persons … of any change in the partnership.

In Business Brief 21/2004, HMRC stress that section 45(1) is not the legal basis for concluding that there is no supply from a partnership to an incoming partner. Nor does it have any bearing on the VAT treatment of the transfer of a partnership interest. These

468. Treating a partnership share as an interest in an entity distinct from the underlying partnership assets is unfamiliar in the UK direct tax context, where there is a tendency to see the partnership as an aggregation of partners' fractional interests in a pool of assets and not as a separate entity. This tendency is influenced heavily by the nature of an English common law partnership. However, analysing a partnership share as a separate asset is not unique to VAT. The United States Tax Court in *Grecian Magnesite Mining, Industrial & Shipping Co, SA v Commissioner of Internal Revenue* 149 TC 3 concluded that, for Federal income tax purposes, the redemption of an interest in a US limited liability company (taxed as a 'transparent' partnership) was not a deemed disposal of a share of the underlying partnership assets, save where the tax rules clearly specified otherwise (as they did for assets such as US real estate). Rather, the redemption of the partnership interest was the sale or exchange of a separate 'indivisible capital asset': the taxpayer's partnership interest. The US Court of Appeals (Washington D.C. circuit) upheld the Tax Court, but on different, narrower grounds: *see* www.cadc.uscourts.gov Decision No. 17-1268. There was no challenge to the Tax Court's finding that the partnership interest was a single 'indivisible capital asset'. The *Grecian Magnesite* decision has been reversed by statute for future years: *see* section 7.2.6.2.1.
469. Dated 19 November 2004.
470. Because of Article 135(1)(f) Directive 2006/112. This has direct effect and applies in particular to 'transactions … in shares, *interests in companies or associations* [emphasis added]'. The UK transposition in Schedule 9 Group 5 VATA is less explicit than the Directive regarding dealings in partnership interests.
471. HMRC consider that section 45(1) allows the partnership to register in the firm name or trading style: *see* VAT Manual on Registration at paragraph VATREG08800 (accessed 18 June 2022). Once a partnership exists, registration under section 45(1) after its formation does not affect the partners' ongoing liability for VAT in respect of the partnership business, although section 45(5) may limit a partner's VAT liability in the period when it joins or leaves the partnership: *Scrace v HMRC* [2007] STC 269.

matters and their EU law analysis have been discussed in section 5.4.2. Rather, section 45(1) deals with the consequences of English common law partnerships having no legal personality and the fact that a partner joining or leaving a partnership technically leads to its dissolution and the formation of a new partnership. Section 45 therefore treats the partners in a partnership from time to time as a separate continuing person for VAT purposes only. Hence, it is a practical solution to discontinuation under English partnership law on a change of partners.[472]

HMRC also consider that the section 45 VAT registration procedure can, and should, be used where property (e.g., land) is co-owned via a trust and is commercially exploited.[473]

Where an English limited partnership is formed under the Limited Partnerships Act 1907, current practice is that VAT registration should only be in the name(s) of the general partner(s) because the 1907 Act actively deters a limited partner from taking part in the management of the partnership business. Therefore, a limited partner cannot be treated as making VATable supplies in the course or furtherance of the partnership's business.[474] An English limited partnership is not a separate legal person,

472. The same discontinuation issues appear to arise under Scottish law even though Scottish partnerships are separate legal persons. There are limits on the extent to which section 45 allows separate registrations for partnerships. In particular, if two individuals are partners in each of two general partnerships, A and B, HMRC is entitled to give them a single registration under section 45 covering both partnerships. There is no need to give each partnership a separate registration. This is because section 45 registers, in the firm name, the partners carrying on the business from time to time but not the partnership business as such: *see Commissioners of Customs and Excise v Glassborrow* [1974] STC 142. The position differs in Scotland where because a partnership is a legal person, each separate business carried on by the same partners may have a separate registration. *Glassborrow* was also distinguished in *Saunders v Sorrell* [1980] VATTR 53, where the same two individuals, X and Y, were partners in two English limited partnerships. X was the general partner of one limited partnership but Y was general partner of the other. For reasons explained in the main text, only the general partners were regarded as carrying on business for VAT purposes. Therefore, a separate registration was required for each general partner. Had there been more than one general partner in either limited partnership, then the general partners of that limited partnership could have been registered as a partnership under section 45.

473. *See* HMRC VAT Manual on Registration at VATREG09100 (accessed 18 June 2022). There is no specific VAT provision for registering trusts, so unless the trust is registered as a partnership under section 45, it must be registered under section 46 as a form of unincorporated association. Registration under section 46 is discussed in section 5.4.4.

474. *See Saunders v Sorrell* [1980] VATTR 53. HMRC accept this decision, although it seems out of line with the cases mentioned in section 5.4.2 and *Larentia and Minerva mbH & Co KG v Finanzamt Nordenham and Finanzamt Hamburg-Mitte v Marenave Schiffahrts AG* Cases C-108/14 and C-109/14 [2015] STC 2101. These treat a partnership as a separate 'person' for EU law purposes, even if it lacks separate legal personality. Furthermore, *Saunders v Sorrell* seems to have been based on the fact that, because the 1907 Act deters a limited partner from taking part in managing the limited partnership, there is therefore no 'business' being conducted for VAT purposes by the limited partner with the general partner. Hence there is no 'business in partnership' for section 45 purposes. Yet, if the arrangement is a partnership at all under the 1890 Act and the 1907 Act, there must be a 'business in common' between the general and limited partners. Besides, 'business' is widely defined for VAT purposes: *see* section 94 VATA based on Article 9 of Council Directive 2006/112. In *Saunders v Sorrell,* the limited partnerships were patent agents.

In VAT Notice 742A - GOV.UK (www.gov.uk) (accessed February 2022), HMRC state, in section 7.4, that a limited partner *will* be treated as a general partner, for VAT registration

and hence, if the limited partners are disregarded for registration purposes, registration can only apply to the general partner(s). A Scottish limited partnership formed under the 1907 Act is a separate legal person. Therefore, registration of a Scottish partnership should, strictly, be in the name of the Scottish firm.

The fact that an English limited partnership is not a separate legal person has also meant in practice that, if the general partner is a 'body corporate', it can join a VAT group. If it does so, the partnership's business activities will be dealt with under the VAT group registration. Treating the corporate general partner alone as a member of a VAT group seems inconsistent with CJEU thinking on partnerships as distinct opaque entities, whether or not they have legal personality. In practice, however, this approach is crucial in avoiding irrecoverable VAT on management fees of partnership-based funds. The corporate general partner typically pays the fund manager, which belongs to the same VAT group, for its services, free of VAT. The general partner itself receives a non-VATable 'priority profit share' from the fund, with which to pay, in particular, management fees. HMRC apparently allows Scottish limited partnerships to join a VAT group, despite their separate legal personality. This concession could be better publicised.

UK LLPs are corporate bodies which are usually treated for UK direct tax purposes (but not VAT) as if they were partnerships. Consequently, a UK LLP should be registered as a separate corporate body for VAT purposes and has always been eligible to join a VAT group. Similar rules may apply, depending on the facts, to non-UK limited liability partnerships which seek a UK VAT registration and/or membership of a VAT group.

For reasons that are unclear, HMRC do not apply their approach based on *Saunders v Sorrell* to non-UK limited partnerships, even if they are structured like an English limited partnership. Instead, such partnerships are to be registered as general partnerships.

5.4.4 Trusts

VAT legislation contains no special rules for registering trusts for VAT purposes. HMRC consider that where a trust is engaged in business activity, it should be registered as a partnership under section 45(1) VATA, discussed in section 5.4.3. However, they accept that a trust could be VAT-registered under section 46 VATA, which provides:

> (2) The Commissioners may by regulations make provision for determining by what persons anything required by or under this Act to be done by a person carrying on a business is to be done where a business is carried on in partnership *or by a club, association or organisation* [emphasis added] the

purposes, if title to land is held jointly by the general partners and the limited partners, because only the titleholders collectively can make 'supplies' together of that land. This limited exception to their *Saunders v Sorrell* approach stems from paragraph 40 Schedule 10 VATA. This treats a person (e.g., a limited partner) as making a 'grant' of land if the benefit of the consideration for the grant accrues to that person.

> affairs of which are managed by its members or a committee or committees of its members.
>
> (3) The registration under this Act of any such club, association or organisation *may* [emphasis added] be in the name of the club, association or organisation; and in determining whether goods or services are supplied to or by such a club, association or organisation ... no account shall be taken of any change in its members ... .

Section 46(3), like section 45(1), ensures that a change of trustees does not affect a VAT registration of a trust under section 46. This is especially relevant to English law trusts which lack separate legal personality.[475] HMRC consider[476] that they cannot refuse applications for separate VAT registrations for trusts, even where each trust concerned has the same trustees. Each trust is to be registered in the names of the trustees and the trust for which they act.[477]

A corporate trustee has in practice been allowed to join a VAT group if it meets the conditions for VAT group treatment in section 43 VATA.[478] This may, for example, apply to the corporate trustee of a pension fund. If such a trustee is allowed to join a VAT group, it will be included in that group in respect of all its business activities (both fiduciary and non-fiduciary) so long as it has been granted 'unitary treatment' under section 45 or 46 VATA by HMRC.[479] While helpful, this practice regarding corporate trustees seems out of line with CJEU thinking (*see* section 5.4.2) that even if a trust lacks legal personality under its governing law, it can be a 'legal person' under EU law.

5.4.5 Conclusion regarding VAT and 'Tax Transparency'

Overall, for the purposes of VAT, the concept of 'tax transparency' has limited relevance. VAT is a tax on transactions and its incidence is closely linked to the nature of those transactions. Consequently, there is less need to 'look through' an entity carrying out a transaction and to tax by reference to those with an interest in it. Hence, the VAT analysis of the acquisition and transfer of partnership interests is in essence the same as the VAT analysis of acquisitions and transfers of company shares. An entity can still be a distinct 'person' for VAT purposes whether or not it has legal personality under its governing law. This makes sense because VAT is a harmonised tax intended to apply in broadly the same way across various states with very different domestic legal traditions.

---

475. A trust under English law is simply a series of obligations imposed on the trustee(s): *see* section 4.1.1.
476. *See* VAT Registration Manual at paragraph VATREG12850 (accessed 18 June 2022). Contrast this with their stance regarding section 45 VATA, which was upheld in *Commissioners of Customs & Excise v Glassborrow* [1974] STC 142. The difference in approach reflects the lack of legal provisions for registering trusts and trustees for VAT, compared to section 45(1).
477. Regulation 8 of the VAT Regulations 1995 SI 1995/2518 makes all members of an entity registered under section 46 VATA jointly and severally liable for VAT-related matters.
478. This is similar to the position discussed in section 5.4.3 regarding the corporate general partner of an English limited partnership.
479. *See* VAT Registration Manual at VATREG13000 (accessed 19 June 2020). If such 'unitary treatment' is unavailable, fiduciary business activities of the corporate trustee fall outside the VAT group registration.

Furthermore, where sections 45-46 VATA apply they are the opposite of 'look through' rules. They create a single enduring person registered for VAT where otherwise (e.g., in relation to a partnership) it could be necessary to change VAT registrations on a regular basis because of changes in entity membership. At the very least, this would be cumbersome.

5.5 STAMP DUTY AND 'TAX TRANSPARENCY'

Stamp duty is a tax on documentation giving effect to certain transactions. Since December 2003, it has been limited to certain transactions (especially transfers on sale) relating to 'stock' or 'marketable securities', and in limited cases, to partnership interests.[480] Before then, it also applied to transfers of interests in land and to the grant of leases. Those transactions are now subject to stamp duty land tax ('SDLT') which is discussed in section 5.7.

5.5.1 Stamp Duty and Partnerships

Historically, for stamp duty purposes, there was no question of 'looking through' to the underlying assets of the partnership. Partnerships were 'non-transparent'. Hence stamp duty was payable at normal rates on a document transferring a partnership interest on sale, without reference to the partnership's underlying assets. The rationale for this is in STSM091040 (accessed 21 June 2022) of the Stamp Taxes on Shares Manual:

> A partnership interest or share is, in law, a separate item of 'property' in its own right. A partner cannot claim to be the owner of any particular partnership asset, nor of any specific share of a partnership asset. Rather, a partnership interest represents a right to control the partnership assets and affairs for as long as the partnership lasts and, upon dissolution, a right to have the assets liquidated, the liabilities discharged and a division of any surplus.

This reflects the case law on partnership interests discussed in section 5.2. However, a partial transparency regime for stamp duty applies on a transfer of a partnership interest, under paragraphs 31-33 Schedule 15 FA 2003, where the partnership assets consist of an interest in land and/or 'stock' or 'marketable securities'.[481] Without paragraphs 31-33, a transfer of a partnership interest would not be subject to stamp duty at all because of section 125 FA 2003, even if its underlying assets included 'stock' or 'marketable securities'. Those assets would be subject to stamp duty if transferred on sale directly, rather than indirectly by selling the partnership interest.

480. Section 125 and paragraphs 31-33 Schedule 15 Finance Act 2003 (FA 2003).
481. Other than stock or marketable securities admitted to trading on a 'recognised growth market' but not listed on any market: *see* paragraph 33(8A) Schedule 15 FA 2003, together with section 99A FA 1986. HMRC do not regard the partnership interest itself (or an interest in a UK LLP) as 'stock' or 'marketable securities' for stamp duty purposes.

Any stamp duty on transferring a partnership interest is charged at the (higher) general rates rather than the 0.5% rate which applies on a direct transfer of 'stock' or 'marketable securities'. However, paragraphs 32-33 are likely to limit any such stamp duty charge.[482]

Paragraph 32 applies where the partnership property includes a 'chargeable interest' in land for SDLT purposes.[483] Because such 'chargeable interests' are dealt with under the SDLT regime, paragraph 32 carves them out of stamp duty, by reducing the stampable amount for the transfer of the partnership interest. The reduction is (broadly) the market value of the 'chargeable interest' in land (less any loan secured on it), multiplied by the percentage interest in the partnership which is being sold.

Paragraph 33 imposes stamp duty where the partnership holds 'stock' or 'marketable securities'.[484] It limits the duty to what it would be if: (i) the instrument transferring the partnership share were a direct transfer of the 'stock' or 'marketable securities' and (ii) the stampable amount was the market value of the 'stock' or 'marketable securities' (less any loan secured on them), multiplied by the percentage interest in the partnership which is being sold. For these purposes, 'stock' or 'marketable securities' will include non-UK 'stock' or 'marketable securities' held by the partnership.[485]

To invoke paragraphs 32 and 33, the relevant instrument of transfer must be submitted to the Stamp Office for adjudication under section 12 Stamp Act 1891.[486]

To sidestep this procedure, parties may choose to execute and retain outside the UK an unstamped instrument of transfer. Unless and until stamped in accordance with paragraph 33, it cannot be used as evidence in UK civil proceedings, nor can it be effectively enforced in the UK.[487] This may not matter if it relates to a partnership interest in non-UK securities. It can later be repatriated without penalty so long as it is stamped within thirty days of being brought into the UK.[488] Interest on unpaid stamp duty will nevertheless accrue from when the instrument is executed.[489]

Paragraphs 32 and 33 partly 'look through' a partnership for stamp duty purposes, although mainly to preserve the stamp duty charge in respect of 'stock' or 'marketable securities' held by the partnership, when a partnership interest is transferred. Generally, a partnership is not 'looked through' for stamp duty. Where a new partner contributes cash or other assets in return for a partnership share and there is no connected withdrawal of capital by an existing partner, HMRC do not regard acquiring

482. If not already reduced to nil under the 'certificate of value' procedure which exempts certain lower-value transactions from the general rates of stamp duty (but not from the 0.5% rate on transactions directly involving 'stock' or 'marketable securities').
483. As discussed in section 5.7, Schedule 15 FA 2003 governs SDLT on transactions in relation to partnerships which hold one or more 'chargeable interests' in land.
484. Other than any stock or marketable securities referred to in fn 481.
485. Such non-UK securities would typically not be subject to stamp duty in practice, if transferred directly.
486. Paragraphs 32(9) and 33(8) Schedule 15 FA 2003.
487. Section 14(4) Stamp Act 1891.
488. Section 15B Stamp Act 1891.
489. Section 15A Stamp Act 1891.

a partnership interest as a stampable sale.[490] In particular, they do not regard the incoming partner as effectively purchasing a fractional interest in any 'stock' or 'marketable securities' already held as partnership assets.[491]

Similarly, when a partnership is dissolved or a partner leaves the partnership, the distribution of 'stock' or 'marketable securities' in proportion to a partner's interest is not a stampable transfer on sale.[492]

5.5.2 Definition of a 'Partnership' for Stamp Duty and SDLT

For stamp duty and SDLT, a 'partnership' is[493] anything counting as a partnership under the 1890 Act, a limited partnership registered under the Limited Partnerships Act 1907, and a UK LLP, as well as 'a firm or entity *of a similar character to any of those mentioned above* [emphasis added] formed under the law of a country or territory outside the United Kingdom'. This last category is broad, given that a UK LLP is a body corporate treated as a partnership for certain UK tax purposes. Does a 'similar character' refer to tax or non-tax characteristics of the relevant non-UK entity? A Delaware LLC, from a non-tax perspective, is similar to a UK LLP which is a UK body corporate without share capital. In practice, HMRC will be reluctant to accept that a Delaware LLC is a 'partnership' for these purposes.

Paragraph 2 Schedule 15 FA 2003 provides that, for SDLT purposes, a 'chargeable interest' in land held by or on behalf of a 'partnership' (as defined above) is treated as held by or on behalf of the partners, even if the partnership is a legal person, or even a body corporate under its governing law. Therefore, this 'look through' rule disregards the partnership and also envisages that some bodies corporate can be partnerships for these purposes (although it is unclear which ones). SDLT in relation to partnerships is discussed in section 5.7, where paragraph 2 relates to the special SDLT computation rules in Schedule 15. Paragraph 2 is, however, not relevant when deciding if a partnership can be 'looked through' for the purposes of claiming SDLT group relief: *see* section 5.5.3. This can have especially odd consequences where the partnership is a UK LLP. It is strange that this 'look through' rule only applies when an interest in land (but not other assets such as shares) is held by a partnership.

Paragraph 3 Schedule 15 ensures that the partnership is regarded as the same partnership despite changes in membership, so long as there is at least one continuing

490. *See* paragraph STSM092020 of the Stamp Taxes on Shares Manual (accessed 19 June 2022). The position would be different if the partner being admitted paid cash or transferred assets directly to the existing partners. In that case, the new partner would be treated as having acquired a partnership interest via a sale. The amount of stamp duty payable on that sale would be subject to paragraphs 32-33. When a partnership converts into a UK LLP (but not any other type of body corporate), there is stamp duty relief under section 12 Limited Liability Partnerships Act 2000. This must be claimed by seeking adjudication under section 12 Stamp Act 1891.

491. Cf. sections 59 and 59A TCGA, discussed in Appendix A.

492. Unless the distribution is in satisfaction of a debt due to the partner from the partnership or the partner assumes a liability in return: *see* paragraph STSM092050 of the Stamp Taxes on Shares Manual (accessed 22 June 2020). In those cases, there is stampable consideration even though the partnership is not 'looked through'.

493. Paragraph 1 Schedule 15 FA 2003.

member. Paragraph 4 Schedule 15 FA 2003 also makes clear that a partnership (as defined in paragraph 1) is not a 'unit trust scheme' or an 'open-ended investment company' for stamp duty or SDLT. Such entities are typically 'opaque' for stamp duty and SDLT.

5.5.3 Partnerships and Stamp Duty/SDLT Group Relief

Paragraphs 31-33 Schedule 15 FA 2003 set out limited situations where a partnership can be treated as 'transparent' for stamp duty purposes. These computational provisions only apply when a partnership interest is transferred. They are usually not relevant for group relief,[494] which exempts from stamp duty certain transfers between 'associated' 'bodies corporate'. There are equivalent group relief rules for SDLT (which is convenient to deal with here). Broadly, bodies corporate are 'associated' if one is a direct or indirect 75% subsidiary of the other or both are direct or indirect 75% subsidiaries of a third body corporate. Whether this 75% threshold is satisfied mainly depends on one body corporate beneficially owning, directly or indirectly, the 'ordinary share capital' of the other.

Because a UK LLP is a body corporate,[495] HMRC accept[496] that it can be the 75% beneficial owner of another 'body corporate' for the purposes of stamp duty group relief. However, because members' interests in a UK LLP are unlikely to be 'ordinary share capital' (or indeed share capital at all), it cannot be the 75% subsidiary of another body corporate for group relief purposes. Therefore, no stamp duty or SDLT group relief is available on an asset transfer from a body corporate which owns the UK LLP, either to that LLP itself or to a third body corporate which is a subsidiary of the UK LLP. In the last scenario, one cannot 'look through' the UK LLP in the same way as for corporation tax group relief because stamp duty has no equivalent of section 1273(1)(c) CTA 2009: *see* Appendix A.8.

The limited 'look through' rule in paragraph 2 Schedule 15 FA 2003 (*see* section 5.5.2) creates further complications but only in relation to SDLT group relief.[497] Paragraph 2 only treats LLP members as owning underlying LLP assets which are 'chargeable interests' in land, not shares. So in the example above, paragraph 2 does not treat the parent of the UK LLP as owning directly the shares of the LLP's subsidiary, so as to establish a group relationship between that parent and the subsidiary. However, if the UK LLP transfers a 'chargeable interest' in land to the subsidiary, paragraph 2 *does* apply. Therefore the land is treated as transferred to the subsidiary not from the UK LLP itself (with which it is grouped) but from the LLP's parent (with which it is not grouped). Hence paragraph 2 denies SDLT group relief where it might be

494. *See* in particular section 42 FA 1930 and the equivalent, but not identical SDLT rules in Schedule 7, Part 1 FA 2003.
495. There is no general rule deeming it to be a partnership for *all* stamp duty purposes, despite paragraph 1 Schedule 15 FA 2003.
496. *See* paragraph STSM093020 in HMRC Stamp Taxes on Shares Manual (accessed 21 June 2022).
497. *See also* Neil Warriner, Michelle Williamson and John Tolman: 'Analysis: LLPs, Groups and Stamp Taxes' (2010) Tax Journal, Issue 1053, at 13.

expected to apply. Paragraph 2 would not have this effect if, instead, the interest in land were merely transferred from one subsidiary of the UK LLP to another.

Paragraph 2 therefore handicaps UK LLPs, for no good reason, when compared to general and limited partnerships formed under English law, which can (at least in practice) be 'looked through' for all purposes.[498] HMRC state that because partnerships formed under English law lack legal personality, they can be 'looked through' to determine whether 'bodies corporate' form a group for stamp duty purposes. In particular, 'as such the companies that are the partners of an English general or limited partnership can, *depending upon the facts* [emphasis added] be grouped with those companies that are below the partnership in the group structure'. These HMRC statements are more tentative than the equivalent guidance on corporation tax group relief (*see* Appendix A.8). While they make practical sense,[499] they sit uneasily with HMRC's accurate analysis of a partner's interest in a partnership.[500] However, if one accepts this guidance, group relief is available for SDLT purposes where a corporate partner has, say, a 75% share in an English partnership which transfers an interest in land to another company whose shares are owned by that partnership. No SDLT group relief would be available if the English partnership were replaced by a UK LLP.

These HMRC statements about 'looking through' an English partnership for group relief purposes do not extend to Scottish partnerships which have legal personality. However, because Scottish partnerships are not 'bodies corporate' (unlike UK LLPs),[501] it is also not possible to form a stamp duty or SDLT group between a Scottish partnership and another company whose shares are wholly owned by it. It is not satisfactory that there should be such divergence between Scottish and English partnerships.[502]

5.5.4 Trusts and Stamp Duty

No rule requires all trusts to be automatically 'looked through' for stamp duty purposes. If 'stock' or 'marketable securities' are held via a trust in which beneficiaries have a vested interest in both trust income and capital (i.e., a 'bare trust'), then a written transfer of a beneficial interest in that trust should be stampable because it transfers a vested beneficial interest in 'stock' or 'marketable securities'. The same applies to a contract for such a transfer. However, the same is not true if the trust is one in which beneficial interests are successive (so that they lack a vested interest in trust capital) or a discretionary and/or accumulation trust. Unless the trust can be 'looked

498. It also disadvantages UK LLPs compared to a UK private limited company, which will be unaffected by paragraph 2, Schedule 15 FA 2003 and typically has 'ordinary share capital'. It can therefore be readily grouped with its parent company.
499. HMRC make similar statements in paragraph SDLTM34360 onwards (accessed 21 June 2022) of the Stamp Duty Land Tax Manual in relation to SDLT group relief.
500. *See* the citation in section 5.5.1 from STSM091040 (accessed 21 June 2022) of HMRC's Stamp Taxes on Shares Manual.
501. *See* fn 33.
502. *See* section 2.9.6. SDLT no longer applies to land in Scotland and Wales. Land and Buildings Transaction Tax applies in Scotland from April 2015 and Land Transaction Tax applies in Wales from April 2018. Both these devolved taxes are largely inspired by SDLT.

through' to the underlying 'stock' or 'marketable securities', a transfer of a beneficial interest in it is not subject to stamp duty since December 2003.

Since February 2000, there has also been no stamp duty charge in respect of transactions involving 'units' in a 'unit trust'.[503]

5.6 STAMP DUTY RESERVE TAX AND 'TAX TRANSPARENCY'

Stamp Duty Reserve Tax (SDRT) is a directly assessable tax on certain transactions involving 'chargeable securities', as defined in section 99 FA 1986. In particular, it is charged at 0.5% on an agreement to transfer such securities.[504] A transaction can be subject to SDRT whether or not documented.

The main definition of 'chargeable securities' is in section 99(3) FA 1986:

(a) stocks, shares or loan capital;
(b) interests in, or in dividends or other rights arising out of, stocks, shares or loan capital;
(c) rights to allotments of or to subscribe for, or options to acquire, stocks, shares or loan capital; and
(d) units under a unit trust scheme.

How does this definition[505] apply to an interest in a partnership? If the partnership is significantly invested in stocks, shares or loan capital, a partnership interest looks very much like an 'interest in' such underlying investments, within section 99(3)(b), especially if the partnership lacks legal personality. To date, HMRC appear not to have argued this for SDRT purposes.[506] This may be because of how they analyse

503. *See* paragraph 1 Schedule 19 FA 1999. There was previously a charge under sections 54-57 Finance Act 1946. For those purposes, a 'unit trust' was defined in essentially the same way as for direct tax purposes (*see* section 4.3.6.1), including carve-outs for, in particular, 'limited partnership schemes' and some employee share incentive plans: *see* Stamp Duty and Stamp Duty Reserve Tax (Definitions of Unit Trust Scheme) Regulations 1988 SI 1988/268 (as amended). Those Regulations still apply for SDRT purposes. The carve-out for 'limited partnership schemes' only applies to an English limited partnership. A partnership with separate legal personality should not give rise to a 'trust' and so cannot be a 'unit trust' anyway.
504. Section 87 FA 1986. Section 92 FA 1986 sets out the main conditions for ensuring that the same transaction does not give rise to both SDRT and stamp duty.
505. This is the basic definition but there are important exceptions to it in section 99 FA 1986, not least where the relevant stocks, shares or loan capital are issued by non-UK persons. Those exceptions are not considered further.
506. In other contexts, HMRC take a different approach. The employment-related securities rules in Part 7 ITEPA 2003 can apply to 'units in a collective investment scheme': *see* section 420(1)(e) ITEPA 2003. The Employment-Related Securities Manual at ERSM20170 (accessed 21 June 2022) states that where a partnership is a collective investment scheme, one should not usually 'look through' to its underlying assets. However, it is appropriate to 'look through' where the partnership invests in so-called restricted securities (whose value is suppressed by restrictions such as forfeiture provisions). This 'look through' is in order to apply the special tax rules in Chapter 2, Part 7 ITEPA 2003.

an interest in a partnership: *see* section 5.5.1.[507] Section 99(3)(b) FA 1986 also covers a vested beneficial interest in stocks, shares or loan capital held on trust, or in the income rights attaching to them.

Where a trust is a 'unit trust scheme', section 99(3)(d) also applies. A 'unit trust scheme' is defined in much the same way as for income tax purposes.[508] A unit in a 'unit trust scheme' also falls potentially within section 99(3)(b) FA 1986. In practice, one would expect HMRC to apply only the specific SDRT rules relating to units in a 'unit trust scheme'. Such a unit is prima facie a 'chargeable security' regardless of the underlying trust property. Section 99(5A)(b) and (5B) FA 1986 treat units in a unit trust scheme as not being 'chargeable securities', where, in particular, that scheme only holds investments outside the charge to stamp duty and SDLT. To this extent, one can 'look through' the unit trust to decide whether units are subject to SDRT.

Section 90(1B) further illustrates the partial 'transparency' of unit trust schemes for SDRT purposes. This removes the 0.5% charge 'as regards an agreement to transfer trust property to the unit holder on the surrender to the managers of a unit under a unit trust scheme if the unit holder is to receive only such part of each description of asset in the trust property as is proportionate to, or as nearly as practicable proportionate to, the unit holder's share'. In short, when surrendered, the unit is treated as equivalent to one or more fractional interests in each of the underlying scheme assets. If the unit holder receives on surrender no more than those underlying fractional interests, the unit is ignored as a separate asset and there is no SDRT charge.

FA 2014 repealed[509] Part II Schedule 19 FA 1999 which imposed SDRT on the surrender of units in a unit trust.

5.7 SDLT AND 'TAX TRANSPARENCY'

SDLT was introduced by Part 4 FA 2003 as a replacement for stamp duty in relation to transactions involving UK real estate. Its scope is broader than its predecessor. It is a directly assessable tax and is not a tax on legal documentation. Slightly different variants of the SDLT legislation apply in Scotland and in Wales, under powers devolved to those parts of the UK. The Scottish and Welsh regimes are not discussed further.[510]

5.7.1 SDLT and Trusts

Section 105 and Schedule 16 FA 2003 deal with SDLT and trusts, subject to the rules regarding 'unit trusts' discussed below. Paragraph 1 Schedule 16 distinguishes

507. Although this is not a convincing reason. If the partnership is a legal person, it is harder to argue that a partnership share is an 'interest in' the underlying partnership investments. However, this risks creating different outcomes depending on whether a partnership is English or Scottish. SDRT applies to the entire UK.
508. *See* paragraphs 14-19 Schedule 19 FA 1999, as well as, in particular, SI 1988/268 *supra*.
509. With effect from 30 March 2014.
510. *See* fn 502.

between 'settlements' and 'bare trusts'. The latter are defined[511] very similarly to section 60 TCGA.

Paragraph 3 sets out a partial 'look through' SDLT regime for 'bare trusts':

(1) Subject to subparagraph (2), where a person acquires a chargeable interest [in UK land] or an interest in a partnership as bare trustee, [SDLT] applies as if the interest were vested in, and the acts of the trustee in relation to it were the acts of, the person or persons for whom he is trustee.
(2) Subparagraph (1) does not apply in relation to the grant of a lease.
(3) Where a lease is granted to a person as bare trustee, he is treated for the purposes of [SDLT], as it applies in relation to the grant of the lease, as purchaser of the whole of the interest acquired.
(4) Where a lease is granted by a person as bare trustee, he is to be treated for the purposes of [SDLT] as it applies in relation to the grant of the lease, as vendor of the whole of the interest disposed of.

The 'look through' means that the bare trustee has no SDLT liability, even if the beneficial owner fails to pay. For anti-avoidance reasons, there is no 'look through' where a lease is *granted* (not assigned) by or to a bare trustee. Where the 'look through' operates, a beneficiary's identity may affect the rate of SDLT payable. The additional 3% SDLT rate may apply if a non-minor beneficiary is treated as owning a residential property via the trust, as well as one which it owns independently. The special 15% SDLT rate on high-value residential properties acquired by certain non-natural persons may well apply if a 'bare trustee' acquires such a property for a corporate beneficiary.

For 'settlements' (all trusts other than 'bare trusts', as defined in paragraph 1), paragraph 4 Schedule 16 provides:

> Where persons acquire a chargeable interest or an interest in a partnership as trustees of a settlement, they are treated for the purposes of [SDLT], as it applies in relation to that acquisition, as purchasers of the whole of the interest acquired (including the beneficial interest).

There is therefore no SDLT 'look through' in relation to a 'settlement' which acquires an interest in land. If there is a vested interest in possession in the trust income, that makes no difference. In practice, the 'settlement' trustees are treated as a single and continuing body of persons distinct from the persons who are trustees from time to time. This is similar to section 69(1) TCGA.

The same non-'look through' approach applies to those trusts which qualify as unit trusts, even if they would otherwise be 'bare trusts'. Section 101(1) FA 2003 provides that SDLT applies to a 'unit trust scheme'[512] 'as if the trustees were a

511. Paragraphs 1(2)-(4) Schedule 16 FA 2003 and *Pollen Estate Trustee Company Ltd v HMRC* [2013] STC 1479. The assets of any such trust will consist of one or more interests in UK land, so the operation of the 'look through' rules regarding such trusts for SDLT purposes may be limited by *Crowe v Appleby* [1975] 3 All ER 529: *see* section 4.3.2.1. *See also* Simon Howley: 'SDLT and Trusts' (22 October 2021) Tax Journal, at 15.
512. As defined in FSMA: *see* section 101(4) FA 2003.

company;[513] and the rights of the unitholders were shares in the company'. Therefore, a 'unit trust scheme' is non-'transparent' for SDLT purposes, which partly explains why investments in UK land via JPUTs have been popular. There is no SDLT in respect of a transfer of units. There is also no SDRT nor (in practice) stamp duty on such a transfer because JPUT units will be registered in a non-UK register of ownership.

This approach in respect of unit trusts should be contrasted with the rules regarding partnerships owning interests in UK land, discussed below.[514] Unit trusts and partnerships can fulfil very similar functions as collective investment vehicles and are both usually income tax transparent. Taxpayers therefore have an effective choice over whether an interest in similar vehicles does or does not give rise to SDLT. This taxpayer choice is not easy to defend on tax policy grounds.

5.7.2 SDLT and Partnerships

Schedule 15 FA 2003 contains complex rules governing the SDLT treatment of transactions involving partnerships. These are summarised below. They apply especially where there is a transfer of a 'chargeable interest' in land to or from the partnership or where there is a transfer of a partnership interest.[515] The definition of 'partnership' for SDLT purposes was discussed in section 5.5.2. In particular,[516] a 'partnership' is not a 'unit trust scheme' for SDLT purposes, so section 101 FA 2003 (*see* section 5.7.1) is not relevant. The definition of 'partnership' seems broad enough to embrace certain 'bodies corporate'. This cuts across the general SDLT approach of not 'looking through' companies. The definition of 'company' in section 100(1) FA 2003 excludes a 'partnership', but the definition of 'partnership' seems to cover companies akin to UK LLPs in particular.

5.7.3 Transfer of a 'Chargeable Interest' to a Partnership

Special computation rules[517] apply where a 'chargeable interest' in land is transferred to a partnership by an existing partner, an incoming partner or a person 'connected'

513. This deemed company status does not entitle the unit trust scheme to certain corporate reliefs (such as SDLT group relief, in Schedule 7 FA 2003): *see* section 101(7) FA 2003. Section 100(1) FA 2003 makes clear that a 'company' for SDLT purposes includes an unincorporated association (*see* section 2.5) but excludes a partnership.
514. The non-'look through' approach is also applied by section 102A FA 2003 to the 'tax-transparent' collective investment schemes known as 'co-ownership authorised contractual schemes': *see* section 235A FSMA. They are not trust-based and hence are not unit trusts. They are also not partnerships although very similar in practice to an investment LP. In fact, an 'authorised contractual scheme' can be set up as a LP (rather than as a purely contractual co-ownership arrangement). In that case it will be a partnership for SDLT purposes. Taxpayers will probably want to avoid this outcome.
515. In those cases, Part 3 of Schedule 15 FA 2003 may apply. The transfer of a 'chargeable interest' in land includes the grant, creation or variation of such an interest (e.g., granting a lease), as well as its surrender or release: *see* paragraph 9(2) Schedule 15 FA 2003.
516. Paragraph 4 Schedule 15 FA 2003.
517. Paragraphs 10-12 Schedule 15 FA 2003.

with an existing or incoming partner. These rules can apply whether the partnership already exists or is being formed.

The aim is to charge SDLT only on that part of the market value of the 'chargeable interest' which is *not* attributable post-transfer to the partnership share[518] of the person who made the land transfer and/or a partner 'connected' with that person.[519] So SDLT only applies to that slice of the value of the 'chargeable interest' given to partners other than the person making the transfer to the partnership or persons 'connected' with that transferor. Unlike a company or 'unit trust scheme', the partnership is therefore 'looked through' so as to treat the person making the transfer, or a person 'connected' with that person, as continuing to own the part of the contributed chargeable interest reflected in their ongoing partnership share. The precise taxable amount is[520] MV multiplied by (100-SLP) %, where MV is the market value of the interest transferred and SLP is the 'sum of the lower proportions'.[521] MV takes no account of leverage within the partnership. Therefore, SDLT may be calculated using an artificially high market value.

Under paragraph 12A Schedule 15, a 'property-investment partnership' (PIP) can elect irrevocably to disapply paragraphs 10-12. A PIP is one whose 'sole or main activity is investing or dealing in chargeable interests (whether or not that activity involves the carrying out of construction operations on the land in question)'.[522] If this election is made, the transfer of the 'chargeable interest' to the partnership is subject to SDLT in the normal way on the full market value of what is transferred. The formula in paragraphs 10-12 is then irrelevant. Making the election can benefit the PIP in relation to subsequent transactions, notably transfers of interests in the PIP itself which could otherwise trigger SDLT: *see* section 5.7.4. To make the election worthwhile, SDLT saved on those later transactions must exceed the extra SDLT incurred upfront because of making the election.

5.7.4 Transfer of Interest in a 'PIP'

With specific exceptions, acquiring an interest in a partnership (e.g., by subscribing money) does *not* give rise to a chargeable transaction for SDLT purposes, even if the partnership property includes land.[523] Hence there is no comprehensive 'look through' treatment of partnerships for SDLT purposes, in contrast to their capital gains tax

518. A person's partnership share is that person's proportionate entitlement at that time to share in the *income* profits of the partnership: *see* paragraph 34(2) Schedule 15 FA 2003. This is odd because a partner's commercial entitlements to 'chargeable interests' owned by the partnership may not be the same as its income entitlement.
519. The definition of 'connected' persons is taken from section 1122 CTA 2010 with modifications. In particular, paragraph 39(2) of Schedule 15 disapplies section 1122(7) CTA 2010, which often treats partners as connected with one another. Otherwise, section 1122(7) could undermine what paragraphs 10-12 Schedule 15 are trying to achieve.
520. Paragraph 10(2) Schedule 15 FA 2003.
521. The detailed rules for determining SLP are in paragraph 12 Schedule 15 FA 2003.
522. Paragraph 14(8) Schedule 15 FA 2003. A PIP should not include, say, a partnership owning and running a hotel. Nor in practice should it include a partnership whose main profit-making activity is a trade of developing property, such as a housebuilder.
523. Paragraph 29 Schedule 15 FA 2003.

treatment (*see* Appendix A, where the pitfalls of a comprehensive 'look through' are discussed).

Paragraph 14 Schedule 15 is a specific exception.[524] It subjects to SDLT the transfer of an interest in a 'PIP', where the 'relevant partnership property' includes a 'chargeable interest' in land in England or Northern Ireland (but not Wales or Scotland). Paragraph 14 is therefore a limited 'look-through' to the underlying real estate assets of that special type of partnership. SDLT is charged on a percentage of the gross market value of the 'relevant partnership property',[525] again ignoring borrowing of the partnership. That percentage corresponds to the partnership share transferred (if the person acquiring it was not previously a partner) or the increase in that person's partnership share (where the acquirer was previously a partner).

5.7.5 Transfer of Interest in a Partnership Pursuant to Earlier Arrangements

Even if the partnership is not a PIP, a transfer of an interest in it can sometimes trigger SDLT under paragraph 17 Schedule 15 where it takes place pursuant to 'arrangements' existing when a 'chargeable interest' was transferred previously to that partnership. That earlier transfer must have been subject to the restricted SDLT charge under paragraphs 10-12 Schedule 15, discussed in section 5.7.3. SDLT on the later transfer is a proportion of the market value (at the time of the later transfer) of the chargeable interest which was previously transferred to the partnership. The proportion reflects the reduction in the transferor's partnership share when the partnership interest is transferred later. These rules tax a two-step realisation of the value of the underlying interest in land, first by transferring it to a partnership with reduced SDLT under paragraphs 10-12 and then disposing of an interest in that partnership.

A similar rule in paragraph 17A Schedule 15 applies where there is a transfer of a 'chargeable interest' to a partnership falling within paragraphs 10-12 Schedule 15 and a 'qualifying event' occurs within three years of that transfer.[526] 'Qualifying events'

---

524. The others are paragraph 10 Schedule 15 (discussed in section 5.7.3) and paragraph 17 Schedule 15 (discussed in section 5.7.5). For further discussion of paragraph 14 Schedule 15, *see* Toby Price and Alexandra Hawkins: 'Practice Guide: Tax Transparent Property Funds' (30 October 2020) Tax Journal, Issue 1507, at 8. The authors note: (i) the reduced range of SDLT reliefs applying to a charge under paragraph 14 and (ii) HMRC's view that in applying paragraph 14, one can look through any intermediate layers of 'property investment partnership' to the underlying 'chargeable interest'. It is unclear how one does this in practice: *see* Crossley and Baldwin *supra*, at 25-46 to 25-48.
525. The meaning of the 'relevant partnership property' varies depending on whether the partnership interest acquired has been directly or indirectly paid for by the acquirer. In any case (*see* paragraphs 14(5) and 14(5A) Schedule 15), 'relevant partnership property' excludes any 'chargeable interest' transferred to the PIP in return for the transfer of the partnership interest; certain leases granted at a market rent; and any 'chargeable interest' not attributable under the partnership agreement to the partnership interest which is being transferred. 'Relevant partnership property' will also not include a 'chargeable interest' previously transferred to the PIP subject to a paragraph 12A election: *see* section 5.7.3.
526. Paragraph 17A does not apply if a paragraph 12A election has been made in respect of the transfer to the partnership. In that case (*see* section 5.7.3), SDLT on that transfer will not be reduced in the first place under paragraphs 10-12.

broadly consist of extracting value[527] from the partnership by reducing a partner's capital account/partnership interest or by securing repayment of a loan made to the partnership by the person in question. SDLT is charged on the value extracted but is capped to the extent that the value extracted exceeds the market value of the 'chargeable interest' in land when it was transferred into the partnership. Therefore paragraph 17A imposes SDLT when the value of the underlying interest in land is indirectly realised, after being transferred to a partnership with the benefit of paragraphs 10-12.

Any paragraph 17A charge is reduced by any concurrent charge under paragraph 14: *see* section 5.7.4.

5.7.6 Transfer of a 'Chargeable Interest' in Land from a Partnership

Paragraphs 18-24 Schedule 15 deal with the opposite situation to paragraphs 10-12. This is where a 'chargeable interest' in land is transferred from a partnership to a present or former partner, or to a person 'connected' with a present or former partner. SDLT is imposed on the market value of the 'chargeable interest' transferred, multiplied by (100-SLP) %.[528] As before, 'SLP' means the 'sum of the lower proportions' but computed under paragraphs 20-24.

The aim is to reduce SDLT to the extent that the 'chargeable interest' is transferred from the partnership to a partner or to certain persons[529] 'connected' with that partner. The rules 'look through' the partnership to treat that partner or 'connected' person as already owning part of the underlying 'chargeable interest', to the extent of the relevant partnership share. There is no SDLT on the transfer from the partnership, to the extent of that share (cf. the equivalent capital gains tax treatment in section 3 of SP D12, discussed in Appendix A). Paragraph 21 prevents this 'look through' applying (and hence more SDLT is due) if the transfer of the 'chargeable interest' into the partnership,[530] and certain subsequent increases in the relevant partnership share, did not trigger stamp duty or SDLT. Hence the 'chargeable interest' cannot be extracted with a reduced SDLT charge unless stamp duty or SDLT was incurred when it was put into the partnership.

Paragraph 24 can apply if a 'chargeable interest' is transferred from a partnership when *all* the partners are bodies corporate. If that is the case and SLP is at least 75, SDLT is charged on the *entire* market value of the 'chargeable interest' transferred, with no SLP discount. However, if the partners are bodies corporate within a group for SDLT purposes, then group relief may be available under Schedule 7 FA 2003,[531] whether or not the entire market value of the transferred interest is otherwise subject to SDLT. For group relief purposes, paragraph 2 Schedule 15 FA 2003 (*see* section 5.5.2) treats the

527. Extracting value which represents 'income profit' does not trigger paragraph 17A.
528. An irrevocable election by a PIP under paragraph 12A overrides these rules.
529. In particular, individuals and certain companies acting as trustee of the 'chargeable interest' and mentioned in paragraph 20(3) Schedule 15.
530. Assuming the 'effective date' of that transfer was after 19 October 2003.
531. As modified by paragraph 27 Schedule 15 FA 2003.

partners as each transferring an appropriate share of the 'chargeable interest' which is being transferred out of the partnership.

5.7.7 Anti-Avoidance

The courts are alert to attempts to exploit the 'transparency' approach of Schedule 15 FA 2003 because it is quite mechanistic. As the Court of Appeal said:

> Schedule 15 should be read, construed and applied in the context of the SDLT legislation as a whole, and should not be treated as if it formed some sort of legislative island all by itself.[532]

In that case, an attempt to avoid SDLT based in part on paragraph 10 Schedule 15 failed, because, under the relevant statutory fictions being invoked, there was no transfer of a 'chargeable interest' by a partner to a partnership, as required by paragraphs 10-12.

The breadth of the SDLT anti-avoidance rule in section 75A-75C FA 2003 has been confirmed by the Supreme Court in *Project Blue Ltd (formerly Project Blue (Guernsey) Ltd) v HMRC.*[533] This needs to be borne in mind when relying on Schedule 15.[534] If section 75A bites so as to reconstitute steps as a single notional transaction subject to higher SDLT, the special computation rules for partnerships in Schedule 15 do not apply to that notional transaction.[535] This may further increase the SDLT charge.

5.8 CONCLUSION ON DIFFERENT TYPES OF 'TRANSPARENCY'

This chapter further illustrates how the term 'tax transparency' in UK tax law contains a number of distinct, if related ideas, which have often evolved independently. These all relate to the extent to which a person holding an interest in an entity or arrangement should be taxed as if that person had a direct interest in its underlying activities and assets. In particular, this chapter shows how the concept of 'tax transparency' is often applied in a more limited way to UK taxes which are not taxes on income and capital gain. There are fewer cases when an entity or arrangement is 'looked through' so as to tax those with an interest in it as if they were carrying on its underlying activities, or had a direct interest in those activities. Generally, the relevant rules have evolved piecemeal, with no single underlying theme. As the IHT 'settlement' rules show, they have even evolved without taking proper account of other rules governing the same tax, which can cause double taxation.

---

532. *See* Lewison LJ in *DV3 RS Ltd Partnership v HMRC* [2013] STC 2150 at 2157.
533. [2018] STC 1355.
534. SDLT also falls within the UK general anti-avoidance rule ('GAAR') in sections 206-215 Finance Act 2013, although in some respects section 75A-C FA 2003 are broader than the GAAR. They do not require proof of a tax avoidance purpose nor that any 'double reasonableness' condition be met.
535. Section 75C(8A) FA 2003, as applied in *Hannover Leasing Wachstumswerte Europa Beteiligungsgesellschaft mbH v HMRC* [2019] SFTD 1231.

In relation to VAT, 'tax transparency' has an especially limited role to play. This is noticeable in relation to the VAT treatment of partnerships, which are regarded for UK income and capital gains tax purposes, for IHT and (to some extent) SDLT as 'flow through'. This is not so for VAT, which characterises a partnership interest (like a company share) as an intangible asset distinct from the underlying partnership assets.

For IHT purposes, 'tax transparency' plays an increasingly limited role. Partnerships can be 'looked through' so as to tax transactions undertaken by the partnership as if undertaken by the partners. In the case of 'close companies', partial 'look through' rules ensure that companies (not normally liable for IHT) cannot be used by those with an interest in them to avoid IHT. These are essentially anti-avoidance rules, although it is not necessary to demonstrate an avoidance motive to trigger them.

A 'look through' approach applies for IHT purposes in respect of those simpler co-ownership arrangements which are not 'settlements'. This approach is shared with income tax and capital gains tax, as well as stamp duty, SDRT and SDLT. However, the concept of a 'unit trust scheme' (often treated as opaque, save for income tax) has no relevance for IHT. Besides, IHT has a broad concept of 'settlement' which covers not just many trusts but some corporate bodies and indeed other commercial arrangements, unlike the 'settlement' concept within income tax or capital gains tax. The IHT 'settlement' rules overlap confusingly with the IHT 'close company' rules but, by contrast, operate mainly on a non-'look through' basis. Since 2006, 'settlements' are increasingly subject to IHT as separate entities, taking no account of the tax profile of the beneficiaries. This approach further complicates the overlap between 'settlements' and 'close companies' because the 'close company' rules do apply 'look through' treatment. The IHT 'settlement' rules need to be reformed so as to better reflect the role of settlements as conditional gifts.

For stamp duty, SDRT and SDLT, arrangements and entities tend (apart from 'bare trusts') not to be 'looked through'. This is especially true of companies and 'unit trust schemes', even though the latter are a sophisticated form of 'bare trust'. Yet there are exceptions where a qualified 'look through' is permitted. However, for stamp duty purposes, the partnership 'look through' is largely a targeted anti-avoidance device while the SDLT rules deliberately fall well short of treating partnerships as fully 'look through' when they engage in real estate transactions. This differs from the capital gains tax approach to partnerships discussed in Appendix A. It thereby avoids a number of complications for partners caused by that more radical 'look through' approach.

The definition of 'partnerships' for stamp duty and SDLT includes some entities (notably UK LLPs) which in essence are private companies. This reflects the extent to which the commercial gap between companies and partnerships has narrowed. It is also confusing: 'partnerships' can sometimes be subject to stamp duty and SDLT on a 'look through' basis, whereas companies and unit trust schemes cannot, even when there are limited differences of substance between these entities. The ability to switch between these entities to achieve a desired tax outcome is well understood by taxpayers and their advisers.

Finally, when deciding whether a group relationship exists between two companies for stamp duty and SDLT purposes, it is very doubtful whether the required affiliation can be traced through a partnership interposed between those two companies on the basis that the partnership is 'transparent'. HMRC sometimes take a more generous approach in practice, but it would be much better if this practice were clearly codified, with proper safeguards against avoidance. The status quo is a reminder that 'transparent' entities are rarely, if ever, tax 'nothings'.

CHAPTER 6

The UK Classification of Entities and 'Tax Transparency' Issues in Relation to Double Tax Treaties and EU Law

6.1 INTRODUCTION AND ARTICLE 1(2) OECD MODEL TAX TREATY 2017

The UK has a very extensive network of double taxation treaties ('treaties') mainly modelled on various versions of the OECD's Model double taxation agreement ('the OECD Model').[536]

Cross-border transactions are especially likely to highlight differences between the UK and non-UK approaches to classifying entities for tax purposes. Such transactions often highlight differences between the UK and other jurisdictions about whether arrangements are 'tax transparent' and, if so, what this means.

Such differences have been actively exploited to avoid tax. To give a simple example, one jurisdiction ('A') may give treaty relief at source in respect of royalty income paid to an entity in another jurisdiction ('B') which it regards as 'transparent' (e.g., a partnership) and all of whose members are individuals resident for tax purposes in B. From A's perspective, income is treated as being currently paid to individual taxpayers resident in B, whether or not the entity distributes that income to its members. However, if B regards the same entity as both non-taxable in its own right and non-'transparent', then the income relieved at source in A may in fact escape current taxation in B, both at the level of the entity and of its members. The differing perspectives of A and B create a risk of double non-taxation (or at last under-taxation), whereas the general aim of a treaty should be to avoid both double taxation and

536. For the most recent post-BEPS version of the OECD Model, *see* the Model Taxation Convention on Income and Capital 2017, dated 21 November 2017 and the accompanying Commentary ('the OECD Commentary') http://www.oecd.org/ctp/model-tax-convention-on-income-and-on-capital-full-version-9a5b369e-en.htm (accessed 23 June 2020).

unintended double non-taxation. Double non-taxation mismatches are a particular target of Action 2 of the BEPS project.[537] However, such situations can also create a risk of double taxation contrary to the aim of a treaty. To reverse the example above, if A regards the payee of royalties as a non-taxable entity, then the risk arises that it will refuse treaty relief even though B regards that entity as a partnership so that its royalty income is currently taxable in the hands of its members who are residents of B.

As discussed in section 5.2, Article 1(2) of the OECD Model goes some way to addressing these issues within treaties. The UK now regularly negotiates language along the lines of Article 1(2) in its treaties.[538] Furthermore, as discussed in section 5.2, the UK is a party to the MLI which is in force in the UK.[539] Article 3(1) of the MLI is in essence the same as Article 1(2) of the OECD Model.

The UK adopted the Article 3 provisions on 'transparent entities'[540] in its list of notifications and reservations, when it deposited its instrument ratifying the MLI. However, some UK treaties which already contained bespoke wording regarding 'transparent entities' (notably, the UK-France and UK-Netherlands treaties) have not been modified by Article 3(1) of the MLI. Those treaties are discussed below.

Article 1(2) is a compromise which does not impose on treaty parties common entity classification standards. It has weaknesses discussed below. However, it represents the current, and most advanced, UK position on how tax treaties should address the allocation of taxing rights where 'transparent' entities are involved and especially

537. Action 2 has been reflected in UK domestic law by the extensive 'hybrid mismatch' rules in Part 6A TIOPA. At EU level, Articles 9-9b of Directive 2016/1164 (as modified by Directive 2017/952) set out how the principles of Action 2 are to be given effect in the domestic law of Member States. This Directive necessitated limited changes to Part 6A TIOPA. A discussion of these rules, which focus on curbing double non-taxation, is beyond the scope of this work. However, while extensive, and in some respects broader than the Action 2 recommendations, Part 6A does not cover all hybrid mismatch situations giving rise to potential double non-taxation. In particular, Part 6A only applies to UK taxpayers subject to corporation tax. It does not generally disturb underlying UK tax thinking on entity classification and the meaning of 'tax transparency'.

538. *See* Article 4(3) of the UK-Uruguay double tax treaty (SI 2016/753) and Article 1(2) of the UK-Uzbekistan treaty of 1993 (SI 1994/770), following amendment in 2018. Most recently, *see* Article 1(2) of the 7 June 2022 UK-Luxembourg treaty, which has yet to be ratified.

539. http://www.oecd.org/tax/treaties/multilateral-convention-to-implement-tax-treaty-related-measures-to-prevent-beps.htm (accessed 23 June 2020). The UK publishes 'conforming' versions of its treaties, as modified by what it and its treaty partners have agreed to, and reserved against, under the MLI procedure. While these 'conforming' versions help understand how the MLI has modified existing treaties, they have no legal authority. Ultimately, each treaty must be compared with the notifications and reservations deposited by the UK and the relevant treaty partner with the OECD under the MLI procedure.

540. The final list was published by HMRC on 17 July 2018: *see* http://www.oecd.org/tax/treaties/beps-mli-position-united-kingdom.pdf (accessed 9 January 2020). The UK did reserve against Article 3(2). This provides that one party to a treaty is not required to grant one of its residents double taxation relief in respect of its income where that treaty permits the other treaty party to tax the same income, as that of a resident of the latter jurisdiction. Such residence-residence-based double taxation could arise because of the 'saving' clause in Article 11 of the MLI, which entitles a contracting state to tax its residents as if the relevant treaty did not apply (with limited exceptions). Paragraph 7.5 of the Explanatory Notes to Double Taxation Relief (Base Erosion and Profit Shifting) Order 2018 (SI 2018/630) states that the UK agrees with the policy of Article 3(2). However, its wording differs from the wording of existing treaties. It might therefore cause uncertainty, which has led the UK to reserve against Article 3(2).

where the parties to the treaty classify an entity differently. The UK position is therefore substantially in line with post-BEPS thinking reflected in the OECD Model and MLI. This chapter explains how the UK got to this position and, in particular, the impact of the current UK-US double tax treaty, which largely foreshadowed, and in some respects goes beyond Article 1(2). Generally, the UK (unlike the US) has not led the debate in this area. It has tended to address such entity classification issues in detail where concerns have been raised by treaty partners (notably, the US, France and the Netherlands).

Article 1(2) of the OECD Model and Article 3(1) of the MLI have been extensively analysed.[541] Without repeating that analysis or the points in section 5.2, it is helpful to summarise some key points, before turning to UK treaty policy in this area.

6.1.1

Article 1(2) only sets a minimum standard. In particular, it only addresses whether a source state should grant treaty relief in respect of source state income paid to or earned *by* an entity which is regarded as 'transparent' by one or other Contracting State. That entity can be in a third state. Article 1(2) does not address the situation where that income is paid *from* a 'transparent' entity. Some countries have negotiated treaties which go beyond this minimum standard, e.g., the US - Canada treaty, whose Article IV(6) and (7) were added in a 2007 Protocol.[542]

Article 1(2) only deals with the attribution of income of a 'transparent' entity to those with an interest in it. Therefore, it does not deal with whether (e.g., in Article 15(2) of the OECD Model) a 'transparent' entity can itself be a 'resident' of a particular state for treaty purposes: *see* section 6.7.2.

6.1.2

Article 1(2) allows the state of source to decide whether an item is taxable income and if so, its amount, when it arises and from whom. The other Contracting State has no say in these matters, even if, for example, it might regard an event as not giving rise to taxable income, such as a 'deemed dividend'. If it takes this position, it will not impose a tax charge. This in turn will prevent Article 1(2) giving relief at source.

6.1.3

As discussed in section 5.2, the meaning of 'fiscally transparent' for Article 1(2) purposes is not clear and using this expression in this context can be unhelpful. Article 1(2) focuses on whether underlying income derived via an entity is taxable in its members' hands on (?) a current basis (even if undistributed by the entity). It does not require those members to be treated for tax purposes as owning the underlying assets

541. *See* 'Some Reflections', *supra*.
542. *See* 'Some Reflections' *supra*, at p. 302.

of the entity. It is unclear whether Article 1(2) applies if the entity's income is currently attributed to its members, or to the settlor of a trust, under anti-deferral rules such as 'controlled foreign company' or 'settlement' rules. Is this scenario 'fiscal transparency'? This question is not answered by the OECD Commentary which simply states that 'controlled foreign company'-type legislation is not contrary to the OECD Model. The fact that such anti-deferral rules do not always operate in the same way adds to the uncertainty.[543] It is also unclear whether Article 1(2) can operate if some prior discretionary step (other than an actual distribution) has to take place at the level of the entity before an income entitlement can arise.[544]

A related point not covered by Article 1(2) is whether treaty benefits should still be granted at source where income is derived via an entity which the source state regards as 'opaque' but where that income would have been exempt from tax anyway if the entity member had received it directly. In treaties based on the OECD Model, the fact that a resident of one jurisdiction is exempt from tax on income in that jurisdiction does not necessarily prevent it claiming treaty relief from source state tax on that income. For example, many pension funds claim treaty relief from dividend withholding tax. If the source state would give treaty relief where a tax-exempt receives income directly, it would be odd for it to deny treaty relief where the tax-exempt derives that income via an interposed 'opaque' entity.

6.1.4

Does Article 1(2) apply if the member of the 'fiscally transparent' entity is fully taxable on a current basis in respect of its allocated share of the entity's income, even if that income share is not treated as having the same character and source in the member's hands as the underlying income of the entity? It seems unobjectionable in policy terms for the source state to grant treaty relief. What matters is whether the entity member is liable for full current taxation. However, this scenario (which partly overlaps with the point in section 6.1.3 about the effect of 'controlled foreign company' legislation) is harder to describe as 'fiscal transparency'. Using that expression in Article 1(2) can therefore cause complications.

6.1.5

It is not clear how Article 1(2) and Article 3(1) of the MLI affect treaties which already adopt a 'partial residence' approach to potentially transparent entities if that approach

543. *See* 'Some Reflections' *supra*, at pp. 315-316.

544. The authors of 'Some Reflections' *supra*, at p. 317 consider that such a scenario is consistent with 'fiscal transparency', whereas an income entitlement which is conditional on there being a distribution is not 'fiscal transparency', if that distribution is treated as a separate income source from the entity's underlying income. This seems right. For a similar argument which may go slightly further, *see* Brabazon *supra*, at p. 208. He states that transparency should depend solely on whether income of the entity is currently attributed to an entity member for tax purposes in that member's home jurisdiction. If there is such current attribution, it is not relevant whether it is in fact triggered by a distribution from the entity.

is not explicitly discarded. Such 'partial residence' provisions often predate the 1999 OECD Partnership Report, which deprecated their use. They operate, in particular, by treating a partnership or trust as resident in a contracting state, to the extent that its income is currently taxable in that state, either at entity or at member level. Hence certain prima facie 'transparent' entities can be wholly or partly treaty-resident: *see* section 6.3.2.

6.1.6

Does Article 1(2) treat as 'beneficial owner' any member of an entity which can rely on it to claim source state treaty benefits? Article 1(2) does not explicitly address the question of 'beneficial ownership' which arises in, for example, Articles 10-12 of the OECD Model. This is a serious weakness. However, a treaty-resident who can otherwise rely on Article 1(2) to claim treaty benefits in respect of income derived via an entity which is 'transparent' in that person's residence state should be treated as the 'beneficial owner' unless additional factors are present, e.g., the entity itself or the treaty-resident receives the income as nominee for a third party.[545] Otherwise, a technical lack of 'beneficial ownership' by the entity member would undermine Article 1(2), even where income derived via the entity is liable to current tax at member level in the non-source state.

Nevertheless, doubts remain, not least because the Technical Explanation of Article 11 of the US Model Treaty says (confusingly) that the *source* state should determine the question of 'beneficial ownership'. The Commentary on Article 1(2) does not expressly contradict this, unlike some comments in the 1999 Partnership Report.[546]

6.1.7

A similar issue arises from the interaction between Article 1(2) and Article 10(2) of the OECD Model. Article 10(2) grants an extra reduction in the permitted withholding tax rate on dividends received by a 'company' resident in one contracting state, where they

545. *See* 'Some Reflections' *supra,* at pp. 333-338. The approach suggested in the main text was adopted by the Australian Taxation Office in 2011 in Interpretative Decision ID 2011/13. This related to interest paid from Australia to a tax transparent New Zealand limited partnership in which the New Zealand-resident taxpayer was a limited partner. Article 1(2) of the 2009 Australia-New Zealand treaty contained a transparent entity clause not dissimilar to Article 1(2) of the OECD Model. The Decision states that it would be inconsistent with the transparent entity clause to interpret 'beneficial ownership' so as to deny treaty benefits to the partners of a fiscally transparent partnership: *see* https://www.ato.gov.au/law/view/document?Mode=type&TOC=%2204%3AATO%20interpretative%20decisions%3ABy%20year%3A2011%3A%230013%23ATO%20ID%202011%2F13%20-%20Interest%20withholding%20tax%26c%20interest%20arising%20in%20Australia%20paid%20to%20a%20New%20Zealand%20Limited%20Partnership%20-%20'beneficially%20owned'%3B%22&DOCID=%22AID%2FAID201113%2F00001%22 (accessed 15 June 2021).

546. *See* Leopoldo Parada: 'Hybrid Entities and Conflicts of Allocation of Income Within Tax Treaties: Is New Article 1(2) of the OECD Model (Article 3(1) of the MLI) the Best Solution Available?'[2018] British Tax Review 335 at 350-358 (hereinafter 'Parada: Article 1(2)').

arise from a substantial shareholding 'held directly' in a company resident in the other Contracting State. Can this last condition ever be satisfied where the first company has an interest in a 'transparent' entity which owns the substantial shareholding in the second company? Is this a 'direct holding'? Article 1(2) does not explicitly attribute ownership of the assets of a 'transparent' entity to its members, although some treaties do address this issue. Despite these ambiguities, the Commentary on Article 10(2) of the OECD Model (2017 version) states that the first company should be regarded as owning the shares in the second company in proportion to its interest in the 'transparent' entity while also encouraging treaty partners to spell this out in the text of the treaty. Article 10(2)(a)(ii) of the 2016 version of the US Model Treaty makes this clearer.

Whether it is appropriate to attribute ownership in this way must surely depend on the facts, despite what the Commentary says. For example, if the shares in the second company are owned by a trust in which all beneficiaries have vested, concurrent interests in trust capital and income, then attributing those shares to a corporate beneficiary in proportion to its beneficial interest makes sense. Such attribution makes less sense where a beneficiary only has a beneficial interest in underlying trust income (not capital) or is a discretionary beneficiary.

It may be easier to conclude that the equivalent of Article 10(2) in a treaty applies where it only requires the substantial shareholding to be subject to the 'control' of the first company, and that shareholding is owned by a 'transparent' entity in which the first company has a significant interest. Even then, depending on the facts, it may be difficult to conclude that the first company has such 'control', e.g., if it is only the income beneficiary of a trust which owns the shares.[547]

6.1.8

If a 'transparent' entity has a 'permanent establishment' in the source state, can that establishment be attributed to those with an interest in the entity when applying Article 1(2)? Policywise, this makes sense if those interest holders are relying on Article 1(2) to claim treaty benefits in respect of income derived via that entity. Otherwise, those

547. *See* 'Some Reflections' *supra,* at pp. 339-342. At p. 366, fn 218, the authors suggest that, by contrast, there is no difficulty tracing the required corporate affiliation through a 'transparent' partnership for the purposes of the EU Parent-Subsidiary Directive 2011/96/EU. Article 3 of that Directive simply refers to a 'holding in the capital' or a 'holding of voting rights' in the putative subsidiary. The author is not aware of this point having been addressed by the CJEU. This reasoning could not apply for the purposes of the EU Interest and Royalties Directive 2003/49/EC, Article 3(b) of which requires a '*direct* minimum holding' [emphasis added] of capital or voting rights by one company in another. A similar issue was considered in Interpretative Decision ID 2011/14, where the Australian Tax Office ruled that a New Zealand corporate limited partner with a majority share in a New Zealand limited partnership did not 'hold directly' a majority voting stake in an Australian company owned by that partnership. The limited partnership had separate legal personality. Hence there was no entitlement to a 5% withholding rate under Article 10(2)(a) of the Australia-New Zealand treaty: *see* https://www.ato.gov.au/law/view/document?LocID=%22AID%2FAID201114%22&PiT=99991231235958 (accessed March 2021). For a further discussion on tracing corporate affiliation through a trust for Article 10(2) purposes, *see* Brabazon *supra,* at pp. 240-243.

interest holders may be in a better position in terms of claiming treaty relief at source than if they had invested directly. Yet it is unclear that Article 1(2) goes that far.[548]

It is doubtful, on both policy and technical grounds, whether one can attribute to the entity a 'permanent establishment' in the source state which an interest holder in the entity may have, independently of the entity.

6.1.9

Where the 'transparent' entity is established in a jurisdiction which requires it to tax its own distributions to those holding an interest in it, Article 1(2) does not apply, e.g., where the entity is non-'transparent' in its home state, even though holders of an interest in it are resident in another state which regards it as 'transparent'. The 'saving' clause discussed in section 6.1.10 also does not apply. It merely preserves the right of the entity's home state to tax the entity itself, rather than distributions to the entity's members.

6.1.10

Article 1(2) sits alongside Article 1(3) which introduces into the OECD Model a 'saving' clause of the type familiar in treaties with the US. This preserves the right of a person's state of residence to tax that person as if the treaty were not in force, with limited exceptions. Those exceptions in particular permit that person to invoke the treaty's elimination of double taxation provisions, the Non-Discrimination Article and the article dealing with mutual agreement proceedings between the treaty parties. Article 11 of the MLI contains a general 'saving' clause which is broadly the same as Article 1(3). Alternatively, Article 3(3) of the MLI contains a short-form 'saving' clause without the exceptions in Article 11. Article 3(3) only ensures that the 'transparent entity' clause in Article 3(1) of the MLI does not prevent a contracting state from taxing its own residents.

Under Article 1(3), if the Contracting State where an entity is established regards it as tax-resident there (e.g., because it is not 'transparent'), that state can tax it. This is so even if members of that entity resident in another jurisdiction can invoke Article 1(2) to obtain treaty benefits in the state where the entity's income is sourced. The 'saving' clause creates the risk that the same underlying income will be taxed twice, on

548. *See* 'Some Reflections' *supra*, at pp. 342-343, where the authors note that the 1999 OECD Partnership Report indicated that a partnership's 'permanent establishment' should be attributed to its partners. Even if this occurs, the tax law of the 'permanent establishment' jurisdiction will dictate how its profits are computed before they are allocated to the partners. In *GE Capital Finance Pty Ltd v Commissioner of Taxation* (2007) 9 ITLR 1083, the Australian Federal Court declined to treat a US unit holder in an *Australian* unit trust as thereby having an Australian 'permanent establishment'. In particular, it refused to apply an Australian rule which treated a non-Australian-resident trust beneficiary as having an Australian 'permanent establishment', where a *non-Australian-resident* trustee had such a 'permanent establishment'. This last kind of rule is standard in Australian tax treaties: *see* Brabazon *supra*, at p. 233 and *see also* (in section 6.7.1) the discussion of the UK-Australia tax treaty.

the basis of residence, in the hands of two different taxpayers: the entity itself and its members.

If the entity is tax-resident in its home state, it may be entitled to treaty benefits in its own right when it receives income from another state. Any such benefits would arise under the treaty between the entity's home state and that source state. Of course, the entity's members may also seek treaty benefits from the source state in respect of the same income. They would rely on the separate treaty between the source state and the residence state of the members, using the equivalent of Article 1(2). Following the 1999 OECD Partnership Report and changes to the OECD Commentaries, the source state is required to give tax relief under whichever of these two treaties is the more favourable, without of course refunding the same tax twice.[549]

Should the source state should have to give treaty relief under whichever of the two treaties is the more favourable? The entity members have only invested indirectly in the source state, via the entity. It is one thing to say, based on Article 1(2), that the source state should not refuse them all treaty relief because it regards the entity as 'opaque' even though it is 'transparent' in the residence state of those members. But why should the source state go further and grant those members a level of treaty relief which they would have obtained only if they had invested directly, and not via the entity? Article 1(2)'s over-encroachment on source state rights is discussed further in section 6.1.12.

6.1.11

Article 1(2) has no bearing on whether the residence state of the members of an entity should give them a foreign tax credit for tax imposed on the entity itself.

Where that residence state regards the entity as 'transparent', then presumably there should be little difficulty giving a foreign tax credit so long as the foreign tax was not imposed on that entity purely because it was a resident of another jurisdiction. In other words, that tax would need to be a source-based tax on the entity's underlying income. The position is more difficult when the residence state of the members regards the entity as 'opaque', even if it is regarded as 'transparent' in its home state or the state where its income is sourced. This in essence is the situation in *Anson v HMRC*.[550]

Article 23A and 23B of the OECD Model have been amended to make clear that one state is not required to give double taxation relief to its residents for tax imposed by the other state in accordance with the treaty but solely on the basis of residence: see the inserted words '(except to the extent that the [...] provisions [of the treaty] allow taxation by that other State *solely* [emphasis added] because the income is also income derived by a resident of that State)'. The word 'solely' should therefore preserve the right to some relief in the residence state where the other state is entitled to tax the

549. *See* 'Some Reflections' *supra*, at pp. 350-352.
550. [2015] STC 1777: *see* section 2.14. The Supreme Court sidestepped the problem by concluding that the LLC was 'transparent' in the state where the members were resident, as well as in the state where it earned its income.

income in question both as local source income and as income of a resident of that state (e.g., under an Article 1(3)-type 'saving' clause).[551]

6.1.12

Article 1(2) has been rightly criticised for not protecting adequately source state taxing rights. It has even been suggested that Article 1(2) is inconsistent with the goals of BEPS: allocating taxing rights to states where income-generating activities take place and curbing unintended non-taxation. The same commentator has criticised Article 1(2), coupled with the 'saving' clause, for creating unrelieved double taxation in situations where the courts had found ways of avoiding it.[552] The court decisions referred to are *Anson v HMRC*[553] and *Bayfine v HMRC*.[554]

The same commentator notes that Article 1(2) removes source state taxation rights simply because of legal fictions on 'transparency' applied to the relevant entity by the Contracting State in which its members are resident. Those fictions may even be applied at the option of that entity's members. Furthermore, if there is active income from business activities in the source state, that state may lose the right to tax that income if the definition of 'permanent establishment' is narrower in its treaty with the state in which the entity's members are resident, when compared to its treaty with the entity's state of residence.[555]

The first of these criticisms is unconvincing: 'opacity' and 'transparency' are inherently legal fictions whose nature will vary between jurisdictions. The essence of Article 1(2) is that the source state should give treaty relief by respecting the 'transparency' fiction in the residence state of the entity's members if it leads to a current tax liability of those members on the entity's income. So long as this is the overall effect, the precise mechanics of that fiction are irrelevant. The second criticism, regarding different 'permanent establishment' definitions, is justified. It is one thing to use Article 1(2) to give a degree of treaty relief to members of an entity which is regarded as 'transparent' in the members' jurisdiction of residence. It is another thing to ignore altogether the treaty between the home state of the entity and the state of source, bearing in mind that those relying on Article 1(2) invested in the source state via that entity. They did not invest in the source state directly.

---

551. For more on the changes to Article 23A and B, *see* Christopher Bergedahl: 'Hybrid Entities and the OECD Model (2017): The End of the Road?'. Bulletin for International Taxation (July 2018) 417 and especially 421-428.
552. *See* discussion of Article 1(2) in Dhruv Sanghavi: 'Structural Issues in the Income Tax Treaty Network: Towards a Coherent Framework'. Ipskamp Printing BV 2018. ISBN 978-94-028 0-972-5 https://cris.maastrichtuniversity.nl/portal/en/publications/structural-issue.
553. [2015] STC 1777.
554. [2011] STC 717. The reference to this case is strange because, as discussed in section 6.4.3, the courts concluded that the UK did *not* need to give credit to a UK-resident company for US tax imposed on its parent company under the 'saving' clause in the then UK-US treaty.
555. The treaty with the entity's residence state may, for example, contain an expanded definition of 'permanent establishment' covering the provision of services related to activities in the source state. For an example, *see* Article 5(2)(k) of the UK-India treaty SI 1993/1801 (as amended).

Another commentator has even suggested that, for ease of administration and partly to protect the source state, Article 1(2) should be replaced by a rule whereby the domestic law of each state accepts the tax characterisation of the entity in the state where it is 'formally and legally established or incorporated'.[556] Yet that state could be a third country (including a tax haven) where the entity has little real presence. Moreover, its rules (if any) for characterising entities may be uncertain or may radically differ from those of the source state and the state where the entity's members are resident. That third country may give taxpayers a lot of freedom to choose the entity's tax characterisation from time to time. It may give them the right to make the entity only partly transparent. The rules in that country could also be changed unilaterally, e.g., to accommodate tax planning. It is therefore doubtful whether the source state or the state where the entity's members reside will want to delegate to a third country, which is not party to the treaty, control over what entities it treats as opaque or transparent.[557]

6.1.13

One point raised[558] is whether treaty relief should be denied in the source state under Article 1(2) where the same income flow is non-deductible under anti-hybrid mismatch rules which give effect to BEPS Action 2. To deny treaty benefits as well as a tax deduction risks overkill.

6.1.14

A final point relates to practical problems in applying Article 1(2). As one commentator has put it recently: '... neither the Partnership Report nor the new OECD Commentary on the fiscally transparent entity provision [i.e. Article 1(2)] explains exactly how in practice a source country can give treaty benefits to the members of a legal entity when it taxes the entity and not the members'.[559] Applying Article 1(2) may also be especially complex when dealing with an entity (such as a collective investment fund) with a large and shifting cast of members and of underlying income-producing investments.

---

556. *See* Parada: Article 1(2) *supra* [2018] British Tax Review 335 at 358 et seq. This rule would apply whenever there was a transaction involving income passing from one state to the other via an entity.
557. The same commentator has suggested that to be fully effective, all states would have to adopt the rule for classifying entities by reference to the law in their state of formation. This rule would also be disapplied where it incentivised entity formation in jurisdictions with advantageous tax treatment: *see* Leopoldo Parada: 'Hybrid Entity Mismatches: Exploring Three Alternatives for Coordination' (2019) Intertax, Volume 47, Issue 1, at 24 and in particular, Parts 3.3.1 and 3.3.2.
558. *See* 'Some Reflections' *supra* (at fn 91, p. 318).
559. *See* Richard Vann commenting on *Resource Capital Fund IV LP v Commissioner of Taxation* 21 ITLR 655 at 660. That case is discussed in section 6.3.2. It involved two limited partnerships which were transparent in the US but taxable entities in Australia.

While there may be opportunities for streamlining treaty relief applications via the manager of that entity, the source state is likely to play safe, by initially withholding tax on income of the entity and then dealing with refund applications from entity members. Securing treaty relief under Article 1(2) is unlikely to be quick or simple, although HMRC plans to improve and digitalise the process for issuing Certificates of Residence.

Therefore, a collective investment fund which is transparent will probably invest indirectly through an intermediate asset holding company which is opaque in all relevant jurisdictions. Such companies are often resident in jurisdictions such as Luxembourg, with a low effective corporate tax rate while still benefiting from a treaty or EU Directive with the state where the underlying investment is located. The UK introduced from April 2022 its own equivalent: the Qualifying Asset Holding Company or 'QAHC'. Being opaque, Article 1(2) will not apply to such a company. However, it must show enough economic substance to demonstrate that it 'beneficially owns' its income and to avoid tax relief being denied under a 'principal purpose test' such as the one in Article 29 of the OECD Model, Article 7(1) of the MLI or Article 1(2) of the EU Parent-Subsidiary Directive.

6.2 PERSONS: DO THEY INCLUDE PARTNERSHIPS AND TRUSTS?

6.2.1 Background

Historically, most UK treaties did not deal directly with potentially tax transparent entities such as partnerships or trusts. A UK treaty typically defines the 'persons' to which it applies using the language in the OECD Model. Article 1(1) states:

> This Convention shall apply to persons who are residents of one or both of the Contracting States.

Article 3 provides that 'unless the context otherwise requires':

> (a) the term 'person' includes an individual, a company *and any other body of persons* [emphasis added];
> (c) the term 'company' means any body corporate or any entity that is treated as a body corporate for tax purposes.

This definition of 'person' is not exhaustive. The Commentary to the OECD Model incorporates the 1999 OECD Partnership Report ('the Partnership Report'),[560] in which paragraph 30 stresses that a partnership is a 'person' for treaty purposes either because it is 'any other body of persons' or because (in some cases) it falls within the second part of the definition of 'company'. The Commentary will be especially relevant when interpreting 'person' in any UK treaty concluded since it was amended to reflect the Partnership Report. Even in respect of older treaties, the UK courts are likely, in the

560. https://read.oecd-ilibrary.org/taxation/the-application-of-the-oecd-model-tax-convention-to-partnerships_9789264173316-en#page1 (accessed 23 June 2020).

light of the *Padmore* decision[561] discussed below, to conclude that a 'person' includes a 'partnership'. They are also likely to conclude that a 'person' includes a trustee or a body of trustees.[562]

Occasionally, a UK treaty will explicitly exclude partnerships from the standard definition of 'person'. For example, Article 3(1)(e) of the UK-Mexico treaty SI 1994/3212 (as amended) adds the proviso 'but does not include a partnership which is not treated as a body corporate for tax purposes in either Contracting State'.

6.2.2 *Padmore v IRC*

Padmore ended any perception that partnerships and trust are 'nothings' for the purposes of the UK's treaties. In *Padmore*, a UK-resident partner in a Jersey partnership relied on the old UK-Jersey treaty[563] to avoid UK tax on his partnership income. The then treaty[564] exempted the profits of a 'Jersey enterprise' from UK tax provided that its business was not being conducted through a UK 'permanent establishment'. It was accepted that there was no UK 'permanent establishment'. Article 2(1) defined a 'Jersey enterprise' as an 'industrial or commercial enterprise or undertaking carried on by a *resident of Jersey* [emphasis added]'.

Article 2(1)(f) defined a 'resident of Jersey' as 'any *person* [emphasis added] who is resident in Jersey for the purposes of Jersey tax and not resident in the United Kingdom for the purposes of United Kingdom tax'. This did not require the 'person' to be liable to tax in Jersey.[565] Hence, although the partnership was not a taxable entity in Jersey,[566] the courts ruled that it could be 'resident' in Jersey for the purposes of this treaty because it was managed and controlled there.[567]

561. [1987] STC 36 upheld in [1989] STC 493.
562. *See* Philip Baker QC: 'The Application of the Convention to Partnerships, Trusts and Other Non-corporate Entities' (2002) Gray's Inn Tax Chambers Review, Volume II, Issue 1, 1 at 15-16. That author notes that where there is more than one trustee, it is advisable to see the trustees as a single 'body of persons', and hence a single 'person' for treaty purposes, rather than treating each trustee as a separate 'person'. This gives the trust a single place of treaty residence even where different trustees are resident, from time to time, in different jurisdictions. It also reflects that fact that a trust, once created, is an ongoing arrangement (with or without legal personality) despite trustee changes. This approach also ensures that the Article 4 residence 'tiebreaker' clause which applies to trusts is the one which applies to 'persons' other than individuals. This makes most sense and ensures a consistent tiebreaking approach where a trust has both corporate and non-corporate trustees.
563. SI 1952/1216, now superseded by SI 2018/1348.
564. Article 3(2).
565. As discussed in section 6.3.1, this definition of treaty 'residence' is archaic and out of line with the OECD Model.
566. As in the UK, a Jersey partnership's profits are apparently currently taxable at the level of its members, and the partnership entity is not a separate taxpayer.
567. In reaching this conclusion, they relied on what is now section 857(1)(b) ITTOIA, with its suggestion that 'control and management' is key when deciding whether a partnership has a *specific* place of non-UK residence (rather than just being resident anywhere 'outside the UK'). For a decision that a partnership was controlled and managed wholly outside the UK for section 857(1)(b) purposes, even though one of the two partners was UK-resident, *see Mark Higgins Rallying (a firm) v HMRC* [2011] SFTD 936. No tax treaty was relevant in that case.

That left the question of whether the partnership was a 'person' at all. Article 2(1)(d) of the UK-Jersey treaty defined 'person' to include 'any body of persons, corporate or not corporate'. This differs from the OECD Model to which the courts in *Padmore* did not refer. It was, however, very similar to Schedule 1 of the Interpretation Act 1978 which provides 'unless the context otherwise requires', that '"person" shall include any body of persons corporate or unincorporated'. Both definitions are expanded by the closing words. Therefore, the courts ruled that the Jersey partnership was an unincorporated 'body of persons' and hence a 'person' for treaty purposes. It was therefore exempt from UK tax on its profits, as was the UK-resident partner. The courts drew no distinction between the partnership itself and the partnership share of the partner, not least because the Jersey partnership resembled a classic English general partnership, lacking a legal personality distinct from its partners. Fox LJ in the Court of Appeal said:[568]

> [The UK-Jersey treaty] relieves from United Kingdom taxation all the profits of a Jersey enterprise ... That enterprise in the present case is a partnership. The partnership is not an entity distinct from the partners. The profits belong to them. As a matter of construction ... I see no words which exclude the individual partner's share of the profits from the exemption. The exemption is in general terms and I see no reason why the greater does not include the less.

The tax authorities also argued that the relevant definition of 'body of persons' was the very old UK definition in what are now section 118(1) TMA, section 989 ITA and section 1119 CTA 2010. This defines 'body of persons' as 'any body politic, corporate or collegiate, and any company, fraternity, fellowship and society of persons, whether corporate or not corporate'.[569] It was argued that this definition was narrower than the definition of 'person' in the UK-Jersey treaty and that it excluded partnerships. The Court of Appeal assumed that it was narrower but decided that it was displaced by the wider definition of 'person' in the treaty.[570]

Article 3 of the OECD Model and the Commentary on it (in particular, paragraph 2) are consistent with *Padmore*.

The effect of *Padmore* in exempting the UK-resident partner from tax on partnership income was reversed retrospectively by what is now section 858 ITTOIA,

568. [1989] STC 493 at 500.

569. This early nineteenth-century definition dates back to the origins of UK income tax. It is mainly relevant when deciding how 'bodies of persons' can be assessed to UK income tax (not corporation tax) under section 71 TMA.

570. The sole basis for importing this definition of 'body of persons' was that a 'body of persons' was an otherwise undefined term. Hence, a reference to domestic law was appropriate under Article 2(3) of the UK-Jersey treaty. The courts decided that 'body of persons' in this treaty was not otherwise undefined. Even if it had been, John Avery Jones has argued (*see* [1990] British Tax Review 453) that the context indicates that the relevant UK domestic law definition for the purposes of Article 2(3) is not section 118(1) TMA, etc., but the definition of 'person' in Schedule 1 Interpretation Act 1978, which closely resembles the definition in the UK-Jersey treaty. He has also argued that the section 118(1) TMA, etc., definition of 'body of persons' probably includes partnerships, because 'companies' at the start of the nineteenth century were in effect large partnerships (*see* [1987] British Tax Review 88 at 89-90).

which[571] overrode the UK's treaties. It was extended in 2008 to counter arrangements whereby UK-resident persons tried to rely on *Padmore* by investing in a non-UK partnership indirectly via a trust.[572]

UK treaties typically provide (e.g., Article 23 of the 1994 UK-Mexico treaty (as amended)) that a UK-resident partner cannot invoke the treaty to avoid UK tax in circumstances akin to *Padmore*. This avoids double non-taxation of UK income and is more diplomatic than simply relying on the UK treaty override. It is consistent with the Commentary on the OECD Model as amended to reflect paragraph 128 of the Partnership Report. Besides, Article 1(3) of the OECD Model is a US-style 'saving' clause[573] and Article 11 of the MLI (which the UK has adopted) covers the same ground. This 'saving' clause allows each Contracting State to tax its residents as if the treaty did not apply, with limited exceptions.[574] Hence, the scope for UK-residents to run *Padmore*-type argument is now very limited.

6.3 CAN A PARTNERSHIP OR TRUSTEE(S) BE A 'RESIDENT' OF A CONTRACTING STATE UNDER A MODERN UK TREATY?

6.3.1 Article 4(1) of the OECD Model

While a partnership or trustee(s) can be a 'person' for UK treaty purposes, that is usually of little benefit unless the 'person' is also a 'resident' of a treaty state and hence entitled to its benefits.[575] The treaty in *Padmore* contained a definition of 'resident' which is obsolete because it did not require the Jersey partnership to be liable to Jersey tax on the basis that it was formed and established in Jersey.

By contrast, Article 4(1) of the OECD Model now states:

> For the purposes of this Convention, the term 'resident of a Contracting State' means any person who, under the laws of that State, is *liable to tax*[576] *therein by*

571. There have been unsuccessful challenges to the retrospective legislation, notably *Padmore v IRC (No 2)* [2001] STC 280.
572. *Padmore* might still exempt the trustees of a non-UK trust which is resident in a jurisdiction with an appropriate treaty, and consequently, might exempt the trust income of a UK-resident life interest holder. This is on the basis that the trustees, like the partners in *Padmore*, are a 'body of persons' and hence a 'person'. *Dawson v IRC* [1989] STC 473 at 475 gives support to this analysis but in practice, the UK would legislate to negate any such outcome.
573. See Article 1(4) and (5) of the 2001 UK-US treaty: SI 2002/2848, discussed in section 6.4.2.
574. Notably, the articles dealing with elimination of double taxation, non-discrimination and the mutual agreement procedure.
575. Being a 'resident' of a contracting state is usually a necessary, but not a sufficient condition for treaty protection. That 'resident' may also need to show, for example, that it is the 'beneficial owner' of the relevant income.
576. In UK tax law, 'liable to tax' does not necessarily mean that actual tax is chargeable, not least because a tax exemption may apply in the circumstances, e.g., to a pension fund. It simply means that the income in question must potentially be within the relevant tax charge ('within the tax net'). For the distinction between 'liable to tax' and 'subject to tax' in the treaty context, *see* the UK First-Tier Tribunal (Tax) decision in *Weiser v HMRC* [2012] SFTD 1381. This related to the 'Pensions' article in the then UK treaty with Israel but the judge also took into account international case law, academic commentary and the OECD Commentary. He endorsed published UK guidance stating that to be "subject to tax", a person must actually pay tax on the

reason of his domicile, residence, place of management or any other criterion of a similar nature [emphasis added], and also includes that State and any political subdivision or local authority thereof as well as a recognised pension fund of that State. *This term, however, does not include any person who is liable to tax in that State in respect only of income from sources in that State or capital situated therein* [emphasis added].

Similar wording is now standard in UK treaties. Unless a partnership or group of trustees is taxable as such[577] and that tax liability does not depend on the tax characteristics of its partners/beneficiaries, then it will not satisfy this definition. In particular, paragraph 40 of the Partnership Report indicates that a partnership is not 'liable to tax' if any tax payable by it or its partners is determined by the tax characteristics of the partners themselves.[578] The same approach should apply to trustees where there is a vested interest in possession in the trust income so that the beneficiary is taxed as if the underlying income arose directly to that beneficiary.[579] In

income in question, unless the income is low enough to be covered by a "de minimis" exclusion such as the UK "personal allowance". Until 1966, it was standard UK treaty practice to include a "subject to tax" proviso.' The thinking in *Weiser* may not be accepted in other jurisdictions: *see* the 2015 decision of the French Conseil d'Etat in *Ministre du Budget v Landesarztekammer Hessen Versorgungswerk; Ministre du Budget v Société Santander Pensiones* (Joined Cases Nos 370054 and 371132) 18 ITLR 554. The French court ruled that two pension funds were not 'liable to tax' (and were therefore not 'residents' of Germany and Spain for treaty purposes) because they were effectively exempt from tax in those jurisdictions because of their 'status or activity'. The 'Conclusions' of the Rapporteur public suggest (at 569) that the decision partly reflected a French policy of treating non-French tax-exempts as 'resident' in a treaty state only on a case-by-case basis (unlike the general inclusion of pension funds in Article 4(1) of the OECD Model). A recent example of this policy is paragraph 6 of the Protocol to the 2021 France-Belgium treaty, which also deals with treaty benefits for certain collective investment vehicles. For discussion of conflicting views and the limited OECD Commentary on the 'liable to tax' condition, especially regarding collective investment funds, *see* Martine Merten: 'Taxation of Investment Funds following the OECD Base Erosion and Profit Shifting Initiative: Part 1'. Bulletin for International Taxation (February 2019) 76 at 79-80 (hereinafter 'Merten I'). Some Luxembourg treaties address this issue specifically in relation to Luxembourg investment funds which may not otherwise be regarded as 'liable to tax': *see* Martine Merten: 'Taxation of Investment Funds following the OECD Base Erosion and Profit Shifting Initiative: Part 2'. Bulletin for International Taxation (May 2019) 252. Paragraph 2 of the Protocol to the 7 June 2022 UK-Luxembourg treaty now deals with certain Luxembourg collective investment vehicles treated for tax purposes as bodies corporate (e.g., Undertakings for Collective Investment in Transferable Securities, Reserved Alternative Investment Funds and Specialised Investment Funds) UK-Luxembourg Double Taxation Convention and protocol – not in force – GOV.UK (www.gov.uk) (accessed 20 July 2022). Paragraph 2 treats these vehicles as Luxembourg-resident individuals and beneficial owners for treaty purposes, with exceptions to limit treaty-shopping. Unfortunately, there are no equivalent provisions in favour of UK funds, such as UK UCITS. The 7 June 2022 treaty has yet to be ratified.

577. Some limited partnerships are taxed in Australia as companies: *see* the Commentary on *Resource Capital Fund IV LP v Commissioner of Taxation* (2019) 21 ITLR 655 at 659.
578. This is so even if, for assessment purposes, partnership income is computed at partnership level before being allocated to the partners, and even if the tax on this income is physically paid over by the partnership.
579. In other words, a trust falling within *Baker v Archer-Shee* [1927] AC 844. In the case of a UK trust, this approach should apply even though the trustees can be taxed on the trust income because they 'receive or are entitled to it'. This is a representative charge whose incidence depends on the tax characteristics (and especially the residence) of the beneficiary: *see* section 4.3.3.1 above. Even if there is a vested interest in possession, some items of taxable income,

that situation, the key question is whether the income beneficiary, not the trustees, can satisfy Article 4(1).

What about an interest in possession trust which falls outside the rule in *Baker v Archer-Shee* because of the trust's governing law? For example, an interest in possession trust with UK-resident trustees, where *Garland v Archer-Shee* 15 TC 693 applies. In such cases, the beneficiary's 'source' of income is *not* the underlying trust income but its rights against the trustee(s) to have the trust enforced. In that case, the trustees will be taxable because they 'receive or are entitled to' the underlying trust income, but this charge is not a purely representative charge whose incidence depends on the tax characteristics of the beneficiary. The trustee(s) and the beneficiary are in this case being taxed on different sources of income. The trustee(s) should be regarded as taxable in their own right and therefore resident within Article 4(1) of the OECD Model, even though such a case is little different from one within the *Archer-Shee* rule.[580] Trusts subject to *Garland v Archer-Shee* are not discretionary trusts so the non-UK-resident income beneficiary cannot use ESC B18 (*see* section 4.3.5) to get relief for UK tax borne by the trustees on the underlying trust income. This is harsh. The UK treaty with the beneficiary's home jurisdiction is unlikely to give relief for tax paid by the trustees, because standard UK policy is to exclude trust distributions from the 'Other Income' Article.

What about a trust which is in whole or part a discretionary or accumulation trust?[581] In an accumulation trust, trustees can retain trust income and add it to trust capital. If the beneficiaries are not taxed on the retained income as it arises and if any tax charged on the trustees in respect of that income is a stand-alone charge unaffected by the beneficiaries' position, those trustees should be 'resident' within Article 4(1) of the OECD Model. If the trust is a pure discretionary trust (which is unlikely),[582] the answer should be the same as for an accumulation trust, if the trustee tax charge is unaffected by the beneficiaries' position.[583] This is typically the case in relation to a UK-resident discretionary trust: *see* section 4.3.5. In particular, there is no deduction at trustee level in respect of any distribution to a discretionary beneficiary. Furthermore, apart from 'bare' trusts, all UK-resident trusts are separate taxable entities in respect of

---

which are not income for trust law purposes, may be taxable at the level of the UK trustees only. This is *not* a representative charge: *see* section 4.3.5. If such income exists, one can therefore argue that a trust with a vested income interest is a 'resident' of a contracting state for treaty purposes.

580. This fine distinction further illustrates the flaws in *Garland v Archer-Shee* 15 TC 693. There are doubts whether the rule in *Garland v Archer-Shee* can apply at all where UK-resident trustees receive non-UK-source income for a non-UK-resident vested income beneficiary: *see* section 4.3.3.2.

581. A trust can have a vested interest in possession in part of its income while the remaining income is subject to a discretionary and/or accumulation trust.

582. In a pure discretionary trust, income must be distributed in full over a specified period, but the trustees can decide how to allocate income between beneficiaries. In practice, a discretionary trust is likely to have an accumulation feature.

583. There is risk of avoidance here because of ESC B18 (*see* section 4.3.5). If UK-resident trustees of a discretionary and accumulation trust claim treaty relief because they are 'resident' in the UK, the UK's treaty partner may lose out if a subsequent trust distribution to a non-UK-resident beneficiary allows the latter to claim relief from UK tax on the trustees' underlying income by relying on ESC B18.

chargeable gains, without reference to the beneficiaries' position: *see* sections 4.3.4 and 4.3.5.

Partnerships and some trustees may therefore be unable to claim the benefits of the UK's treaties because they are not 'residents' of the other Contracting State. In their Double Taxation Relief Manual,[584] HMRC stated that, where there is no specific treaty provision dealing with partnerships and a partnership is not a 'resident' of the other Contracting State, 'the partnership should be treated as transparent for the purpose of claims to relief under a double taxation agreement. Where a partnership is treated as transparent, claims may be made by a partner who is a resident in a country with which the United Kingdom has a double taxation agreement in respect of his share of partnership income as if he had received that income direct'. This statement oversimplifies the situation, although presumably it is inspired by the Partnership Report. This approach does not work well if the partner's residence state regards the 'partnership' as non-'transparent'. In that case, the UK may give treaty relief for UK-source income which is not currently taxable at partner level. Double non-taxation is a real risk. Of course, Article 1(2) of the OECD Model is meant to address this more effectively, especially where the two Contracting States characterise the entity differently: *see* section 6.1.

It has been argued that an entity is 'resident' for the purposes of a treaty based on Article 4(1) of the OECD Model, even if it is not liable to tax on all of its income in a particular jurisdiction, so long as that income is currently taxable there, at entity level or in the hands of residents of that jurisdiction with an interest in the entity (e.g., the partners in a partnership). The UK courts have yet to consider this argument. However, non-resident partnership-type entities have been treated as treaty-'resident' on this basis by the Tax Court of Canada in *TD Securities (USA) LLC v Her Majesty the Queen,*[585] and also by the Indian Income Tax Appellate Tribunal in *Linklaters LLP v Income Tax Officer – International Taxation Ward 1(1)(2), Mumbai.*[586] In *TD Securities,* a US LLC sought treaty protection from the Canadian branch profits tax. The Canadian court ruled in its favour, even though it was a single-member 'disregarded entity' with no entity level US tax liability. It won because the entity's sole member was a US corporation whose income was fully liable to current US taxation. The Canadian court was not prepared to treat the LLC as 'resident' in the US simply because it was formed there.[587] In *Linklaters,* the Indian court applied similar thinking to a UK LLP which had given legal advice to Indian clients. The court noted that India had not accepted the approach of the Partnership Report.[588] Hence:

584. Formerly at DT1750, although no longer available at 24 June 2020, perhaps because of Article 1(2) of the OECD Model.
585. (2010) 12 ITLR 783.
586. (2010) 13 ITLR 245.
587. The case predated a Fifth Protocol to the US-Canada treaty. This was agreed in 2007 which introduced a new Article IV(6) and (7). These are similar to (although more elaborate than) Article 1(2) of the OECD Model: *see* 12 ITLR 783 at 809, and section 6.1.1. Article 1(2) does not treat a 'transparent' entity as itself being 'resident' for treaty purposes.
588. The same is apparently true of Canada: *see* Angelo Nikolakakis in 12 ITLR 783 at 799.

> [T]he assessee was indeed eligible to [sic] the benefits of India-UK tax treaty, as long as entire profits of the partnership firm are taxed in UK – whether in the hands of the partnership firm though the taxable income is determined in relation to the personal characteristics of the partners, or in the hands of the partners directly.[589]

Treating the 'transparent' entity itself as 'resident' for treaty purposes is not consistent with HMRC's position to date, which is more aligned with the Partnership Report and Article 1(2) of the OECD Model. Article 1(2) may also make the UK courts less receptive to such arguments. Neither the Canadian nor the Indian court had to address the more difficult situation where the LLC/partnership had members resident in more than one jurisdiction. Would the courts have taken a 'partial residence' approach in such cases, which are more effectively dealt with under Article 1(2) of the OECD Model?

The approach of the Canadian and Indian courts nevertheless has similarities with Article 4 of the former UK-US treaty, which is analysed next.

6.3.2 Article 4 of the 1975 UK-US Treaty

The UK has experimented with other definitions of 'resident' for treaty purposes which do not depend on a partnership or trust itself being liable to tax. An important example was the 'partial residency' wording in the 1975 UK-US treaty.[590] Article 4(1)(b)(i) of that treaty defined 'resident of the United States'[591] as:

> (i) any person, other than a corporation, resident in the United States for the purposes of United States tax; *but in the case of a partnership, estate or trust, only to the extent that the income derived by such partnership, estate or trust is subject to United States tax as the income of a resident, either in its hands or in the hands of its partners or beneficiaries* [emphasis added]; and (ii) a United States corporation.

This definition permitted, for example, a US partnership[592] to be 'resident' in the US for treaty purposes if and to the extent that its income was subject to US tax either at entity level (unusual) or in the hands of US-resident partners. This meant that a US

589. (2010) 13 ITLR 245 at 321. The Mumbai Income Tax Appellate Tribunal has followed the *Linklaters* decision in *Deputy Director of Income Tax (International Taxation) AP Møller-Maersk A/S* 16 ITLR 392 and more recently, in *ING Bewaar Maatschappij I BV – as trustees of ING Emerging Markets Equity Fund v Deputy Commissioner of Income Tax International Taxation Circle 2(2)(1), Mumbai* ITA No. 7119/Mum/2014. In *ING*, a Dutch 'Fonds Vor Gemene Rekening' or FGR was treated as a resident of the Netherlands for the purposes of the Dutch-India tax treaty. The entity assessed to Indian tax was the Dutch corporate custodian of the FGR. The FGR, under Dutch law, was not an entity in its own right but simply a contractual arrangement all of whose participants were Dutch-resident taxable entities. The authors of 'Some Reflections' *supra* have queried, at pp. 326-332, the correctness of *TD Securities* and *Linklaters*.
590. SI 1980/568. This has been superseded by the 2001 treaty.
591. Article 4(1)(a) contained a similar definition of a 'resident of the United Kingdom'.
592. There were technical concerns about whether this definition would apply to a US LLC which was taxed as a partnership in the US. In practice, the UK tax authorities ignored these concerns and treated such a company as a partnership purely for the purposes of applying Article 4(1)(b). This practice was first published in the June 1997 edition of HMRC's 'Tax Bulletin'.

partnership with some non-US-resident partners would only be regarded as 'partially resident' in the US for treaty purposes. Therefore, the definition addressed the problem of members' mixed residence which was not expressly addressed by the Canadian and Indian court decisions mentioned in section 6.3.1.

This provision was rare in UK treaties and has not been replicated in the 2001 treaty discussed in section 6.4.[593] Article 4(1)(b)(i) was *not* simply a 'look through' rule. If it applied to a partnership, estate or trust, then that entity itself (and not its members/beneficiaries) was the 'person' 'resident in the United States' which could claim treaty benefits. That could affect what treaty benefits were available compared to the position if the entity was simply 'looked through'. For example, suppose that a US partnership was owned 50:50 by two US corporations, A and B, and that the partnership itself owned all of a UK-resident company, C. Therefore, A and B each had indirect economic ownership of 50% of C via the partnership. The effect of Article 4(1)(b)(i) was that the partnership was not 'looked through' but was itself a resident of the US, because all its partners were taxpaying US corporations. As a resident of the US, the partnership was entitled to a partial refund[594] of the UK imputation 'tax credit'[595] which attached to any dividend paid by C to the partnership. However, although treated as a resident of the US, the US partnership remained a partnership, not a corporation for treaty purposes. Hence it could not claim the larger refund of the imputation 'tax credit' which was only available for dividends *paid to US corporations* [emphasis added] controlling a significant shareholding in a UK-resident company.[596] Because (i) Article 4(1)(b)(i) did not 'look through' the US partnership to its corporate partners, A and B, and (ii) the US partnership would typically have legal personality, there was no clear way for either corporate partner to claim its share of that larger refund even though each effectively owned 50% of C via the partnership.

It would have been different if A and B had formed a contractual joint venture (falling short of partnership) to co-own C directly in equal shares.

593. A similar, but not identical provision still applies, for partnerships only, in Article 4(1) of the current (1996) UK-Argentina treaty SI 1997/1777: '... in relation to taxes on income in the case of partnerships, the term ["resident of a Contracting State"] applies only to the extent that the income derived by the partnership is subjected to tax in that Contracting State *in the hands of its partners* [emphasis added] who are liable to taxation in that State as residents of that State. In relation to taxes on capital or assets, in the case of a partnership the term applies only to the extent that the capital or assets of the partnership are subjected to tax in that State as the capital or assets of a resident'. *See also* section 6.7.1 regarding the revised UK-India treaty. The Partnership Report disliked (*see* paragraphs 45-46) 'residence' definitions such as Article 4(1)(b). Other US treaties then contained language similar to Article 4(1)(b): *see* Richard O. Loengard, Jr: 'Tax Treaties, Partnerships and Partners: Exploration of a Relationship' (1975) Tax Lawyer, Volume 29, 31 at 37 (hereinafter 'Loengard'). Article 4(1)(b) of the US Model Income Tax Treaty of 1981 was similar to Article 4(1)(b), but such language has not featured in the US Model since 1996. 'Partial residence' articles are further discussed in 'Some Reflections' *supra*, at 326-332.

594. Under Article 10(2)(a)(ii) of the 1975 treaty. It is assumed that for these purposes, the US partnership would be the 'beneficial owner' of the dividends from C and that the anti-avoidance rules in Article 10(7) would not apply.

595. Formerly available under section 231 Income and Corporation Taxes Act 1988 and now abolished.

596. *See* Article 10(2)(a)(i) of the 1975 treaty.

For a partnership to be a 'resident of the United States' under Article 4(1)(b)(i), it was, strictly, not enough for all its partners to be US-resident taxpayers. The opening words of the paragraph apparently also required the partnership itself to be 'resident in the United States for the purposes of United States tax'.[597] If that was correct, a partnership in a third state all of whose partners were US-residents would not fall within Article 4(1)(b), further illustrating its non-'look through' nature.

This last point has been considered by the Australian courts. While Article 4(1) has not been litigated in either the UK or the US, the Australian Federal Court (Full Court) considered a similar definition of a 'resident of the United States' in Article 4(1)(b)(iii) of the US-Australia treaty, in *Resource Capital Fund IV LP v Commissioner of Taxation.*[598] This related to gains on selling shares in a Toronto-listed, Australian lithium mining company. The sellers were Cayman Island LPs, many of whose partners were apparently US tax-resident. It was accepted that these partnerships were 'transparent' for US tax purposes, but were taxable entities in Australia. The majority read the relevant definition of 'resident of the United States' quite restrictively.[599] First, the court ruled (harshly) that there was no evidence that the partnerships' income was subject to US tax. In any case, Article 4(1)(b)(iii) required the partnership to meet two conditions: it had to be a resident of the US itself for tax purposes *and* its income had to be subject to US tax. A partnership formed in the Cayman Islands could not be a resident of the US and so the first condition was not met. Hence neither partnership could rely on Article 4(1)(b)(iii) to show that it was treaty-resident.[600] The majority indicated that each US-resident partner in either partnership could claim treaty relief but not in these proceedings which involved a tax assessment on the LP itself.[601]

597. Under US tax law, the concept of the 'residence of a partnership' has limited significance. It is defined, for example, in regulations under section 861 Internal Revenue Code specifying what is US-source income. Using this definition to interpret Article 4(1)(b)(i) could mean that some US-formed investment partnerships were not US-resident, because they lacked a US trade or business. To the same effect, *see* Blanchard *supra,* at p. 47.
598. (2019) 12 ITLR 655. The High Court of Australia refused leave to appeal.
599. (2019) 12 ITLR 655 at 695-699.
600. In this respect, the majority followed the first instance judge in *Resource Capital Fund III LP v Commissioner of Taxation* (2013) 15 ITLR 814 ('*RCF III*'). They noted that treating the Cayman LP as a taxable entity, despite the US-Australia treaty, was consistent with the Full Federal Court when *RCF III* was appealed: *see Commissioner of Taxation v Resource Capital Fund III LP* (2014) 16 ITLR 876. For further discussion of *RCF III, see* John Azzi: 'Impact of the OECD Multilateral Convention to implement tax treaty related measures to prevent Base Erosion and Profit Shifting on the Taxation of Fiscally-Transparent Entities under the Australia-UK Double Tax Agreement' [2018] British Tax Review 556. That article (which predates the decision of the Full Federal Court in *RCF IV)* notes that the High Court of Australia refused special leave to appeal in *RCF III.* The High Court questioned whether individual partners could contest the Australian tax assessment on the partnership and even suggested that the only way to do so was via the treaty-based mutual agreement procedure. The UK-Australia treaty is discussed in section 6.7.1.
601. The court indicated that a partner could rely on the treaty in recovery proceedings or when seeking a declaration that the treaty protected that partner's profit share. These suggestions apparently overlook the fact that, outside a formal tax appeal, a notice of assessment is conclusive: *see* Mark Brabazon: 'After the Flood: Transparent and Hybrid Entities in Australian Tax Treaties after the MLI' (hereinafter 'Brabazon: Australian Treaties') (2019) eJournal of Tax Research, Volume 17, Issue 1, 1-34, at 19.

The court did not mention the mutual agreement procedure: *see* the previous footnote.

The majority interpretation is both restrictive and impractical, not least because of the procedural restrictions it imposes on each partner when claiming treaty benefits. An alternative, and superior, interpretation was put forward in Davies J's partial dissent.[602] This rejected the two-condition approach and, in particular, the idea that Article 4(1)(b)(iii) required the partnership itself to be a resident of the US. Rather:

> [A]lthough under United States tax law a partnership is a fiscally transparent entity, the proviso in Article 4(1)(b)(iii) would attribute a residency status to a partnership separate from its partners for the purposes of the application of the [treaty] where income of the partnership is taxable in the hands of the United States partners (or if exempt from United States tax, it is exempt other than because such partners are not United States residents). On this construction, it is the residency of the United States partners for United States tax law purposes which would dictate whether a partnership is a resident of the United States for the purposes of the [treaty]. On this construction also, there is no separate and additional requirement that partnerships be recognised by the United States as a resident of the United States. *Rather, partners who are United States residents and taxable in the United States on the partnership income may claim through the partnership to get the benefit of the [treaty] whether or not the partnership is a United States domestic partnership* [emphasis added].

This alternative interpretation does not have the same 'look through' effect as Article 1(2) of the OECD Model because it recognises that Article 4(1)(b)(iii) confers treaty residence on the partnership itself, to the extent that its income is liable to tax in the hands of its US-resident partners. However, it gives treaty relief to partnerships formed outside the US to the extent that their partners are US-residents. This is sensible: partnerships are 'transparent' anyway for US income tax purposes, and the concept of a partnership's 'residence' has little independent significance. Nothing is achieved by reading the treaty so as to require the partnership itself to be formed in the US.

Article 4(1)(b) of the 1975 treaty also applied to trusts and estates. The US Technical Explanation of that treaty stated that, consequently, 'the treatment of income received by a trust or estate will be determined by the residence and taxation of the person subject to tax on such income, which may be the grantor [i.e., the settlor], the beneficiaries or the trust or estate itself, as the case may be'.[603] While the US Technical Explanation is a purely unilateral commentary by one state on the treaty, and therefore of little or no persuasive authority before a UK court, this statement seems sensible. It caters for the different ways in which trust income may be taxable in the hands of US persons, whether at trust level or in the hands of others linked to the trust. However,

602. (2019) 12 ITLR 655 at 758-763. Davies J's interpretation is consistent with the interpretation of Article 4(1)(b)(i) of the 1975 UK-US treaty in the US Treasury's Technical Explanation: https://www.irs.gov/pub/irs-trty/uktech.pdf (accessed 24 June 2020). The *RCF* litigation is discussed in Mark Brabazon: 'The Oracle, Transparent Entities and Access to Tax Treaties' (2020) AT Rev, Volume 49, 250, which analyses three different types of 'partial residence' clause in US treaties, as well as the precise wording of Article 4(1)(b)(iii) of the US-Australia treaty. This wording arguably made it harder for Davies J to reach her conclusion. Those wording issues are not relevant to Article 4(1)(b)(i) of the 1975 UK-US treaty.

603. https://www.irs.gov/pub/irs-trty/uktech.pdf (accessed 24 June 2020).

the strict letter of the treaty does not envisage settlor taxation of trust income (as opposed to beneficiary taxation) being enough to trigger Article 4(1)(b). As with partnerships, the US Technical Explanation does not suggest that Article 4(1)(b)(i) requires the trust or estate itself to be a resident of the US.

A final weakness of Article 4(1)(b) of the 1975 UK-US treaty was that it did not apply easily where the two Contracting States had different ideas of what amounted to a 'partnership, estate or trust'.

With this in mind, one commentator stressed a long time ago the need for a solution focused on a partner's residence, rather than the entity itself, when taxing partnership income, thereby avoiding abuse and excessive emphasis on whether a partnership exists. This is especially important because (*see* section 7.2) the US defines a partnership more broadly than many jurisdictions, and in particular treats as a partnership many joint venture/co-ownership arrangements, provided that they amount to more than mere investment.[604]

Consequently the 2001 UK-US treaty takes a different approach to these issues, tracking changes to the US Model treaty since 1996. Article 1(2) of the OECD Model has now gone down the same road.

6.4 THE APPROACH OF THE 2001 UK-US TAX TREATY TO 'TAX TRANSPARENT' ENTITIES

6.4.1 Introduction

The treatment of 'transparent' entities was a key issue when the UK last renegotiated its tax treaty with the US.[605] The 2001 UK-US treaty[606] takes a very different approach to the 1975 treaty, echoing the Partnership Report and anticipating Article 1(2) of the OECD Model and Article 3 of the MLI. Article 1(1) provides:

> Except as specifically provided herein, this Convention is applicable only to persons who are residents of one or both of the Contracting States.

Article 3(1)(a) and (b) then provide that 'unless the context otherwise requires:

> (a) the term "person" includes an individual, *an estate, a trust, a partnership* [emphasis added] a company and any other body of persons; (b) the term "company" means any body corporate or any entity that is treated as a body corporate for tax purposes'.

604. *See* Loengard *supra*, at p. 43. This comment foreshadows Article 1(2) of the OECD Model and Article 3 of the MLI. The problem highlighted by this comment affected whether a US LLC treated as a partnership for US tax purposes could claim the benefit of the 1975 UK-US treaty because the UK does not generally regard such entities as partnerships. UK published practice glossed over this issue: *see* fn 592. For further discussion of the US entity classification rules, *see* section 7.2.

605. Not least because of the 1997 changes (*see* section 7.2) to the US entity classification rules and the introduction of UK LLPs in 2000.

606. SI 2002/2848.

Trusts and partnerships are therefore 'persons'. It is standard US treaty practice to be so explicit. Article 4(1) defines 'resident of a Contracting State' very differently from Article 4(1)(b) of the 1975 treaty:

> [T]he term 'resident of a Contracting State' means, for the purposes of this Convention, any person who, under the laws of that State, is liable to tax therein by reason of his domicile, residence, citizenship, place of management, place of incorporation, or any other criterion of a similar nature.

This resembles Article 4(1) of the OECD Model and means that a partnership whose income is taxable only at partner level, by reference to the personal characteristics of the partners, is not a 'resident of a Contracting State'. But this is not the end of the story.[607]

6.4.2 Article 1(8) and Article 1(4)

Article 1(8) of the 2001 treaty[608] provides:

> An item of income, profit or gain derived through a person that is *fiscally transparent under the laws of either Contracting State* [emphasis added] shall be considered to be derived by a resident of a Contracting State to the extent that the item is treated for the purposes of the taxation law of such Contracting State as the income, profit or gain of a resident.

This rule is a type of 'look through', conferring treaty benefits on the resident of a treaty state who derives, and is liable to tax as a resident, on the relevant income, if that income is derived via a person regarded as 'fiscally transparent' in either the UK or the US. Article 1(8), unlike Article 4(1) of the 1975 treaty, does *not* make the 'fiscally transparent' person itself a resident of either the UK or the US. Indeed, it applies even where the 'fiscally transparent' person is established in a third state.[609] The entire focus is on the tax treatment of those deriving income via that person. Crucially, Article 1(8) operates even if only one of the treaty partners regards the person as 'fiscally

607. One assumes, because of Article 1(8), that the UK courts would not interpret Article 4(1) in the same way as the Canadian and Indian courts in the cases mentioned earlier.
608. Article 1(8) is based on the US domestic withholding tax regulations under section 894(c) Internal Revenue Code 1986 and the 1996 US Model treaty: *see* Avery Jones: Partnerships *supra*, at 430-431.
609. This is what the treaty says and is the view of the US Treasury Technical Explanation of the 2001 treaty https://www.treasury.gov/resource-center/tax-policy/treaties/Documents/teus-uk.pdf (accessed 24 June 2020). That document is the view of one Contracting State and hence has negligible weight in a UK court, unlike the Exchange of Notes discussed below. A decision which contradicts this interpretation of Article 1(8) is the 2013 German Federal Tax Court decision in *Re US S Corporation's German withholding tax status* 16 ITLR 428. This related to an equivalent of Article 1(8): Article 1(7) of the 1989 US-Germany treaty, as amended in 2008. The German court granted, under Article 10(2)(a), the 5% withholding tax rate for German dividends paid on a 50% shareholding to a US corporation which had elected for 'look through' US treatment as a S Corporation. The court ruled that under German standards, the US corporation was a corporate shareholder for Article 10(2)(a) purposes and the beneficial owner of the dividends, despite being 'look through' in the US. Furthermore, although not 'resident' in the US because it had no US tax liability, it could be deemed treaty-resident because of the

transparent'. It is not necessary that the UK and the US see eye to eye on classifying it. This sidesteps a flaw in Article 4(1)(b) of the 1975 treaty. Unlike Article 1(2) of the OECD Model, Article 1(8) does not expressly cover cases of 'partial transparency'.

Article 1(8) operates in tandem with the Article 1(4) 'saving' clause which is a feature of all modern US tax treaties:[610]

> Notwithstanding any provision of this Convention except paragraph 5 of this Article, a Contracting State may tax its residents (as determined under Article 4, (Residence)), and by reason of citizenship may tax its citizens, as if this Convention had not come into effect.

Article 1(5)(a) provides that Article 1(4) does not prevent a resident of a contracting state from invoking 'the benefits conferred ... under paragraph 2 of Article 9 (Associated Enterprises), sub-paragraph (b) of paragraph 1 and paragraphs 3 and 5 of Article 17 (Pensions, Social Security, Annuities, Alimony and Child Support), paragraphs 1 and 5 of Article 18 (Pension Schemes) and Articles 24 (Relief from Double Taxation), 25 (Non-discrimination), and 26 (Mutual Agreement Procedure) of this Convention'.

The interplay between Article 1(8) and the 'saving' clause, plus other aspects of Article 1(8), is explained in the Exchange of Notes signed in conjunction with the 2001 treaty:

> It is understood that where an item of income, profit or gain is derived through a person which is a resident of a Contracting State the provisions of [Article 1(8)] shall not prevent that Contracting State from taxing the item as the income, profit or gain of that person.[611]
>
> It is further understood that, where, by virtue of [Article 1(8)], an item of income, profit or gain is considered by a Contracting State to be derived by a person who is a resident of that Contracting State and the same item is considered by the other Contracting State to be derived by that person or by a person who is a resident of that other Contracting State, [Article 1(8)] shall not prevent either Contracting State from taxing the item as the income, profit or gain of the person considered by that State to have derived the item of income, profit or gain.[612]

'transparent entity' clause in Article 1(7), to the extent that its income was taxable in the hands of its US shareholders. So the S Corporation ended up with the best possible outcome, partly because Article 1(7) was interpreted as deeming that company itself to be US-resident. This reading of Article 1(7) is hard to justify.

610. And which is now included in Article 1(3) of the OECD Model and Article 11 of the MLI.
611. If all else fails, by relying on Article 1(4).
612. This is consistent with Article 1(8) not being listed in the Article 1(5) exceptions to the 'saving' clause. Consequently Article 1(8) creates a significant risk of double taxation because of conflicting characterisations by the UK and the US, e.g., if one state taxes the fiscally transparent entity as a resident and the other state taxes its members on that entity's underlying income. A good example would be where income is earned by a UK-resident unlimited liability company whose sole shareholder is a US corporation. This double taxation risk is part-mitigated via Article 24 (Relief from Double Taxation) as explained by the Exchange of Notes: *see* section 6.4.3.

> It is further understood that, in applying [Article 1(8)], the United Kingdom shall, *exceptionally,* [emphasis added] regard an item of income, profit or gain arising to a person as falling within [Article 1(8)] where another person is charged to United Kingdom tax in respect of that item of income, profit or gain:
>
> (a) under section 660A or 739 Income and Corporation Taxes Act 1988;[613] or
> (b) under section 77[614] or 86 Taxation of Chargeable Gains Act 1992.
>
> It is further understood that, in applying [Article 1(8)], a person shall be regarded as fiscally transparent under the laws of the United Kingdom in relation to an item of income, profit or gain where a charge is made on another person on that item either:
>
> (a) by virtue of section 13 Taxation of Chargeable Gains Act 1992;[615] or
> (b) because that other person has (or under section 118 Finance Act 1993, is treated as having) an equitable right in possession in a trust.[616]

This part of the Exchange of Notes is a novel attempt by the UK in particular to clarify and expand what 'fiscal transparency' means for Article 1(8) purposes. 'Fiscal transparency' is otherwise undefined. Article 1(8) is regarded ('exceptionally') by the UK as applying where income or gain of a person is imputed to a UK-resident under various anti-avoidance or anti-deferral rules, even though these rules would not ordinarily be seen as making that person 'fiscally transparent'.[617] The anti-deferral rules listed are not an exhaustive list. They do not include the UK 'controlled foreign company' rules, for reasons which are unclear but which may be linked to the US section 894 Regulations perceiving such rules as anti-deferral rules and not 'transparency' rules.[618] However, the overall approach is sensible: if clearly identifiable income

613. Section 660A has been repealed and replaced by the similar sections 624-628C in Part 5 Chapter 5 ITTOIA. These impose income tax on the 'settlor' of arrangements amounting to 'settlements', where the 'settlor' retains an interest in the 'settlement'. Part 5 Chapter 5 contains further rules attributing income of a 'settlement' to the 'settlor', notably under section 629 ITTOIA, where income is paid to relevant minor children of the settlor. These other rules existed in 2001 but are not listed in the Exchange of Notes, for reasons which are unclear. Section 739 has been repealed and replaced by the similar 'Transfer of Assets Abroad' rules in Part 13 Chapter 2 ITA. Section 739 is replaced by the income tax charge in sections 720-721 ITA on a UK-resident individual with 'power to enjoy' income arising from certain transfers of assets outside the UK.
614. Section 77 was repealed in 2008. It became redundant when UK-resident trusts became taxable on their capital gains at the highest marginal UK rate for individuals. Section 86 taxes a UK-resident settlor of a non-UK-resident trust in respect of that trust's capital gains.
615. Section 13 TCGA has been replaced by sections 3-3G TCGA, although the substance remains essentially the same. The effect is usually to attribute the *actual* capital gains of a non-UK-resident, closely held company to its UK-resident shareholders and certain other UK-residents ('participators') with a significant interest in it.
616. This refers to the rule in *Baker v Archer-Shee*: *see* section 4.3.3. Section 118 Finance Act 1993 (now section 464 ITA) applies that rule to trusts formed under the law of Scotland: *see* section 4.3.3.2.
617. The US Treasury Technical Explanation of the 2001 treaty *supra* states that for US purposes, 'fiscally transparent' persons will include partnerships, common investment trusts under section 584 Internal Revenue Code, grantor trusts and US limited liability companies which are treated as partnerships for US tax purposes.
618. The UK 'controlled foreign company' rules are now in Part 9A TIOPA. Technically they do not charge directly the company's underlying income: *see* fn 7. However, underlying income is not

or gain of an entity is effectively liable to current UK tax in the hands of a person with an interest in it, then the goal of Article 1(8) is being met, even if that entity (e.g., a non-UK-resident closely held company) would not be regarded, classically, as 'transparent' in the same way as a partnership.

One commentator[619] has suggested that Article 1(8) (or Article 1(2) of the OECD Model) should not give treaty relief at source to a UK-resident if anti-deferral rules of the kind discussed in the previous paragraph do not attribute the *actual* income or gain of a person to a UK-resident but only a *notional amount* computed by reference to that income or gain. This distinction is unconvincing. The UK attribution rules referred to in the Exchange of Notes often, although not always, attribute notional income or gain to a UK-resident yet this is not a bar to applying Article 1(8) of the UK-US treaty. This is sensible. The UK has often drafted its attribution rules in this way, so that they apply even if the underlying income or gain used to measure the notional amount is the actual income of a treaty-protected non-UK-resident. Hence such drafting defeats *Padmore*-type arguments (*see* section 6.2.2) by UK-residents. But why should such drafting, which a taxpayer with an interest in a 'transparent' entity avoiding *residence*-based tax, lead to treaty relief being denied in the *source* state under a provision such as Article 1(8)? The source state's concern is that an amount clearly corresponding to source state income derived by or through that entity is liable to current taxation in the hands of a resident of the treaty partner. If that current taxation occurs by attribution under, say, a 'controlled foreign company' rule, it is the rule's effect that matters, not its linguistic structure. If its structure better ensures a current tax liability in the taxpayer's residence state, that further protects the source state from double non-taxation.

Article 1(8) will give effect to one state's analysis of an entity as 'fiscally transparent' but only if this leads to residents of a contracting state being liable to current taxation on the entity's underlying income. Therefore, when giving treaty relief

directly charged under the 'Transfer of Assets Abroad' rules mentioned in fn 613. Yet, the successor of section 739 Income and Corporation Taxes Act 1988, the 'Transfer of Assets Abroad' rules *are* presumably covered by the Exchange of Notes. For further discussion of whether a 'controlled foreign company' charge activates Article 1(8) (or Article 1(2) of the OECD Model), *see* Joanna Wheeler: Chapter 2: 'Some Thoughts about Transparency, Attribution and CFC Regimes and Their Interaction with Tax Treaties'. The Aftermath of BEPS: ed. Joanna Wheeler, International Bureau of Fiscal Documentation 2020. The author is most grateful to Dr Wheeler for her insights. One point she raises is whether a 'controlled foreign company' charge can activate Article 1(2) where it is only designed to tax the company's income at a prescribed level *without* treating it effectively as the income of the shareholder, etc. (either directly or as a deemed dividend). If so, the person taxed is then simply a tax debt collector for the targeted company. This is a fair point but it is unusual for 'controlled foreign company' rules to be structured in this way. However, an exception may be the proposed 'income inclusion rule' in the OECD's December 2021 'Pillar 2' proposals: *see* 'Tax Challenges Arising from the Digitalisation of the Economy – Global Anti-Base Erosion Model Rules (Pillar Two): Inclusive Framework on BEPS)'. https://www.oecd.org/tax/beps/tax-challenges-arising-from-the-digitalisation-of-the-economy – global-anti-base-erosion-model-rules-pillar-two.htm.

619. *See* Brabazon *supra,* at pp. 226-229. While the author queries the main point made by Brabazon, Article 1(8) (or Article 1(2) of the Model) should not apply if an attribution rule does not clearly link: (i) specific underlying income of an entity and (ii) notional income attributed to a taxpayer by reference to that underlying income. Whether the link exists is a matter of evidence and precisely how the attribution rule works.

on that income, the source state can be confident that double non-taxation should not arise, unless there are separate policy-based reasons for not taxing those with an interest in the entity (e.g., entity members which are recognised tax-exempts). Because of its right to tax its own residents (in Article 1(4)), the source state can also be confident that the treaty will not restrict its taxing powers in a purely domestic situation where source state income flows to an entity regarded as resident in the source state.

6.4.3 Article 24 and the Exchange of Notes

Article 1(4) creates a risk of double taxation if one state taxes an entity as a resident taxpayer under its own domestic laws while the other state regards that entity as 'fiscally transparent' and therefore taxes the entity's members resident in that other state on their share of the entity's underlying income as it arises. For example, consider the facts of *Bayfine UK v HMRC.*[620] This involved a tax avoidance scheme based on the 'saving' clause (Article 1(3)) in the 1975 UK-US treaty coupled with the elimination of double taxation article in that treaty (Article 23). A US corporation wholly owned a UK unlimited company, which made a profit from entering into a derivative contract. The UK taxed the profit of what it perceived to be a UK-resident company (either under the 'Business Profits' Article of the treaty or by relying on the 'saving' clause). However, the US treated the unlimited company as 'fiscally transparent': it 'disregarded' it under US domestic tax rules because it was unlimited and had only one member.[621] The US therefore treated the income of the unlimited company as belonging to its US parent and taxed it under the 'saving' clause. Hence each jurisdiction was taxing the same pool of profit in a situation which would now fall under Article 1(4) and 1(8) of the 2001 treaty. The UK courts ultimately refused the unlimited company a foreign tax credit for the US tax incurred by its US parent solely because it was US-resident. The Exchange of Notes to the 2001 treaty addresses this economic double taxation risk, to a degree not encountered in other UK tax treaties, or indeed in tax treaties generally.[622] It states the following in relation to Article 24 (Relief from double taxation):

> It is understood that, under paragraph 4 or 8 of Article 1 ..., the provisions of the Convention may permit the Contracting State of which a person is a resident (or, in the case of the United States, a citizen), to tax an item of income, profit or gain derived through another person (the entity) which is fiscally transparent under the laws of either Contracting State, and may permit the other Contracting State to tax (a) the same person; (b) the entity; or (c) a third person with respect to that item.
>
> Under such circumstances, *the tax paid or accrued by the entity shall be treated as if it were paid or accrued by the first-mentioned person for the purposes*

620. [2011] STC 717 reversing [2010] STC 1379 and upholding [2009] STC (SCD) 43.
621. *See* section 7.2.5 for the relevant US tax rules.
622. Article 3(2) of the MLI makes clear that a residence state is not expected to give double taxation relief for tax imposed on the same income by the other Contracting State where the latter taxes *solely* on the basis of residence. The UK reserved against this part of the MLI but as *Bayfine* illustrates, the UK agrees with the underlying policy. For a fuller discussion of the limited extent to which treaties address double taxation where two states each tax solely on the basis of residence, *see* Brabazon *supra,* at pp. 246-250, which points out that such situations are especially likely to arise in respect of trusts.

> *of determining the relief from double taxation to be allowed by the State of which that first-mentioned person is a resident (or, in the case of the United States, a citizen), except that, in the case of an item of income from real property to which paragraph 1 of Article 6 ... of the Convention applies, or a gain from the alienation of real property to which paragraph 1 of Article 13 ... applies, the tax paid or accrued by the person who is a resident of the Contracting State in which the real property is situated shall be treated as if it were paid or accrued by the person who is a resident of the other Contracting State* [emphasis added].
>
> In the case where the same income, profit or gain derived through a trust is treated by each Contracting State as derived by different persons resident in either State, and (a) the person taxed by one State is the settlor or grantor of a trust; and (b) the person taxed by the other State is a beneficiary of that trust, the tax paid or accrued by the beneficiary shall be treated as if it were paid or accrued by the settlor or grantor for the purposes of determining the relief from double taxation to be allowed by the State of which that settlor or grantor is a resident (or, in the case of the United States, a citizen), except that, in the case of an item of income from real property to which paragraph 1 of Article 6 ... of the Convention applies, or a gain from the alienation of real property to which paragraph 1 of Article 13 ... applies, the tax paid or accrued by the person who is a resident of the Contracting State in which the real property is situated shall be treated as if it were paid or accrued by the person who is a resident of the other Contracting State.
>
> It is further understood that paragraphs 2 and 5 of Article 24 shall apply to such an item of income, profit or gain to the extent necessary to provide relief from double taxation.[623]

The highlighted words apply directly to the *Bayfine* situation. The UK tax payable by the UK unlimited company is to be treated as 'paid or accrued' by the US company[624] when determining what double taxation relief the latter can claim in respect of the income on which it is taxed under the 'saving' clause when the US 'disregards' the UK subsidiary. The special rule for real estate income and gain was not relevant in *Bayfine.*

623. This sentence refers to the rules in Article 24 which define the 'source' of items taxable under the allocation rules in the 2001 treaty. Those rules make it easier to claim double taxation relief, by treating an item taxable in a contracting state under the treaty as having a 'source' in that state for the purposes of granting double taxation relief in the other state.

624. The US company would *not* be entitled to double taxation relief for any withholding tax payable on a distribution to it by its 'disregarded' UK subsidiary. It can only claim a credit for what would otherwise be underlying tax on the profits of the UK subsidiary. This distinction is odd. The overall goal seems to be that a resident ('A') of the jurisdiction which perceives the entity to be 'transparent' should not suffer double taxation simply because the other jurisdiction perceives the entity differently, so long as A is currently taxed in its state of residence on its share of the entity's income. In that case, *any* taxation on the entity's profits (distributed or undistributed) should surely generate double taxation relief in A's jurisdiction of residence. Paragraph 133 of the Partnership Report draws a similarly odd distinction in its Example 18. It argues that because the residence state of A sees the entity as 'transparent' and therefore does not tax a distribution from the entity, it should not be required to give double taxation relief for any withholding tax on that distribution. This is unconvincing. For budgetary reasons, A's right to claim relief for withholding on a distribution should be limited to distributions paid within a set time period. The Netherlands-Belgium treaty of 2001 apparently gives relief from double taxation when there is a distribution by an entity treated as 'transparent' in the state where its members are resident. It does this by making the residence state of that entity waive its tax on such a distribution: *see* Verhoog & Breuer: 'Hybrid Entity Issues in a Tax Treaty Context: OECD Approach Versus Actual Tax Treaties' Intertax, Volume 44, Issue 8 and 9, 684 at 694.

This Exchange of Notes was briefly considered by the Court of Appeal in *Anson v HMRC*,[625] where the taxpayer sought to rely on it in respect of that part of its UK foreign tax credit claim which fell within the 2001 treaty.[626] *Anson* was analysed in section 2.14. The attraction to the taxpayer of relying on the Exchange of Notes was that, if relevant, a UK foreign tax credit was available for the taxpayer's share of the US taxes on the income of the LLC, whether or not that income belonged to the taxpayer as it arose. In short, it was not necessary to show, for UK foreign tax credit purposes, that UK and US tax had been paid on *the same* profits. The Court of Appeal prevented this point being introduced. Arden LJ (as she then was) stated, in paragraph 92:

> There is clearly some dispute as to the mischief to which the exchange of notes is directed .... Moreover, the words 'with respect to that item' [at the end of the first paragraph of the part of the Exchange of Notes dealing with Article 24] ... are, on the face of it, consistent with [HMRC's submission] that no change is made in the requirement for the profits taxed in each jurisdiction to be the same profits in order to qualify for [double taxation relief]. If an alteration to Article 23 [sic] was intended, it is surprising that it was dealt with in this oblique way.

This seems to ignore much of what the Exchange of Notes is trying to achieve. Because of the way Article 1(8) and the 'saving' clause interact, different persons may be taxed as residents in respect of the same profits (as in *Bayfine*), not least because of differences between UK and US domestic tax rules on entity classification. Those rules may mean that one jurisdiction perceives the profits to be the income of one legal person while the other jurisdiction regards them as the profits of a different person. There could therefore be unrelieved double taxation,[627] which the part of the Exchange of Notes dealing with Article 24 seeks to remedy. It cannot address this problem effectively[628] if no change can ever be made to the requirement for the profits taxed in each jurisdiction to be the same profits in order to qualify for UK double taxation relief. For example, one jurisdiction may tax actual income, while the other taxes notional income under an anti-deferral income attribution rule.

However, the Court of Appeal correctly rejected the taxpayer's submission. The relevant part of the Exchange of Notes only addresses a situation where the person claiming double taxation relief is resident in a treaty jurisdiction which regards the relevant entity as 'transparent' while the other jurisdiction regards it as 'opaque' and hence taxable in its own right. Those facts are the opposite of *Anson*. Mr Anson was a

625. [2013] STC 557 and, in particular, paragraphs 87-93.
626. Most relevant years fell under the 1975 treaty to which the Exchange of Notes does not apply.
627. The UK gives a unilateral foreign tax credit for non-UK tax imposed on income or gain of a UK taxpayer, even if that non-UK tax is imposed on a different person. In each case, the UK and non-UK tax must be calculated by reference to the same income or gain, and the income must arise or the gain accrue in the jurisdiction imposing the non-UK tax. Hence, identity of taxable income or gain is required and the non-UK tax must be imposed by the jurisdiction of source, and not just on the basis of residence. Identity of taxable persons is not required: *see* section 9 TIOPA.
628. The Exchange of Notes should have the same force in UK domestic law as the main body of the treaty. The concept of 'arrangements' in the treaty-enabling legislation in section 2 TIOPA is wide enough to include a contemporaneous Exchange of Notes signed by both Contracting States together with the treaty itself.

resident of the UK which sought to treat the LLC as 'opaque', while the US regarded it as 'transparent' so that its income was only taxable for US purposes at the level of its members. The Exchange of Notes would have been relevant if Mr Anson had invested in a Delaware LP (usually recognised as 'transparent' in the UK) which had elected to be taxed as a corporation in the US.[629] The fact that the Exchange of Notes does not cover the *Anson* situation is a weakness.[630]

The US Treasury Technical Explanation makes interesting comments[631] about how the US regards the Exchange of Notes as operating in respect of Article 24. First, it discusses the effect of the Exchange of Notes in cases involving real property, where primary taxing rights with respect to real property income must rest with the Contracting State where that property is located.[632] It gives the following example:

> [A] UK unlimited liability company ('ULC') with U.S. resident partners derives gain from the sale of U.S. real property. The ULC has elected to be treated for U.S. tax purposes as a partnership and, therefore, the U.S. taxes the U.S. resident partners on the gain derived. However, because the United Kingdom treats the ULC as a company resident in the United Kingdom, the saving clause ... ensures that the United Kingdom may continue to tax the company as a U.K. resident. Because the notes provide that the United States retains primary taxing rights with respect to real property located in the United States, the United Kingdom will treat the tax paid by the U.S. resident partners as having been paid by the ULC[633] for the purposes of providing the foreign tax credit to the ULC with respect to the gain derived from the sale of U.S. real property.

The US Treasury Technical Explanation also discusses how Article 1(8) and Article 24 apply to trusts. As in the UK, some US trusts are taxable as such while income and gain of others are attributed to the 'grantor' (i.e., the 'settlor').[634] US-taxpaying beneficiaries can also be taxable on underlying trust income. Unrelieved double

629. This is the mirror image of the first example on p. 95 of the US Treasury Technical Explanation of the 2001 treaty *supra*, towards the start of the discussion of Article 24. For the relevant US entity classification rules, *see* section 7.2.4. Where the UK regards the US partnership as 'transparent' but the US does not, a UK foreign tax credit should be available in any case to a UK-taxpaying partner, subject to the conditions in fn 627 and especially the condition that the non-UK tax be based on source.
630. Similar criticisms have been made of Article 1(2) of the OECD Model: *see* 'Some Reflections' *supra*, at pp. 357-358.
631. *Supra* on pp. 95-96. Being a unilateral publication of the US Treasury, the Technical Explanation has very low status, for interpretation purposes.
632. 'Real property' has an expanded definition here because of Article 13(1) of the 2001 treaty. It includes certain indirect real property interests: on the US side, a 'United States real property interest' and, on the UK side, certain shareholdings, partnership or trust interests deriving their value from UK real estate.
633. This scenario is quite similar to *Bayfine* [2011] STC 717, but, unlike that case, the Exchange of Notes expressly requires the UK to give credit for the US tax imposed on the US members of the ULC in respect of the US real property gain. This part of the Exchange of Notes should be consistent with the normal UK approach. The UK requires that the income or gain arise or accrue in the relevant non-UK jurisdiction and that non-UK tax be computed by reference to the same gain as the UK tax. However, the UK does not require that the UK and non-UK tax liabilities should arise at the same time nor be charged on the same person: section 9 TIOPA and Statement of Practice 6/88.
634. For further discussion of the US tax treatment of trusts, *see* section 7.2.2.

taxation may arise where one Contracting State taxes trust income at, say, the level of the trust itself or of its beneficiaries, while the other Contracting State taxes the grantor on the same income. The Technical Explanation states:

> [A] U.S. company pays interest to a U.S. complex trust ('UST') with UK beneficiaries. The UST is treated for U.K. tax purposes as a fiscally transparent entity. ... the U.K. beneficiaries claim an exemption from U.S. withholding tax with respect to that interest. However, because the United States treats the UST as a taxable entity resident in the United States ..., the saving clause ... ensures that the United States may continue to tax the trust as a U.S.-resident. Pursuant to the notes, the United Kingdom will treat the tax paid by the UST as having been paid by the U.K. beneficiaries for purposes of providing a foreign tax credit to the U.K. beneficiaries with respect to the interest income.[635]
>
> [I]f a trust is a grantor trust for U.S. tax purposes, the income of the trust is included in the income of the U.S. grantor, and the grantor is taxed on the income. However, for U.K. tax purposes the trust income may be included in the income of the beneficiaries of the trust so that the beneficiaries pay tax on the income in the U.K. *Thus each country will have a different view regarding the identity of the taxpayer* [emphasis added]. The [Exchange of Notes] provide[s] that if the person taxed by one State is the grantor of the trust and the person taxed in the other State is a beneficiary of the trust, the tax paid or accrued by the beneficiary will be treated as if it were paid or accrued by the grantor for the purposes of determining the relief from double taxation allowed by the State of which the grantor is a resident. Thus, in the case of the trust described above, the United States would provide a credit to the U.S. grantor for the U.K. tax imposed upon the U.K. beneficiaries of the trust. An exception to this special rule applies with respect to an item of income from real property ... or gain from the alienation of real property ... [In that case] the tax paid by the resident of the Contracting State in which the property is located will be treated as if it were paid by the person who is a resident of the other Contracting State.

6.4.4 The Limits of Article 1(8), Etc.

Article 1(8) is consistent with US treaty policy since the US Model Treaty abandoned the 'partial residence' approach reflected in Article 4 of the 1975 UK-US treaty. Article 1(8) avoids double taxation or unintended double non-taxation without one Contracting State's entity classification rules prevailing over those of the other. So long as the members of a 'transparent' entity resident in the non-source state are liable to tax on a current basis in respect of an item of income derived via that entity from the source state, the latter should be prepared to give treaty relief. This is subject to any other preconditions for relief in the treaty, and to the right of the source state to decide the incidence and timing of its tax charge. This is consistent with the Partnership Report, Article 1(2) of the OECD Model and the related Commentary.

Article 1(8) is similar to Article 1(2) of the OECD Model and Article 3(1) of the MLI. There is no attempt to define fully what is meant by 'fiscally transparent' for

635. Giving a UK foreign tax credit for US tax paid on the US-source interest in these circumstances is consistent with standard UK foreign tax credit policy: *see* fns 627 and 633.

Article 1(8) purposes.[636] Apparently, the US withholding tax regulations under section 894(c) Internal Revenue Code 1986 regard an entity as 'tax transparent' only if holders of interests in it must treat its underlying income as theirs regardless of distributions, and the character and source of the holders' income is determined by the original item of underlying income.[637] In fact the focus on 'fiscal transparency' is a distraction. What is important when deciding whether the source state should grant treaty relief is whether the members of the intermediate entity are liable to current taxation in respect of their shares of its income for whatever reason. That may be because the entity is regarded by a contracting state as 'fiscally transparent' in the fairly narrow sense described in the US withholding tax regulations. However, the source state should also grant treaty relief if the entity is not regarded as 'fiscally transparent' in this way, but its members are currently taxable on its income for other reasons, e.g., under a 'controlled foreign company' or 'grantor trust' regime for attributing income. In that case too, there is no unintended double non-taxation in respect of the income item. This point is not fully reflected in the 2001 treaty. However, the Exchange of Notes partly recognises it by expanding the concept of 'tax transparency' to include some UK anti-deferral rules in respect of the income and gains of UK and non-UK entities.[638]

Article 1(8) leaves unresolved other issues arising in respect of Article 4(1)(b) of the 1975 UK-US treaty. It only provides a limited 'look through' of the 'tax transparent' entity. Suppose that two UK-resident companies set up a UK partnership (in which they share 50:50) to own 100% of a US subsidiary which then pays dividends. It is not clear that Article 1(8) disregards the partnership sufficiently to enable each of the UK-resident corporate partners to claim the 5% rate of US withholding tax under Article 10(2)(a) on the basis that it is the 'beneficial owner' of shares representing at least 10% of the voting power of the US subsidiary.[639] Article 1(8) also does not resolve other issues which equally arise in relation to Article 1(2) of the OECD Model: *see* sections 6.1.6, 6.1.8, 6.1.10 and 6.1.12.

Article 1(8) does not attempt to resolve other potential entity classification conflicts elsewhere in the 2001 treaty, and especially in its distributive Articles dealing with taxing rights over particular types of income. These are discussed in section 6.8.

Article 1(8) does not alter the characterisation and quantification of income by the source state, nor the persons which it taxes and when it taxes them. The source state's rules on these issues prevail even if the other Contracting State might have characterised and/or quantified that income differently. In this respect, Article 1(8) resembles Article 1(2) of the OECD Model and Article 3(1) of the MLI.

636. The limited guidance on this topic in the Commentary on Article 1 of the OECD Model may be of some help: that part of the Commentary postdates the 2001 UK-US treaty but it also develops aspects of the Partnership Report which predates the 2001 treaty.
637. *See* Avery Jones: Partnerships *supra*, at 430.
638. *See* section 6.4.2 above.
639. At the end of Article 10(10), there is a special 'look through' rule which treats a 'pooled investment vehicle' holding a partnership interest as thereby owning directly a proportion of the partnership's interests in real property. There is nothing so explicit in Article 1(8) and it is doubtful (*see* section 5.2) whether a partner 'beneficially owns' specific items of partnership property, even if the partnership lacks legal personality.

Finally, the 2001 treaty is not affected by the MLI, to which the UK, but not the US, is a party.

6.5 THE UNIQUE APPROACH OF THE 2008 UK-FRANCE TREATY TO 'TAX TRANSPARENT' ENTITIES[640]

6.5.1 Introduction: The French Taxation of Partnerships

The UK-France double tax treaty (SI 2009/226) took effect in the UK from April 2010. It is notable for an expanded Article 4 ('Residence') which deals in particular with 'any partnership, group of persons or any other similar entity'. Both the UK and France are parties to the MLI, but this part of Article 4 is not altered by the MLI.[641]

France has historically adopted an unusual position regarding the taxation of partnerships. In particular, it regards a partnership (especially a French partnership) as a taxable person in its own right even though the partnership's tax liability on its income is collected from the partners, and each partner's liability in respect of that income is computed taking into account the personal circumstances and tax attributes of that partner (e.g., whether the partner is an individual or a company). This approach is usually described in French legal literature as treating partnerships as 'translucent' ('translucidité'). Hence under French domestic law, a non-resident partner in a French partnership will be taxable in France even if that partnership earns purely passive income and has no French 'permanent establishment'.[642] That partner is not entitled to treaty protection from French tax, unless the treaty specifically provides otherwise. To that extent, the French partnership is a taxpayer in its own right and not transparent. France equally regards French partnerships as 'resident in France' for treaty purposes. France does not accept that income 'flows through' a partnership to its partners, even though the partners are taxable on their share of the partnership's income in accordance with their personal circumstances. France reserved its position accordingly in the Partnership Report, and has usually required specific provisions in French tax

640. *See* Nicolas De Boynes and Andrew Howard: 'Treatment of Partnerships in the 2008 France-UK Tax Treaty' (2009) Tax Notes International, Volume 54, Issue 5, at 401; and John F. Avery Jones: 'The Revised UK-France Tax Treaty' (2008) Bulletin for International Taxation, Volume 62, Issue 10, 457.
641. *See* the synthesised text of the UK-France treaty published by HMRC, Multilateral Instrument and the 2008 France-UK Double Taxation Convention (publishing.service.gov.uk) (accessed 15 December 2019). France relied on Article 3(5)(a) of the MLI to disapply Article 3 to all of its tax treaties which are otherwise affected by the MLI: *see* France's instrument of ratification, etc., dated 26 September 2018 in 'Signatories and Parties to the Multilateral Convention to implement tax treaty-related measures to prevent base erosion and profit shifting' at www.oecd.org (accessed 29 June 2022).
642. *See* the decision of the Conseil d'Etat in *Re Société Kingroup Inc.* Case No. 144211 (1997/98) 1 OFLR 399. The French entity in that case was a 'groupement d'intérêt économique' (GIE), which had legal personality and received royalty income, but which was not liable to French tax in its own name. A Canadian-resident member of the GIE could not rely on the France-Canada treaty to avoid French tax on its share of the GIE profits derived from those royalties.

treaties to give effect to the Partnership Report.[643] These ideas are reflected in the 2008 treaty with the UK and in particular Article 4(5). France has not changed its stance in the light of Article 1(2) of the OECD Model and Article 3 of the MLI.

Since *Kingroup,* the Conseil d'Etat has shed further light on 'translucence'. In 1999, in *Re SA Diebold Courtage* Case No. 191191,[644] the Conseil d'Etat *was* prepared to 'look through' a 'closed' *Dutch* LP (a 'besloten commanditaire vennootschap' or CV),[645] whose partners were Dutch-resident private limited companies (besloten vennootschaps (BVs)). It relied on the fact that, while the CV itself was not liable to Dutch tax and, importantly, lacked legal personality, this was not true of its Dutch-resident corporate partners who could therefore be treated, under Article 12 of the then France-Netherlands treaty, as receiving French-source royalties earned by the CV.

This decision initially seems at odds with *Kingroup,* because the French court 'looked through' the non-French partnership. However, it related to a non-French partnership lacking legal personality, as noted by the Conseil d'Etat in its 2014 decision in *Re Artemis SA* Case No. 363556.[646] In that case, the court decided that the French 'participation exemption'[647] did not apply where a French-resident taxpaying company owned almost all of a Delaware general partnership which in turn owned more than 10% of a US corporation. In particular, the French exemption only applied to dividends paid directly to the French company from the other company. That condition was not met because the interposed general partnership had legal personality under Delaware law, unlike the CV in *Diebold.* The fact that it was 'tax transparent' in the US was irrelevant. The US-France tax treaty regarded US-source dividends as being distributed to the French partner in the Delaware partnership to the extent of its partnership share. However, this fell short of treating those dividends as paid 'directly' for the purposes of the French domestic 'participation exemption'.

In deciding whether a non-French partnership is not just 'translucent' but may be 'looked through' for French income tax purposes, it is therefore important whether it has legal personality under its governing law (whether or not it is a taxable entity under

643. In 2010, France published a proposal for reform of its tax treatment of partnerships. This was abandoned but had it been adopted, France would have regarded certain non-French partnerships 'equivalent' to French partnerships as fully 'transparent' where their French-source profits were regarded as the profits of the partners, both in the jurisdiction where the partnership was formed and in the jurisdiction where the partners were resident. Therefore, non-French-resident partners would have been able to claim treaty protection from French tax unless the partnership was carrying on business through a French 'permanent establishment'. This treatment would only have been available to partnerships established in EU Member States or in a third country with a tax treaty with France providing for comprehensive information exchange. *See* G.K. Fibbe and A.J.A Stevens eds: 'Hybrid Entities and the EU Direct Tax Directives'. Wolters Kluwer, 113 and 115.
644. (2000) 2 ITLR 365.
645. *See also* section 7.3.2.
646. 17 ITLR 582. *See* the analysis of *Diebold* at p. 600 in the 'conclusions' of the Rapporteur Public. These 'conclusions' are not part of the judgment but a detailed opinion to assist the court. In *Artemis,* the court's decision was consistent with those 'conclusions'. For a critique of *Artemis, see* Philippe Derouin: 'Régime des sociétés mères et société de personnes interposée' (13 January 2015) Revue de Droit Fiscal, No. 3. This does not consider 'translucence' in detail.
647. Articles 145 and 216 Code Général des Impôts.

non-French law).[648] This is not ideal, not least because different jurisdictions may interpret legal personality differently. Some jurisdictions (e.g., the UK) regard an entity with full legal capacity to own assets and incur rights and liabilities as therefore being a legal person. Others may not always regard full legal capacity as synonymous with legal personality. This seems to be the case for certain German and Dutch entities.[649]

'Translucence' has been analysed as follows by one Luxembourg commentator[650] as being equivalent to what counts in Luxembourg as fiscal transparency.[651] This involves in particular an entity level calculation of partnership profits, which are then divided among the partners for the purpose of taxing them. Each partner's tax liability depends on the particular rules applicable to the partner's tax circumstances.

This commentator identifies two competing schools of thought regarding the nature of 'translucence'. The first sees there as being a single tax debt of the partnership, which is then simply collected from the partners: *see* Professor Jean-Pierre Le Gall in Part I.A.3 of his General Report on the Worldwide Taxation of Partnerships for the 1995 Congress of the International Fiscal Association. This comes close to seeing the partnership as opaque, which seems to go too far. The second school sees 'translucence' as a two-stage process, whereby the tax base and the nature of the partnership's income are worked out at partnership level but where each partner is then taxable individually, by reference to its circumstances, on its share of the partnership profits ascertained at stage one. The second school of thought seems correct. This differs from the classic 'opaque' entity, which is a taxpayer in its own right in respect of its own separately computed income, and whose tax base and tax liability are unaffected by the characteristics of its members.

While this second school of thought defines 'translucence' in a manner more closely resembling what other jurisdictions (including the UK) regard as income tax 'transparency', 'translucence' still treats the partnership, obliquely, as having its own tax liability, even if this is collected from the partners and reflects each partner's personal circumstances. Hence the court in *Kingroup*[652] regarded the Canadian partner in the French GIE as being liable for French tax on its share of the entity's French-source income, even though there was no French 'permanent establishment'. The

648. *See* section 2.9.5 for the problems which arise for UK entity classification purposes, if one focuses on whether or not an entity has legal personality.
649. *See* the findings of fact regarding the Dutch VOF in the UK Court of Appeal decision in *Rowan Companies Incorporated v Lambert Eggink Offshore Transport Consultants VOF* [1998] CLC 1574. The same seems to be true of the Luxembourg 'société en commandite spéciale' which lacks legal personality under Luxembourg law but has rights and powers equivalent to legal personality, from a common law perspective.
650. Jean Schaffner: 'Droit Fiscal International'. Editions Promoculture 2005, at 582.
651. It also seems very similar to the way in which income profits of a partnership are taxed in the UK, which is regarded as a form of UK tax 'transparency', even though the tax base is first established at partnership level: *see* sections 846-858 ITTOIA. Article 8 Code Général des Impôts is regarded as codifying the 'translucency' principle, for both French and non-French partnerships: *see* 17 ITLR 582 at 593, 604.
652. (1997/8) 1 OFLR 399. For the implications of *Kingroup* when applying a tax treaty's Non-Discrimination Article to a 'translucent' partnership, *see* Mark L. Brabazon: 'Non-discrimination and Transparent Entities' Bulletin for International Taxation, Volume 76, Issue 3, at 3.1 (hereinafter, 'Brabazon: Non-discrimination').

non-French-resident, treaty-protected partner was liable for its share of what, indirectly, was the tax liability of the GIE itself.

In one limited situation France regards an entity as fully 'transparent'. This entity is a 'société immobilière de copropriété', whose role is to acquire or build property to be leased to, or otherwise used by, its members.[653] The Luxembourg commentator quoted earlier points out[654] that such entities are not taxable persons separate from their members, who are treated as owning the entity's assets directly, in proportion to their rights in the entity.[655] Hence France reserves the concept of 'transparency' for the (rare) situation where an entity is literally 'looked through' for tax purposes and where its members are treated as having a direct share in the entity's underlying assets and income, and not just in its net profit computed at entity level. The closest UK analogy to this is the capital gains tax treatment of 'bare' trusts under section 60 TCGA. This is yet another reminder that 'transparency' can mean different things in different contexts. One jurisdiction's concept of 'transparency' may be broader or narrower than that of another. Indeed a single jurisdiction may, concurrently, use different meanings of 'transparency', in different situations. This is certainly true of the UK.

The uniquely French thinking discussed above permeates the UK-France double tax treaty.

6.5.2 Article 3

Article 3(1)(e) and (f) define 'person' and 'company' in the same way as the OECD Model.

6.5.3 Article 4: General

Article 4(1) provides a definition of a 'resident of a Contracting State' which is very similar to Article 4(1) of the OECD Model. However, Article 4(4) then provides:[656]

> The term 'resident of a Contracting State' shall include where that Contracting State is France any partnership, group of persons or any other similar entity:
>
> (a) which has its place of effective management in France;
> (b) which is subject to tax in France; and
> (c) all of whose shareholders, associates or members are, pursuant to the tax laws of France, personally liable to tax therein in respect of their share of the profits of that partnership, group of persons or other similar entity.

653. Article 1655ter Code Général des Impôts.
654. Schaffner *supra,* at p. 583.
655. There is a similar analysis in the 'conclusions' of the Rapporteur Public in *Artemis: see* 17 ITLR 582 at 593-594.
656. This kind of provision exists in several French treaties, e.g., Article 4(6) of the France-Japan treaty: *see* De Boynes and Howard: *supra,* at p. 402 fn 11. *See also* Article 4(4) of the 2021 France-Belgium treaty where it is explicitly applied by paragraph 4 of the Protocol to various fiduciary structures ('patrimoines fiduciaires').

This reflects France's stated position on the 'translucence' of French partnerships and on the treatment of partnerships under double tax treaties. It is not clear what is meant by a partnership, etc., being 'subject to tax in France'. The more normal formulation 'liable to tax' is not used. The discussion above of 'translucence' suggests that Article 4(1)(b) is expressing the idea that a 'translucent' partnership has, obliquely, its own tax liability, even though this is given effect (*see* Article 4(4)(c)) as the personal tax liability of shareholders, associates or members in respect of their share of the entity's profits. Presumably Article 4(4) does not extend to a 'société immobilière de copropriété' which France regards as 'transparent', not merely 'translucent'.

While Article 4(4) requires all shareholders, etc., to be liable to French tax on their share of partnership, etc., profits, it does not require any of them to be French resident. Hence Article 4(4) would apply to the French GIE with a Canadian-resident member which featured in *Kingroup*.

Article 4(4) should also be read in the light of paragraph 3 of the Protocol where the French-resident partnership has a UK 'permanent establishment'. This is regarded as a 'permanent establishment' of each member of the partnership who is entitled to treaty benefits. Hence, in this situation, 'translucency' is replaced with full 'transparency'.[657] The same applies in the converse situation, i.e., a UK partnership with a French 'permanent establishment'. It is rare in a UK tax treaty for the 'permanent establishment' of a partnership or trust to be expressly attributed to those with an interest in the entity.[658] However, this approach makes sense: *see* section 6.1.8.

The 2008 treaty does not attempt to define 'partnership' and the English courts have had difficulties characterising entities which France would regard as partnerships.[659] The use of the phrase 'partnerships, groups of persons or any other similar entity' should go some way to ensuring that such characterisation conflicts do not cause problems applying Article 4.[660] The breadth of that phrase should limit the situations where each state finds it necessary to fall back on its domestic law to interpret the treaty, as per Article 3(2). Does this phrase covers trusts, which can now exist under French law too? Given recent pronouncements by the CJEU regarding trusts,[661] there is much to be said for applying this phrase to a trust, at least if it makes profits to which beneficiaries have a vested entitlement and it has at least two trustees.

657. This is consistent with paragraph 81 Example 12 of the Partnership Report, where the majority view was that the activities of that 'permanent establishment' should also be attributed to the partners.
658. As in many Australian treaties, there is a similar provision in the UK-Australia treaty of 2003, dealing with the 'permanent establishment' of a trust: *see* Brabazon *supra*, at p. 233. However, it does not extend to other transparent entities such as partnerships. By contrast, the 1982 US-Australia treaty extends this provision to other transparent entities, consistently with US treaty practice, reflected in the expanded meaning of 'enterprise' in Article 3(1)(c) of the 2016 US Model Treaty: *see* Brabazon: Australian Treaties *supra*, at p. 15. There is no equivalent in Article 3(1)(c) of the 2001 UK-US treaty.
659. *See Dreyfus v IRC* 14 TC 560, discussed in section 2.10.
660. The equivalent French phrase is 'toute société de personnes, groupement de personnes ou autre entité analogue'. However, paragraph 3 of the Protocol only applies to 'partnerships'.
661. *See Trustees of the P Panayi Accumulation and Maintenance Settlements v HMRC* (Case C-646/15) [2017] STC 2495. *See also* fn 656 regarding the 2021 France-Belgium treaty.

6.5.4 Article 4(5)

This contains six scenarios and sets out how the 2008 treaty should apply to each. The outcomes broadly reflect the Partnership Report. This detailed, prescriptive approach is consistent with the French reservation to that Report.

6.5.4.1 Article 4(5)(a)

> [A]n item of income, profit or gain:
>
> (i) derived from a Contracting State through a partnership, group of persons or other similar entity that is established in the other Contracting State; and
> (ii) treated as the income of beneficiaries, members or participants of that partnership, group of persons or other similar entity under the laws of that other Contracting State;
>
> shall be eligible for the benefits of the Convention that would be granted if it were directly derived by a beneficiary, member or participant of that partnership, group of persons or other similar entity who is a resident of that other Contracting State, to the extent that such beneficiaries, members or other participants are residents of that other Contracting State and satisfy any other conditions specified in the Convention, without regard to whether the income is treated as the income of such beneficiaries, members or participants under the tax laws of the first-mentioned State.

In this scenario, the source state does not recognise the transparency of the partnership 'established' in the other Contracting State, while that other state does recognise it. In practice, because France does not regard partnerships as 'transparent', this scenario will apply where the source state is France, and the partnership is 'established' in the UK. The outcome is consistent with the Partnership Report, Article 1(2) of the OECD Model and Article 3(1) of the MLI. It should not give rise to unintended double non-taxation. The source state grants treaty relief and accepts the characterisation of the entity by the other Contracting State because the partners, etc., resident in that other state are liable to tax on their share (distributed or otherwise) of the entity's income and gains.[662]

Interestingly, the words 'fiscally transparent' are not used, unlike Article 1(8) of the 2001 UK-US treaty, Article 1(2) of the OECD Model and Article 3(1) of the MLI. Article 4(5)(a)(ii) appears to apply even if the other Contracting State does not regard the partnership as 'transparent' but nevertheless taxes partners currently on its income via a CFC-type or other income attribution regime.[663]

662. The treaty in this respect underpins the practice of the French tax authorities, in Guideline 4 H-5-07 published in March 2007 following *Diebold supra*: *see* BOI-INT-DG-20-20-20-10, paragraph 110 (for dividends) and BOI-INT-DG-20-20-30, paragraph 120 (for interest and royalties). Unlike the treaty, those guidelines only apply where the French-source income is interest, dividends or royalties: *see* De Boynes and Howard: *supra*, at p. 404.
663. If that regime deems the partners to receive the actual underlying income of the partnership. This would not be so under the UK CFC regime in Part 9A TIOPA. However, it can be the case

Like the other limbs of Article 4(5), Article 4(5)(a) applies on a 'per item of income' basis.

There is also no definition of when a partnership, etc., is 'established' in a contracting state. The views of France and the UK may not coincide. One view is that it is enough for a partnership to be 'established' in a contracting state if it is formed under the law of that state.[664] However, given the relative ease with which the governing law of a partnership may be changed, this would be a weak treaty nexus with a contracting state. A better approach would be to read 'established' as connoting some level of senior management in the relevant Contracting State. This is consistent with the wider context of the treaty and with Article 4(4), which focuses on the place of 'effective management' of a partnership and not on its governing law. It appears (*see* Brabazon: Australian treaties *supra* at page 23) that the equivalent provisions of the France-Australia treaty focus on the partnership's 'effective management'.

Paragraph 3 of the Protocol permits a French 'permanent establishment' of the UK partnership to be attributed to the partners. This may limit their treaty relief under Article 4(5)(a).

Article 4(5)(a) shares some of the weaknesses of Article 1(8) of the 2001 UK-US treaty, and of Article 1(2) of the OECD Model and Article 3(1) of the MLI. It does not disregard the partnership altogether. Consequently, it is not clear that two UK-resident corporate partners, sharing 50:50 in a UK partnership owning a French company, can claim the special nil rate of French withholding tax on dividends. This applies under Article 11(1)(c) where the 'beneficial owner' of those dividends is 'a company liable to corporation tax which *holds, directly or indirectly,* [emphasis added] at least 10 per cent of the capital of the company paying the dividends'. The words 'directly or indirectly' probably save the day for the UK partners, as does the fact that Article 4(5)(a) treats income as being 'derived directly' by them. The 'directly derived' wording may also address the type of concern raised in *Artemis.*[665] In that case, the legal personality of the Delaware general partnership prevented the domestic French participation exemption from applying. If the UK partnership is an English general or limited partnership (but not a UK LLP), it will lack legal personality under English law. Therefore a French court may more readily accept, for treaty purposes, that a UK-resident corporate partner in that partnership 'holds, directly or indirectly', shares in the underlying French company.[666]

---

under the 'close company' capital gains attribution rules in sections 3-3G TCGA 1979. The reference in Article 4(5)(a) to current taxation of 'beneficiaries, members or participants' suggests that, if a trust is covered, Article 4(5)(a) cannot apply where there are no beneficiaries resident in France or the UK but instead the settlor is taxable on the trust income and is resident in France or the UK. It is hard to describe the settlor as a 'participant' for these purposes.

664. This is the view expressed in Avery Jones: 'The Revised UK-France Tax Treaty', *supra*.
665. 17 ITLR 582: *see* section 6.5.1.
666. Such an approach would resemble that in *Diebold* 2 ITLR 365, although that case did not address whether shares could be 'held' through the Dutch CV. This approach would probably not work if the partnership were a Scottish partnership, which has legal personality. *See* fn 547 regarding the (greater) scope for tracing corporate affiliation through a 'transparent' partnership when relieving double taxation on distributed profits under the EU Parent-Subsidiary Directive.

6.5.4.2 *Article 4(5)(b)*

This states that:

> An item of income, profit or gain:
>
> (i) derived from a Contracting State through a partnership, group of persons or other similar entity that is established in the other Contracting State; and
> (ii) treated as the income of that partnership, group of persons or other similar entity under the tax laws of that other Contracting State;
>
> shall be eligible for the benefits of the Convention that would be granted to a resident of that other Contracting State, without regard to whether the income is treated as the income of that partnership, group of persons or other similar entity under the tax laws of the first-mentioned State, if such partnership, group of persons or other similar entity is a resident of that other Contracting State and satisfies any other conditions specified in the Convention.

This approach reflects Example 5 in the Partnership Report. The characterisation of the partnership in the source state is ignored. Treaty relief is available in the source state for the partnership if it is taxable in the other state and regarded as resident there for treaty purposes (which it should be on the basis that it is a 'body of persons', and hence a 'person', 'established' in that state, thereby satisfying Article 4(1)).

This is a sensible answer because there is no risk of unintended double non-taxation if the source state's characterisation of the partnership is set aside in this way.

'Established' remains undefined. If the UK is the source state, a French partnership should satisfy Article 4(5)(b) because French domestic tax law treats it as 'translucent', and it should be a 'resident of France' under Article 4(4) so long as its 'place of effective management' is there. On the basis of *Kingroup,*[667] third-country partners in the French partnership should be subject to French tax on their shares of the partnership's income. This reduces the risk of the UK effectively giving treaty benefits to third-country residents via the French partnership.

What if France is the source state? Under French domestic rules on entity classification, unlimited liability of members is important when deciding that an entity is a partnership. Suppose that French-source income is paid to a UK-resident unlimited company, which is taxable as a body corporate in the UK, is not a partnership for UK tax purposes and should be a 'resident of the UK' for treaty purposes. Does this mean that it is not a 'partnership, group of persons or other similar entity' at all so that Article 4(5)(b) does not apply? If that is correct, the unlimited company can rely on all other relevant treaty protections; and, if it receives dividends on a 10% or greater shareholding in a French company, it can claim the Article 11(1)(c) nil withholding tax rate because, on UK principles, it is a 'company subject to corporation tax'. This is the ideal answer from the unlimited company's perspective, especially as the dividend income should be exempt under UK domestic law.[668] However, it is not clear which state's

---

667. *See* section 6.5.1.
668. Part 9A Chapters 2-4 CTA 2009.

definition of 'partnership' determines what 'partnership' means in Article 4(5)(b).[669] Arguably, under Article 3(2), France's should prevail because the relevant income is French source. Even if it does, nothing in the treaty prevents the unlimited company from also being a 'company' for Article 11(1)(c) purposes. The treaty definition of 'company' in Article 3(1)(f) does not carve out 'partnerships' as such, and covers a UK unlimited company.

Article 4(5)(b) does not address the situation where UK-source passive income is paid to a French partnership (regarded by the UK, if not by France, as 'transparent') whose partners are resident in a third country, which has a double tax treaty with the UK and which also regards the French partnership as 'transparent'. However, as the UK generally has no domestic withholding tax on dividends, and the 2008 treaty provides for nil withholding on interest and royalties, it is less likely that the members of the French partnership would want to invoke the treaty between the UK and the third country. It would of course be different if the third-country treaty provided better reliefs from UK tax than the UK-France treaty.[670]

6.5.4.3 Article 4(5)(c)

This provides that:

> [A]n item of income, profit or gain:
>
> (i) derived from a Contracting State through a partnership, group of persons or any other similar entity that is established in that Contracting State;
> (ii) treated as the income of the beneficiaries, members or participants of that partnership, group of persons or other similar entity under the tax laws of the other Contracting State; and
> (iii) treated as the income of that partnership, group of persons or other similar entity under the tax laws of the first-mentioned State;
>
> can be taxed under the tax laws of the first-mentioned State without any restriction.

This recognises, in particular, that France regards a partnership as a taxable person. Hence, if French-source income is paid to a French partnership, that is perceived as an entirely domestic matter which should not give rise to treaty relief in France.[671] This is so even if the other Contracting State regards the partnership as transparent, some of the partners are resident in that other state and are currently

669. The phrase 'group of persons or other similar entity' in Article 4(5)(b) seems inadequate anyway to describe an unlimited company which has full corporate personality, with a clear distinction between the rights of the entity and those of its members.
670. In that situation, the Partnership Report indicates that both the UK-France treaty and the UK-third country treaty would apply. Consequently, the source state should grant the more generous of the two relief packages under these treaties. Not all countries accept this approach because of concerns about possible duplicate claims for treaty relief. *See also* section 6.1.10.
671. There is no 'saving' clause in the UK-France treaty akin to Article 1(4) of the UK-US treaty, Article 1(3) of the OECD Model or Article 11 of the MLI. In Article 4(5)(c), the broad effect of such a 'saving' clause is replicated, but there is no equivalent of, say, Article 1(5) of the UK-US

taxable there on their shares of partnership income. The issue is one of fiscal sovereignty: France is not willing to accept the UK transparency analysis if that would render cross-border a situation which France regards as purely domestic.

A UK-resident partner in the partnership will therefore be taxed in France without restriction, even in respect of purely passive income of the partnership. This is consistent with *Kingroup.*[672] Paragraph 5 of the Protocol preserves the concurrent right of the UK to tax the UK-resident in respect of his partnership share. It also confirms that this income will be treated as having a French source for UK foreign tax credit purposes, which should ensure a credit.

The scenario can also apply in theory where UK-source income is paid to a UK entity regarded as non-'transparent' by the UK but 'transparent' by France. However, this is harder to envisage because the French concept of 'translucency' means that France may well not regard Article 4(5)(c)(ii) as being satisfied in respect of the UK entity. Article 4(5)(c)(ii) might be satisfied if, under a CFC-type regime, France treated its residents as entitled to the actual underlying income of the UK entity, which was not treated as 'transparent' in the UK. In that case, the UK tax charge would be fully preserved.

As noted elsewhere,[673] this scenario seems to be based on example 17 in the Partnership Report. However, that example presupposes an entity in the state of source which is fully non-'transparent', whereas Article 4(5)(c) envisages, if France is the state of source, a French entity which is 'translucent'. Because of this, some commentators disagree with the solution in Article 4(5)(c).[674] In particular, they regard this situation as cross-border, not purely domestic, because the French partnership pays no tax but its partners do, whether or not they are French resident. This criticism is partly justified because, under French law, the computation of the 'translucent' partnership's tax liability fully reflects the tax characteristics of the partners.[675] Furthermore, partners are taxed on their allocated share of partnership profit whether or not it is distributed. In short, French tax law does not treat the partnership as an entirely separate taxpayer from its partners. On the other hand, *Kingroup* means that the French tax liability of the non-French-resident partner arises whether or not there is a French 'permanent establishment'. Therefore, Article 4(5)(c) is consistent with the fact that 'translucency' falls short of full 'transparency'.

Again, 'established' and 'partnership' are not defined.

---

treaty, or the carve-outs in Article 11(1) of the MLI, which preserve some treaty protections for a resident taxpayer. This seems to be French treaty policy: *see* paragraph 1 of the Protocol to the 2021 France-Belgium treaty.

672. *See* section 6.5.1.
673. *See* De Boynes and Howard: *supra,* at 406.
674. *See* De Boynes and Howard: *supra,* at 406.
675. In particular, this is the case when the partner is a corporation subject to French corporate income tax, or is an individual conducting business activity who has booked his partnership share as an asset on the balance sheet of that person's enterprise: Article 238 bis K of the French Tax Code – *see* the country report on France by Anne-Sophie Coustel: 'Cahiers de Droit Fiscal International: Qualification of Taxable Entities and Treaty Protection'. Volume 99b Stu Uitgevers on behalf of International Fiscal Association 2014 335 at 336. *See also* the discussion of 'translucency' in section 6.5.1.

6.5.4.4 *Article 4(5)(d)*

This provides that:

> [A]n item of income, profit or gain:
>
> (i) derived from a Contracting State through a partnership, group of persons or other similar entity that is established in that Contracting State; and
> (ii) treated as the income of that partnership, group of persons or other similar entity under the tax laws of the other Contracting State;
>
> shall not be eligible for the benefits of the Convention.

This scenario is based on example 6 in the Partnership Report. Treaty relief should be denied in cases which otherwise trigger unintended double non-taxation, not least where income derived through a partnership, etc., 'established' in the source state is not currently liable to tax at the level of partners resident in the other state because the latter perceives it to be 'opaque'.

While the basic principle is understandable,[676] Article 4(5)(d) is excessively wide. If the partnership is a general partnership established in the UK but some or all of the partners are individuals[677] resident in France, France will in fact tax such a partner on its share of the partnership income because the partner is taxable on a worldwide basis. To that extent, there is no risk of double non-taxation,[678] yet treaty benefits may still be denied, creating possible double taxation. It is also doubtful whether France will grant the French partner relief for UK tax on the income of the UK partnership, unless the partnership has a UK permanent establishment. If it is a UK limited partnership deriving only investment income from the UK, there may be no UK permanent establishment. If there is one, paragraph 3 of the Protocol treats the French partners themselves as having that permanent establishment. Any income attributable to it will then be exempt in France.

Article 4(5)(d)(ii) does not cater well for the situation where the partnership, etc., is regarded as non-'transparent' in the other Contracting State (so that (ii) is satisfied), but nevertheless its income can be currently taxed at, say, partner level under a CFC-type regime. Where this is the case, there is again no effective double non-taxation, and treaty benefits should not be denied.

'Established' is not defined.

---

676. Apparently, before this provision was introduced, there was potential double non-taxation where a French resident was a member of a UK LLP, which was seen as a partnership for UK tax purposes but as a company in France because of its members' limited liability. Article 4(5)(d) now entitles the UK to deny treaty relief in such cases and France will give the French-resident LLP member no credit for that UK tax where there is a distribution from the LLP. To complicate matters further (!), France has apparently chosen to tax French-resident members of a UK LLP which is a law firm on the basis that the LLP is a partnership, not a company for French tax purposes: *see* De Boynes and Howard: *supra,* at p. 407.
677. Where the partners are companies subject to French corporate income tax, income from the UK partnership is not taxed under the French 'territoriality' principle.
678. *See* De Boynes and Howard: *supra,* at 407-408.

6.5.4.5 *Article 4(5)(e)*

This provides that:

> [A]n item of income, profit or gain:
>
> (i) derived from a Contracting State through a partnership, group of persons or any other similar entity that is established in a State other than the Contracting States; and
>
> (ii) treated as the income of the beneficiaries, members or participants of that partnership, group of persons or other similar entity under the tax laws of the other Contracting State *and under the tax laws of the State where the entity is established* [emphasis added];
>
> shall be eligible for the benefits of the Convention that would be granted if it were directly derived by a beneficiary, member or participant of that partnership, group of persons or other similar entity who is a resident of that other Contracting State, to the extent that such beneficiaries, members or participants are residents of that other Contracting State and satisfy any other conditions specified in the Convention, without regard to whether the income is treated as the income of such beneficiaries, members or participants under the tax laws of the first-mentioned State *provided that the State where the partnership, group of persons or other similar entity is established has concluded with the first-mentioned State an agreement containing a provision for the exchange of information with a view to the prevention of fiscal evasion* [emphasis added].

This scenario covers certain cases where the partnership, etc., is 'established' in a third country. Treaty benefits remain available in the source state so long as *both* the state of the partnership's 'establishment' *and* the other Contracting State regard the partnership as 'transparent'. There must also be an effective exchange of information agreement between the source state and the third state where the 'partnership' is 'established'. It is not clear why both the third state and the other Contracting State must regard the partnership as 'transparent'.[679] Surely the views of the third state on 'transparency' should be irrelevant? Indeed, if it is a tax haven (which is common) it may not have any views on this issue. The EU law implications of Article 4(5)(e) are discussed in section 6.7.6.5.1.

'Established' is again not defined. Similar comments to those made in relation to Article 4(5)(a) also apply. In particular, is Article 4(5)(e)(ii) satisfied if the partners, etc., are subject in the other Contracting State to a CFC-type regime in respect of the

679. The January 2009 protocol to the treaty between France and the US does not require the third state in this triangular scenario to regard the partnership as 'transparent'. Nor does Article 29(2) of the 2006 Australia-France treaty, although Article 29(2) does not apply where there are 'contrary provisions' in a treaty between Australia or France and the third country: *see* Brabazon: Australian Treaties *supra*, at pp. 24-25. Article 1(2) of the recent 2021 France-Belgium treaty is a 'transparent entity' clause modelled on Article 1(2) of the OECD Model but less broad, covering only an 'entité' but not 'arrangements'. It also makes clear that French-resident entities remain 'translucent' for treaty purposes. In the triangular scenario mentioned above, the third state must regard the entity as 'totally or partly tax-transparent' ('totalement ou partiellement transparent sur le plan fiscal') if treaty relief is to apply. It must also have an administrative assistance agreement (not just an exchange of information agreement) with the source state.

partnership income? In any case, the requirement for taxation of 'beneficiaries, members or participants' of the entity means that the current taxation of trust income in the hands of a settlor resident in France or the UK will not readily satisfy Article 4(5)(ii).

Is the effect of Article 4(5)(e) to treat partners as owning the partnership's underlying assets (e.g., in order to invoke the lower dividend withholding rate under Article 11(1)(c))? For the reasons given in section 6.5.4.1, this is arguable given the reference to granting treaty benefits as if income were 'directly derived'. These words go some way to address the concerns raised in the *Artemis* case discussed earlier.

6.5.4.6 *Article 4(5)(f)*

This provides that:

> [A]n item of income, profit or gain:
>
> (i) derived from a Contracting State through a partnership, group of persons or any other similar entity that is established in a State other than the Contracting States; and
> (ii) treated as the income of that partnership, group of persons or other similar entity under the tax laws of the other Contracting State;
>
> shall not be eligible for the benefits of the Convention.

Therefore if the partnership is 'established' in a third state, there is no treaty relief if it is not 'transparent' from the perspective of the Contracting State which is not the source state.

This scenario resembles example 7 in the Partnership Report (at paragraphs 68-69). It is a logical extension of Article 4(5)(d). As before, 'established' is not defined.

As in Article 4(5)(d), (ii) does not deal clearly with the situation where the third-country partnership, etc., is regarded as non-'transparent' in the other Contracting State but its income can still be currently taxed at partner level under an attribution regime in that other Contracting State. Where this is the case, it is not clear why source state treaty benefits should be denied.

6.5.5 Conclusion on UK-France Treaty

The 2008 UK-France treaty is a notable example of a fairly recent UK tax treaty which regulates in detail the availability of treaty relief where the two Contracting States have different views on the classification of entities and their tax 'transparency' or otherwise. The treaty reflects in particular the special position of France regarding the taxation of partnerships, which led to France's reservation in the Partnership Report and which it has maintained ever since. However, Article 4(5) is unsatisfactory in a number of respects. Specific criticisms aside, its approach to granting treaty relief at source is fairly restrictive, bearing in mind the slender distinction between the French concept of 'translucency', and what many other jurisdictions regard as 'transparency', when taxing entity income at member level. Now that the approach of the Partnership Report has been made more explicit and extended via Article 1(2) of the OECD Model and Article 3(1) of the MLI, Article 4(5) of the UK-France treaty looks even more restrictive.

Having said that, Article 4(4) of the 2013 UK treaty with Spain (SI 2013/3152) closely resembles Article 4(5) of the UK-France treaty. So French thinking on these matters has influenced at least one of France's neighbours. Unlike Article 4(5), Article 4(4) of the UK-Spain treaty refers expressly to 'trusts' as well as partnerships, groups of persons and 'any other similar entity'.

6.6 THE APPROACH OF THE 2009 UK-NETHERLANDS TAX TREATY[680] TO 'TAX TRANSPARENT' ENTITIES

6.6.1 'Person' and 'Residence'

This treaty took effect in the UK from April 2011. It defines a 'person' and a 'company' in the same way as the OECD Model.

Similarly, Article 4(1) defines a 'resident of a Contracting State' as 'any person who, under the laws of that State, is liable to tax therein by reason of his domicile, residence, place of management, place of incorporation or any other criterion of a similar nature, and also includes that State and any political subdivision or local authority thereof'.

6.6.2 Article 22

However, Article 22(2)-(4) contains provisions regarding partnerships and 'fiscally transparent' entities, no doubt reflecting the Dutch reservation in the Partnership Report about not applying the approach of that Report without explicit treaty language:[681]

> (2) Where a resident of a Contracting State is a member of a partnership established under the laws of the other Contracting State, nothing in this Convention shall prevent the first-mentioned Contracting State from taxing that resident on his share of any income, profits or gains of that partnership.
>
> (3) In the case of an item of income, profit or gain derived through a person that is fiscally transparent under the laws of either State, such item shall be considered to be derived by a resident of a State to the extent that the item is

680. SI 2009/227.

681. Apparently, less than ten of the ninety or so Dutch tax treaties have language similar to Article 22, although this also includes the Dutch treaties with the US, Japan, Germany and Belgium. The 2001 Netherlands treaty with Belgium provides the most comprehensive resolution of issues in relation to hybrid entities. It differs somewhat from Article 22: *see* Verhoog & Breuer: 'Hybrid Entity Issues in a Tax Treaty Context: OECD Approach Versus Actual Tax Treaties' *supra*; and Michael L. Molenaars: 'The Tax Significance of Legal Personality: A Dutch View' (December 2014) Tax Review, Issue 316, at 4.2. The Netherlands-Belgian treaty is also discussed in Avery Jones: Partnerships *supra*, at pp. 431-436.

treated for the purposes of the taxation law of such State as the income, profit or gain of a resident.

(4) Where, by virtue of paragraph (3) ..., an item of income, profit or gain is considered by a State to be derived by a person who is a resident of that State and the same item is considered by the other State to be derived by a person who is a resident of that other State, that paragraph shall not prevent either State from taxing the item as the income, profit or gain of the person considered by that State to have derived the item of income.

(5) The competent authority of a State may grant the benefits of the Convention to a resident of the other State with respect to an item of income, profit or gain, even though it is not treated as income, profit or gain of the resident under the laws of that other State, in cases where such income would have been exempt from tax if it had been treated as the income of that resident.

While both the UK and the Netherlands are parties to the MLI, the Netherlands has made a reservation under Article 3(5)(d) of the MLI, which preserves Article 22(2)-(5). They therefore continue to apply under Article 3(6) of the MLI, notwithstanding the general 'transparent entity' clause in Article 3(1). The Netherlands has also reserved the right not to apply to its treaties the 'saving' clause in Article 11 of the MLI.[682]

Article 22(2) reverses *Padmore* and is a standard feature of UK treaties. It does not define a 'partnership' so, 'unless the context otherwise requires', Article 3(2) presumably requires that concept to be defined by reference to the domestic law of the state which wishes to tax its resident's partnership share. As Article 22(2) upholds that state's right to tax its resident, it would be strange if the context did 'otherwise require'. There is considerable overlap anyway between Article 22(2) and the partial 'saving' clause in Article 22(4).

Article 22(3) and (4) are similar to Article 1(8) of the 2001 UK-US treaty,[683] and to Article 1(2) of the OECD Model. There is no equivalent of the Exchange of Notes in the UK-US treaty which develops Article 1(8), interprets it and clarifies how double taxation should be eliminated where each Contracting State taxes the same income in the hands of the same or a different person. Therefore, the issues already discussed in relation to the 2001 UK-US treaty are pertinent in relation to the 2008 UK-Netherlands treaty, but resolving them may be less straightforward.

The 'look through' permitted by Article 22(3) is limited. Hence it is not clear whether, if shares in a Dutch company are owned by a UK partnership whose two equal partners are UK-resident companies, those partners can claim the nil dividend withholding rate in Article 10(2)(b)(i). This would require, in particular, each corporate partner to 'control, directly or indirectly, at least 10 per cent of the voting power in the company paying the dividends'. That may not be the case under the partnership

682. *See* www.oecd.org/tax/tax treaties/ Multilateral Convention to Implement Tax Treaty Related Measures to Prevent BEPS/Signatories and Parties (MLI Positions)/the Netherlands - beps-mli -position-netherlands-instrument-deposit.pdf (oecd.org) (accessed 7 January 2020).

683. Article 22(3) is identical to Article 24(4) of the US-Netherlands treaty: *see* G.K. Fibbe and A.J.A Stevens eds: 'Hybrid Entities and the EU Direct Tax Directives'. Wolters Kluwer, 229. Article 22(3) does not address the situation where the relevant entity is not 'transparent', but its members are currently taxed on its income because of a CFC-type attribution regime.

arrangements and Article 22(3) does not disregard the 'fiscally transparent' entity altogether. Now that the UK is no longer party to the EU Parent-Subsidiary Directive, this point is more important.

Article 22(3) also does not attribute a 'permanent establishment' of that entity to its members.

There is no equivalent in the UK-Netherlands treaty of the general 'saving' clause in Article 1(4) of the UK-US treaty, or in Article 1(3) of the OECD Model and Article 11 of the MLI. However, Article 22(4) fulfils a similar function in relation to a fiscally transparent entity but without preserving for a treaty-resident even a limited number of treaty protections. This differs from Article 1(3) of the OECD Model but is similar to Article 3(3) of the MLI.

Article 22(5) is unusual in UK double tax treaties. It permits treaty relief, via the competent authority procedure, where, for example, income is derived via an entity (a 'reverse hybrid') regarded as 'transparent' in the source state but non-'transparent' in the state where the entity's members are resident. This situation would normally trigger unintended double non-taxation, and the source state would deny treaty relief.[684] However, Article 22(5) recognises that this non-taxation risk disappears if the income would have been exempt anyway in the entity member's hands, even if the entity had been 'transparent' in the state where its members are resident.[685] Article 22(5) could apply where a UK-registered tax-exempt pension fund derives Dutch dividend income via an entity which the Netherlands regards as 'transparent' but the UK does not. A similar relaxation to Article 22(5) has now been inserted in the UK domestic anti-hybrid mismatch rules in Part 6A TIOPA.[686]

The UK and the Netherlands have used the competent authority procedure to agree that certain fund vehicles should be regarded as 'transparent' for treaty purposes. An August 2010 agreement relates to the Dutch mutual account called a 'closed' FGR ('fondsen voor gemene rekening').[687] That agreement states that 'since a closed FGR is fiscally transparent, all income and gain derived by the fund from the fund assets are allocated to the investors in the closed FGR in proportion to their participations in the fund'. The agreement envisages that, in some cases and subject to safeguards against duplicate claims, the fund manager or depositary can make treaty relief claims on behalf of the investors. The Netherlands routinely seeks such agreements with its

684. Unless the entity was itself a taxable resident of the Contracting State which was not the state of source.

685. In 'Some Reflections', *supra,* at pp. 324-326, the authors note, and regret, the lack of a provision like Article 22(5) in what is now Article 1(2) of the OECD Model. They also suggest that such a provision should extend to an item of income which would not be recognised anyway in the state of an entity member's residence (e.g., a deemed dividend in the source state), even if one ignored entirely the entity. It is less clear that the Article 22(5) approach should apply in that case, which involves an income classification mismatch. The OECD Model provides that in such cases, the source state's classification should govern.

686. This relaxation applies where certain tax-exempts are members of a 'reverse hybrid' entity: *see* section 259BC(8A), 259EB(4A), 259GB(2A) and 259NDA TIOPA. The relevant tax-exempts (*see* paragraph 30A, Schedule 7AC TCGA) are certain tax-approved UK and non-UK pension funds, life assurance companies, sovereign wealth funds, charities, various widely held UK 'approved' investment funds and widely held 'exempt' unauthorised unit trusts.

687. *See* fn 589 and section 7.3.2 for the nature of a FGR.

treaty partners. Paragraph 4 of the Protocol to the 7 June 2022 UK-Luxembourg treaty (as yet unratified) envisages similar arrangements for treaty claims. This helps to address the practical problems mentioned in section 6.1.14.

An agreement dated September 2014 gives a similar result in relation to certain UK Common Investment Funds deriving income and gains from the Netherlands.[688]

6.7 FURTHER THOUGHTS AND CONCLUSION ON UK TAX TREATIES AND 'TAX TRANSPARENT' ENTITIES

6.7.1 Introduction

Unlike France and the Netherlands,[689] the UK did not register any reservations regarding the Partnership Report[690] and appears to have broadly acquiesced in that Report's conclusions and its implementation[691] by amending the Commentary on the OECD Model, rather than the Model itself.[692]

However, even before the 2017 changes to the OECD Model and the MLI, UK treaty-making suggested a greater willingness to address explicitly concerns regarding 'transparent' entities. Yet what was achieved pre-2017 often reflected the specific concerns of UK treaty partners. The 2001 UK-US treaty dealt with these issues in detail because of US policy on tax treaties and hybrid entities, reflected in the US Model and the Regulations under section 894(c) Internal Revenue Code. The current treaty with France reflects France's long-standing reservations about the 'flow through' nature of partnerships and how treaties should address these issues. The UK-Dutch treaty reflects the Dutch view that such issues can only be effectively tackled by explicit treaty language. The bespoke provisions on 'transparent' entities in the UK's treaties with the US, France and the Netherlands have not been displaced by Article 3(1) of the MLI.

688. Such Funds typically act as a pooled investment vehicle for the assets of UK-registered pension schemes or charities.

689. The Netherlands expressed doubts about whether the OECD Model could be interpreted in the way the Partnership Report suggested so as to give effect to the Report's conclusions.

690. For interpretational concerns which the UK might have had with that Report's conclusions, *see* Murray Clayson: 'OECD Partnerships Report: Reshaping Treaty Interpretation?' [2000] British Tax Review 71. This predates several UK treaties discussed above which have explicitly addressed issues dealt with in that Report. It obviously predates the 2017 OECD Model and Article 3 of the MLI.

691. *See* Clayson *supra*, at p. 71. Part 2 of the UK report in Volume 99b (2014) of the IFA Cahiers de Droit Fiscal International offers answers to a number of problem questions sent to all country reporters contributing to that volume. Those questions related to treaty entitlement where one Contracting State regards an entity as 'transparent' while another does not. Some of the answers in Part 2 of the UK Report suggest that the UK position may be out of line with the Partnership Report, emphasising the tax analysis in the source state and not that of the state of residence of the entity's members. No further explanation is given for these answers, which were not authored by HMRC. They are surprising given the lack of a UK reservation in the Partnership Report.

692. The Partnership Report proposed one change to the OECD Model: Article 23A(4) requires the state of residence to give double taxation relief by credit, not exemption, where the state of source/situs exempts income or capital from tax or reduces the rate of withholding in reliance on a treaty.

France and the Netherlands are parties to the MLI which suggests that they are not satisfied that the revised OECD Model and the MLI address their concerns in full.[693]

Despite the changes introduced by Article 1(2) of the OECD Model and Article 3(1) of the MLI, other UK treaties with major trading partners often remain relatively silent on these issues. The UK-Italy treaty of 1988[694] simply carves out from the OECD Model-style definition of 'person'[695] 'partnerships which are not treated as bodies corporate for tax purposes in either Contracting State'. It says nothing about how either state should treat residents of one state deriving income from the other state via an intermediate entity (which could also be a trust rather than a partnership). The 2010 UK treaty with Germany[696] also says very little.[697]

The UK treaties with Australia and New Zealand[698] have been amended by the MLI. In both cases, the 'transparent entity' clause in Article 3(1) has been adopted, as has the comprehensive 'saving' clause in Article 11 of the MLI. In the UK treaty with Australia, Article 11 of the MLI displaces the old Article 24 which was the usual treaty reversal of *Padmore*. The old Article 24 made clear that tax imposed in the state of residence of a partner on its share of partnership income would be treated, for double taxation relief purposes in the state of residence, as tax on income sourced in the other Contracting State. This helpful clarification has not been replicated in the post-MLI treaty. Another useful provision unaffected by the MLI is paragraph 3(b) of the Exchange of Notes. Where a trust is carrying on a business in a Contracting State through a permanent establishment, paragraph 3(b) attributes that permanent establishment to a beneficiary resident in the other Contracting State, but only where the beneficiary is directly or indirectly 'beneficially entitled' to a share of the business profits. Hence paragraph 3(b) does not operate in respect of a discretionary trust. It is a standard feature of Australian treaties but is confined to trusts. It partly clarifies one

693. The US is not a signatory to the MLI. The 2001 UK-US treaty largely mirrors Article 1(2) of the OECD Model and Article 3(1) of the MLI, while dealing more comprehensively, via the Exchange of Notes, with related issues.
694. SI 1990/2590. Although this treaty is regarded by the UK as a 'covered tax agreement' for MLI purposes, Italy has not, as at 1 September 2022, deposited its instrument of ratification, acceptance or approval of the MLI: *see* Signatories and Parties (MLI Positions) (oecd.org) (accessed 1 September 2022).
695. In Article 3(1)(d).
696. SI 2010/2975. The UK-Germany treaty is a not a 'covered tax agreement' for MLI purposes and in any case Germany has reserved against Article 3 of the MLI: *see* Signatories and Parties (MLI Positions) (oecd.org) (accessed 30 June 2022).
697. Article 21(2) ('Other Income') 'looks through' a trust or estate to its underlying income sources where the trustees or personal representatives are UK-resident and the beneficiary is German resident. This is consistent with ESC B18 (*see* section 4.3.5). Article 23(1)(e) also requires Germany to give double taxation relief by credit (not exemption) in certain cases where the two Contracting States classify items of income differently or attribute them to different persons (cf. the *Columbus Containers* case discussed in section 6.7.6.3). Hence, the conflict of classification or attribution does not lead to unintended double non-taxation.
698. SI 2003/3199 and SI 1984/365 respectively. In the UK-Australia treaty, partnerships are excluded from the meaning of 'person' unless they are Australian limited partnerships, which are typically taxable corporate entities in Australia. A non-Australian limited partnership can sometimes irrevocably elect for 'transparent' status as a 'foreign hybrid limited partnership', if it is transparent in other relevant jurisdictions and is not caught by the Australian controlled foreign company rules.

of the uncertainties surrounding Article 3(1) of the MLI and Article 1(2) of the OECD Model: *see* section 6.1.8.

Paragraphs 1(d) and (e) of the Exchange of Notes prevent the UK-Australia treaty from restricting the impact of rules which prevent 'the avoidance or evasion of taxes'. Such rules include 'controlled foreign company, transferor trust and foreign investment fund rules'. Paragraphs 1(d) and (e) only partly affect the new 'transparent entity' clause. In particular, they need not prevent an entity from being 'fiscally transparent' purely because its members are fully taxable in respect of its income under 'controlled foreign company', etc., rules. The impact of those rules is not being restricted by the 'transparent entity' clause. It may even be enhanced if applying that clause minimises source state tax which would otherwise be creditable against the entity members' tax liability.

The UK treaty with Canada[699] has been less heavily amended by the MLI, not least because Canada has reserved the right not to apply Articles 3 and 11 of the MLI to its 'covered tax agreements'.[700] The amended treaty explicitly includes 'trusts' and 'partnerships' in the definition of 'person' (and regards a trust as an entity). Article 27(3) gives each state the right to tax its residents on their share of the profits of a 'partnership, trust or controlled foreign affiliate in which that resident has an interest'. Paragraph 1 of the Interpretative Protocol requires Canada to treat as fully 'transparent' a UK LLP 'effectively managed' and tax-'transparent' in the UK, but only to the extent that the LLP's income is treated as the income of a UK-resident for UK tax purposes.[701] Nor does this obligation restrict the right of either Contracting State to tax its own residents.

A final example of an important UK treaty which has not been significantly amended by the MLI to deal with 'transparent' entities is the 1993 treaty with India,[702] as amended by a Protocol.[703] Partnerships were originally carved out of the definition of 'person', unless treated as a 'taxable unit' in India. This has changed. 'Person'[704] now 'includes an individual, a company, a body of persons and any other *entity which is treated as a taxable unit under the taxation laws in force in the respective Contracting States* [emphasis added]'. This presumably does not mean that 'a body of persons' must be a taxable unit in order to be a 'person', because Article 4(1) now reads:

> [T]he term 'resident of a Contracting State' means any person who, under the laws of that State, is liable to tax therein by reason of his domicile, residence, place of management, place of incorporation or any other criterion of a similar nature, provided, however, that:

699. SI 1980/709, as amended by various Protocols.
700. *See* Signatories and Parties (MLI Positions) (oecd.org) (accessed 30 June 2022).
701. This approach is not a total 'look through' but goes beyond that of Article 4(1)(b) of the 1975 UK-US treaty (*see* section 6.3.2) and of the Canadian courts in *TD Securities (USA) LLC v Her Majesty the Queen* (2010) 12 ITLR 783 (*see* section 6.3.1). In particular, it treats the income of the UK LLP as being the income of its UK-resident members, rather than just treating the UK LLP itself as UK treaty-resident to the extent of its UK-resident membership.
702. SI 1993/1801.
703. SI 2013/3147.
704. Article 3(1)(f).

(a) this term does not include any person who is liable to tax in that State in respect only of income from sources in that State; and
(b) *in the case of income derived or paid by a partnership, estate or trust, this term applies only to the extent that the income derived by such partnership, estate or trust is subject to tax in that State as the income of a resident, either in its hands or in the hands of its partners or beneficiaries* [emphasis added].

The wording in the revised Article 4(1)(b) is not dissimilar to the 'partial residence' approach of Article 4(1)(b) of the 1975 UK-US treaty,[705] discussed in section 6.3.2. It is also consistent with the approach of the Indian courts, although it requires income to be 'subject to tax', not just 'liable to tax'.[706] India seems more comfortable with this older approach to 'transparent' entities. While acceding to the MLI, it has chosen not to apply Article 3 to its covered tax agreements, unlike the UK.[707]

6.7.2 Other Treaty Issues on Entity Classification: The Income from Employment Article

There are further areas where the classification of entities, and their 'transparency' or otherwise, impinges on the interpretation of UK treaties. These areas remain untouched by recent UK treaties, case law, Article 1(2) of the OECD Model and Article 3(1) of the MLI. Some of these areas are discussed below. For additional commentary, *see* Brabazon: Non-discrimination *supra.*

The 'Income from Employment' Article raises a difficult entity classification issue when exempting from tax those short-stay employees resident in one Contracting State who perform work in the other state. Ordinarily, that other state ('the Work State') would have the right to tax, but this is subject to Article 15(2) of the OECD Model, whose material parts read:

> [R]emuneration derived by a resident of a Contracting State in respect of an employment exercised in the other Contracting State shall be taxable only in the first-mentioned State if:
>
> (a) the recipient is present in the other State for a period or periods not exceeding in the aggregate 183 days in any twelve month period commencing or ending in the fiscal year concerned; and
> (b) the remuneration is paid by, or on behalf of, *an employer who is not a resident of the other State* ... [emphasis added], and
> (c) the remuneration is not *borne by a permanent establishment which the employer has* [emphasis added] in the other State.

This language is the same, for example, as Article 14(2) of the UK-Netherlands treaty.

705. Article 25 of the UK-India treaty has now been removed, because both the UK and India have adopted the general 'saving' clause in Article 11 of the MLI. Article 25 restated the UK statutory reversal of *Padmore* [1989] STC 493.
706. *See* section 6.3.1 and also fn 576.
707. *See* Signatories and Parties (MLI Positions) (oecd.org) (accessed 30 June 2022).

In Article 15(2)(b), how does one determine that employer's 'residence' if the employer is a partnership which is not itself liable to tax? It cannot be a 'resident of a contracting state' within the normal Article 4 meaning so how does one apply Article 15(2)? Should one look instead at the residence of the partners and, indeed, should the partners, not the partnership, be treated as the 'employer(s)'? Treating them as the 'employer' seems problematic because the partnership is not a 'nothing'. It is a 'person' for treaty purposes. There is no authority for disregarding it in Article 15(2) nor in Article 1(2) of the OECD Model. If one assumes the partnership entity is the employer, determining its residence by reference to that of its partners also creates difficulties, especially if they are resident in more than one jurisdiction.[708] Changes in the partnership membership could mean recurring changes in the employer's residence, which would create an unstable position regarding relief under Article 15(2). Besides, what if one Contracting State regards the partnership as 'transparent' and the other does not? A compromise is needed.[709] The OECD Commentary on Article 15(2) suggests:

> While [an interpretation which focusses solely on the residence of the partners/members] could create difficulties where the partners or members reside in different States, such difficulties could be addressed through the mutual agreement procedure by determining, for example, the State in which the partners or members who own the majority of the interests in the entity or arrangement reside (i.e. the State in which the greatest part of the deduction [for employment income] will be claimed).

In an age when major international partnerships are significant employers of internationally mobile staff, it would be better if this approach could be embedded, for consistency, in Article 15(2) of the relevant treaty and the OECD Model, and not left to the mutual agreement procedure. Such partnerships often have a fluctuating group of partners resident in various jurisdictions. There may be no one state in which the holders of a majority of partnership interests reside. Hence a better approach would treat the partnership as *not* resident in the Work State, *provided that* no more than a specified percentage of interests in it (by value) are held by residents of that state. The percentage threshold should not be too low. It makes no sense to disapply Article 15(2) entirely simply because a smallish percentage of interests in the partnership are held by residents of the Work State. It would also make sense to permit that percentage threshold to be accidentally exceeded by small amounts for a grace period without

708. Although this approach is recommended in paragraphs 88-92 of the Partnership Report and the OECD Commentary on Article 15(2) of the OECD Model. The Commentary states that its approach is consistent with Article 1(2). This overlooks the different issues which Article 15(2) must address. It requires the residence of the partnership entity to be determined, in order to decide whether the Work State has the right to tax, at source, an employee of the partnership, not a member of the partnership. Article 1(2) focuses instead on whether the source state can tax income derived by a particular entity member (e.g., a member of a partnership) through that entity. It does not focus on the entity's own residence.
709. *See also* Loengard *supra*, at 60-61.

forfeiting Article 15(2) relief. Otherwise, transitory, non-tax-motivated changes of partnership members could prevent Article 15(2) from applying.[710]

Article 15(2) should also make clearer that, if the Work State alone regards the employer as being a resident taxpayer there,[711] the protection of Article 15(2) should fall away because the entity will then presumably be claiming a deduction in the Work State for the short-term employment income. This approach is consistent with Article 15(2)(b) and with the 'saving' clause in Article 1(3) of the OECD Model.

If the partnership has a 'permanent establishment' in the Work State, Article 15(2) should also fall away because Article 15(2)(c) will not be satisfied. A local tax deduction is likely to be claimed in that state for the short-term employment cost, when computing the profits of that 'permanent establishment'. If the partnership is the 'employer' but is not a taxable entity, one can argue that it cannot have a 'permanent establishment' in the Work State for Article 15(2)(c) purposes, because a 'permanent establishment' (*see* Article 5 of the OECD Model) must belong to an 'enterprise', which (*see* Article 3(c)) requires the 'carrying on of any business'. Furthermore, in Article 7 (where the 'permanent establishment' concept has greatest significance), that 'enterprise' must be carried on by a 'resident of a contracting state' (*see* Article 3(d)). The non-taxable partnership is not such a 'resident'.

However, unlike Article 7, Article 15(2)(c) strictly does not require the 'permanent establishment' to be owned by a 'resident of a contracting state' but merely by the 'employer'. Therefore, if employment costs are attributed to ('borne by') the partnership's 'permanent establishment' in the Work State, Article 15(2) should not provide relief because Article 15(2)(c) is not satisfied.

6.7.3 Other Treaty Issues Regarding Entity Classification: The Capital Gains Article

The Capital Gains Article raises entity classification issues. It typically preserves the taxing rights of the Contracting State in which immovable property is situated, whether

710. Germany has added an observation to the OECD Commentary regarding Article 15(2). It considers that a partnership, and not the partners, should be regarded as an 'employer' for these purposes, even if it is not a taxable entity. The partnership's 'residence' would be determined hypothetically as if it were liable to tax on the basis of Article 4 of the OECD Model. This approach does not work well if the partnership is 'transparent' and a significant percentage of the partnership interests are held by residents of the Work State, even if the partnership is not 'resident' in that state using the German approach. For further discussion of Article 15(2) and, in particular, criticism of the German approach, *see* Frank P.G Pötgens, – 'Income from International Private Employment', Books IBFD, Chapter VII sections 3.5.3, 4.3.2.1 and 4.3.3.2 (accessed 1 July 2020). Germany's approach has been reflected in some of its treaties, even though it is hard to justify on the wording of Article 15(2). Until 2014, Germany also made a more radical reservation on Article 4 of the OECD Model. This stated that a 'transparent' partnership should generally be treated as a 'resident' of the Contracting State where its actual management is located. This went beyond a definition of 'residence' for the limited purposes of Article 15(2) and was reflected in the old 1959 Netherlands-Germany treaty.
711. Even if the other Contracting State perceives it to be 'transparent' and so incapable of being resident there.

that property is alienated directly, or indirectly by disposing of interests in an intermediate property-owning entity. Entity classification issues arise in relation to such indirect disposals.

The relevant paragraph of Article 13 (Capital Gains) of the OECD Model reads:

> Gains derived by a resident of a Contracting State from the alienation of *shares or comparable interests* [emphasis added], such as interests in a partnership or trust, may be taxed in the other Contracting State if, at any time during the 365 days preceding the alienation, those shares or comparable interests derived more than 50 per cent of their value directly or indirectly from immovable property, as defined in Article 6, situated in that other State.

This is more or less mirrored in Article 13(2) of the 7 June 2022 UK-Luxembourg treaty, which has yet to be ratified. However, as the OECD Commentary on Article 13(4) anticipates, specific treaties introduce refinements, for example, by broadening or narrowing the scope of the Capital Gains Article. So Article 14(2) of the UK-France treaty reads:

> Gains derived from the alienation of:
>
> (a) shares, other than those regularly traded on an approved Stock Exchange, or rights deriving their value or the greater part of their value directly or indirectly from immovable property … . situated in a Contracting State; or
>
> (b) an interest in a partnership or trust the assets of which consist principally of immovable property … situated in a Contracting State, or of shares or rights referred to in subparagraph (a) of this paragraph;
>
> may be taxed in the State in which the immovable property is situated.

The reference to 'shares' in Article 14(2)(a) implies that subparagraph (a) is directed at interests in a 'company', especially given the wording of Article 14(2)(b). The company, partnership or trust need not be established in a contracting state. However, the underlying immovable property must be situated in such a state.

Only the first limb of Article 14(2) excludes stock exchange-traded members' rights. Therefore, much depends in the UK-France treaty on whether gains arise from 'shares' or from 'an interest in a partnership or trust'.[712] Article 13 of the OECD Model avoids these classification issues by treating 'shares or comparable interests' in the

712. There is an equivalent issue in the UK rules for taxing capital gains of non-UK-residents disposing of interests in UK real property. This issue arises independently of any UK treaty. A partnership is 'transparent' for UK capital gains tax purposes under sections 59-59A TCGA (*see* Appendix A) and a 'bare' trust is usually 'transparent' under section 60 TCGA (*see* section 4.3.2). Hence a disposal of an interest in a partnership or 'bare' trust by a non-UK-resident typically equates to a pro rata disposal of underlying real estate within that partnership or trust. It is different where an interest in a 'company' holding UK real estate is disposed of by a non-UK-resident, who will only be taxable if at least 75% of the value of that interest derives directly or indirectly from UK land. Furthermore, if the 'company' is not a collective investment fund, the non-UK-resident must have had at least a 25% voting entitlement or economic equity interest in that 'company' within the two years leading up to the disposal. For further detail, *see* sections 1A, 1C, 1D, 2B and Schedule 1A TCGA. There is therefore an incentive for non-UK-residents to avoid UK tax on capital gains by holding interests in UK real property through 'companies' (as defined for UK tax purposes) and not through partnerships or 'bare' trusts.

same way. This is sensible, not least because there is often little real commercial difference between a company and a limited partnership.

Article 14(2) focuses on preserving the taxing rights of the state in which the immovable property is situated. It is consistent with that focus for that state to have the last word on whether the rights disposed of are 'shares' or 'interests in a partnership or trust',[713] even if its view differs from the state where the alienator of those shares or interests is resident. However, this point could be made more explicit.

6.7.4 Other Treaty Issues on Entity Classification: The Directors' Fees Article

Similar points to those in section 6.7.4 arise in relation to the Directors' Fees Article. Article 15 of the OECD Model reads:

> Directors' fees and other similar payments derived by a resident of a Contracting State in his capacity as a member of the board of directors of a company which is a resident of the other Contracting State may be taxed in that other State.

Article 16 of the UK-France treaty is identical.

This article also preserves the taxing rights of the source state. The relevant concepts ('company' and 'a resident of the other Contracting State') are defined in the treaty itself. Hence it should be easier to identify whether the entity in question is a 'company' resident in the other Contracting State without needing to resolve a classification conflict between the treaty partners. The reference to membership of the 'board of directors' also suggests that entities of a non-corporate nature are not covered by this article.

If a corporate entity is 'transparent' in the state where it is established, e.g., a EEIG (*see* section 2.7), then it will not be a 'resident of the other Contracting State' as per Article 4 of the OECD Model. Prima facie, that displaces the Article 15 taxing rights of the source state. It has, however, been argued that the source state should tax the management fees if the corporate entity has enough connecting factors with that jurisdiction to be resident there (setting aside the fact that it is not a taxable entity).[714] This is questionable. If the entity is 'transparent' (e.g., a UK LLP), fees paid to its management are better dealt with under the 'Business Profits' Article because they are effectively distributions of profits which have usually already been taxed.

6.7.5 Other Treaty Issues: Some Further Comments Regarding Trusts

Much of this chapter has focused on 'transparent' entities which are partnerships. However, treaties impact on other potentially 'transparent' arrangements and in particular, trusts.[715] Depending on the nature of their beneficial interests, trusts may

713. This seems consistent with the Partnership Report. This issue should not arise under Article 13 of the OECD Model.
714. *See* the General Report in Volume 99b Cahiers de Droit Fiscal International *supra*.
715. For an extended discussion, *see* Brabazon *supra*, at Chapter 8.

not be entirely 'transparent', e.g., where part of the trust income is held for a fully vested income beneficiary, but the rest is held on discretionary and accumulation trusts, where no appointment of income has yet been made.

The treatment of trusts has already been discussed in relation to Article 4(1) of the OECD Model (*see* section 6.3) and Article 1(8) of the 2001 UK-US treaty (*see* section 6.4). The UK-US treaty makes clear that a trust is a 'person'. That 'person' can be 'resident' in a contracting state because there are situations where trustees can be liable to tax by reason of domicile, residence, place of management, etc. Of course, to the extent that a trust is 'transparent', the beneficiaries may be able to claim treaty benefits directly in respect of underlying trust income by relying on Article 1(8).[716] Article 1(8) will not prevent a contracting state taxing a trust which it regards as a resident of that state: *see* Article 1(4). This creates a risk of double taxation, at both trust and beneficiary levels. The UK-US treaty approach is now reflected in Article 1(2) and (3) of the OECD Model, and increasingly reflected in other UK tax treaties, mainly via Articles 3 and 11 of the MLI.

There is limited focus on trusts in those other UK treaties whose 'bespoke' provisions on 'transparent' entities are unaffected by the MLI. It is not entirely clear whether 'partnerships, groups of persons or any other similar entity' in Article 4(5) of the UK-France treaty covers trusts, although it should do so if a trust has more than one trustee: *see* section 6.5.3. Article 4(4) of the UK-Spain treaty covers the point expressly.

Article 22(3) of the UK-Netherlands treaty (*see* section 6.6) focuses on 'a person that is fiscally transparent'. This more closely resembles Article 1(8) of the UK-US treaty, Article 1(2) of the OECD Model and Article 3(1) of the MLI. It may not cover all trusts,[717] such as an accumulation or discretionary trust where income has not been appointed to a beneficiary or (?) a life interest trust where the beneficiary's income entitlement lacks the same character as the underlying trust income.

Article 4(1)(b) of the UK-India treaty treats a trust as a 'resident' of a contracting state if the relevant income is taxable in the hands of the trust itself or its beneficiaries resident in the relevant Contracting State. As discussed in section 6.7.1, this is similar to the 'partial residence' approach of the 1980 UK-US treaty (*see* section 6.3.2). India has not adopted Article 1(2) of the OECD Model or Article 3(1) of the MLI. Indian trust

716. Is a trust with a vested income beneficiary 'transparent' for these purposes if its governing law makes it subject to the rule in *Garland v Archer-Shee* 15 TC 693. Suppose the non-UK-resident income beneficiary of a trust seeks to rely on the equivalent of Article 1(2) of the OECD Model in the treaty between that person's home state and the UK (where the underlying trust income is sourced). Suppose also that the trust's governing law (which is respected in the beneficiary's home state) treats the beneficiary as having no right to underlying income as it arises but only a right to have the trust performed, so as to make net trust income available for the beneficiary. The UK may well take the position (*see* fn 722) that the trust is not 'transparent' for treaty purposes because the governing law treats the beneficiary as having an income source which is not the same as the underlying trust income. This is similar to arguing (*see* section 6.1.3) that a member of an entity who is taxable in respect of its income under 'controlled foreign company' legislation cannot invoke the equivalent of Article 1(2) if that legislation does not directly tax the entity's underlying income but only a notional amount computed by reference to that income. That argument seems weak: *see* section 6.4.2.

717. *See* also the discussion of Article 1(2) in section 5.2 and fn 716.

law apparently follows the rule in *Garland v Archer-Shee*: *see* section 4.3.3.2. Presumably, India will argue that while an Indian-resident income beneficiary of an Indian trust is not taxable on the underlying trust income as it arises, any Indian-resident trustees will be entitled to that income and taxable on it. Therefore, Article 4(1)(b) of the UK-India treaty will be satisfied if there are Indian-resident trustees.

None of these treaties addresses whether trustees can be 'beneficial owners' of income for treaty purposes (and especially for the purposes of Articles 10, 11 and 12 of the OECD Model).[718] On a narrow common law reading of 'beneficial ownership', trustees cannot have 'beneficial ownership'. However, this concept is not intended to bear the common law meaning but an 'international fiscal meaning'.[719] The better view is now that a trustee can be a 'beneficial owner' for treaty purposes where it is 'liable to tax' on trust income in more than a 'purely representative' capacity (*see* section 6.3) and the trust is a discretionary and accumulation trust.[720] Where the trust is a pure discretionary trust (i.e., the trustees must distribute all income within the beneficiary class), it is harder to see how the trustees have 'beneficial ownership', given their fiduciary obligation to pass on all trust income,[721] although a discretionary trust without powers of accumulation is unlikely in practice.

Where the trust is a discretionary and accumulation trust, what if the trust claims treaty relief on its income on the basis that it is a 'resident' and 'beneficial owner' but then makes a distribution enabling the relevant beneficiary to recover tax paid by the trustees on the income underlying that distribution? This can arise where non-UK-source income is distributed by UK-resident discretionary trustees to a non-UK-resident beneficiary: *see* section 4.3.5. Surely the jurisdiction in which the underlying income is sourced should be able to restrict, or at least delay, the UK trustees from claiming treaty

718. Increasingly, the 'Other Income' Article in UK treaties also includes the 'beneficial ownership' condition.
719. This is the view of HMRC, and is likely to be the UK courts' view following *Indofood International Finance Ltd v JP Morgan Chase Bank NA* [2006] STC 1195. It better respects the use, in the French version of the OECD Model, of the term 'bénéficiaire effectif', rather than 'beneficial owner'. The French and English versions have equal weight and the OECD Model is of course intended to apply in civil law jurisdictions.
720. *See also* Prebble: 'Accumulation Trusts and Double Tax Conventions' *supra*. Prebble (whose article predates *Indofood*) notes that New Zealand has, in several treaties, made clear that dividends, interests and royalties on which a trustee is taxable should be treated as beneficially owned by that trustee, although New Zealand may have inserted this language to resolve doubt: *see* Avery Jones: Trusts *supra*, at p. 391. There is an equivalent New Zealand reservation to Article 3 of the OECD Model. *See also* Brabazon *supra*, at pp. 236-240.
721. There may be a difference here between private trusts and trust-based collective investment schemes. HMRC have in the past accepted that a Massachusetts business trust (a form of regulated US collective investment fund) can be the 'beneficial owner' of UK-source dividend income for treaty purposes, even though the US rules on 'regulated investment companies' effectively require the US entity to distribute most of its income to investors on a current-year basis in order to minimise entity level US taxation. This is consistent with more recent OECD statements regarding whether widely held and regulated investment funds 'beneficially own' their income: *see* Merten I *supra*, at 78 and 81. The HMRC International Manual indicates, at INTM339550 (accessed 1 July 2022), that HMRC are more relaxed about treaty claims by the trustees of a non-UK discretionary trust if all the beneficiaries are resident in the same country as the trustees, and the settlor cannot benefit from the trust. In that case, no 'treaty shopping' concern arises and the conclusion that there is no 'beneficial owner' is avoided.

benefits, where that income can effectively pass tax-free to a third-country resident because of the way in which the UK limits tax on subsequent trust distributions?

If the charge on the trustee is purely 'representative', then the 'beneficial ownership' question should be addressed at the level of the beneficiary.[722]

Of course, if a trustee or beneficiary has entered into other arrangements (apart from the trust) which make it an agent, nominee or other conduit in respect of income, then it will lack 'beneficial ownership' for treaty purposes. However, that has nothing to do with the trust itself.

6.7.6 EU Law and Entity Classification Issues

6.7.6.1 EU Law

Despite the UK having left the EU at the end of 2020, no discussion of entity classification and 'tax transparency' would be complete without considering the impact of EU law and in particular, the case law of the CJEU regarding the four 'fundamental freedoms': the freedom of establishment, the freedom to provide services, the free movement of workers and the free movement of capital.[723]

This discussion may also be relevant to Irish tax law whose approach to entity classification overlaps with the UK approach.

6.7.6.2 Lack of Harmonisation Regarding Entity Classification, Etc.

EU law has not imposed on Member States uniform criteria for classifying entities for direct tax purposes. Nor has it sought to dictate when and how specific entities should

722. In the International Manual at INTM339540 (accessed 1 July 2022), HMRC confirm this approach where a treaty claim is made in respect of a trust subject to the rule in *Baker v Archer-Shee*. However, where the governing law of a trust is such that *Garland v Archer-Shee* applies, the trustees are treated as beneficial owners of the trust income because HMRC consider that the beneficiary's right to income from the trust is against the trustees, rather than in the underlying trust assets. This HMRC statement about 'beneficial ownership' is not strictly correct. Even under a *Garland* trust (*see* section 4.3.3.2), the trustees have an absolute obligation to pay net trust income to, or for the benefit of, the vested income beneficiary. That is hard to equate with the trustees being 'beneficial owners' of that income. This HMRC statement is effectively concessionary. They already regard (*see* section 6.3.1) the trustees of a *Garland* trust as 'resident' for treaty purposes, because they are not taxed in a purely 'representative' capacity. If HMRC then refused to treat such trustees (rather than the beneficiary) as 'beneficial owners', neither the trustees nor the beneficiary could claim treaty relief from UK tax at source.

723. *See* Articles 45-66 Treaty on the Functioning of the European Union ('TFEU'). The EU state aid rules in Articles 107-108 TFEU have also been considered in relation to a tax-advantaged structure relying, at least in part, on a 'transparent' entity (a EEIG): *see* the General Court in *European Commission v Kingdom of Spain, Lico Leasing SA and others* (Case C-128/16 P). State aid is not considered further in this work, although a Member State's rules on entity classification and 'transparency' may have state aid implications: *see* Mart Van Hulten and Ton Stevens: 'Is the Symmetrical Classification Method EU Proof?' (forthcoming article in EC Tax Review) (hereinafter 'Symmetrical Classification').

be treated as 'transparent' or not for tax purposes.[724] These are matters left to the domestic tax law of Member States.

However, several Directives regulate certain consequences of entities being treated as 'transparent' in a Member State. This is true of the Parent-Subsidiary Directive,[725] the Mergers, etc Directive[726] and the Anti-Tax Avoidance Directive.[727] As already noted,[728] the Parent-Subsidiary Directive and the Mergers, etc Directive seem to assume that 'fiscal transparency' is driven by an entity's legal characteristics. This is not always so, because it may depend on whether an election has been made.[729]

Article 9a of the Anti-Tax Avoidance Directive imposes a rule to avoid mismatches arising in respect of a 'reverse hybrid' entity within the EU. Article 9a can require a Member State to treat that entity as non-'transparent'. It departs from the general approach of that Directive which neutralises double non-taxation risk from an entity classification mismatch, but does not generally require Member States to treat an entity as 'transparent' or not. Article 9a applies, in particular, where one or more 'associated' non-resident 'entities' hold(s) in aggregate, directly or indirectly, at least 50% of the voting rights, capital interests or profit-distribution rights in a 'hybrid

724. Leaving aside EEIGs (*see* section 2.7) and Article 9a of the Anti-Tax Avoidance Directive (discussed below).
725. 2011/96/EU as amended.
726. 2009/133/EC as amended.
727. 2016/1164/EU, as amended by 2017/952/EU.
728. *See* fn 155.
729. A wider EU law question arises, especially in relation to Articles 9-9b of the Anti-Tax Avoidance Directive. These counteract mismatches arising from an entity being classified differently in separate jurisdictions or from it being dual-resident. They apply if certain objective conditions are met, including certain affiliation tests. Do these Articles restrict the four freedoms (in particular the freedom of establishment and the free movement of capital) without justification and disproportionately? This Directive was enacted under the procedure in Article 115 of the TFEU. The TFEU contains the 'four freedoms' and is the highest source of EU law. A Directive must in principle respect the 'four freedoms': *see* Advocate-General Alber in paragraph 58 of his opinion in *Bosal Holding BV v Staatssecretaris van Financien* Case C-168/01 [2003] ECR I-9409. The CJEU has in the past defined narrowly the grounds on which a Member State can invoke tax avoidance to justify restricting the 'four freedoms': *see Cadbury Schweppes Overseas Ltd and Cadbury Schweppes plc v HMRC* C-196/04 [2006] STC 1908, which requires the relevant arrangement to be 'wholly artificial'. It is not clear that Articles 9-9b of the Anti-Tax Avoidance Directive fully respect this CJEU reasoning, although in a 2019 case regarding free movement of capital, the CJEU seemed willing to admit tax avoidance as a justification in a wider range of cases: *see X GmbH v Finanzamt Stuttgart – Körperschaften* Case C-135/17. It would be surprising if the CJEU significantly limited the Anti-Tax Avoidance Directive. It is aware of that Directive and seems to regard curbing double non-taxation (e.g., double deduction of losses) as a justification for restricting the four freedoms: *see NN A/S v Skatteministeriet* Case C-28/17 and the UK Upper Tribunal in *HMRC v Volkerrail Plant Ltd and others* [2022] UKUT 78 (TCC). The tensions between *Cadbury Schweppes* and the Anti-Tax Avoidance Directive are discussed in Christiana HJI Panayi: 'Cadbury Schweppes and Cadbury Schweppes Overseas (2006): CFC Rules under EU Tax Law'. Chapter 19. Landmark Cases in Revenue Law: eds John Snape and Dominic de Cogan. Hart Publishing 2019. *See also* Alexander Rust: 'BEPS Action 2: 2014 Deliverable – Neutralising the Effects of Hybrid Mismatch Arrangements and its Compatibility with the Non-discrimination Provisions in Tax Treaties and the Treaty on the Functioning of the European Union' [2015] British Tax Review 308.

entity'[730] which is incorporated or 'established' in a Member State. If any of those 'associated' holders are 'located' in a jurisdiction(s) which regard(s) the 'hybrid entity' as a taxable person in its own right, the Member State in which that entity is incorporated, etc., must tax it as a resident of that state, to the extent that its income is not already being taxed either in that state or any other jurisdiction. Therefore Article 9a should not apply if a payment to the 'reverse hybrid' cannot be deducted by the payer. Furthermore, Article 9a should arguably not apply where the income of the 'reverse hybrid' is being taxed under an income attribution regime such as 'controlled foreign company' legislation. The aim of Article 9a is that the entity's income does not escape taxation at either entity level (because it would otherwise be 'transparent') or at member level (because the entity is opaque in the members' home jurisdictions, so they are not taxed on its undistributed income).[731]

Whether entities are 'fiscally transparent' is also addressed in the October 2016 draft Directives on a Common Corporate Tax Base (CCTB) and a Common Consolidated Corporate Tax Base (CCCTB). Both deal with tax mismatches arising from entity classification differences between jurisdictions, but do not impose uniform entity classification rules nor uniform criteria for deciding whether an entity is 'transparent'. Article 62(1) of the CCTB states that where an 'entity' (undefined) is treated as 'transparent' in the Member State where it is 'established', a taxpayer holding an interest in it must include in its tax base its share of that entity's income. Article 62(2) treats transactions between such a taxpayer and that entity as, effectively, transactions between the taxpayer and third-party owners of that entity. 'Transparent' and 'established' are not defined. Article 63 then provides that whether a non-EU 'entity' is 'transparent' must be determined according to the law of the Member State of the taxpayer subject to CCTB.

Under Article 27 of the CCCTB, the classification of a non-EU entity in which at least two group members hold an interest is to be agreed between the relevant Member

730. A 'hybrid entity' is an entity or arrangement treated as taxable in one jurisdiction but whose income or expenditure is treated as that of one or more other persons (i.e., it is 'transparent') in another jurisdiction.

731. There is a carve-out for widely owned, regulated 'collective investment vehicles' which hold a diversified portfolio of securities (but not real estate assets). This exclusion does not cover all collective investment vehicles. Article 9a can be a particular problem for those with minority interests in the relevant entity. Their tax treatment may alter adversely if Article 9a makes the entity non-'transparent' because of a change, which the minority investor cannot control, in the other holders of interests in that entity. To alleviate such problems in its anti-hybrid-mismatch rules in Part 6A TIOPA, the UK now disregards, with safeguards, minority interests which do not comprise equity (e.g., a commercial loan) or which comprise an equity interest of no more than 5%. A less-than-10% interest in a CIS or Alternative Investment Fund (AIF) will also be ignored for these purposes if the CIS or AIF is 'transparent' within *Baker v Archer-Shee.* For details, *see* Part 6A Chapter 13A and Matthew Mortimer and Kirsten Hunt: 'UK Loan Structures: Changes to the Anti-hybrid Rules' (26 November 2021) Tax Journal, 11 at 12-13. Luxembourg has adopted a similar relaxation when applying Article 9a.

By changing the tax classification of an entity because of a change in the holders of interests in it, Article 9a may also give rise to discrimination issues, under EU law or a double tax treaty: *see* Leopoldo Parada: 'Hybrid Entity Mismatches and the International Trend of Matching Tax Outcomes: A Critical Approach' (2018) Intertax, Volume 46, Issue 12, 971 at 991 (hereinafter 'Parada: Hybrid Entity Mismatches').

States. Classification is to be decided by the so-called principal tax authority if there is no agreement. Article 31 then provides how income of a 'transparent' entity is to be apportioned to a member of the group which (for CCCTB purposes) holds an interest in it.

In 2021, the EU Commission announced that it planned to withdraw the CCCTB and replace it by 2023 with a (seemingly similar) corporate tax rulebook called 'Business in Europe: Framework for Income Taxation'. Full details are awaited.

Last but not least, special allocation rules apply to 'flow-through entities' in the December 2021 draft Directive on ensuring a global minimum level of taxation for multinational and other groups in the EU ('the Pillar II Directive'). Article 3(9) defines a 'flow-through entity' as:

> [A]n entity [i.e., any legal person or legal arrangement that prepares separate financial accounts] that is considered as a fiscally transparent entity with respect to its income, expenditure, profit or loss in the jurisdiction where it was created and which is not tax resident and subject to a covered tax on its income or profit in another jurisdiction.
>
> For the purposes of this definition, a fiscally transparent entity means an entity whose income, expenditure, profit or loss is treated by the laws of a jurisdiction in the same manner as if it were derived or incurred directly by the owner of that entity.

This definition of 'fiscally transparent' does not require a full disregard of the entity in question.

A 'hybrid entity' is defined in Article 23(4) as an entity treated as a separate person for income tax purposes in the jurisdiction where it is 'located' but as 'fiscally transparent' (*see* above) in the jurisdiction in which its owner is 'located'.

6.7.6.3 CJEU Decisions Relating to Entity Classification, Transparency and 'Hybrid Mismatches'

The CJEU has considered in detail an entity classification mismatch in *Columbus Container Services BVBA & Co v Finanzamt Bielefeld-Innenstadt* (Case C-298/05) [2008] STC 2554. This involved a Belgian limited partnership taxable as a separate entity in Belgium, but at a low rate because it carried on business as a so-called co-ordination centre. The interests in the Belgian entity were held directly or indirectly by German-resident members of a family. Under the then Belgium-Germany treaty, there was a German exemption for income of a German resident (in this case, its share of partnership profits) which were derived and taxed in Belgium. This exemption caused effective double non-taxation because of the very low rate of Belgian tax. Therefore Germany unilaterally overrode the treaty so that it only granted the German-resident partners a credit for the (low) Belgian tax on their partnership profits. This produced a German tax outcome similar to the outcome where a German resident had a share in a low-taxed 'controlled foreign company'. The German override was challenged as an unjustifiable restriction on the German partners' freedom to establish in Belgium and as an unjustifiable restriction on the free movement of capital.

Advocate-General Mengozzi stressed that the entity classification mismatch between Germany and Belgium was not an issue in and of itself: Member States were not required to recognise for their own tax purposes the legal and tax status conferred by other Member States on entities carrying on business in those other states.[732] However, he considered[733] that the German override restricted the 'freedom of establishment' of a German resident and could only be upheld if the underlying arrangements satisfied the 'wholly artificial' standard required to justify restricting 'freedom of establishment' because of tax avoidance. The Advocate-General referred to *Cadbury Schweppes*[734] and was unpersuaded that this standard could be met. A particular concern was that the German override applied only to the extent that the Belgian partnership's income was low-taxed passive income. Because the override was targeted in this way, the case was not one where an unfavourable outcome arose simply because the tax legislation of two sovereign Member States was different.

The CJEU also had no concern with the underlying entity classification mismatch. This simply reflected differences between the entity classification rules of two sovereign Member States. However, the CJEU did not adopt[735] the Advocate-General's position on the four freedoms. The German override did not restrict those freedoms. All that mattered was that profits of a German resident from a non-German partnership were being taxed no less favourably than profits of a German resident from a ('transparent') German partnership. That condition was met. It was irrelevant that Germany would not have taxed in the same way an investment by a German resident in an entity which (by German standards) was not 'transparent' (e.g., a Belgian company). Member States were free to decide how to tax different types of foreign 'establishment' (including subsidiaries or branches) set up by their residents provided that they were taxed no less favourably than equivalent domestic 'establishments'.

The CJEU stressed[736] that there was limited EU harmonisation regarding methods of eliminating double taxation, e.g., the Parent-Subsidiary Directive 2011/96/EU and the 1990 Arbitration Convention (the latter now superseded by the Directive on Tax Dispute Resolution Mechanisms in the European Union 2017/1852/EU). Otherwise, Member States were free to conclude bilateral double tax treaties. Generally, the CJEU

732. *See* [2008] STC 2554 at p. 2563. The CJEU has also refused to apply the EU 'abuse of law' doctrine to a deliberately created VAT mismatch: *see HMRC v RBS Deutschland Holdings GmbH* (Case C-277/09) [2010] ECR I-13805. This VAT mismatch did not exploit entity classification differences but, rather, differences in the way in which the UK and Germany had transposed into domestic law the Sixth Council Directive 77/388/EEC of 17 May 1977 (in particular, Article 5 on 'place of supply'). The CJEU focused on the fact that lessor and lessee were unaffiliated and that the transaction, even though structured to be tax-efficient, was not 'an artificial arrangement that does not reflect economic reality and the sole aim of which is to obtain a tax advantage'. This conclusion seems generous.
733. *See* [2008] STC 2554 at 2573-2585.
734. [2006] STC 1908.
735. *See* [2008] STC 2554 at 2590-2593. This has prompted one commentator to propose an EU Directive on Mutual Recognition of Entities within the EU. This would require mutual recognition, within the EU, of the classification of an entity in its 'host' country: *see* Parada: Hybrid Entity Mismatches *supra*, at p. 992, fn 136.
736. *See* [2008] STC 2554 at 2591.

had no jurisdiction to interpret those treaties or to rule on whether Member States had infringed their terms (e.g., by treaty override).[737]

6.7.6.4 *Other Issues Regarding the Four Freedoms and Bilateral Double Tax Treaties*

The CJEU has considered other issues regarding the impact of the four freedoms on bilateral tax treaties between Member States. Of particular importance is *D v Inspecteur van de Belastingdienst/Particulieren/Ondernemingen buitenland te Heerlen*[738] which established that the EU freedoms do not prevent Member States from entering into bilateral tax treaties allocating tax jurisdiction on the basis of nationality and residence. Such treaties are a legitimate method of achieving a balanced allocation of taxing power between states.[739] Because such treaties create an overall balance of rights and obligations between the two states in relation to their residents, those rights cannot be

737. The CJEU has taken into account the OECD Model and Commentary when interpreting the Interest and Royalties Directive 2003/49/EC and the Parent-Subsidiary Directive 2011/96/EC. Generally, the CJEU regards the four freedoms as not affecting how Member States relieve double taxation on their residents provided that they tax cross-border situations no less favourably than purely domestic situations, which was the case in *Columbus*. Whether such double taxation is relieved in whole or in part will then depend on the interaction between the separate domestic taxing rules of the relevant Member States. A disparity between the rules of two sovereign Member States may lead to unrelieved double taxation. For example, in *Kerckhaert and Morres v Belgian State* (Case C-513/04) [2007] STC 1349, the CJEU did not object to Belgian taxation of its residents in respect of *all* dividends at a (lower) flat rate, with (usually) no credit for any non-Belgian tax on cross-border dividends. This approach led to unrelieved double taxation but was confirmed in *Damseaux v Belgium* (Case C-128/08) [2009] STC 2689, even though Belgium had overridden its own treaty-based obligation to give a foreign tax credit. The approach was also confirmed in 2009 in *Margarete Block v Finanzamt Kaufbeuren* (Case C-67/08) and in *Daniel Levy, Carine Sebbag v Etat Belge* (Case C-540/11), where it was held that there was no duty of EU loyalty to give double taxation relief. More recently, in *Societe Generale SA v Ministre de l'Action et des Comptes publics* (Case C-403/19), the CJEU held that the French foreign tax credit for dividend withholding tax imposed in other Member States could be limited to French tax on the net dividend income, rather than the gross dividend income, derived by a French company from non-French sources. The ruling assumed that France would tax dividend income of its residents on a net basis, whether sourced in France or not. In *Gilly v Directeur des Services Fiscaux du Bas-Rhin* (Case C-336/96) [1998] STC 1014, the CJEU recognised that under Article 293 EC Treaty (repealed in 2009), Member States merely had an obligation to *negotiate* to remove double taxation. They were not required to guarantee such an outcome. For a critique of the CJEU's 'hands off' approach regarding double taxation relief and the four freedoms, *see* Sandra Eden: 'The Obstacles Faced by the European Court of Justice in Removing the "Obstacles" Faced by the Taxpayer: The Difficult Case of Double Taxation' [2010] British Tax Review 610. By contrast, where non-residents are being taxed differently to residents of a Member State, the four freedoms may well be relevant, e.g., in relation to dividend withholding taxes. The effect of a relevant tax treaty will be important when deciding if the non-resident is being treated less favourably in a Member State than an equivalent resident: *see Bouanich v Skatteverket* (Case C-265/04) [2008] STC 2020 and *Denkavit Internationaal BV and another v Ministre de l'Economie, des Finances et de l'Industrie* (Case C-170/05) [2007] STC 452.
738. Case C-376/03 [2006] All ER (EC) 554.
739. The CJEU noted that as per *Gilly* [1998] STC 1014, a difference in treatment between nationals of two Contracting States because of a treaty-based allocation of taxing rights is not prohibited discrimination.

invoked by a third-country EU resident on the basis of the four freedoms. This would amount to cherry-picking parts of the overall treaty package and would undermine the bargain between the Contracting States. Hence the four freedoms do not create a form of 'most favoured nation' clause in tax treaties between Member States.[740] *D* is a pragmatic response to questions about whether tax treaties discriminate against residents of Member States which are not party to the relevant treaty.[741] Hence 'bespoke' provisions regarding 'transparent' entities such as Article 4(5) of the UK-France treaty cannot be invoked by a national of another Member State who is not resident in the UK or France for the purposes of that treaty. Of course, with Article 3(1) of the MLI modifying many other UK treaties, this issue should become less significant.

Despite the decision in *D*, residents of Member State C may sometimes be able to invoke the protection of a tax treaty between Member State A and another jurisdiction, B, especially if the Member State C-resident has exercised its freedom of establishment via a 'permanent establishment' in A. In *Compagnie de Saint-Gobain, Zweigniederlassung Deutschland v Finanzamt Aachen-Innenstadt,*[742] the German branch of a French company successfully relied on the 'freedom of establishment' to invoke German relief under two German tax treaties with non-EU Member States. The CJEU stressed that in neither case was the non-EU Member State required to give treaty relief to the French company. The latter simply claimed relief in Germany because it had exercised its EU right of establishment there by setting up a German branch, rather than a subsidiary. Under EU law, the form of its German establishment should not negatively affect its German tax treatment. German domestic law was changed to reflect the CJEU decision.[743]

740. In *D*, a German resident subject to Dutch wealth tax claimed an exemption from that tax which the Netherlands granted to Belgian-residents in its treaty with Belgium, via that treaty's Non-Discrimination Article. There was no equivalent provision in the Dutch treaty with Germany. The CJEU rejected the claim, which was based on the free movement of capital.

741. *D* has been followed in *Test Claimants in Class IV of the ACT Group Litigation v Inland Revenue Commissioners* (Case C-374/04) [2007] STC 404, which raised issues regarding the freedom of establishment and the free movement of capital, in respect of UK-source dividends paid to non-UK-residents. The CJEU ruled that the freedoms were not infringed simply because the UK granted a treaty-based refundable 'tax credit' in respect of dividends paid to residents of Member State A, but offered no refund to residents of Member State B with which it had a different treaty. Residents of Member States A were not in the same position as residents of Member State B. Furthermore, the freedoms were not infringed where the UK treaty with Member State A contained a 'limitation of benefits' clause. This denied a refund to a corporate resident of Member State A which was controlled by residents of other jurisdictions whose treaties with the UK did not offer such refunds. The CJEU's approach to a 'limitation of benefits' clause in *Test Claimants* has been queried, not least because of an earlier conflicting decision in relation to a 'limitation of benefits' clause in international aviation treaties. However, it appears to be CJEU policy to encourage Member States to make tax treaties without being excessively tied down by EU law in doing so. *Test Claimants* ensures that the tax treaty package cannot be indirectly exploited by residents of other jurisdictions whose treaties with the UK are less beneficial. Hence it is a logical development from *D*. For further discussion, *see* F. Debelva, D. Scornos, J. Van den Berghen and P. Van Braband: 'LOB Clauses and EU-Law Compatibility: A Debate Revived by BEPS?' (2015) EC Tax Review, Volume 24, Issue 3.

742. Case C-307/97 [2000] STC 854.

743. Following *Saint-Gobain,* the UK enacted section 30 TIOPA which allows a UK branch or permanent establishment to claim a UK foreign tax credit. It does not matter whether the branch or permanent establishment belongs to a national of a Member State.

Had the relevant treaties in *Saint-Gobain* been between Germany and other Member States, the German 'permanent establishment' of the French company should also have been entitled (despite *D*) to the same treaty benefits from the source state as that state would have granted to a German resident. Otherwise, the EU source state would be restricting the claimant's freedom to establish in Germany through a branch rather than a subsidiary.[744] Therefore, the German 'permanent establishment' in *Saint Gobain* could claim the benefit of any 'bespoke' 'transparent' entity clause in the relevant German treaty, even if there was no such clause in France's treaty with the EU source jurisdiction.

6.7.6.5 *Unjustified UK Restrictions of the Four Freedoms in Relation to 'Transparent' Entities?*

Brexit aside, it is interesting to consider whether existing UK rules relating to 'transparent' entities breach the four freedoms.

6.7.6.5.1 Article 4(5)(e) of the UK-France Treaty?

Article 4(5)(e) of the UK-France treaty may restrict freedom of establishment without justification. Where a partnership is 'established' in a third country, source state treaty benefits are only available under Article 4(5)(e) if both the state of the partnership's establishment and the non-source Contracting State regard it as 'transparent'. If the partnership happens to be established in another Member State which does not regard it as 'transparent', Article 4(5)(e) renders investment via that state less attractive because it denies treaty relief. There is no obvious justification for this, especially as the US-France treaty does not require the third state in this triangular scenario to regard the partnership as 'transparent'. Furthermore, ignoring this restrictive aspect of Article 4(5)(e) under EU law is proportionate because it does not upset the overall balance of the UK-France treaty. This situation is not simply one where two sovereign Member States have differing views on whether an entity is 'transparent', so *Columbus Container Services* (*see* section 6.7.6.3) is not relevant. Instead, the UK and France have negotiated an additional condition which expressly restricts treaty relief by reference to the entity classification rules of a third state.

6.7.6.5.2 The UK Tax Treatment of a UK LLP?

As discussed in section 2.7, a UK LLP is a form of company which is normally treated for UK direct tax purposes as a partnership. In particular members of the UK LLP within

744. Suppose a treaty contains a 'limitation of benefits' clause denying source state benefits to a resident of the other Contracting State which is controlled by one or more third-state entities (EU or non-EU). Presumably, those benefits should also be denied to a 'permanent establishment' in that other Contracting State which belongs to such a third-country entity? This seems consistent with *Test Claimants in Class IV of the ACT Group Litigation* discussed above. It maintains tax consistency between a third-country-controlled branch and a third-country-controlled subsidiary.

the UK tax charge can claim a share of its losses which they may be able to set against other non-LLP-related income and gains.[745] Suppose that X and Y are German residents who wish to set up a joint venture to carry on a trade solely in the UK. X and Y each have other UK income sources outside the joint venture. If their joint venture takes the corporate form of a UK LLP and produces losses, then each may be able to set its share of those losses against its other UK income and at the same time enjoy the benefit of limited liability. This ability to use losses while enjoying limited liability would not be available if X and Y conducted their UK trade through a purpose-formed German GmbH with no other activity. The fiction which treats a UK LLP as a partnership for UK tax purposes does not apply to any other form of company (apart from EEIGs in corporate form). In particular it does not apply to non-UK companies, such as a GmbH. The UK rules on loss utilisation may therefore make it more favourable to establish a UK joint venture through a UK LLP rather than through, say, a German GmbH, even though both are forms of private limited company and even though both conduct business solely in the UK. This appears to be a restriction on the freedom of X and Y to establish in the UK which is very difficult to justify.

This criticism of the UK rules is supported by the recent CJEU decision in *A SCPI v Veronsaajien oikeudenvalvontayksikkö*,[746] which related to the Finnish rules for taxing 'transparent' investment funds investing in Finnish real property. They were entitled to a Finnish tax exemption in respect of rental income and profits from disposing of real property and shares in companies owning real property. However, the exemption was limited to funds (Finnish or non-Finnish) formed under contract law, not statute, and which lacked legal personality. Apparently, most Finnish funds took this form. The CJEU ruled that restricting the exemption in this way to one type of entity was an unjustifiable restriction of the free movement of capital. While it did not discriminate against non-Finnish funds as such, it denied the exemption in practice to investment funds in other Member States which were 'objectively comparable', in 'transparency' terms, to a Finnish contract-based fund but which were unlikely to be structured in the same way. The CJEU's ruling was not highly technical when defining 'transparency'. The French fund in question was formed by statute as a variable capital property-investment company ('société civile de placement immobilier à capital variable'). It was 'transparent' in France only in the sense that there was no French entity level taxation, it lacked legal capacity and it distributed most of its profits yearly to investors, following their approval. Members had secondary liability for its obligations. The CJEU regarded this as enough to make the French fund comparable, in 'transparency' terms, with a Finnish fund based purely on contract. It made no difference that only investors in the contract-based fund had a proprietary interest in its assets.

745. *See* fn 273 and the accompanying main text.
746. Case C-324/20, decided on 7 April 2022. *See also* the Advocate-General's opinion (in French) of 6 October 2021.

6.7.6.5.3 *Imprecise Nature of UK Rules for Classifying Non-UK Entities (But Not UK Entities) for Tax Purposes?*

As discussed (e.g., at section 3.9), the UK approach to classifying UK entities for tax purposes is fairly prescriptive; the 'resemblance' approach in relation to non-UK entities is much more fluid, fact-sensitive and indeed confused.

A UK taxpayer investing 'outbound' in a non-UK entity may therefore have problems, and a considerable administrative burden, working out its UK tax position accurately. This lack of clear, binding guidance and entity classification criteria can in theory impede UK-residents exercising their 'freedom of establishment' or their right to the free movement of capital. The same is true in 'inbound' situations, e.g., if residents of other Member States seek to establish in the UK using non-UK entities. Were the UK still a Member State, EU law (notably *Futura Participations SA v Administration des Contributions* (Case C-250/95) [1997] STC 1301) would reinforce the case for clearer, objective binding entity classification rules applying similarly to both UK and non-UK entities.

6.8 MECHANICS OF CLAIMING TREATY RELIEF

Even if the members of an entity can claim treaty benefits from the jurisdiction where that entity's income is sourced, by invoking a 'transparent entity' provision, the source state may prefer to give such relief only by refunding tax withheld, rather than giving upfront relief from such withholding. This will have cash flow implications for entity members, which are less likely to arise where an entity is 'opaque'. HMRC's International Manual at INTM335530 states:[747]

> [A]lthough HMRC is willing to entertain any application for relief at source from partnerships, it should be understood that we will be likely to give relief in this way chiefly where:
>
> - We are able to obtain satisfactory assurances about the membership of the partnership.
> - The number and type of partners is not such as to cause concern in the first place - for example, a small and fixed number of participators ...
>
> Where [we] conclude that relief at source cannot be authorised,[748] the partnership will only be able to obtain treaty benefits on behalf of its members by making a series of repayment claims and by providing supporting evidence about the identity of its partners with each claim.

If the entity in question is a collective investment fund which is 'transparent', it may therefore choose to hold its underlying investments via an intermediate company

747. INTM335530 (accessed 13 January 2020).
748. Upfront relief at source is given at HMRC's discretion under Double Taxation Relief (Taxes on Income) (General) Regulations 1970: SI 1970/488. Crossley and Baldwin *supra* note at 17-46 that expedited relief can be granted to a partnership under the Double Tax Treaty Passport scheme if *all* beneficial owners of the interest income are entitled to the same treaty benefits under the *same* treaty (e.g., a partnership all of whose partners are Luxembourg-resident).

resident in a jurisdiction (e.g., Luxembourg) where effective tax rates are low and that company can claim the benefit of a tax treaty with the jurisdiction where the underlying investment is located. Use of such an intermediate company will raise other questions when accessing treaty relief, which are not discussed here. However, that company itself will be unaffected by the 'transparent entity' provision.

6.9 FINAL REMARKS

A double tax treaty tends not to impose on the two Contracting States comprehensive rules on entity classification and tax 'transparency' because these are key structural questions for the domestic tax law of each state. Thinking on these issues within each jurisdiction is likely to evolve over the life of a treaty, making it even harder for them to be effectively addressed in a treaty and for potential classification tensions to be eliminated. The treaty merely aims to ensure that these issues, and any resulting mismatches, do not give rise to double taxation or unintended double non-taxation, where income flows via an entity which may not be classified the same way in each state. Despite their limitations, treaty provisions such as Article 1(8) of the UK-US treaty and Article 4(5) of the UK-France treaty have refocused the UK treaty network more effectively on such questions, although the impetus for such measures has tended to come from UK treaty partners.

Article 1(2) of the OECD Model, together with Article 3(1) of the MLI, should take that process further, even if Article 1(2) has certain weaknesses (*see* section 6.1). Further work is needed on rather different entity classification/'transparency' issues in the distributive articles of a treaty (such as Article 13 (Capital Gains) and Article 15(2) (Employment Income) of the OECD Model).

CHAPTER 7

Entity Classification in the US and the Netherlands

7.1 INTRODUCTION

Other jurisdictions besides the UK have of course wrestled with how best to classify entities for local tax purposes. It is instructive to consider how other jurisdictions have addressed such questions, in particular for US Federal tax purposes. The first part of this chapter therefore focuses on the distinctive US approach to these questions, which the UK tax authorities (among others) are known to dislike. The second part looks at the approach of the Netherlands. Here civil law thinking colours the classification of Dutch and non-Dutch entities for Dutch tax purposes, although the Dutch approach has a certain amount in common with the UK approach. Neither the US nor the Netherlands takes account of the tax treatment of a non-US or Dutch entity in its home jurisdiction when classifying it for US or Dutch tax purposes.

7.2 THE US ENTITY CLASSIFICATION RULES

7.2.1 1997 Reform

The US Federal tax rules[749] on entity classification were significantly overhauled from the start of 1997, including the introduction of the (in)famous 'check-the-box' feature. However, that feature is one part of a bigger picture.

7.2.2 Trust or Business Entity?

The first question to ask for US tax purposes is whether an organisation or arrangement is a stand-alone entity at all, separate from its owners, for Federal income tax purposes

749. Most states have based their state income tax rules on the Federal approach.

(rather than simply being disregarded). Some arrangements (e.g., those based on contract such as a Luxembourg 'fonds commun de placement') may be regarded as a separate entity for US tax purposes if the parties carry on a business and share profits (which they often do). It is irrelevant that arrangement would not be a separate legal person for non-tax purposes or for non-US tax purposes. Other arrangements (e.g., cost-sharing arrangements, the relationship of lessor and lessee) may be 'nothings' for US tax purposes, although US courts fight shy of treating arrangements as a 'nothing', rather than a stand-alone entity. Apparently, joint decision-making is enough for a co-ownership arrangement to be a business entity (and probably a partnership) for US tax purposes.[750]

Whether there is a separate entity, and if so, how many entities, is determined under Federal tax law for Federal tax purposes, and not by reference to state law.[751] There is debate about the ongoing relevance of pre-1997 court decisions on whether a separate entity exists for US tax purposes.[752]

If there is a separate entity, is it a trust or a 'business entity'? The borderline between the two is not simple. A trust for these purposes is an arrangement created by will or 'inter vivos' whereby trustees take title to property so as to protect or conserve it for beneficiaries. An arrangement which is a trust from a formal legal perspective can nevertheless be treated[753] as a separate business entity for Federal tax purposes. This is true in particular of business or commercial 'trusts', where the trustee's role involves more than simply protecting or conserving a more or less static pool of trust assets.[754] A good example is the Massachusetts Business Trust, a popular vehicle for the US

750. *See* Blanchard: *'The Tax Significance of Legal Personality: A US View', New York University School of Law Spring 2015 Colloquium on Tax Policy and Public Finances* at 18-20. That author suggests that the US bias in favour of recognising entities, not 'nothings', ensures that more arrangements can be brought within Subchapter K (partnerships) of the Internal Revenue Code. This prevents artificial income shifting among entity members. In the UK, co-ownership arrangements often do fall short of partnership status, and are not regarded as an entity. Each participant is separately taxed on its share of income and gains. There is therefore a mismatch here between the UK and US entity classification rules. The UK concept of partnership for tax purposes is narrower than its US equivalent, although it extends to LPs which are used for passive investment and which, in practice, may be little more than co-ownership arrangements. This particular mismatch between the UK and US rules has nothing to do with 'checking the box'.
751. Treas. Reg. 301.7701-1(a)(1).
752. *See* the United States country report (by Anthony C. Infanti and Bernard Moens) in Volume 99b (2014) of the International Fiscal Association Cahiers de Droit Fiscal International, p. 859 at pp. 861-862. In particular, there is debate about the relative importance of two US Supreme Court decisions in the 1940s: *Moline Properties, Inc. v Commissioner* 319 US 436 and *Commissioner v Culbertson* 337 US 733. *Moline* set an especially low threshold for deciding that an entity or arrangement formed under state law was a separate entity for Federal tax purposes, requiring only a business purpose or activity.
753. Treas. Reg. 301.7701-4(b).
754. The UK treats certain trusts ('unit trusts') as business entities (namely, companies) for the purposes of both corporation tax and capital gains tax, as discussed in section 4.3.6.2. However, whether a trust is a 'unit trust' depends on the regulatory definition of a 'unit trust scheme'. This concept does not distinguish clearly between those trusts which are more dynamically managed and those which are more like asset protection mechanisms. A trust which conducts a trade remains a trust for UK tax purposes, unless it is a 'unit trust scheme', which is not always the case (e.g., a private trust).

collective fund known as a 'Regulated Investment Company' (RIC) (*see also* section 7.2.4.1). It is usually regarded as a 'business entity' (indeed a corporation) for US tax purposes.

This chapter only summarises the US Federal income tax treatment of trusts which are not 'business entities'. Under the 'grantor trust' rules in Internal Revenue Code Part 1, Subpart E, the income and activities of such a trust can be attributed to the 'grantor'. Such a trust is 'looked through' in its entirety and the trust income and capital are regarded for Federal tax purposes as owned by the 'grantor'. Hence there is no gift tax unless and until the grantor ceases to hold the rights and powers in relation to the trust which trigger grantor taxation. The 'grantor' is a person with a specified degree of power over the trustee or the trust property (broadly, the equivalent of the 'settlor' for UK tax purposes). However, there are limits on the attribution of income and capital to the 'grantor', not least to ensure that in most cases, items are only attributed directly or indirectly to a US taxpayer.[755]

The Internal Revenue Code also has a 'simple trust' concept.[756] This is a trust other than a 'grantor trust' where the trustee is required to make current distributions of income and/or capital. The trust is a separate taxable unit. However, the trust income which must be currently distributed retains its character, timing and source in the hands of the beneficiaries. Therefore, there is considerable 'transparency', although less so than in relation to a 'grantor trust', because this type of trust is not 'looked through' in the same way.

The Internal Revenue Code recognises a third type of trust, the 'complex trust'. This is a taxable unit, but the trustee has significant discretion regarding trust distributions. This type of trust is the least 'transparent' of the three, but it can deduct income distributed to beneficiaries. That distributed income retains its underlying character and source for US tax purposes in the hands of beneficiaries, although not always its timing. In particular, it is only attributed to beneficiaries in the tax year when the distribution is made (or required to be made). If the trust income is not distributed in a timely manner, it is taxed in the hands of the trustees.

7.2.3 What Kind of 'Business Entity'?

Having identified a separate entity which is a 'business entity' rather than a trust, one must decide whether it is created or organised 'in the United States, or under the law of the United States or of any State' or in the District of Columbia.[757] If so, that 'business

755. For further details, *see* fn 73 of 'Some Reflections' *supra*, and Brabazon *supra*, at pp. 32-34, 39-40 and 43-48, in relation to 'grantor trusts'. As is pointed out in Brabazon *supra*, at p. 39, there are important exceptions (e.g., a simple revocable trust) where income can be attributed to a *non*-US grantor under the 'grantor trust' rules.

756. *See* Brabazon *supra*, at pp. 296-300 for further discussion of the US taxation of beneficiaries of non-'grantor trusts'. Time limits for making distributions may need to be met to ensure 'transparent' treatment of trust income and gain at beneficiary level.

757. But not created or organised in a US possession (e.g., Guam) or Puerto Rico.

entity' will be 'domestic'. Sometimes, 'non-domestic' entities may elect to be treated, or must be treated as 'domestic' entities for Federal tax purposes.[758]

'Domestic' or 'non-domestic' status has consequences. The entity classification rules for Federal tax purposes apply to both 'domestic' and 'non-domestic' entities, with relatively few differences. Therefore, the US (unlike, say, the UK and the Netherlands) has a single, largely harmonised set of tax rules for classifying all entities and not just those which are 'foreign'.

7.2.4 Classifying a 'Domestic' 'Business Entity'

7.2.4.1 'Domestic' 'Per Se' Corporations

The US legislation provides an exhaustive list of 'domestic' business entities which are always regarded as corporations (and hence typically tax-'opaque') for Federal tax purposes. These are often referred to as corporations 'per se'. In particular, this category includes any entity organised under a statute of one of the states which 'describes or refers to the entity as incorporated or as a corporation, body corporate or body politic' or 'as a joint-stock company or joint-stock association'.[759]

Also regarded invariably as corporations for Federal tax purposes are insurance companies, state-chartered banks and entities wholly owned by a state or non-US government.[760] The same applies to certain 'publicly-traded partnerships'.[761]

A number of these categories of 'per se' corporation are set out in the Internal Revenue Code itself, so they cannot readily be altered by Treasury Regulations. It is not easy to justify such blanket exclusions from the elective part of the US entity classification regime.[762]

In any case, the Internal Revenue Code, in Subchapter S, has long permitted certain small, privately held US corporations to elect for 'transparent' treatment. Detailed conditions must be met before a corporation can make such an election. With limited exceptions, a S Corporation pays no US tax on its income.[763]

758. For example, 'stapled entities' (section 269B(a)(1) Internal Revenue Code) and some 'inverted corporations' created via transactions whereby a non-US corporation acquires a US corporation (section 7874(b) Internal Revenue Code).
759. Treas. Reg. 301.7701-(2)(b)(1), (3).
760. Treas. Reg. 301-7701-2(b)(4)-(6). State-chartered banks are those whose deposits are insured by the Federal Government.
761. Section 7704 Internal Revenue Code. These must have interests traded on an established securities market or readily tradeable on a secondary market. Section 7704 does not impose corporate status where the publicly traded partnership receives predominantly passive income (e.g., interest, dividends or royalties). This has enabled certain private equity funds to list interests in entities qualifying as partnerships for US tax purposes without being caught by section 7704. The logic of section 7704 is open to question: why should a partnership always be treated as a corporation simply because it sources capital in public markets rather than privately?
762. *See* Heather M. Field: 'Checking in on Check: The-Box' (2009) Loyola. L.A. L. Rev. Volume 42, 451 http://digitalcommons.lmu.edu/llr/vol42/iss2/4 (accessed 7 July 2022) (hereinafter 'Field') at 505-520.
763. The need for S Corporation status has been questioned now that limited liability companies (*see* section 7.2.4.2) can readily be set up as 'tax-transparent' partnerships or disregarded entities

The Internal Revenue Code also contains bespoke and largely 'pass-through' taxation regimes for certain corporations engaged in specified activities, e.g., RICs, Real Estate Investment Trusts and Real Estate Mortgage Investment Conduits. These special regimes are unaffected by the general rules on elective entity classification.[764] They are bespoke tax regimes for collective investment vehicles, whose economic rationale would be undermined if the entity itself paid significant tax on its profits.

7.2.4.2 'Domestic' 'Eligible Entities'

If a 'business entity' is domestic and not a 'per se' corporation, then it will be an 'eligible entity'. This enables it to elect its US tax classification. The most important 'domestic' 'eligible entity' is the LLC. Almost all US states have legislation permitting the creation of these hybrid limited liability entities. They combine the legal personality and limited liability of a corporation, without being incorporated. They also have the internal organisational flexibility of a partnership. In particular, LLC members' interests usually do not take the form of share capital.[765] The closest analogue to a LLC in UK law is the UK LLP, which typically lacks share capital and is deemed to be a partnership for certain tax purposes.[766] However, unlike a LLC, it is an incorporated entity, quite deliberately and for non-tax reasons.

'Domestic' 'eligible entities' also include limited partnerships, limited liability partnerships and limited liability limited partnerships formed under the laws of various states. LPs, LLPs, LLLPs and LLCs are now largely interchangeable for US tax and non-tax purposes, although none of a LLC's members need have any degree of unlimited liability. Classically, a LP required at least one general partner with unlimited liability for partnership obligations, although in practice that partner's exposure could be contained. However, under the 2001 Uniform Limited Partnership Act, limited liability is apparently extended to all partners of a LP, whether or not they take part in management.[767]

---

for US tax purposes. However, S Corporations remain quite common. The US tax treatment of a S Corporation is similar, but not identical, to a partnership or a disregarded entity.

764. Treas. Reg. 301.7701-1(b) and 2(a).
765. This was true of the LLC in *Anson v HMRC*: *see* section 2.14. HMRC consider that it is possible for interests in a Delaware LLC to be structured as 'ordinary share capital' for UK tax purposes: *see* section 2.14.6. When tracing a UK group (e.g., for corporation tax, stamp duty and SDLT purposes) via an intermediate LLC, it will be very important to demonstrate that it has 'ordinary share capital' for UK tax purposes. Nevertheless, the idea of members' interests being share capital is largely alien to the LLC concept.
766. The author has been told in the past by US advisers that the LLC is similar to the 'limitada' in Spain and Latin America. Parallels have also been drawn with the German Gesellchaft mit beschränkter Haftung or GmbH, which is often viewed as equivalent to a UK private limited company. However, the division between ownership and management in a GmbH is much less clear-cut than in a UK private limited company. GmbH members can, for example, issue detailed, binding directions to its managers on a very wide range of issues: *see* Dr Christoph Schulte: 'Legal Forms in German Corporate Law'. Cross-Border Investments with Germany: Tax, Legal and Accounting – Essays in Honour of Detlev J. Piltz: ed. Flick Gocke Schaumburg. Verlag Dr Otto Schmidt KG 2014.
767. *See* Blanchard, 'The Tax Significance of Legal Personality: A US View' *supra*, at p. 9.

LLPs and LLLPs bear an even closer resemblance to LLCs, not least because all members benefit from limited liability even if they take part in firm management. What limited liability amounts to varies from state to state. So-called first generation LLPs only protect innocent partners from liability for malpractice of their fellow partners. This is true of New York and California, which also limit LLP structures to professional firms. However, 'second generation' LLPs go further and provide partners with a 'full shield', not only from the malpractice of other partners but also from debts arising in the ordinary course of business. Delaware is a 'full shield' state although a Delaware LLP does not limit a member's liability for personal negligence, unlike a Delaware LLC.

A LLLP is a form of LP which provides all partners with limited liability, not only for each other's wrongdoing but also for debts arising in the ordinary course of business. Like the LLP, it continues the trend of limiting the liability of partners who take part in firm management.[768]

A 'domestic' 'eligible entity' with more than one member can elect to be treated as a partnership or a corporation for US tax purposes.[769] If no election is made, then that entity is classified as a partnership.[770] Therefore, it remains an entity for US tax purposes but is taxed under Subchapter K of the Internal Revenue Code. A 'domestic' 'eligible entity' with a single member can elect to be treated as a corporation or to be disregarded for US tax purposes.[771] If no election is made, then the entity is disregarded.[772] Such disregarded entities are treated as a sole proprietorship (if the single member is an individual) or as a branch or division of the member (if the latter is an entity).[773] This capacity to disregard altogether a single-member entity is a distinctive feature of the US entity classification rules. It is a major cause (deliberate or not) of classification mismatches with the tax laws of other jurisdictions. Where it applies, the entity's income and assets are treated as those of its member. Transactions and income flows between entity and member are ignored.

Entity classification elections, on IRS Form 8832, are effective on the date filed unless a different effective date is specified. The effective date cannot be more than seventy-five days' prior to the filing date nor more than twelve months after it.[774] An entity which files an election to change its existing classification cannot normally file another such election for sixty months following the effective date of that earlier election.[775]

768. *See* Blanchard, 'The Tax Significance of Legal Personality: A US View' *supra*, at pp. 9-11. New York and California prohibit the LLLP form.
769. Treas. Reg. 301.7701-2(a).
770. Treas. Reg. 301.7701-3(b)(1)(i).
771. Treas. Reg. 301.7701-2(a).
772. Treas. Reg. 301.7701-3(b)(1)(iii).
773. Treas. Reg. 301.7701-2(a).
774. Treas. Reg. 301.7701-3(c)(1)(iii).
775. Treas. Reg. 301.7701-3(c)(1)(iv). This sixty-month rule does not apply to an election which is effective from an entity's formation. Nor does it apply where the election is to change the entity's default classification. The IRS also has discretion, via private letter ruling, to relax the sixty-month limitation.

7.2.5 Classifying a 'Non-domestic' 'Business Entity'

7.2.5.1 'Non-domestic' 'Per Se' Corporations

There is a list which specifies by country a number of non-US legal entities which are invariably corporations for US Federal tax purposes.[776] These tend to be corporate entities in major non-US jurisdictions which have the right (whether or not they exercise it) to offer their securities to the public, e.g., the UK public limited company, the French société anonyme, the German Aktiengesellschaft and the Dutch NV. Canada enjoys a special status: although Canadian corporations are listed as 'per se' corporations, this does not apply to any Canadian company, all of whose members have unlimited liability (e.g., a Nova Scotia unlimited liability corporation).[777]

Importantly, this 'per se' list for non-US entities leaves out many corporate bodies (notably, corporate bodies formed in tax havens), unlike the 'per se' rules for 'domestic' entities: *see* section 7.2.4.1.

This list includes non-US corporate entities which could offer their securities to the public, whether or not they do so. This differs from the 'publicly-traded partnership' rule: *see* section 7.2.4.1. The reasons for this difference are unclear.

7.2.5.2 'Non-domestic' 'Eligible Entities'

Non-domestic business entities which are not 'per se' corporations are 'eligible entities' which can elect their US tax classification in much the same way as 'domestic' 'eligible entities': *see* section 7.2.4.2. The default classification rules for 'non-domestic' entities are, however, different. If an entity with more than one member does not elect its classification, then it will be a corporation if all its members have limited liability and a partnership if at least one member lacks limited liability.[778] If a single-member entity does not elect its classification, then it will be a corporation if the single member has limited liability and disregarded if it does not.[779] For these purposes, 'a member of a foreign eligible entity has limited liability if the member has no personal liability for the debts of or claims against the entity by reason of being a member'.[780]

There is evidence of non-US entities electing in large numbers to be disregarded for US tax purposes.[781] This may be explained in part by the different default entity

776. Treas. Reg. 301.7701-2(b)(8).
777. Treas. Reg. 301.7701-2(b)(8)(ii)(A)(1). The UK unlimited liability company is not a 'per se' corporation because only a UK public limited company is and a UK unlimited company cannot be a public limited company.
778. Treas. Reg. 301-7701-3(b)(2)(i)(A)-(B).
779. Treas. Reg. 301.7701-3(b)(1)(ii).
780. Treas. Reg. 301.701-3(b)(2)(ii), which determines whether there is unlimited liability purely by reference to the governing law and constitutional documents under which the entity is organised. It does not take account of the actual economic capacity of an entity member to make good that entity's loss. So the 'unlimited liability' condition can be met even if the entity with unlimited liability is, in fact, a purpose-formed limited company with very low net worth (so that its unlimited liability does not amount to much).
781. *See* Field *supra*, at p. 527.

classification rules which apply to non-US entities. Hence there are more cases where an election is needed for disregarded entity status.

The US tax classification of a 'non-domestic' entity is only relevant when it affects the liability of any person for US Federal tax or information-reporting purposes.[782]

7.2.6 Implications of the US Entity Classification Rules

7.2.6.1 Building on the Effective Choice Available under the pre-1997 Rules

The US Federal tax rules for entity classification are not entirely elective. The automatic 'opaque' status of domestically incorporated US business entities is similar to the way in which the UK characterises entities incorporated under UK domestic law (except UK EEIGs and the misleadingly named UK LLP). The US rules also mandate 'opaque' status for many non-US entities. However, it is striking that the US rules do not mandate 'opaque' status for more non-US incorporated entities, including UK private limited companies, the French Sàrl, the Dutch BV, the German GmbH and a number of entities incorporated in tax havens. All US-incorporated entities are invariably 'opaque' if they are not S corporations. Hence there is asymmetry in the treatment of US and non-US incorporated entities although this is partly offset by the widespread availability within the US of LLCs. These are not regarded as 'incorporated' under state law. Therefore they are not automatically 'opaque'.

The US is unusual in allowing taxpayers an administratively simple choice about whether 'eligible entities' should be treated as transparent for Federal tax purposes. The practical benefits of this choice are magnified by the availability within the US of the LLC. This offers an attractive combination of full legal personality, perpetual succession and member limited liability as well as great constitutional flexibility. Commercially, it is a halfway house between a 'classic' partnership (including a Scottish partnership) and a corporation. Tax-wise, it can decide whether it should be taxed as a corporation, a partnership or (if it has a single member) a disregarded entity.

The most novel substantive effect of the US elective regime is the ability to 'disregard' single-member 'eligible entities'. Whereas a partnership is not a 'nothing' for Federal tax purposes,[783] a disregarded single-member entity is. The single member is regarded, for most tax purposes, as directly owning the assets, and assuming the liabilities of that entity.[784] This is quite radical. It does not merely provide[785] that the

782. Treas. Reg. 301.7701-3(d)(1)(i).
783. Sometimes Federal tax law treats a partnership simply as an aggregate of its members' interests and activities, while in other situations, it regards it as an entity. For example, a US partnership which holds shares in a non-US corporation can itself be a '10% US shareholder' in that corporation when deciding if the latter is within the US controlled foreign corporation rules ('Subpart F'). That partnership can still be a '10% US shareholder' even if its partners are not US persons at all or they include US persons with, indirectly, less than a 10% partnership share. However, this entity theory only goes so far: the US partnership itself is not subject to US tax under Subpart F. Only its US-taxpaying partners are. This approach does not apply to non-US partnerships. This has given scope for sidestepping Subpart F by using a non-US partnership.
784. The single-member entity may not be a 'nothing' regarding obligations to collect third-party tax liabilities; e.g., it must operate employee payroll withholding.

entity's profits are to be taxed solely at member level, as they arise and by reference to that member's fiscal characteristics. The disregard can affect parties other than the single member and the 'disregarded' entity. For example, if the single member of a disregarded non-US entity is a US corporation and the disregarded entity owns another US corporation, the two US corporations can form a 'consolidated group' for US tax purposes because the intermediate non-US entity is ignored.

The 1997 rules often build on pre-1997 features. The elective regime for 'eligible entities' was a deliberate decision to make more readily accessible the benefit of rules which were already giving taxpayers considerable choice over US tax classification.

Pre-1997, there were also business entities which were corporations per se, although there was no equivalent of the current 'per se' list for non-US entities. Pre-1997, it was increasingly possible for many other business entities to secure partnership treatment for US tax purposes if they *failed* to meet two out of four prescribed corporate characteristics. These were fairly formalistic and each had equal weight. They were (i) limited liability (i.e., no member was liable without limit for the debts of the entity); (ii) free transferability of members' interests (i.e., substantially all of the ownership interests - meaning *all* legal rights of the member in the entity - were transferable without the consent of the other members); (iii) centralised management (i.e., the entity was managed by one or more persons similar to a board of directors, and not by the members themselves) and (iv) continuity of life (i.e., the entity's existence did not cease because of the resignation, bankruptcy, etc., of any member). The four factors were contained in the then Treasury Regulations[786] which distilled several decisions of the US courts. No one factor was decisive, not even continuity of life.[787] Separate legal personality was not a factor at all. Almost all US partnerships have legal personality anyway, so the presence or absence of legal personality could not sensibly be a differentiating factor. For historic reasons, three out of four factors had to be present to achieve corporation status.[788] An entity seeking partnership status

785. As is the case with a partnership.

786. The 'Kintner Regulations': Treasury Decision 6503: Treas. Reg. 301.7701-1 to 301.7701-11 (1960). These were a legislative response to *Morrissey v Commissioner* (1935) 296 US 344 and especially *United States v Kintner* 216 F. 2d 418 (9th Circuit 1954). Technically, these Regulations set out six factors but the first two ('associates' and 'an objective to carry on a business and divide the gains therefrom') were only relevant in deciding whether an entity was a 'business entity' or a trust. The 'Kintner Regulations' did not adopt a further factor mentioned in *Morrissey v Commissioner:* the ability of the entity to hold title to property. This was presumably because almost all entities (including partnerships) in the US can own property in their own name because they have legal personality. For a recent UK discussion of the pre-1997 US entity classification regime (and especially the 'continuity of life' factor), *see* Montagu: '*Anson* and Entity Classification Revisited in Light of Brexit' *supra,* in particular, at pp. 471-476.

787. The decision to avoid a single conclusive criterion was sensible, given the wide range of legal systems regulating business entities, both within and outside the US. In any case, as one commentator has pointed out: continuity of life was largely a formalism, because most state laws allowed the remaining partners to reconstitute the partnership and continue in business as though nothing had happened: Kimberly Blanchard: 'The Significance of Legal Personality for US Tax Purposes': Business Entities March/April 2016 p. 5 at p. 11 (hereinafter 'Blanchard: Significance').

788. It was made harder to achieve corporation status because, *inter alia,* in 1960, corporations enjoyed certain tax advantages, such as lower tax rates than individuals and the opportunity to set up a qualified pension plan.

therefore had to lack at least two factors. For example, a UK unlimited liability company achieved partnership status for US tax purposes by limiting the transferability of its shares. It therefore lacked limited liability and free transferability of its members' interests.

Well-advised and well-resourced taxpayers could therefore structure entities so as to give themselves effective choice pre-1997 over their US tax characterisation. This gave them an unfair advantage, especially in relation to non-US 'eligible entities'.[789] The simpler, more explicitly elective rules adopted in 1997 made such choice available to the many, not the few. It also created simplicity and certainty for taxpayers, as well as being simpler for the IRS to administer.

When introducing the new regime, the US Treasury highlighted another key reason for turning its back on the 'four factor' test which focused on structural features of business entities and whether they 'resembled' a partnership or a corporation. As it noted, 'many states have revised their statutes to provide that partnerships and other unincorporated organisations may possess characteristics that traditionally have been associated with corporations, *thereby narrowing considerably the traditional distinctions between corporations and partnerships under local law* [emphasis added]'.[790] This narrowing has not been confined to the US. By introducing the UK LLP, the UK has travelled the same route, in a slightly different way.

The new rules made clear that a single-member entity could be disregarded. Even this change was based to some extent on pre-1997 authority.[791]

7.2.6.2 Lessons from the US Experiment

7.2.6.2.1 How Much US Tax Has Been Avoided?

The elective regime for 'eligible entities' has been widely used in US tax planning, especially cross-border planning. The US Treasury has on occasion made changes to combat less welcome side effects of increased planning based on entity classification.

There has been much debate[792] about the extent to which this regime has led to additional US tax avoidance, given the practical ability to choose entity classification pre-1997. Of course, the new rules enable more taxpayers to take advantage of entity

789. In relation to such entities, a detailed understanding of the relevant non-US law governing the entity would be necessary, requiring detailed local law advice. There would often be a language barrier too.
790. US Treasury, 26 CFR Pt 301 [PS-43-95] RIN 1545-AT91 'Simplification of Entity Classification Rules', cited in Montagu, '*Anson* and Entity Classification Revisited in Light of Brexit' *supra,* at p. 475. As has been pointed out, US tax law largely ignores limited liability in relation to entity classification, because almost all US entities can now obtain virtually complete liability protection: Blanchard: Significance *supra,* at p. 8. Blanchard describes how, under current US partnership law (in particular, section 303 of the 2001 Uniform Limited Partnership Act), *all* partners in a US LLP or a LLLP are shielded from liability arising from the bad acts of other partners or from debts arising in the ordinary course of partnership business. *See also* section 7.2.4.2.
791. *See* Michael L. Schler: 'Initial Thoughts on the Proposed "Check The Box" Regulations' May 1996 unpublished paper for the New York Tax Club, at p. 15.
792. *See* Field *supra,* at pp. 486-495.

classification choices. For that reason alone, the revised rules have probably facilitated avoidance. Furthermore, the post-1996 regime clearly allows a single-member 'eligible entity' to be disregarded. Hence the use of disregarded entities in US tax planning has proliferated, especially where this relates to the US 'controlled foreign corporation' rules and to the foreign tax credit rules.

It is interesting to consider the US Federal tax treatment of a non-US person investing in the US via a partnership rather than a corporation (although for reasons given below, investment in the US directly via a partnership is in practice unlikely).

An investor in the US which invests via a US LLC, treated as a partnership, rather than via a US corporation, will be fully taxable in the US on the net 'effectively connected income' (distributed or undistributed) which it derives by carrying on a US trade or business via the LLC. So investing via the LLC, rather than a US corporation, does not remove the investor's US tax liability. If the investor is a corporation by US standards, it will be taxed at regular US corporate income tax rates on this 'effectively connected income'. If it is an individual, it will be taxed at progressive US personal income tax rates on that net income. In certain cases involving non-US corporate investors, the US branch tax will also apply.[793] Where it applies, it will cancel out (at least in part) any US dividend withholding tax saving which a non-US corporate investor might otherwise achieve by investing in the US through a branch or a transparent entity, rather than through a US corporation. However, once any treaty relief is taken into account, the rate of any branch tax on a less-than-10% investment in a LLC may be lower than the US dividend withholding tax rate on a less-than-10% shareholding in a US corporation.

A sale of shares by a non-US investor in a US corporation will not normally give rise to US tax on any gain.[794] The same is not true of a sale by a non-US partner of an interest in a US LLC taxed as a partnership. In 2017, the US Tax Court in *Grecian Magnesite Mining*[795] decided that a sale by a non-US investor of an interest in a US LLC (taxed as a partnership) did not automatically amount to a disposal of a corresponding share of each of the underlying assets of the LLC. The same result would not have been reached if the investor had been the sole member of a disregarded US LLC. This shows how for US tax purposes, a partnership (unlike a disregarded entity) is not a tax 'nothing'.

The IRS unsuccessfully appealed the Tax Court's decision.[796] However, the US Tax Cuts and Jobs Act 2017 has reversed the effect of *Grecian Magnesite Mining* for future years.[797] An equivalent effect can still be secured if the non-US investor invests

793. This is an additional tax charge of up to 30% under section 884 Internal Revenue Code, where a non-US corporation invests in the US via a branch. It taxes a 'dividend equivalent amount', i.e., the after-tax amount of certain US-taxable income of the branch which is not treated as reinvested in a US trade or business. It is US policy to amend the 'Non-Discrimination' Article in its treaties so as to preserve its right to impose the branch tax.
794. Unless the US corporation is US real estate-'rich': a US Real Property Holding Corporation.
795. *See* fn 468.
796. *See* fn 468.
797. The 2017 Act in effect codifies Revenue Ruling 91-32 (which the Tax Court and the US Court of Appeals (Washington, D.C. Circuit) declined to follow) in a new section 864(c)(8) Internal Revenue Code 1986 (as amended). Gain or loss from the sale or exchange of a partnership

in the US LLC through a US 'blocker' corporation. This is typically a corporation (by US standards) whose sole asset is the LLC interest. The non-US investor would then exit by selling an interest in the 'blocker', rather than selling directly the underlying LLC interest. By using a US 'blocker' in this way, the non-US investor need not file a US tax return and branch tax is also avoided.[798]

Hence, one should not overstate the tax difference between investing in the US via a US LLC treated as a partnership, rather than via a US corporation. Direct investment into the US via a partnership is rare and each case will be fact-sensitive. An important development is the reduction to 21% (from 35%) of the headline Federal corporate income tax rate for US corporations in the Tax Cuts and Jobs Act 2017.[799] For a US individual investing in a US corporation, the 21% rate means that the effective Federal tax rate on *distributed* corporate profits is 36.8% (21% at the level of the corporation with a further 20%, in most cases, on the after-tax profits of the corporation, but *only* if distributed).[800] This compares with a maximum 37%[801] if the same underlying income is earned through a US partnership (in which case it will be taxed at that rate whether or not distributed).[802]

If the US corporation or partnership has an interest in an entity which is a controlled foreign corporation, then the individual would be well advised to invest in a US corporation rather than a US partnership, to avoid tax costs described in sections 7.2.6.2.3-7.2.6.2.4.

7.2.6.2.2 Use of 'Check-the-Box' Elections for Cross-Border Tax Planning

Much 'check-the-box' planning has historically occurred when US taxpayers invest *outside* the US. A key objective was to minimise the extent to which profits from the US taxpayer's non-US operations were subject to US tax before being physically repatriated to the US, under the various US anti-deferral regimes (and especially under

interest by a non-US partner will henceforth be US-taxable 'effectively connected income', to the extent that the investor would have had effectively connected income or loss if the partnership had sold all of its underlying assets for cash at fair market value when the sale or exchange of the partnership interest took place.

798. *See* Kimberly S. Blanchard: 'What is the Government's Appeal in "Grecian" About?' (10 August 2018) Tax Management International Journal, Volume 47, Issue 8, 546.
799. The formal title of this Act is 'An Act to provide for reconciliation pursuant to Titles II and V of the concurrent resolution on the budget for fiscal year 2018, H.R. 1, 115th Congress (2017)'. The reduction in the headline corporate income tax rate was accompanied by important base-widening measures: notably, a cap on overall deductible interest, and extensions to anti-deferral rules (notably GILTI - *see* section 7.2.6.2.3 below). These base-widening measures can also apply to individual taxpayers.
800. If the investor were non-US, that 20% tax rate on distributions would rise to 30%, subject to treaty relief. There could also be tax on that distribution in the investor's home jurisdiction.
801. The rate in respect of income earned through a partnership can be reduced to 29.6% because of the Pass-Thru Deduction. However, this is not available in respect of income from partnerships providing law or accounting services, or engaging in investing or financial trading. The Pass-Thru Deduction is scheduled to end after 2025.
802. If the investor were non-US, one would also have to take into account 'branch tax' (up to 30%, subject to treaty relief) as well as any tax in the investor's home jurisdiction, potentially reduced by relief for US tax.

Subpart F, the US controlled foreign corporation rules). Subpart F taxes certain profits of a 'controlled foreign corporation' at regular US corporate income tax rates in the hands of certain US persons with an interest in it ('10% US shareholders').[803] Taxpayers often elected to disregard single-member non-US affiliates which were directly owned by a non-US subholding entity, while electing to treat that subholding entity as a corporation. This structure treated the lower-tier disregarded affiliates as branches of the non-US subholding entity. Hence income flows (especially interest, dividends and royalties) from those lower-tier affiliates, to that subholding entity, were ignored for Subpart F purposes.

There was a tacit acceptance of this planning by the US tax authorities. Before the 2017 Act, US multinationals long complained that the previous US corporate income tax rate (35%), coupled with Subpart F, eroded their competitiveness. 'Check-the-box' planning of the kind described above reduced Subpart F's impact on non-repatriated earnings from outside the US. It also led to low-taxed cash accumulating in non-US subsidiaries which were 'controlled foreign corporations'.

This structuring was also adopted to reduce the non-US tax liabilities of the lower-tier disregarded affiliates which were directly owned by the non-US subholding entity. Those affiliates were paid interest and royalties to low-taxed affiliates not resident in the payer's home jurisdiction. Those payments would be disregarded for US purposes but would be deductible in the payers' home jurisdictions. Hence, a 'deduction/non-inclusion' mismatch would arise: interest and royalties would be deducted for non-US tax purposes without giving rise to US tax as long as no cash was repatriated to the US. This mismatch largely relied on the ability to 'disregard' entities for US tax purposes.

'Check-the-box' planning was also used to structure investment into the US. In the early 2000s, some UK parent companies used 'deferred share subscription' structures to fund US subsidiaries in return for the latter making capital contributions into a special-purpose UK subsidiary of the UK parent company. Economically, these structures were amortising loans to the US subsidiary. However, no interest income was recognised by the UK parent because the periodic capital contribution payments by the US subsidiary were respected as non-taxable deferred subscriptions for shares in the special-purpose UK subsidiary. They were not treated as interest and principal repayments on a loan. From a US tax perspective, the structure *was* treated as a loan to the US subsidiary by the UK parent because an election was made to 'disregard' the special-purpose UK subsidiary. Hence the periodic payments were treated as direct payments of interest and principal by the US subsidiary to the UK parent. The interest component was deductible for US tax purposes,[804] even though it was not treated as income for UK tax purposes.

803. Subpart F applies in particular to 'passive' income of a controlled foreign corporation (or, to be more precise, 'foreign personal holding company' income).

804. The UK legislated to tax the interest element: *see* section 91A Finance Act 1996, re-enacted as section 524 CTA 2009 and now replaced by Part 6 Chapter 2A CTA 2009.

This last example shows how the US entity classification rules make it easier to engineer cross-border tax mismatches.[805] A taxpayer which wants to create an 'eligible entity' mismatch between the US and another jurisdiction can do so by altering the entity's structure to achieve the desired non-US classification while simply electing to achieve the desired US classification. Hence a taxpayer can structure an entity to achieve the desired non-US tax classification, without compromising the desired US tax classification.[806]

7.2.6.2.3 Further Effects of the 2017 US Tax Reforms

The Tax Cuts and Jobs Act 2017 is the most significant US tax reform since 1986 and impacts US tax planning, as regards both investment into and out of the US.[807] The following paragraphs focus on investment out of the US. Besides reducing the corporate income tax rate to 21%, unrepatriated non-US earnings of non-US subsidiaries were taxed on a 'one-off' basis in the hands of US shareholders treated as holding at least 10% of the relevant subsidiary.[808] Section 245A Internal Revenue Code now exempts non-US dividends received by US *corporate* shareholders[809] with actual or deemed equity of at least 10% in the distributing non-US corporation ('10% US shareholders').[810] However, this exemption is counterbalanced by a new charge on such 10% US shareholders in respect of 'global intangible low-taxed income' (or GILTI)

805. However, Blanchard: Significance *supra,* at p. 53 considers that the BEPS project exaggerates the extent to which the 'check-the-box' rules create hybrid mismatches and underestimates the more important cause of mismatches, which is divergent law between countries. In particular, hybridity is caused by using per se rules and comparability tests to classify entities, together with concepts, like legal personality, which have little relevance in many countries. The comparability approach should focus on substance rather meaningless legal forms. This author agrees that the 'check-the-box' rules are not the root of all evil and are often used to divert attention from the deficiencies of other countries' entity classification rules, notably the UK's. However, the point in the main text about the different approach of the US rules remains important.
806. Reconciling US and non-US rules pre-1997 would have been harder because the then US entity classification rules also focused on structural features, as discussed in section 7.2.6.1.
807. This Act passed very rapidly through Congress. The result was many legislative uncertainties, which are gradually being resolved via administrative guidance and further legislation. The discussion of the Act in this chapter is largely based on TCJA Navigator - Final Bill (davispolk.com) (accessed 6 July 2020).
808. The tax charge was levied at 8% to 15.5%. The 'one-off' tax could be paid in eight, equal annual interest-free instalments. If the US shareholder was a S Corporation (but not a partnership), it could defer this tax charge further.
809. S Corporations and partnerships cannot use this exemption, nor can RICs and Real Estate Investment Trusts. However, a 'look-through' rule permits a regular US corporation, which is a partner in a partnership, to claim the exemption in respect of its share of a non-US dividend paid to the partnership (cf. the French decision in *Artemis* – *see* section 6.5.1). The section 245A exemption does not apply to Subpart F inclusions nor to any dividend which gives rise to a non-US deduction or other tax benefit. The company paying the dividend must not be a 'passive foreign investment corporation'. This exemption only applies to dividends and not to capital gains on disposing of shares in the non-US corporation, except where that gain is treated as a dividend under section 1248 Internal Revenue Code.
810. The US corporate shareholder must meet a minimum one-year holding period to qualify for the exemption.

of a 'controlled foreign corporation'.[811] This GILTI charge applies to distributed or undistributed income. Despite its name, it is in fact imposed on the total net income of the 'controlled foreign corporation' in excess of 10% of its aggregate tax basis in its *tangible, depreciable* property (less any relevant net interest expense).[812] GILTI is a new, wide-ranging US tax charge on outbound investment.

It is unlikely that the GILTI charge can be avoided by making the lower-tier 'disregarded entity' elections which have been used in the past to accumulate low-taxed income outside the US without triggering Subpart F. However, the GILTI charge applies in addition to the existing Subpart F rules. Managing existing Subpart F exposure in a manner which minimises relevant non-US taxes remains important, especially as the tax rate on GILTI is significantly less than for Subpart F inclusions (which are taxed at regular US corporate income tax rates). 'Disregarded entity' planning may have ongoing relevance in managing Subpart F exposure.[813]

Managing non-US taxes of a US multinational group will become even more important for two reasons. The new dividend exemption in respect of non-US dividends means that any non-US tax on non-US distributed profits is an absolute cost. Besides, at most 80% of any non-US tax on GILTI can be credited in the US, and in practice it may be difficult to credit even that much. Entity classification is likely to be important when managing such non-US taxes.

7.2.6.2.4 Entity Classification Decisions in the Light of the 2017 Changes

The 2017 Act is likely to drive other tax-planning responses, which may require US entity classification choices.

The GILTI charge on a *non-corporate* US shareholder in a controlled foreign corporation is very high (although an individual US shareholder can elect to be taxed at corporate rates under section 962 Internal Revenue Code). Hence, a non-corporate US shareholder may want its interest in the controlled foreign corporation to be held through an entity which is a domestic corporation for US tax purposes.

If, however, that shareholder is determined to own directly its interest in a non-US business, it may want to reclassify any controlled foreign corporation in which it invests as a partnership or disregarded entity. Any tax costs of that reclassification

811. The GILTI charge does not only apply to 10% US shareholders which are corporations. It also applies to an individual 10% US shareholder but at regular progressive tax rates for individuals. Unlike corporate shareholders, the individual shareholder does not benefit from an effective GILTI tax rate of 10.25% until 2025 (and thereafter 13.125%). Only corporate 10% US shareholders can claim a US credit for non-US tax on income subject to GILTI. That credit is capped at 80% of the relevant non-US tax. There is a separate GILTI 'basket' for US foreign tax credit purposes, which makes it harder to use any excess foreign tax credits relating to GILTI.
812. That tax basis will be computed on US tax principles. It is easier for GILTI to arise if the controlled foreign corporation has valuable intangibles and/or fully depreciated tangibles.
813. The GILTI rules differ in key respects from Subpart F. Broadly, Congress intended the tax burden in respect of GILTI to be less than in respect of Subpart F income, at least for 10% US shareholders which are corporations. However, sometimes it makes sense to structure so that income falls within Subpart F or the 'high tax' exclusion from Subpart F, rather than GILTI: *see* Libin Zhang: 'To the Frying Pan: New Virtues of Subpart F Income over GILTI' (2 July 2018) Tax Notes, at 73.

must be evaluated.[814] Assuming they are acceptable, owning through a partnership or disregarded entity will give that US person greater scope for using losses, claiming capital gains treatment and obtaining foreign tax credit relief. It will avoid GILTI (and Subpart F in general) although it will be currently taxable in the US on income and capital gains of the partnership or disregarded entity, whether or not distributed.

While the US has created a dividend exemption for certain non-US dividends paid to a US corporation, a controlled foreign corporation may not be able to rely on this exemption when computing its own Subpart F income or GILTI, if it receives a dividend from a lower-tier, non-US subsidiary. Hence, it may make sense to elect to disregard that lower-tier subsidiary. The question of dividend exemption is then unnecessary.

Whether an entity is a partnership or a disregarded entity may also be relevant in relation to section 163(j) Internal Revenue Code, which now introduces an overall cap on deductible interest expense for all US taxpayers. This cap is set at 30% of 'adjusted taxable income', which is initially defined as EBITDA but in later years as EBIT.[815] Either way, the US taxpayer will be able to take into account its interest in the income of a non-US partnership or disregarded entity when computing 'adjusted taxable income'. That increases its 'adjusted taxable income', which limits the impact of section 163(j).

7.2.6.2.5 *Final Thoughts on the US Entity Classification Rules*

While significant tax planning has been based on the US entity classification rules introduced in 1997, not all of that planning should be seen as abusive. In any case, those rules illustrate some broader themes. The US has recognised that classifying entities for tax purposes by reference to non-tax structural features is an increasingly flawed and arbitrary approach, especially when the structural and other differences between a corporation and a partnership have been greatly eroded. The old approach is also a poor use of taxpayer and IRS time and resources.

However, while the non-tax differences between corporations and partnerships are increasingly insignificant, the Internal Revenue Code still distinguishes between them and taxes them very differently. US corporations and their members are subject to two levels of taxation under Subchapter C[816] of the Internal Revenue Code: at entity level on all their profits and again at member level, on distributed profits. There is limited relief against the tax at member level for US or non-US tax borne at entity level. By contrast, under Subchapter K, partnerships are subject to a single US tax charge on their profits (whether or not distributed) but calculated by reference to the tax position of the partnership members and charged on them. Relief for non-US tax on those profits is more readily available. In short, the partnership is 'transparent'.

The contrast between Subchapter C and Subchapter K is an entrenched feature of the US tax system. Any line drawn between entities to determine which Subchapter

814. For example, tax on any deemed liquidation of the 'controlled foreign corporation'.
815. This is less generous than the equivalent UK rules introduced in 2017.
816. There is of course an exception for smaller US corporations which elect for 'pass-through' taxation under Subchapter S.

governs is likely to be somewhat arbitrary.[817] The ability to elect classification gives the taxpayer leeway to avoid an arbitrary outcome being imposed on it. That leeway is not total because many US and non-US entities are corporations 'per se'. The rules on 'per se' corporations sometimes draw odd distinctions but are likely to endure, to protect the scope of Subchapter C taxation.

From the US Government's perspective, avoidance issues raised by elective entity classification are often better dealt with by tackling them directly rather than by denying taxpayers their limited right to elect. The fact that an entity falls within Subchapter K (or is disregarded) does not prevent the US from limiting consequences which might otherwise flow automatically from a 'transparent' approach. Of course, counteracting specific avoidance issues further complicates the US tax code. This partly offsets the simplification benefits of the 1997 changes.

7.3 THE DUTCH ENTITY CLASSIFICATION RULES

7.3.1 Introduction

As a civil law jurisdiction with its own distinct views on aspects of entity classification and its impact on double tax treaties,[818] the Netherlands offers an interesting contrast to both UK and US entity classification methods.

7.3.2 Classification of Domestic Dutch Entities

Article 2(1) of the Netherlands Corporate Income Tax Act 1969[819] lists the entities that are taxable on their worldwide income if resident in the Netherlands. This list includes Dutch corporate entities[820] such as a public limited company ('naamloze vennootschap' or 'NV'), a private limited company ('besloten vennootschap' or 'BV'),

817. This is true, for example, of the US default classification rules in respect of 'eligible entities' e.g., their focus on limited or unlimited liability in relation to non-US entities.
818. *See* the Dutch observations on Articles 1, 23A and 23B of the OECD Model. These are cited by De Graaf and Gooijer in their country report on the Netherlands in Volume 99b Cahiers de Droit Fiscal International (2014), *supra,* at pp. 566-567.
819. Wet op de vennootschapsbelasting 1969 (hereinafter 'CITA').
820. Being a civil law jurisdiction, Dutch domestic law recognises both 'formal' and 'informal' partnerships, a distinction not known in common law jurisdictions. It turns largely on the extent to which, under civil law agency concepts, members of the partnership are sufficiently disclosed to third parties that they can incur obligations to them because of partnership activities. The Dutch 'formal' partnership is the 'Vennootschap onder firma' or 'VOF'. The 'informal' Dutch partnership is the 'maatschap' whose members may or may not be fully disclosed to third parties. If not fully disclosed, the 'maatschap' will be a form of 'silent' partnership, where the 'silent' partners will not incur obligations to third parties. For further discussion, *see* Part II of Avery Jones: Partnerships *supra* [2002] British Tax Review 375. The UK Court of Appeal has considered a VOF in a non-tax case, *Rowan Companies Incorporated v Lambert Eggink Offshore Transport Consultants VOF* [1998] CLC 1574. Relying on expert evidence, it concluded that a VOF was similar to a Scottish, rather than an English general partnership. Although not a 'complete' legal person like a body corporate, it could contract, sue and be sued in its own name because it represented the partners 'taken as a whole' and was not

co-operative associations, mutual insurance organisations, as well as foundations ('Stichtingen') and other associations ('Verenigingen').[821]

However, the list of Dutch entities taxable on their worldwide income under CITA also includes an 'open' limited partnership ('commanditaire vennootschap' or 'CV') CV.[822] This is one in which limited partners can be admitted without the prior consent of all other partners.[823] An 'open' CV enjoys a hybrid, 'part-transparent' tax status. It is a separate taxpayer under CITA in respect of the share of its profits allocable to the limited partners, but its general partners are taxable directly on their (typically small) share of those profits.[824] The general partner's profit share is deductible in computing the taxable profits of the 'open' CV. Like an English LP, a CV (whether 'open' or 'closed') is merely an agreement between its members which creates no legal personality. Hence one party to the agreement will usually act as general partner, and will hold the assets of the CV and incur its liabilities.[825]

It has therefore been possible to alter the classification of a CV for Dutch tax purposes by amending its rules on admitting limited partners. This is similar to the pre-1997 ability to change an entity's US tax classification by dropping or retaining structural features (notably, free transferability of members' interests). However, expert advice is needed when structuring a CV so as to make it 'open' or not.[826]

Similar tax rules apply to Dutch mutual investment funds (FGRs), even though such funds are typically contractual agreements, rather than legal entities or (perhaps) partnerships under Dutch company law. A FGR is therefore a separate entity for CITA if participations in it can be disposed of without the consent of all investors.[827] This is

just an aggregation of individual partners. Those individual partners were jointly and severally liable for the VOF's obligations under Article 18 of the Dutch Commercial Code.

821. For a broader discussion, *see* De Graaf and Gooijer *supra*, at p. 559. A co-operative does not normally have share capital. Therefore, subject to anti-avoidance rules, its distributions to members are free of Dutch dividend withholding tax although the entity remains subject to Dutch corporate income tax: Michael L. Molenaars: 'The Tax Significance of Legal Personality: A Dutch View' (December 2014) Tax Review, Issue 316, at 2.2.3. By contrast, the UK tax authorities regard some Dutch co-operatives as partnerships for UK tax purposes – International Tax Manual INTM 222000 (accessed 11 July 2022). 'Stichtingen' are legal entities with no members, created for a defined purpose, often charitable. They may not distribute to their founder: *see* Molenaars *supra*, at 2.1(i). However, the formal lack of members can be sidestepped by the Stichting issuing depositary receipts (a so-called Stichting administratiekantoor or STAK). Each receipt confers a proprietary interest in the underlying assets of the Stichting. A STAK is therefore regarded as 'transparent' for Dutch (and indeed UK) tax purposes.
822. Apart from 'open' CVs, Dutch general and limited partnerships are not regarded as separate taxable entities for CITA, although Dutch company law regards them as separate entities.
823. That is, admitted for reasons other than inheritance: *see* Article 2(3)(c) of the 1959 Algemene wet inzake rijksbelastingen (General Taxes Act) which defines an 'open' CV, whose most important features are described above. This applies to the CITA (and also to the personal income tax act/Wet inkomstenbelasting 2001).
824. This hybrid 'part-transparency' stems from the decision of the Hoge Raad (Supreme Court) of 7 July 1982, No. 20 655, *BNB* 1982/268.
825. *See* Molenaars *supra*, at 2.1(ii).
826. For a fuller discussion, including the 2007 'CV Decree' of the Dutch Ministry of Finance, *see* Molenaars *supra*, at 2.2.1.
827. This will not be the case if participations can only be transferred back to the fund itself or to certain close relatives of the relevant investor. For further discussion, including the 2007 'FGR Decree', *see* Molenaars *supra*, at 2.2.2.

so even though its assets will be held by a separate depositary with legal personality (often a 'stichting') for the risk and account of the FGR members (the investors).

If interests in a CV or FGR are not freely transferable in this way, it will be 'transparent' for Dutch tax purposes. This is the usual situation and merely means that its profits will be taxable only at the level of its members, based on their specific fiscal characteristics. It does not mean that the CV or mutual fund will be 'disregarded' or a fiscal 'nothing'.

In March 2021, the Dutch Ministry of Finance announced a consultation on proposals to change the Dutch entity classification rules. These changes seek to limit the situations where the Dutch rules create hybrid mismatches with other jurisdictions.[828] If they take effect, all CVs will become 'transparent' for Dutch tax purposes. An 'open' CV will no longer be a separate Dutch taxpayer. This will apply for Dutch income tax, corporate income tax and withholding tax on dividends, interest and royalties. The changes also affect FGRs. These will be 'transparent' for Dutch tax purposes, unless the FGR is obliged to repurchase participations regularly (i.e., it is 'open-ended') or those participations are 'publicly traded' on a regulated market or trading platform (cf. the US 'publicly-traded partnership' concept). Such repurchase obligations would be ignored if the repurchased participation can only be transferred to other FGR members or to members of the family of the person whose participation is repurchased. Family-controlled FGRs may still be 'transparent'. Existing 'open' CVs which cease to be 'opaque' because of these changes may be taxable on a deemed disposal of assets at fair market value. Their members may also be taxable on a deemed disposal of their interests in the 'open' CV. The proposals allow a 'rollover' of these liabilities or, at least, payment of these tax charges in equal instalments over ten years. It is currently unclear when the changes will come into force, although the proposals should be reintroduced in the Dutch Parliament in 2023.

Dutch tax law permits certain Dutch-resident companies to form a tax consolidation, or 'fiscal unity', for corporate income tax purposes. This does not lead to the members of the fiscal unity being 'disregarded' for such purposes. They remain as theoretical taxpayers, which can, for example, invoke tax treaties. However, their transactions, assets and liabilities are attributed to the parent company of the 'fiscal unity', which is the sole taxpayer.

7.3.3 Classification of Non-domestic Dutch Entities[829]

Dutch tax law adopts a 'resemblance' approach akin to UK tax law when classifying, for Dutch tax purposes, entities not formed under Dutch law.[830] It classifies them by

828. https://www.loyensloeff.com/en/en/news/news-articles/the-netherlands-brings-entity-tax-classification-rules-in-line-with-international-standards-n22176/?utm_medium = email&utm_source = newsletter&utm_campaign = tax_classification_rules_30032021_en_en&msdynttrid = KeHeo2CbsS5LP7KLUYnCqJb45U6s5u5-cWsVGWRLBtg.
829. For a fuller decision, *see* G.K. Fibbe and A.J.A. Stevens eds: 'Chapter 12. The Netherlands, in Hybrid Entities and the EU Direct Tax Directives'. Wolters Kluwer.
830. The basis for this is Article 2(1)(a) CITA mentioned above providing that domestic taxpayers include *inter alia*, Dutch NVs, BVs and other entities that have a capital divided into shares. The last category may include a limited company incorporated in another jurisdiction.

comparing them with Dutch entities.[831] Hence it focuses on the non-Dutch entity's characteristics under its governing law[832] and constitutional documents. The entity's non-Dutch tax classification is irrelevant.[833]

As in the UK, there are no hard and fast classification criteria for non-Dutch entities and case law guidance is limited. The Dutch Ministry of Finance has nevertheless published a Decree setting out relevant criteria. This Decree[834] distils relevant case law principles and is in practice very important. A taxpayer can invoke it under administrative law because it creates a legitimate expectation of particular tax treatment. It does not apply to the classification of non-Dutch foundations, mutual funds, trusts and similar entities.[835]

The Dutch Decree sets out four key factors:

(1) Can the non-Dutch entity legally own the assets with which it performs its activities, i.e., does it have separate legal personality ('the ownership factor')?
(2) Do all members of the entity enjoy limited liability for its obligations to third parties ('the liability factor')?
(3) Does the entity have the equivalent of share capital ('the share factor')?
(4) Can new members be admitted without the consent of all other members (ignoring cases where a member's interest passes by inheritance) ('the free transferability factor')? This factor will be downgraded if the proposed Dutch entity classification changes become law.

Echoing the pre-1997 US entity classification rules, the Decree considers the non-Dutch entity to be non-transparent only if the answer to at least three of the four

831. It does not follow the Italian approach of treating all such entities as corporations.
832. The governing law for these purposes is the law of the place of the entity's incorporation or formation, rather than the law where it has its 'seat'.
833. Unlike, for example, Denmark, which in some cases takes into account the tax classification of an entity in another jurisdiction, so as to avoid a classification mismatch: *see* Parada: Article 1(2) *supra,* at pp. 370-371. In a Report for the Dutch Association of Tax Science (Vereniging voor Belastingwetenschap), G.K. Fibbe and A.J.A. Stevens argued that Dutch domestic law should apply the Danish approach in addition to the corporate resemblance approach. In case of a mismatch, the Netherlands would follow the other state's entity classification. Fibbe had already argued in his PhD thesis that a symmetrical approach should be enshrined in a EU Directive. *See* G.K. Fibbe and A.J.A. Stevens: 'Internationale Fiscal Aspecten'. Chapter 6. Belastingheffing van personenvennootschappen. Rapport van de Commissie Personenvennootschappen 2020, 151 et seq.
834. Decree of the State Secretary of Finance of 11 December 2009, CPP2009/519M BNB 2010/58 (Kwalificatie buitenlandse samenwerkingsverbanden). There is no formal English translation of this Decree. It supersedes and amends earlier Decrees of 1997 and 2004. In particular, the factors listed in the 2009 Decree no longer include whether a resolution is needed to distribute the entity's profits. This would be a highly relevant factor for UK entity classification purposes: *see Anson v HMRC* [2015] STC 1777 (*see* section 2.14) and *Dreyfus v IRC* 14 TC 560, where the Court of Appeal (*see* section 2.10) concluded (wrongly in the view of HMRC) that such a resolution was needed in relation to a French SNC. The 1997 Decree is discussed in Avery Jones: Partnerships *supra,* at pp. 415-419. Fn 200 of that article refers to a decision of the Court of Appeal of Amsterdam of 4 February 1995, No. 93/1466, Infobulletin 1995/315, which concluded that a French SNC was transparent for Dutch tax purposes, contrary to *Dreyfus* but in line with what HMRC now regard as the correct answer.
835. *See* paragraph 3.4 of the Decree.

questions is 'yes'. This at-least-three-out-of-four approach is more mechanistic than that adopted by HMRC following *Memec.*[836] Unlike the pre-1997 US rules, the Dutch rules place some, but not conclusive emphasis on whether there is legal personality.[837] They do not place any emphasis on whether management is centralised nor on whether the entity has a limited life.

The Decree also states that a non-Dutch entity is non-'transparent' if members' liability is limited to their agreed capital contributions; the entity itself owns its business operation; and that business is not otherwise operated at the risk of, or on behalf of the entity members.[838] This separate rule apparently cuts across the four-factor approach mentioned above.[839]

The Decree also provides that an entity which would prima facie be 'transparent' (on the basis of the four-factor test) is nevertheless non-'transparent' if it is comparable to a Dutch 'open' CV or if its capital is divided into freely transferable shares. As discussed in section 7.3.2, what makes an 'open' CV non-'transparent' for Dutch tax purposes is the free transferability of members' interests. Where that feature is present, the non-Dutch entity will be comparable to a Dutch 'open' CV if it carries on business; there is at least one general partner with unlimited liability; at least one limited partner who cannot bind the partnership by making management decisions; and there is no share capital. If the proposed Dutch entity classification changes take effect, a non-Dutch entity which resembles a Dutch CV for the reasons given above (but ignoring free transferability of interests) will be 'transparent' for Dutch tax purposes.

Finally, the Decree is not decisive where the non-Dutch entity is directly comparable with a Dutch co-operative or mutual insurance association.

The Ministry of Finance's website contains a list of non-Dutch entities whose status has been ruled on by the Dutch tax authorities.[840] This list is indicative, like its UK counterpart: *see* section 2.13. However, it is lengthier than the UK list. It also

---

836. [1998] STC 754. The entity classification criteria produced by HMRC following *Memec* are all potentially relevant although some are more important than others. *See* sections 2.13 and 3.7.
837. As pointed out in Blanchard *supra*, legal personality is not relevant for US entity classification purposes. Hence any focus on it by the UK or the Netherlands in relation to US entities raises the risk of a classification mismatch. Strictly speaking, the Dutch emphasis is on whether a non-Dutch entity is a capital company or a partnership. Hence, a general partnership with legal personality formed under the law of one of the states of the US can be regarded as transparent, because it resembles a Dutch general partnership (a VOF). In particular, its partnership characteristics are more relevant than its legal personality. The distinction between partnerships and capital companies is not always clear as demonstrated by Dutch court decisions on a UK LLP, which does not have a capital divided into shares. Hence from a Dutch perspective, it has characteristics in almost equal measure of a partnership and a capital company. The District Court of The Hague, 26 February 2019, No. 18/1972 and 18/1974, ECLI:NL:RB-DHA:2019:1565 regarded a UK LLP as transparent because it had more characteristics of a partnership. The Court of Appeal of Amsterdam 11 April 2017, No. 16/00225, ECLI:GHAMS:2017:2577 also ruled that the UK LLP was to be considered as transparent.
838. This part of the Decree reflects a decision of the Dutch Supreme Court of 2 June 2006, No. 40,919. BNB 2006/288, in which it confirmed that a US LLC was opaque. The Dutch authorities have apparently ruled that LLCs formed in a number of US states are non-'transparent' for Dutch tax purposes.
839. *See* Blanchard: Significance *supra,* at p. 14.
840. Clarification of 4 May 2016 (Lijst van gekwalificeerde buitenlandse samenwerkingsverbanden) https://www.belastingdienst.nl/wps/wcm/connect/bldcontentnl/themaoverstijgend/brochu

provides some explanation, by reference to the four factors mentioned above, why an entity has been classified in a particular way for Dutch tax purposes, which makes it more useful than the UK equivalent. It has been regularly updated, and the Dutch tax authorities will provide advance rulings on the classification of entities.

Some interesting points emerge from the Dutch list. The fact that an entity can own its own assets clearly does not prevent the Netherlands regarding it as transparent. However, the Netherlands generally regards LLCs formed in various US states as non-transparent, along with some LLPs (e.g., in Delaware but not in the UK) and all US limited liability LPs. This contrasts with the UK's general willingness to treat all types of US partnership as 'transparent': *see* section 2.13.3. It also contrasts with the Supreme Court decision in *Anson* [2015] STC 1777.

Non-Dutch foundations, mutual funds, trusts and comparable entities fall outside the Decree. Such entities are to be classified on the basis of which domestic Dutch entity they most closely resemble. Non-resident non-Dutch mutual funds, trusts and similar entities could be regarded as special-purpose funds, or 'doelvermogens', for Dutch tax purposes.

The Dutch rules on classifying entities therefore do not deal in the same way with those which are and those which are not formed under Dutch company law. This could raise questions about compatibility with EU law: *see* section 6.7.6.

The Dutch 'corporate resemblance' test for classifying non-Dutch entities will change if the proposals published in March 2021 by the Dutch Ministry of Finance take effect in the future.[841] First, as all Dutch CVs will henceforth be 'transparent', the same will apply to equivalent non-Dutch entities. This will reduce the scope for 'hybrid mismatches' which would have arisen in the past because of the Dutch treatment of an 'open' CV as 'opaque'.

Second, there are two proposed default rules which only apply if, under the 'corporate resemblance' test, there is no clearly equivalent Dutch entity. The first default rule applies if the relevant non-Dutch entity owns a participation in a Dutch entity subject to corporate income tax, or vice versa. It requires the Netherlands to follow the entity classification rules (if any) of the non-Dutch entity's incorporation state. The first default rule does not apply if the Dutch and non-Dutch entities enter into a debt transaction or an intangibles licence but there is no equity link between them. The second default rule treats the non-Dutch entity as 'opaque', and a Dutch taxpayer in its own right, but only if it is based in the Netherlands. Such situations may be unlikely. If this second rule applies, it could lead to 'hybrid mismatches' if those with an interest in the non-Dutch entity are regarded, in their home jurisdictions, as members of a 'transparent' entity.

The first proposed default rule is linked to the ongoing debate about whether the existing Dutch 'corporate resemblance' test can create unequal treatment which restricts unjustifiably the EU freedoms. The debate centres on UK LLPs which have no

res_en_publicaties/lijst_van_gekwalificeerde_buitenlandse_samenwerkingsverbanden (accessed 11 July 2022). For an unofficial English translation of this list, *see* the Annex to Molenaars *supra.*

841. *See* fn 828.

Dutch equivalent. Some Dutch courts have treated them as transparent (*see* footnote 837) but others have not.

7.3.4 Lessons from the Dutch Experience

The Netherlands has adopted a method of classifying non-Dutch entities which is similar to the UK method, focusing on structural features of the entity under its governing law and constitutional documents. It then uses these factors to identify the closest equivalent Dutch domestic entity. The factors chosen are not the same as those which are relevant in the UK, and inevitably the choice of factors is somewhat arbitrary.

The Netherlands approach is simpler, and more mechanistic than that of the UK when applying the four classification factors which it often regards as key. No one factor is conclusive under Dutch tax law, and it is possible for an entity to be 'transparent' in the Netherlands by failing to satisfy at least two factors. An example could be an entity which owns its own assets and whose members have limited liability but which lacks share capital and where members' interests cannot be transferred without the consent of other members.

The UK and Dutch approaches are not symmetrical. This alone could lead to entity classification mismatches, even though the two countries' 'resemblance' approaches are philosophically similar.

This more mechanistic Dutch approach provides taxpayers with more certainty about which factors count. To that extent, it is superior to the UK approach. The factors which count for Dutch tax purposes, plus a more mechanistic approach and a more developed ruling practice, affect how easily taxpayers can structure so as to achieve a desired tax outcome (e.g., a cross-border mismatch) in another jurisdiction.

The Dutch Decree on entity classification no longer places any emphasis on whether members are entitled to profits as they arise without an intervening resolution by a third party. Interestingly, that Decree still attaches importance to legal personality, even though this is a highly formalistic criterion, and there are Dutch entities (notably, the 'open' CV) which lack legal personality but are still subject to Dutch corporate income tax.[842]

Limited liability and the free transferability of members' interests remain relevant factors for Dutch tax purposes. They can be readily manipulated by well-advised taxpayers. By contrast, centralised management of an entity is not relevant yet is less easy to manipulate. Hence the Dutch rules have offered significant scope to pick a desired entity classification.[843] This has helped to create cross-border hybrid mismatches, notably with the US. For example, a Dutch 'transparent' entity can be created by forming a 'closed' CV, with significant limitations on transferring members' interests. This can nevertheless elect to be treated as a corporation for US tax purposes.

842. There is draft legislation to change the Dutch Civil Law Code so that all Dutch partnerships will have legal personality. This is not expected to affect the tax transparency of such partnerships, nor the Dutch tax classification of non-Dutch entities.

843. This is now subject to the proposed Dutch reforms.

'Transparency' for Dutch tax purposes means that the profits of the entity are taxable at the level of its members, reflecting each member's tax circumstances. There is nothing akin to disregarded entity status in the US. On the other hand, the Netherlands does not subscribe to the concept of 'translucency' applied to partnerships in France and discussed in section 6.5.1.

Historically, the Netherlands has not had controlled foreign company rules, apart from section 13a CITA which can require marking-to-market of shareholdings of at least 25% in non-Dutch companies which are taxed at an effective rate below 10% and which hold mainly portfolio investments. Therefore, classifying non-Dutch entities so as to avoid exposure under controlled foreign company rules has not been a major issue. That may change now that the Netherlands has enacted such rules to satisfy Article 7 of the EU Anti-Tax Avoidance Directive 2016.[844] The Netherlands does not appear to have enacted especially stringent controlled foreign company rules.

The Netherlands has already taken steps to limit its attractiveness as a location for hybrid structures, in the wake of BEPS and the EU Anti-Tax Avoidance Directive. The 2021 proposals to change Dutch entity classification rules have already been discussed. In any case, anti-'reverse hybrid' rules took effect from 1 January 2020, in line with Article 9a of that EU Directive. These target the hitherto popular CV/BV structures much used by US multinationals.

The Netherlands has broadened its domestic exemption from dividend withholding tax (based on the EU Parent-Subsidiary Directive) so that it also applies to certain corporate shareholders resident in Dutch treaty partner jurisdictions outside the EU. When applying this widened exemption to dividends paid to hybrid entities, the Netherlands will not simply classify the hybrid according to its own domestic entity classification rules. Instead, it will apply the exemption in a manner similar to Article 1(2) of the OECD Model. Hence it will give priority to the classification of that hybrid entity in the jurisdiction where its members are resident.[845] Therefore, the exemption will not apply to Dutch 'reverse hybrid' structures, such as CV/BV structures.[846]

844. Council Directive (EU) 2016/1164 of 19 July 2016, as amended by Council Directive (EU) 2017/952.
845. Article 4(9) and (10) of the Wet op de dividendbelasting 1965 (Dividend Withholding Tax Act 1965).
846. *See* https://www.debrauw.com/articles/proposed-atad-2-hybrid-rules-in-the-netherlands-will-have-far-reaching-impact (accessed 12 July 2022).

CHAPTER 8

Conclusion

8.1 INTRODUCTION

Earlier chapters addressed various questions about the UK approach to entity classification and tax transparency. It is helpful to summarise the answers before setting out some more general conclusions on the UK approach.

8.1.1 How Does the UK Classify Entities, Especially in Relation to Companies, Partnerships and Trusts?

The UK entity classification rules (especially in relation to companies, partnerships and trusts) are summarised in sections 3.9, 4.3.7 and 8.6.1. The connection between classifying entities and 'tax transparency' is summarised in sections 1.2 and 8.3.

8.1.2 What Does 'Tax Transparency' Mean in UK Tax Law? Does It Have More than One Meaning?

'Tax transparency' means a number of different things in UK tax law, in relation to different entities in different contexts and for the purposes of different taxes. These separate meanings have evolved largely independently and piecemeal. The meaning of 'transparency' in relation to trusts depends on the tax and the type of trust. It is summarised in section 4.3.7 for the purposes of income tax and capital gains tax. The special meaning of 'transparency' in relation to partnerships for the purposes of taxing capital gains is discussed in Appendix A.

What 'transparency' signifies, in relation to UK taxes other than those on income and gains, is discussed in section 5.8. This includes the extent to which corporate affiliation can be 'traced' through 'transparent' partnerships. This is further analysed for the purposes of corporation tax in Appendix A.

'Transparency' is a different concept from the (many) rules allowing income and gains of an entity to be attributed to other persons with a link to it (e.g., shareholders of a 'close' company and settlors or beneficiaries of a trust). Those rules are specifically targeted at avoidance, and especially tax deferral, although their effect may be similar to treating an entity as 'transparent'.

8.1.3 How Do UK Double Tax Treaties Address Entity Classification and Tax Transparency Issues, Especially when the UK and Its Treaty Partners Classify an Entity in Different Ways?

The UK has addressed entity classification and 'transparency' issues in its tax treaties broadly along OECD-approved lines since the 1999 Partnership Report. Article 1(2) of the OECD Model and now Article 3(1) of the MLI reinforce this trend. However, there are variations, e.g., the UK-France treaty, which reflects particular French concerns, and the UK-US treaty, which reflects long-standing US treaty negotiation priorities (which now largely coincide with OECD thinking).

8.1.4 Is the UK Approach to Entity Classification Affected by EU Law?

In some respects, the UK rules regarding the classification of entities and their 'transparency' seem inconsistent with the EU 'fundamental freedoms', although the practical impact of this is limited now that the UK has left the EU.

8.1.5 Is the Approach of Other Jurisdictions (In Particular, the US and the Netherlands) to These Issues Instructive?

The Netherlands operates (*see* section 7.3) a 'resemblance' test (not dissimilar to the UK's) for classifying non-Dutch entities. It exhibits many of the weaknesses of such tests but is more clearly articulated and easier to administer than the UK equivalent. The Netherlands is planning more extensive reform in this area in the near future.

The US abandoned its old 'four factor' resemblance test in 1997 and moved to the (in)famous 'check-the-box' system. Descriptions of that system have tended to exaggerate its features, but it is a fertile source of entity classification mismatches in cross-border transactions. However, with modifications, it offers a basis for reforming the UK entity classification rules so that they are more user-friendly, without encouraging mismatch-based avoidance activity. This is discussed further below.

8.2 THE RELEVANCE OF 'ENTITY CLASSIFICATION'

Entity classification is crucial when defining the boundaries of a tax system, which depend on defining those persons which: (i) are liable for the relevant tax or (ii) even if they are not taxable (e.g., partnerships and some trusts) are still treated for tax purposes as separate entities whose status can affect the tax liability of others (e.g., the members of a partnership or, in the case of a trust, the settlor and beneficiaries).

Defining natural persons (i.e., individuals) as taxpayers is straightforward, although they may have different (in)capacities from time to time, such as when they are minors, mentally ill or act as trustees. It is harder to define those arrangements which should be treated as legal entities, not 'nothings', for relevant tax purposes. Some such legal entities may be liable for direct taxes in their own right (e.g., companies, UK 'authorised unit trusts' or discretionary trusts with UK-resident trustees), if they have the necessary link to the taxing jurisdiction. Other entities may not be direct taxpayers (e.g., partnerships or trusts within section 60 TCGA), even if they have that link. Nevertheless, their existence may affect the liability of others, especially those with an economic interest in them. Hence these other entities are not tax 'nothings'. An example is where two companies are regarded as 'related' or 'connected' because they are under the common ownership or control of a third entity (such as a partnership) which has no substantive tax liability. The partnership, which has a tax identity, creates a connection between the two companies. That connection may then affect how transactions between those companies are taxed.

A tax system will need to define whether arrangements outside its territorial jurisdiction amount to legal entities and if so, what sort. This will be essential when taxing investment into that jurisdiction, as well as investment by its residents in other jurisdictions. A good example is when taxpayers resident in one jurisdiction, A, have economic interests in an entity or arrangement located outside A and which may pay tax elsewhere on its activities. The way in which A defines that entity or arrangement will affect how A's own residents are taxed and, in particular, their right to any double taxation relief from A in respect of non-A tax on that entity or arrangement. Double taxation relief may vary a lot depending on whether A treats that entity or arrangement as a company, rather than a partnership or a trust.

8.3 THE MULTIFACETED CONCEPT OF 'TAX TRANSPARENCY'

If an entity is classified in its home jurisdiction as having no tax liability of its own, that raises the further question of whether and how it is 'tax-transparent'.

'Tax transparency' is shorthand for situations where persons with an 'interest' in an entity or arrangement are taxed as if they were carrying on the underlying activities of that entity or arrangement or at the very least owning its income and assets. Hence the tax liability on that entity is determined at the level of those with an 'interest' in it, taking account of their tax profile. The meaning of an 'interest' can vary. It will usually include a legal and economic interest such as a share or a beneficial interest under a trust. It may (?) include less direct links, e.g., that of a settlor or a discretionary beneficiary under a trust. The entity itself will typically have no substantive liability of its own. It may have a 'representative' liability, e.g., the liability of UK-resident trustees of an English law trust with a vested income beneficiary. If so, tax can be provisionally collected from the entity on behalf of those with an interest in it, but the tax characteristics of those interest holders will shape the ultimate tax liability in respect of that entity's activities.[847] So if those with a relevant interest are tax-exempt, that may trigger a refund of tax provisionally collected at entity level.

'Tax transparency' classically means that entity profits are taxed at the level of those with an interest in it, whether or not they are distributed. Those persons may have to fund from other sources the tax on any undistributed income and gain. 'Tax transparency' of this kind can be problematic where an entity has a large and fluctuating body of members, especially if each member has limited influence over its affairs. Such members may have liquidity issues when paying tax on their share of undistributed profits, unless the entity commits to distribute enough money to fund such tax. Tax authorities will also want to avoid pursuing a large and fluctuating body of members of a 'transparent' entity for tax on smallish profit entitlements. This collection problem can be resolved by imposing on the entity a representative liability, on behalf of its members, to collect most, if not all, of their ultimate tax liability. Members can then seek refunds if that representative liability turns out to be too high, as it often will.

'Tax transparency' does not work easily in relation to trusts with discretionary beneficiaries, whose 'interest' in trust profits is highly contingent. Taxing them on undistributed profit would make little sense.

'Tax transparency' is the opposite of the way in which companies are normally taxed. With limited exceptions, the UK, like most jurisdictions, treats companies as taxable entities in their own right, notably in respect of their income and gains. The company's tax liability is not normally affected by the tax characteristics of the company's members, e.g., where they are resident and what reliefs and exemptions they are entitled to.

Members of a company are therefore usually exposed to economic double taxation of income and gain: once at the level of the company itself and then again if and when income and gain (net of company-level tax) is distributed to members, or value is otherwise realised by them (e.g., when they sell shares in the company). Some jurisdictions (notably, the US) do relatively little to alleviate economic double taxation of distributed profit.[848] Their systems of taxing corporate profits are often referred to as 'classical systems'.

The UK began with such a system in 1965 when corporation tax was first introduced. For the purposes of taxing non-corporate shareholders, it largely reverted to such a system in 2016, but UK corporate shareholders typically benefit from an exemption on distributed profit. From 1973 until 2016, the UK experimented with various devices to give non-corporate members some relief, against their own tax liability on distributed profits, for tax at company level. Such devices never gave members of a company full relief for company-level tax. While members were not usually taxed on undistributed corporate profits, the company was taxed on them. However, that company liability was typically imposed at rates well below marginal income tax rates for individual members. Hence if company profit was not distributed,

847. As in *Williams v Singer* 7 TC 387: *see* section 4.3.3.1.
848. For a summary of the competing arguments about dealing with economic double taxation of corporate profit, *see* Glen Loutzenhiser: 'Tiley's Revenue Law'. 10th edition, at pp. 984-990.

the company's lack of transparency reduced the economic burden of taxation on those members.[849]

'Tax transparency' also usually means that a person with an interest in an entity is treated as entitled to income or gain of the same character as the underlying income or gain of the entity. However, for an entity to be 'tax transparent', must the interest holder be taxable on a percentage of underlying income or gain exactly corresponding to its pro rata 'interest' in the entity? Moreover, must it become entitled to that income or gain for tax purposes as soon as it arises to the entity, even if it is not then distributed?

The classic answer to both these questions is 'yes'. However, 'transparency' is a number of variations on a theme. One limited form of UK tax transparency is where a life interest holder in an English law trust is regarded as entitled to distributed or undistributed income of the same *character* as that arising to the trustees from their activities, even if the *quantum* of that entitlement is reduced by taxes and other trust expenses.[850] It can also be argued that, if trust beneficiaries are entitled to income and gain of the same character as that arising to the trustees, it matters less whether that entitlement arises precisely when the income or gain arises to the trustees. Hence another, modified form of 'tax transparency' is where beneficiaries of a discretionary trust are treated as entitled to a blended mix of the underlying trust income, but only if and when that income is distributed to them.[851]

More radical variants of 'transparency' exist, depending on the rules being applied. Hence, when taxing partnership income in the UK, partners are regarded as carrying on the underlying business of the partnership collectively so that they are entitled to the distributed and undistributed profits of that business, and incur its losses, in proportion to their profit-sharing entitlements. Those income profits (receipts less expenses) are first computed at partnership, not partner, level before being allocated to partners. Hence the partnership is not ignored, but this form of 'transparency' goes beyond simply treating the source and character of income as unaffected by interposing the partnership.[852]

When taxing partnership capital gains, UK tax law goes even further (in sections 59 and 59A TCGA, amplified by Statement of Practice D12). It treats each partner as having a fractional interest in each underlying partnership asset, consistent with the partnership's profit-sharing arrangements. This is a tax fiction because a partner cannot usually say that it is entitled to a specific undivided interest in a particular partnership asset.[853] Sections 59 and 59A TCGA are burdensome because each partner must keep track of its fractional interests in underlying partnership assets, its base cost

849. Of course, a low headline rate of corporation tax is only one factor in determining whether there is a low effective tax rate.
850. *See Baker v Archer-Shee* 11 TC 749 and related cases in section 4.3.3 above.
851. *See Drummond v Collins* 8 TC 525, and ESC B18.
852. *See*, for income tax purposes, sections 846 et seq. ITTOIA and, for corporation tax purposes, sections 1259 et seq. CTA 2009.
853. This is true in relation to both English and Scottish partnerships. Section 60 TCGA adopts a similar and potentially more radical 'look through' approach to 'bare trusts'.

in each of those interests as well as any relevant increases or reductions. Such increases and reductions can sometimes trigger an unfunded tax liability.[854]

Occasionally, UK tax law adopts a less radical transparency analysis when taxing partnership capital gains: *see* Schedule 7AD TCGA, where an insurance company is a limited partner in a 'venture capital investment partnership'.[855] In that case, section 59 TCGA 1992 is largely disapplied and the partnership interest is treated as a separate asset.

'Tax transparency' very rarely means that one can disregard altogether an entity or arrangement, i.e., treat it as a 'nothing' so that one can trace the affiliation of other persons through that entity or arrangement as if it did not exist. A rare non-UK example of such a tax 'nothing' is where, under the US 'check-the-box' regulations, a single-member 'eligible entity', is 'disregarded' for Federal tax purposes. In that case, the entity is simply treated as a branch of the single member,[856] while transactions between the entity and the single member are in principle ignored.

'Transparency' is not a concept confined to taxes on income and gains, but that is where it is mainly encountered. By contrast, entities are not usually regarded as 'transparent' for VAT purposes, and this is increasingly true in relation to IHT, since the 2006 changes to the taxation of 'settlements'.

8.4 'TAX TRANSPARENCY' VERSUS ANTI-AVOIDANCE ATTRIBUTION RULES: WHAT IS THE DIFFERENCE AND WHEN DOES IT MATTER?

Whether there is transparency, and what form it takes, are policy choices about taxing entities in a particular way. Where 'transparency' leads to the holder of an interest in an entity being entitled to underlying income or gain, whether or not distributed, then its effect is similar to tax rules (e.g., the UK 'controlled foreign company' rules[857] and the income tax 'settlement' rules)[858] which combat tax deferral or avoidance by imposing current taxation on an entity's undistributed income or gain. That tax is imposed on persons linked, to varying degrees, with the entity.

However, the effect of 'tax transparency' differs from those other rules ('*attribution rules*'), and it helps to distinguish between the two. Attribution rules often contain carefully designed exceptions, including defences based on the taxpayer lacking an avoidance motive.[859] Attribution rules usually only attribute income to a UK-resident taxpayer. Where an arrangement is treated as 'tax transparent', such exceptions are less likely. Tax on distributed or undistributed income and gain will simply be charged by reference to the pro rata legal and economic interest of the taxpayer in the

854. Statement of Practice D12 partially mitigates this tax exposure, especially when partnership sharing ratios change, e.g., on the departure of a partner or the admission of a new partner. *See* Appendix A.
855. *See* paragraph 2, Schedule 7AD. *See* Appendix A.
856. *See* section 7.2.4.2.
857. Part 9A TIOPA.
858. Part 5 Chapter 5 ITTOIA.
859. For example, section 742A ITA in relation to the 'transfer of assets abroad' rules.

'transparent' entity, whether or not the taxpayer is UK resident. All that matters is that the relationship of the member with the entity's underlying activity is sufficiently intertwined that the member should be taxed as if it were engaging in that activity.

Where attribution rules bite, their effect may be quite harsh because they have an explicit or implicit[860] goal of counteracting avoidance. For example, where the 'settlement' rules in Chapter 5 Part 5 ITTOIA bite, the 'settlor' can be taxed on attributed 'settlement' income even if the 'settlor' has no legal claim on that income.[861] The 'settlor' charge applies because the 'settlor' has instigated the arrangement, and is regarded as having ongoing influence over it, even if others can only ever be its economic beneficiaries. By contrast, where an arrangement is 'tax transparent', the tax liability of a person with an interest in that arrangement will be more tightly linked to an actual legal and economic stake in the underlying activities. This is because arrangements are not usually treated as 'tax transparent' to combat avoidance. Hence the income tax liability of a partner in a partnership will be measured by reference to that partner's profit-sharing entitlement,[862] whether or not the partner has significant influence within the partnership. Under the rule in *Baker v Archer-Shee,* the holder of the interest in possession is only entitled for tax purposes to underlying income which would also be income for trust law purposes. In short, the income which it could demand from the trustees as income beneficiary.[863]

Furthermore, attribution rules do not always treat the taxpayer as entitled to the actual underlying income or gain of an entity or arrangement. The UK 'controlled foreign company' rules[864] tax a separate notional amount computed by reference to certain types of income, but not capital gains, of the 'controlled foreign company'.

UK attribution rules do not usually disregard the entity or arrangement at which they are targeted.[865] Hence they stop short of the more radical variants of 'tax transparency'. They usually operate asymmetrically, attributing income and gain, but not losses, to affected taxpayers. This is consistent with their anti-avoidance rationale. By contrast, in cases of 'tax transparency', it is more common to treat the interest holder as entitled to relief for underlying losses of the entity, in proportion to its legal and economic interest, as well as being taxable on its share of underlying profits. This is true in relation to partnerships as well as trusts with vested concurrent beneficial interests in both income and capital. It is not the case in relation to vested interests in trusts which only extend to income.[866]

860. Such rules are not always explicit about an anti-avoidance purpose. This is true of the 'settlement' rules in Part 5 Chapter 5 ITTOIA (unlike the 'transfer of assets abroad' rules in Part 13 Chapter 2 ITA). However, they require a non-arm's length arrangement (an 'element of bounty').
861. Other than in highly contingent situations.
862. *See,* for example, section 850 ITTOIA, together with section 12ABZB TMA.
863. *See* section 4.3.3.
864. *See Bricom Holdings Ltd v IRC* [1997] STC 1179. A similar approach is now adopted by the 'transfer of assets abroad' rules in Part 13 Chapter 2 ITA: *see* section 721(3B) and section 728(1A) ITA.
865. Unlike, for example, the US 'grantor trust' rules.
866. Under the rule in *Baker v Archer-Shee.*

There is therefore a meaningful distinction in UK tax law between 'tax transparency' and attribution rules. However, there is one area where it makes sense to treat attribution rules as a form of 'tax transparency'. This area involves 'fiscal transparency' clauses of the kind which are increasingly widespread in UK tax treaties, reflecting Article 1(2) of the OECD Model and Article 3(1) of the MLI.

Article 1(2) has been discussed in sections 5.2 and 6.1. For reasons given in section 6.4.2, when interpreting Article 1(2) purposively,[867] such attribution rules (including rules attributing trust income to a settlor) are a form of 'fiscal transparency'. Otherwise, the underlying purpose of Article 1(2) may be frustrated. Article 1(2) applies if the income in question is liable to current taxation in the hands of a resident of the non-source Contracting State. It should not matter how that liability is achieved mechanically, so long as it is achieved in substance. The words 'fiscally transparent' should be interpreted accordingly. If the non-source state attributed income to its residents on an entirely outlandish basis, the source state could make clear in treaty negotiations that it did not regard that attribution rule as triggering Article 1(2).

Consequently, if an entity is regarded as 'opaque' in the residence state of an entity member (e.g., a shareholder), but that member is currently taxable in that state on an attributed amount reflecting that entity's income from the other Contracting State, failing to apply Article 1(2) would largely frustrate its purpose.

If Article 1(2) is interpreted in this way, does this limit the scope of a domestic anti-avoidance regime? Such concerns can be addressed, not least by the type of 'saving' clause now widespread because of Article 1(3) of the OECD Model.[868] 'Saving' clauses preserve the right of the state where the entity member is resident to tax that member as if the treaty did not exist. A 'saving' clause will usually preserve the right of a resident to claim double taxation relief (by credit or exemption) under that treaty.

8.5 ENTITY CLASSIFICATION AND 'TAX TRANSPARENCY': KEY ASPECTS OF TAX SOVEREIGNTY

If a jurisdiction is to define its own tax sovereignty and tax base, it must define those entities which are relevant when imposing its taxes, especially those which it regards as taxpayers in their own right. Ceding control of those definitions to other jurisdictions, or to supranational laws and courts, means losing control of the shape and structure of its tax system. For example, if the UK does not have the final say over what is a 'company' for the purposes of corporation tax, it lacks control over the extent of that tax. Deciding what is a 'company' may also determine other aspects of the UK tax

867. *See* Mummery J (as he then was) in *IRC v Commerzbank AG* [1990] STC 285. His exposition of the purposive UK approach to interpreting tax treaties, based on Articles 31-32 of the 1969 Vienna Convention on the Law of Treaties, has been frequently cited as a classic summary, although limited aspects of it are debatable. For a full discussion, *see* Philip Baker: 'The *Commerzbank Litigation (1990)* UK Law, Tax Treaty Law and EU Law'. Chapter 15. Landmark Cases in Revenue Law: eds John Snape and Dominic de Cogan. Hart Publishing 2019 and especially at 335-341.
868. Also Article 11 of the MLI.

base, notably, double taxation relief where a UK-resident bears the economic burden of non-UK tax on profits of a non-UK entity in which it has invested.

Some jurisdictions (e.g., South Africa in some cases)[869] have nevertheless part-aligned their own rules on defining entities with those of other jurisdictions, when deciding the tax treatment of cross-border arrangements. The extent of such alignment varies. Clearly, it can reduce entity classification mismatches which otherwise lead to tax avoidance. However, this approach is not common. The author is not aware of any jurisdiction whose entity classification rules are mainly based on this approach. It erodes tax sovereignty by tying the boundaries of one jurisdiction's tax system to the entity classification choices (present or future) of another jurisdiction. It may also trigger further mismatches in situations involving third countries, unless selectively overridden. Even within the EU, this approach has not found much favour. When the EU Anti-Tax Avoidance Directive[870] was first mooted, suggestions were made[871] that it should impose on Member States uniform entity classification rules so as to avoid double non-taxation. Article 10 of the original draft read:

> Where two Member States give a different legal characterisation to the same taxpayer (hybrid entity), including its permanent establishments in one or more Member States, and this leads to a situation where a deduction of the same payment, expenses or losses occurs both in the Member State in which the payment has its source, the expenses are incurred or the losses are suffered and in another Member State or a situation where there is a deduction of a payment in the Member State in which the payment has its source without a corresponding inclusion of the same payment in the other Member State, *the legal characterisation given to the hybrid entity by the Member State* [emphasis added] in which the payment has its source, the expenses are incurred or the losses are suffered shall be followed by the other Member State.

This language only targeted mismatches giving rise to a double deduction or a deduction by the payer which was not matched by a payee income inclusion. It gave precedence to the entity classification in the Member State where a payment was sourced but would not have addressed mismatches with non-EU jurisdictions. The draft Article 10 was abandoned.[872] Instead, Article 9 of the final Directive counteracts some of the double non-taxation effects of classification mismatches, without altering

869. Notably, its 'foreign partnerships' rules in section 1 of the South African Income Tax Act. These incentivise inbound investment by ensuring that entities such as US LLCs and UK LLPs which are in essence 'transparent' outside South Africa are treated as partnerships, not companies, for South African tax purposes, despite having legal personality.
870. Directive 2016/1164, as amended by Directive 2017/952.
871. *See* G.K. Fibbe and A.J.A. Stevens: 'Hybrid Mismatches under the ATAD I and II' (2017) EC Tax Review, Volume 3, 153 at 154.
872. *See* Parada: Article 1(2) *supra*, at pp. 372-373. For the practical problems in removing mismatches by harmonisation, *see* Ruth Mason and Pascal Saint-Amans: 'Has Cross-Border Arbitrage met its match?'. Thinker, Teacher, Traveller: Reimagining International Tax – Essays in Honour of H. David Rosenbloom: eds Kofler, Mason, Rust. IBFD September 2021, 355 at 361-362. Parada has made further suggestions for preventing abuse if a tax treaty contains a rule requiring both parties to accept an entity's tax classification in the jurisdiction where it is 'formed': *see* Leopoldo Parada: 'Hybrid Entity Mismatches and the MLI: A Tax Policy Assessment' (2021) Intertax, Volume 49, Issue 10, at 786. If an EU Member State unilaterally introduces a rule similar to the rejected Article 10, it must not restrict the EU fundamental

entity classification. Article 9a (*see* section 6.7.6.2) imposes 'opaque' treatment on 'reverse hybrids' in certain situations. Where it applies, it takes priority over Article 9.[873] Therefore, the Directive in its final form (like BEPS Action 2) does not significantly challenge the sovereign right of Member States to classify entities.

Of course, if a jurisdiction retains control over classifying legal persons and arrangements for tax purposes, classification differences may well arise with other jurisdictions. That creates scope for planning. Those planning opportunities are partly addressed in the first part of the October 2015 recommendations regarding BEPS Action 2, and in Articles 9 and 9a of the EU Anti-Tax Avoidance Directive.

Particular problems always arise when classifying entities or arrangements formed outside the relevant taxing jurisdiction. It is often hard to apply that jurisdiction's criteria for classifying its domestic entities to those formed under another system of law. Other jurisdictions' laws will often be based on a different legal culture. In Europe and the US, it is important to distinguish between common law entities and those based on the civil law tradition. Besides, within both common law and civil law traditions, jurisdictions differ about what entities can be formed and their attributes. For example, an English general partnership is never regarded as an entity distinct from its partners, but this is not true of partnerships formed under the laws of US states, or of Scotland (a 'mixed system' based on both the common law and the civil law).

As part of its tax sovereignty, a jurisdiction must also be free to decide when and how to treat an entity or arrangement as 'transparent', whether formed under the laws of that jurisdiction or elsewhere. The question of whether an entity is 'transparent' need not always involve definitively classifying it. The Supreme Court in *Anson v HMRC*[874] concluded that the nature of an interest in a particular Delaware LLC made it 'transparent' for foreign tax credit purposes. The court did not definitively conclude[875] whether that LLC was a 'company' or a 'partnership' for UK tax purposes, because it was considering a narrow point which did not require it to do so. However, the way in which an entity is classified is likely to affect precisely when, and how, to treat it as 'transparent'. Transparency is a key characteristic of some entities. If an entity is a 'partnership', rather than a 'company' for UK tax purposes, it will be 'transparent' for the purposes of taxing both its income and gains. The form that transparency takes is set out for (for income) in section 850 ITTOIA and (for capital gains) in section 59 TCGA. Those forms are different. Neither form is available unless the entity concerned is a 'partnership'. So classifying the relevant entity determines exactly what form of transparency, if any, can apply to it.

---

freedoms. If it does, it may be justifiable if it prevents mismatches causing double taxation or double non-taxation: *see* Van Hulten and Stevens: 'Symmetrical Classification' *supra*, at 3.2.1.

873. Article 9a resembles earlier Danish rules to counteract mismatches involving Danish hybrid and 'reverse hybrid' entities – *see* Parada: Article 1(2) *supra*, at 370-371.

874. [2015] STC 1777: *see* section 2.14.

875. The Supreme Court chose not to delve deeply into wider entity classification questions, such as the nature of a Scottish partnership versus a Delaware LLC. It was able to do this by focusing closely on the factual findings of the FTT regarding Delaware law, together with the precise wording of the UK-US tax treaty.

8.6 WEAKNESSES IN THE UK APPROACH TO ENTITY CLASSIFICATION AND 'TAX TRANSPARENCY', AND SUGGESTED IMPROVEMENTS

8.6.1 Entity Classification

The existing UK entity classification rules comprise specific statutory rules (of limited ambit),[876] some judicial decisions mainly regarding non-UK entities (and fact-dependent) plus published HMRC guidance (which purports to interpret the judicial decisions). There is a statutory requirement to distinguish, for corporation tax purposes, between 'companies' on the one hand and partnerships and trusts on the other.[877] 'Companies' include the problematic category of 'unincorporated associations'.[878] Non-UK entities with a UK tax presence (especially those trading through a UK 'permanent establishment'[879] or centrally managed and controlled in the UK) can be subject to corporation tax, but only if they are 'companies'. Therefore, these classification categories also apply to entities formed outside the UK.

The rules for classifying entities or arrangements formed under English (or Scottish) law are fairly prescriptive. Hence, there should be a lot of certainty about whether such entities or arrangements are 'companies', partnerships or trusts for UK tax purposes.[880] This is not true of entities or arrangements formed outside the UK. In such cases, the rules are vaguer, largely judge-made and more fact-sensitive. Classification usually depends on what English law entity most closely resembles the non-UK entity. This may not be easy to decide, not least because non-UK entities or arrangements may have no clear UK analogue. A good example is the foundation, or 'Stiftung', well known in some civil law countries. Is this a company or is it a trust or is it something else[881]? If the question is being asked in the context of IHT, is it a 'settlement'[882] even if it is not a trust?

There is no settled hierarchy of criteria for comparing a non-UK entity or arrangement with any UK entity. In contrast with the Netherlands (*see* section 7.3), there is a non-exhaustive list of guidelines from HMRC. With limited exceptions, there is no clear ranking within these guidelines, which only address 'transparency' questions where there is outbound investment from the UK. They do not tackle entity classification overall. Their status after *Anson* is unclear. The UK's more nebulous approach to classifying non-UK entities and arrangements may breach EU law.

876. For example, the rules deeming a UK LLP to be a partnership for direct tax purposes.
877. Although some trusts, e.g., 'authorised' unit trusts and some 'unauthorised' unit trusts, are subject to corporation tax.
878. *See* section 2.5.
879. Section 5 CTA 2009.
880. Despite some uncertainty about the meaning of 'unincorporated association': *see* section 2.5.
881. *See* the discussion of *Sommerer* in section 4.1.2.
882. Within section 43(2) IHTA: *see* section 5.3.2. *Sommerer* suggests that an entity can be both a 'settlement' and a 'company' for Inheritance Tax purposes.

Existing classification criteria focus mainly on matters which resonate from the perspective of UK corporate and partnership law,[883] but do not necessarily reflecting important issues under non-UK legal systems. Dutch law also classifies non-Dutch entities by seeking analogies with Dutch entities but currently places much greater emphasis than the UK on whether entity members can freely transfer their membership interests.

Analysing the governing law of the non-UK entity and seeking its closest UK analogue is also very cumbersome. It depends heavily on the quality of expert evidence on relevant aspects of the relevant non-UK law. The lack of clear classification criteria for non-UK entities, and their focus on UK preoccupations, may also mean non-UK experts are asked questions about non-UK legal rules which are especially hard for those experts to understand,[884] quite apart from any language barrier.

The result is an expensive and protracted process which may well produce unsatisfactory answers to key questions. Expert evidence is only as good as the questions which the experts are asked. Experts often disagree. The UK tribunal (which is not expert in the relevant non-UK law) must often adjudicate between expert opinions in order to make key findings of fact about the non-UK legal position. Those findings may be contested by the parties (yet, being findings of fact, are much harder to appeal). For example, HMRC reject the key finding by the FTT in *Anson*, that the LLC members in that case were entitled, under Delaware law, to underlying LLC profits as they arose, even though the LLC was a separate legal person.

Even if the evidence of non-UK law is clear or uncontested, it has no weight as precedent because it is a finding of fact and no two cases are the same. Therefore, a decision in one entity classification case may not avoid the same laborious procedure in a later case. Well-resourced and well-advised taxpayers have a clear advantage when navigating the UK rules on classifying non-UK entities. This is the imbalance between taxpayers which the US sought to address by introducing the 'check-the-box' rules. It is hard to justify in a globalised world. However, it creates a 'benefit', at least from HMRC's perspective: taxpayers' ability to choose their preferred entity classification with ease and certainty is limited.

The UK approach to classifying non-UK entities risks basing important distinctions on abstract points with little real-world relevance. *Anson* is a good illustration. The Supreme Court ruled in favour of 'transparency' for UK foreign tax credit purposes because LLC members were entitled to the underlying LLC profits as they arose (at least as a matter of contract), and were therefore not in the same position as company shareholders, whose entitlement to profits requires a prior corporate decision to

883. For example, the focus on the presence or absence of legal personality as a dividing line between companies and partnerships, although this focus should have lessened after *Anson*. In the US, the presence or absence of legal personality has little relevance for classification purposes, although it has some relevance in France.

884. Such questions may only make (some) sense to those versed in UK law, e.g., whether, for the purposes of the rule in *Baker v Archer-Shee*, a life interest holder in a trust is entitled to trust income as it arises to the trustees, or is only entitled to a net sum from the trustees comprising trust income less certain trust expenses.

distribute profits,[885] which initially belong to the company, not its members. Yet in practice the LLC members in *Anson* were not much better placed than shareholders of a company. Would their theoretical profit entitlement in the LLC's books ever be satisfied by an actual distribution? In a world where the substantive difference between partnerships and companies is increasingly hard to pinpoint, the UK entity classification rules seem to rely on criteria with limited business significance.

In order to escape from these problems, and to protect the UK corporate tax base, the UK should be slower to confer on business entities (UK or non-UK) a status (in particular, partnership status) which leads to 'transparency'. This would require reversing trends which have seen the UK treat large, centrally managed UK and non-UK business entities (notably, UK and non-UK LLPs) as partnerships for most tax purposes. The result has been that, while such entities are effectively private companies, that is not how they and their members are taxed.

Instead, 'transparency' should be reserved for business organisations which are much smaller and looser-knit aggregations of persons, and in particular which are not 'centrally managed' to any significant degree. This would be more faithful to the concept of 'partnership' which the draftsman probably had in mind when introducing the 'partnership' carve-out from corporation tax in 1965.[886] It would also greatly reduce the need for arcane legal analysis of non-UK entities to determine their UK tax classification. All other business entities (including business trusts) outside this limited 'transparency' category would be regarded as companies for tax purposes. 'Unincorporated associations' could be dispensed with as a relevant category.

This approach would also protect the employment income tax and National Insurance base.[887] There would be fewer opportunities for senior personnel in 'partnerships' to use their 'partner' status[888] to reduce income tax and National Insurance

885. *Re Accrington Corporation Steam Tramways Company* [1909] 2 Ch 40 and *Re Buenos Ayres Great Southern Railway Co. Ltd, The Company v Preston* [1947] 1 All ER 729, following *Bond v Barrow Haematite Steel Co.* [1902] 1 Ch 353. In those cases, preference shareholders were only entitled to a dividend paid out of (any) profits remaining after reserving or carrying forward in the accounts such amounts as the directors thought appropriate. Hence, preference shareholders had no unqualified right to a distribution of the positive balance on the company's profit and loss account.

886. A decision would also need to be taken about which 'transparent' entities or arrangements were regarded as a partnership for tax purposes, because there are special taxing rules for partnerships and not all 'transparent' arrangements (e.g., simple co-ownership) are partnerships. It may be appropriate to confer 'transparency' on a business arrangement falling short of partnership under current standards, e.g., barristers' chambers.

887. However, by limiting the number of transparent entities, this approach may narrow the scope of UK tax on non-UK-residents' chargeable gains from UK real property. That charge covers gains from direct disposals of interests in UK land (including an interest in a partnership to the extent that it holds UK real property, because partnerships are 'transparent'). It also covers indirect disposals of UK real property, such as certain disposals of interests in a company, but only where at least 75% of that company's gross assets comprise interests in UK real property. Hence the UK charge on non-UK-residents is less likely to apply if they own UK real property via a non-UK 'company', rather than via a 'transparent' partnership.

888. Such arrangements are routinely used to remunerate senior UK-based personnel working in professional services and the fund management industry, especially where those who are non-UK 'domiciled' for tax purposes. Such arrangements may include 'carried interest' partnership allocations which entitle senior staff to what is effectively remuneration for

contributions on their remuneration. One can therefore expect stiff opposition to any such change[889] so an intermediate solution is set out below. The author prefers this 'halfway house', on grounds of feasibility and outcome. It mitigates many problems with classifying non-UK entities by analogy with UK entities.

This intermediate solution would involve switching to an entity classification regime which resembles the US 'check-the-box' regime by being partly elective. While HMRC is opposed, this switch need not involve wholesale adoption of the US system. Like the US, there could be 'per se' lists of UK and non-UK entities which would always be treated as companies for UK tax purposes. Those lists could be updated periodically to take account of new business entities. 'Per se' categorisation is somewhat arbitrary but so are existing classification criteria for non-UK entities. Besides, this solution ensures that the corporate tax base can only be modified by election within limits.

While the US 'per se' list for non-US entities is quite limited, this need not be the case under a modified UK 'check-the-box' approach. A UK 'per se' list could include all entities formed under both UK and non-UK incorporation procedures, whether or not such entities were capable of offering securities to the public. Hence, a Dutch BV or a Luxembourg Sàrl could be a 'per se' company for UK tax purposes. The same could be true of a US LLC, although this raises harder questions. There is little meaningful legal and commercial difference between a US LLC and US LLPs yet HMRC have historically treated the latter as partnerships for UK tax purposes. Treating all US LLCs as 'per se' companies would therefore create a difficult distinction between them and US LLPs, unless they too were treated as 'per se' companies. However, to do that would greatly devalue any classification election feature.

There is no need to replicate the US disregard of a single-member 'eligible entity'. That has been an especially fertile source of US mismatch planning. On the other hand, there is no need to replicate the US 'publicly traded partnership' concept.

Adopting a system more like the US system would provide a less costly, less time-consuming and clearer approach to entity classification issues, while reducing the existing advantage conferred on well-advised and well-resourced taxpayers. It would also steer classification away from detailed analysis of non-UK law, and from esoteric classification criteria often based on an incomplete understanding of the relevant non-UK legal system. There would of course need to be transitional rules if such a system were implemented. However, experience suggests that this is entirely feasible.

---

services but in a form taxed at much lower rates as capital gain, and with much lower National Insurance liabilities. They may also include special partnership allocations of non-UK-source income and gain. UK tax on non-UK-domiciled staff in respect of such non-UK-source profits can be deferred indefinitely, if they are not 'remitted' to the UK. There are no National Insurance liabilities on such allocations so long as, in particular, they represent 'profits of a trade, profession or vocation carried on *wholly* outside the United Kingdom': *see* section 15(1)(c) Social Security Contributions and Benefits Act 1992 (SSCBA). A non-UK partnership with UK operations needs to consider carefully whether this condition is met.

889. A 'transparency' regime, with safeguards, is needed for some kinds of investment fund where professional investors value a fully 'flow through' tax treatment. Any such regime should not extend to a management vehicle for that fund, nor to fund managers' remuneration arrangements.

The HMRC concerns about elective entity classification should be put in context. The UK has already radically extended its rules for counteracting the tax avoidance effects of 'hybrid mismatches', including any mismatches created because of an elective system for classifying entities. Those rules in Part 6A TIOPA would still apply. Part 6A's features have caused many headaches (notably, its broad scope, uncertainty about how parts of it operate and the fact that it can apply automatically, even to commercially motivated structures). Hence it continues to be modified regularly. However, these concerns exist with or without a more elective classification regime.

Part 6A does not address all hybrid mismatches for UK tax purposes. For example, it only applies for corporation tax. However, a 'targeted anti-avoidance rule' (TAAR) could also restrict significantly tax-motivated entity classification elections, if a more elective system were adopted. That TAAR would need to be drafted so as to avoid making all entity classification elections ineffective for tax purposes.[890] However, 'regime TAARs' already exist, e.g., in the 'loan relationship' rules in Parts 5 and 6 CTA 2009,[891] the 'derivative contract' rules in Part 7 CTA 2009,[892] and the Finance Act 2011 bank levy rules.[893] These useful precedents try to ensure that the language of the TAAR does not prevent taxpayers making certain tax-efficient choices consistent with the policy of the relevant rules. Something similar could be developed in relation to entity classification. It could, for example, disallow (in whole or in part) an election where one of its 'main purposes' was to create a mismatch resulting in unintended double non-taxation between jurisdictions and/or to share between taxpayers savings from a mismatch. There would therefore be similarities with the 'structured arrangement' concept already used in Part 6A TIOPA (e.g., section 259CA(7) and section 259DA(7) TIOPA).

The HMRC hostility to elective entity classification is less easy to understand, given that well-informed taxpayers already have significant freedom under existing rules to choose the desired UK tax classification of their preferred entity, without altering its key commercial features. There are few substantive differences between a UK LLP and a UK private limited company. Both are quite easy for a taxpayer to set up. Yet the former is taxed as a partnership in most situations[894] while the latter is subject to corporation tax.

In relation to non-UK entities, HMRC have consistently taken the position that a US LLC is a company for UK tax purposes (despite *Anson)*, while generally accepting that a US LLP is 'transparent', on the basis that it is a partnership. Yet there is usually

890. The UK courts have interpreted very expansively the 'main purpose' form of words used in most TAARs: *see* '*HMRC v Lloyds Bank Leasing (No 1) Ltd*: The Troublesome Increase in the Scope of the "Sole or Main Object" Test' [2015] British Tax Review 649, as well as *Travel Document Service v HMRC* [2018] STC 723.

891. *See* sections 455B-D CTA 2009.

892. *See* sections 698B-D CTA 2009.

893. *See* paragraph 47, Schedule 19 Finance Act 2011, where care is taken to ensure that the anti-avoidance rule does not undermine activities and structures which reduce bank credit risk, even if they also reduce the bank levy.

894. In limited situations, a UK LLP ceases to be taxed as a partnership and becomes subject to corporation tax.

little real difference between the two, not least in terms of setting them up. Well-advised taxpayers can therefore already set up non-UK entities with a local law constitution, tailored to achieve an 'opaque' or a 'transparent' UK tax outcome,[895] without altering the essential business structure. Hence the current UK system is largely elective already, but mainly for the benefit of a privileged minority.

If a modified elective classification system is a bridge too far, the existing rules could still be significantly improved, although only in a way which still requires considerable focus on the legal system under which a non-UK entity is formed. A less parochial approach can be adopted when classifying entities as 'companies' versus 'partnerships'. There is no reason why a non-UK legal system will define a 'partnership' in the same way as English or Scottish law, with its central concept of a 'business in common with a view of profit'[896] and the English law insistence that a partnership is not a legal person. A non-UK legal system may well confer on a putative 'partnership' a legal personality which is more fully fledged than that which applies to Scottish partnerships. Following *Ryall v The DuBois Company Limited*,[897] 'partnership' needs to be interpreted in a more nuanced and context-sensitive way. It would be better to focus on the role an entity fulfils (compared to other entities) under the commercial law of the relevant non-UK jurisdiction, when deciding if it is a 'partnership', rather than trying to shoehorn it into UK concepts of 'partnership' without reference to the local law context.[898] The fact that the entity has features (a more fully fledged legal personality; creation of the entity by registration) which are inconsistent with the English law 'partnership' paradigm should not be the end of the story, especially where civil law jurisdictions are concerned. Their narrower concepts of agency law have given rise to different types of arrangement which can legitimately be regarded as 'partnerships': formal and informal partnerships. There is no precise analogue for either in English partnership law, where the law of agency applies differently to partnerships. Yet that should not prevent these non-UK arrangements being 'partnerships' for UK tax purposes.

One area where UK tax legislation has travelled in a less parochial direction relates to 'settlements'. For anti-avoidance reasons, these include more than common law trusts for both IHT purposes[899] and for the purposes of the income tax and capital

895. In the aftermath of *Anson*, some taxpayers looked closely at the structure of their US LLCs to ensure that they would continue to be regarded as 'opaque' for UK tax purposes. This aligns with HMRC's preferred classification of a US LLC. By contrast, the successful taxpayer in *Anson* is believed to have switched anyway to a US LLP structure.
896. Section 1 Partnership Act 1890.
897. 16 TC 431.
898. This alternative approach already applies in relation to 'unilateral' foreign tax credit relief. Following *Yates v GCA International* [1991] STC 157, Statement of Practice 7/91 states that, when deciding if a non-UK tax is an 'income tax' for 'unilateral relief' purposes, the answer 'will be determined by examining the tax *within its legislative context in the foreign territory and deciding whether it serves the same function as income and corporation tax serve in the UK in relation to the profits of the business*' [emphasis added]. The UK abandoned an earlier approach under which '... the proportion of the gross amount charged to [non-UK] tax prompted the view that the [non-UK] tax could not reasonably be regarded as corresponding to UK income tax or corporation tax on net profits'.
899. Section 43(2) IHTA.

gains tax 'settlement' rules[900] (but not for all income tax and capital gains tax purposes). Those broader definitions can cover non-trust-based civil law arrangements such as foundations ('Stiftungen') with similar wealth preservation and distribution effects to a trust, despite their structural differences and their roots in a different legal tradition.

More recently, there are limited signs of movement in terms of defining a 'partnership' less narrowly for UK direct tax purposes. In Finance Act 2015, the UK enacted the 'diverted profits tax' (DPT). This is a tax, akin to corporation tax, on certain transactions aimed at eroding the UK corporation tax base by creating certain mismatches, or by structuring UK business activity so that it avoids being a taxable 'permanent establishment'. For DPT purposes, a company is defined according to section 1121 CTA 2010.[901] However, this is supplemented by a non-exhaustive definition of 'partnership' which reads:[902]

> 'Partnership' includes (a) a limited liability partnership to which section 1273 of CTA 2009 applies [i.e., a UK LLP], and (b) *an entity established under the law of a territory outside the United Kingdom of a similar character to a partnership* [emphasis added], and 'member' of a partnership is to be read accordingly.

'Of a similar character' invites a court, in a DPT context, to interpret 'partnership' in a manner which does not cling too closely to the English law paradigm. This makes sense because DPT is most likely to apply to cross-border arrangements. Will the UK courts accept this invitation? So far, HMRC seem very hesitant.

8.6.2 'Tax Transparency': How Far Should It Apply to Partnerships?

The UK approach to classifying entities could therefore be greatly improved, without triggering significant avoidance. This could strengthen the UK tax base. However, even if an entity is classified so that it is prima facie 'tax transparent', that need not lead to such treatment in all situations. 'Transparency' is a tax policy choice, and it can be implemented in different ways mechanically. The different strands of the 'transparency' concept have evolved piecemeal, which is not ideal.

The 'transparency' of partnerships is a good example of this. Classically, if an entity is a 'partnership', it enjoys a high degree of UK tax transparency, especially when taxing its income and gains. These are taxed at partner level only, on the basis that each partner (however lowly and wherever located) helps carry on its business and has a direct entitlement for tax purposes to its underlying assets and income. A similar approach applies in respect of partnership losses. Furthermore, an individual partner in

900. In Part 5 Chapter 5 ITTOIA, and especially section 620(1) ITTOIA.
901. Section 114(1) FA 2015.
902. Section 114(1) FA 2015. This is identical to the 'partnership' definition in the anti-hybrid mismatch rules in Part 6A TIOPA: *see* section 259NE(4)(a) TIOPA. The new section 259GB(4C) TIOPA suggests that HMRC regard neither section 259NE(4)(a) TIOPA nor section 114(1) FA 2015 as covering a LLC which is 'transparent' in the US. The SDLT definition of 'partnership' in paragraph 1, Schedule 15 FA 2003, moves even further from the English law paradigm: *see* section 5.5.2.

a partnership is regarded as self-employed. Hence that partner is subject to a significantly lower National Insurance liability than an employee or director of a company with equivalent status.

This largely all-or-nothing transparency approach overlooks the increasingly strong commercial similarities between LLPs and private limited companies.[903] LLPs are commonplace, especially where the 'partnership' engages in active business (notably, professional and financial services). General services partnerships where partners retain unlimited liability for the firm's obligations are now the exception in these sectors. Is it appropriate that the tax treatment of a member of an LLP[904] should always differ so radically from that of a senior shareholder-employee or director of a limited company, when there are few significant commercial distinctions between these two types of entity?

Not least because of the UK approach to 'transparency', partnership structures are routinely used to remunerate UK-resident high-earning individuals at low effective tax rates, even where their role mainly involves providing services in the UK to clients of the partnership. Partners in a partnership pay National Insurance at lower rates than similarly remunerated employees, and there is no equivalent for partners of the separate employer's National Insurance liability.[905] Where the partnership is 'controlled and managed outside the UK',[906] despite carrying on business in the UK, its 'transparent' status enables it to allocate non-UK-source partnership income to UK-resident, but non-UK-domiciled partners. Those allocations are taxed on the much more generous 'remittance' basis (i.e., if and when directly or indirectly repatriated to the UK). The 'remittance' basis is available even if those profits have not suffered significant non-UK taxation and are not sourced in the jurisdiction where the partner is domiciled. The result is often low effective UK taxation on income which is technically 'non-UK source' (because of 'transparency') but which, in reality, is usually being paid

903. The UK courts have been slow to adjust their thinking to reflect evolving business realities in relation to so-called partnerships. In *MacKinlay v Arthur Young McLelland Moores & Co* [1989] STC 898, the House of Lords reversed the Court of Appeal's decision in favour of the taxpayer. Lord Oliver said at pp. 903-904, '... I am unable to accept that the purpose of "the partnership", considered as if it has a separate legal identity, and the purpose of the individual partners for whose benefit the payment [of business-related removal expenses] enured can be segregated in this way. ... [T]he Court of Appeal ... appear to have been influenced by the sheer size of the partnership [which was a large nationwide firm of accountants] ... and to have considered that a large partnership falls in some way to be treated differently from a small partnership. ... Partners are partners, however numerous; and mere numbers cannot in itself justify an attribution of a "collective purpose" unjustified in the case of a small partnership.' This case related to expenses payments by a large nationwide accounting partnership to its partners. Even though the partnership was very large, payments by it to cover partners' business-driven moving costs were taxed as profit distributions paid to the partners as such. *MacKinlay* was followed in *HMRC v Lansdowne Partners Limited Partnership* [2012] STC 544. *See also Morgan v HMRC, Self v HMRC* [2009] SFTD 160 and *AB v HMRC* [2011] UKFTT 685 (TC).

904. The introduction in 2000 of UK LLPs followed intensive lobbying for an entity where the liability of members involved in firm management could be limited but which was still 'transparent', not 'opaque', for UK direct tax and National Insurance purposes. Use of the UK LLP is not in fact confined to professional services businesses.

905. This 15.05% liability (as of April 2022) on all employee remuneration is a very significant extra tax cost for employers, even though deductible for income tax/corporation tax purposes.

906. *See* section 857(1)(b) ITTOIA and *Mark Higgins Rallying (a firm) v HMRC* [2011] SFTD 936.

to UK-resident partners for rendering services in the UK. Were those individuals receiving that remuneration from a non-UK company (e.g., a bank) carrying on UK business, then they would probably be subject to UK employee income tax on an arising basis, as well as employer and employee National Insurance contributions, as employees performing UK services.[907] This better reflects economic reality. It is hard to justify such a radical difference in individual tax treatment simply because an individual is a partner in a 'transparent' partnership, especially when the business difference between partnerships and companies is increasingly narrow.

Some would argue that there is a fundamental difference between the status of partner and of employee, because the former, but not the latter, is an entrepreneur. This justifies the difference in tax treatment described above. However, this argument is not strong, especially when comparing partners with senior employees. LLPs are now widespread. LLP status ensures that 'partners' typically bear levels of liability for the LLP's obligations which are not radically different from those which a senior employee, with a large holding of incentive shares in its employer, would bear in relation to that employer company. Indeed in industries such as financial services, regulatory changes have significantly increased the risk to senior employees of financial and other sanctions, including possible remuneration 'clawback'. Senior employees' significant shareholdings in their employers are often 'locked in' over an extended period, just as partners contribute long-term capital to a partnership. Hence a partner in a LLP and a senior employee of a company performing similar roles may nowadays be exposed to very similar business and legal liability risks. Both are remunerated mainly on a performance-related basis. While partners are technically remunerated with a share of profits, that share, like a senior employee's remuneration, will usually be heavily tied to prescribed, and variable individual performance targets. A centralised management committee of the LLP or the employing company is likely to have very wide discretion to fix that remuneration. Indeed management centralisation is now the norm in major partnerships (e.g., law firms and accounting firms). Such management is typically secretive and it is ever rarer for major decisions to be put to a meaningful partnership vote.

Therefore the effective status of most partners within major partnerships is similar to that of senior company employees on performance-related pay. It is anomalous that the tax classification of a business entity, as a 'transparent' partnership rather than a company, can lead to much more favourable tax treatment for relevant senior staff than if they were formally employees. A more level playing field is appropriate, better reflecting economic reality, even if the basic principle that the partnership is 'transparent' for tax purposes is respected.

Legislation has tried to correct some distortions which can arise if the 'transparency' which typically flows from classifying an entity as a partnership with limited liability is applied too widely. The 'salaried member' legislation introduced in 2014[908]

907. Non-UK-domiciled employees have much less scope to be taxed on the 'remittance' basis.
908. Section 863A-G ITTOIA, section 4A SSCBA and Regulation 3 Social Security Contributions (LLP) Regulations 2014. This legislation is discussed in detail in Crossley and Baldwin *supra*, at 8-14 to 8-56. For the first judicial decision on it, *see Bluecrest Capital Management (UK) LLP*

treats certain members of a UK LLP on relatively fixed remuneration, and with a relatively small say in the running of the LLP, as if they were employees, not partners, for income tax and National Insurance purposes. This change (which better reflects the real economic and management status of many LLP members) was hotly contested when introduced but partially addresses the distortions described above. However, it is complicated, fact-sensitive legislation whose impact is limited. It does not in particular apply to non-UK LLPs, a number of which operate very successfully in the UK.

Very similar points can be made about the UK taxation of 'carried interest'. This complex topic can only be discussed here in summary. 'Carried interest' is a method of paying what are in effect performance-related fees to fund managers (notably, in the 'private equity' industry). The fee entitlement can be very large. It is typically structured as a grant to the manager of a special partnership interest (in a special 'carry partnership'), which is supposed to have a very low value when granted. Because partnerships are 'transparent' for income tax and capital gains tax purposes, it is therefore treated as an interest in underlying investments of the fund which is being managed. One aim may be to characterise much of any profit from that special partnership interest as capital gain from underlying managed assets, so that the recipient can access much lower effective tax rates than if it were simply paid a performance-related fee for management services. Another aim may be for 'carry' to be treated as derived (in whole or in part) from underlying non-UK-source income of a partnership, so that a non-UK-domiciled recipient can claim the 'remittance' basis of taxation in respect of it.

Yet the widely recognised reality is that 'carry' is fee income for providing services. Therefore, using 'transparent' partnerships to create 'carry' structures lies at the root of highly favourable tax treatment of such fee income. Such arrangements have been vigorously defended by the investment funds industry and its well-paid advocates. Legislation[909] has reduced somewhat the tax privileges of 'carried interest',

v HMRC [2022] UKFTT 204 (TC), where the court tried to interpret it not too expansively. Even before this legislation was introduced, there was debate about whether a member of a UK LLP could be its employee. This debate centred on the obscure section 4(4) Limited Liability Partnerships Act 2000. The debate is largely irrelevant for tax purposes because, unless the 'salaried member' rules apply, UK LLP members are typically *deemed* to carry on the LLP's business as partners: *see* section 863 ITTOIA and the FTT in *Peter Wilson v HMRC* [2020] UKFTT 230 (TC). The Tribunal also ruled (obiter) that, because of section 4(4), a member of an *English law* UK LLP could never be its employee, following Lady Hale in the employment law case, *Clyde & Co v Bates van Winkelhof* [2014] 1 WLR 2047. Lady Hale disagreed with an earlier interpretation of section 4(4) in *Tiffin v Lester Aldridge LLP* [2012] IRLR 391. The Upper Tribunal in *Peter Wilson v HMRC* [2021] UKUT 0239 (TCC) chose not to decide on the effect of section 863 ITTOIA and of Lady Hale's dicta. Lady Hale seems to draw a distinction between English and Scottish LLPs. However, the LLP is a new UK-wide company with a special tax status. Its legal treatment should not be coloured by historical differences between England and Scotland about whether a general partnership, not a company, can employ one of its members (*see* fn 42). English partnerships and LLPs now also appear to be in a different position from the many non-UK LLPs operating in the UK, which typically have legal personality but are unaffected by section 4(4). Therefore, their members may, depending on the facts, be employees of the non-UK LLP, for both tax and employment law purposes. Non-UK LLPs are of course unaffected by the 'salaried members' legislation.

909. *See* section 103KA-KH TCGA and section 809EZA-FZZ ITA. For a detailed analysis of these complex rules, *see* Crossley and Baldwin *supra*, Chapters 21-24. While Parts 7 and 7A ITEPA

without denying the basic 'transparency' of the partnerships in question. That legislation limits the benefits of capital gains tax treatment on such profits. However, it is complex, not least because it limits but does not reverse the unequal tax treatment mentioned above. 'Carry' structures continue to generate considerable planning activity, not least to limit the impact of recent legal changes.[910]

Changes are therefore required to better reflect the limited difference between a LLP and a company. These should also include relaxation of the rules which usually treat partners in a partnership as 'connected' for capital gains tax purposes and as 'associates' in relation to a 'close company'. Those rules reflect a conception of partnership which is outdated.

Lastly, statute should clarify when and how an affiliation between two companies can be traced through a partnership or a LLP, given the nature of a partnership and a partnership interest. Rather than uncertain published guidance, rules are needed similar to those permitting one company to establish its indirect 'beneficial ownership' of ordinary share capital in another company, by tracing ownership through intermediate companies.[911]

8.6.3 'Tax Transparency': Trusts

In relation to partnerships, 'transparency' has been applied too generously for UK tax purposes, especially as the commercial differences between companies and partnerships have been eroded. It has also been applied inconsistently, because 'transparency' does not mean the same thing when taxing partnership income rather than capital gain: *see* Appendix A. It has yet another meaning in relation to SDLT: *see* section 5.7.

By contrast, 'tax transparency' has been applied much more restrictively to UK trusts, especially since the IHT changes in 2006. The reasons for this have not always been clearly articulated. It is unsatisfactory that holding assets via UK trusts often carries a significant extra tax cost when compared to owning those assets directly. Trusts have of course been used for tax planning. However the pendulum has now swung too far the other way, given the legitimate non-tax reasons for using trusts (notably, to protect assets and/or vulnerable beneficiaries).

'Bare trusts' aside, the clearest situation in which a beneficiary of a trust enjoys 'look through' treatment for income tax purposes is under the rule in *Baker v Archer-Shee*. The oddities of this rule have already been explored in section 4.3.3.2. It means that a beneficiary with a vested interest in possession can be taxed on both

aim to tax as employment income at least some of the growth in value of 'securities' granted to employees as an incentive, there is no direct equivalent where an interest in a 'carry' partnership is granted to a self-employed executive. However, ongoing litigation may impact the tax position on granting an interest in a 'carry' partnership: *see HMRC v Bluecrest Capital Management LP and others* [2022] STC 1696, *Odey Asset Management LLP v HMRC* [2021] UFTT 31 (TC) and *HFFX LLP v HMRC* [2021] UKFTT 36 (TC).

910. In the US, limits on 'long-term capital gain' treatment of 'carried interest' were contained in the US Tax Cuts and Jobs Act 2017, discussed in section 7.2.

911. *See* Part 24 Chapter 3 CTA 2010.

distributed and undistributed trust income. By contrast, beneficiaries under a discretionary trust should not be taxed on undistributed trust income on a fully 'transparent' basis, because they may never be entitled to that income. It is also sensible that the trust, if UK-resident, is taxable on that income because otherwise there would be significant scope for deferral by allowing income to build up in the trust. However, when discretionary beneficiaries do receive income from a UK-resident trust, the mechanism for linking that income to underlying trust income is deficient. This leads to inefficiencies, including economic double taxation as well as the beneficiary being unable to access preferential tax rates on certain types of underlying income (e.g., dividends). These weaknesses are alleviated, but only in part, by concession and statute.[912]

For capital gains tax purposes, unless a UK-resident trust is a section 60 TCGA 'bare trust', then it is a taxable entity in its own right, and not on a 'representative' basis.[913] Therefore tax can arise, both at trust level and again at the level of the beneficiaries. For example, the disposal of a beneficial interest in a non-'bare' trust is not always exempt from tax on chargeable gains.[914] The tax burden if assets are held in trust seems heavier than it would be if beneficiaries owned those assets directly. Unsurprisingly, such rules encourage setting up trusts in low-tax jurisdictions. This largely eliminates UK tax at the level of the trust, unless the trustees derive income and gain from UK real property.[915]

As for IHT, far more 'settlements' are now taxable under the UK's highly unusual 'relevant property' regime.[916] IHT is then charged on the settlement on a basis which takes very little account of the IHT status of the beneficiaries and of any reliefs to which they may be entitled.[917] The result is typically more onerous taxation. If the assets were instead held directly by the beneficiaries, headline IHT rates would be higher but would be counterbalanced by more generous reliefs (notably, the 'potentially exempt transfer' and the exemption for transfers between spouses).

There is one type of UK trust where economic double taxation problems are less pronounced. This is the UK 'authorised' unit trust, a regulated retail collective investment fund. Economic double taxation must be eradicated for such a vehicle to be viable. This is not achieved by making it 'tax transparent' on a 'look through' basis. Instead the trust is treated as a company for UK tax purposes but enjoys certain entity level exemptions from tax on income and gain, provided that it does not engage in trading activity (which is unlikely). Normally there is taxation only at investor level on

912. ESC B18 and section 111 TIOPA.
913. This means that its tax liability is largely unaffected by the tax status and attributes of its beneficiaries.
914. Under section 76 TCGA but *see also* section 76A and Schedule 4A TCGA.
915. The various anti-deferral rules for taxing UK-resident settlors and beneficiaries on the undistributed gains of a non-UK trust need to be taken into account: *see* sections 86-98A TCGA.
916. Part III Chapter III IHTA.
917. HMRC saw the 2006 changes as addressing abuse of the more generous rules in Part III Chapter II IHTA. In the limited cases where they still apply, those rules produce a tax outcome closer to what would apply if the beneficiaries owned the trust assets directly.

distributions.[918] There is scope to characterise these, for UK tax purposes, in the same way as the fund's underlying income. Investors' holdings are treated as shares in a company. There is no 'look through' to the underlying assets of the unit trust.[919] Therefore, investors cannot claim relief for any non-UK tax on the income and gains of the unit trust. Also, its losses (if any) are not investors' losses for tax purposes, although no doubt reflected in the value of investors' units.

8.6.4 'Tax Transparency': Conclusion

Even if an entity is classified in a way which typically entails 'tax transparency',[920] the precise consequences of that transparent treatment need careful consideration. Judging how far the concept of 'transparency' should be allowed to run, and the form it should take, is a tax policy question at least as important as deciding how to classify an entity or arrangement in the first place. The classification question has absorbed much time and energy, not least because of the weaknesses of the UK entity classification rules. Those rules need a thorough overhaul and some suggestions have been made about ways to achieve this.

However, the tax policy consequences of classifying entities in certain ways need equal scrutiny, especially where 'transparency' is the expected outcome of a particular classification. Currently, well-advised taxpayers retain too much scope to use, in particular, partnerships to achieve very low effective taxation. By contrast, the UK taxation of trusts and equivalent wealth protection mechanisms needs to move towards a more broadly applicable, but modified version of 'transparency'. This would ensure that trust income, gains and assets are taxed in a way which better reflects the source of the trust's underlying profits and the tax profile of its beneficiaries.

918. Where income is undistributed, investors can be taxed on deemed distributions so as to avoid tax deferral.
919. This greatly simplifies investor tax compliance, when they dispose of interests in the trust.
920. Whatever that means in the particular context.

APPENDIX A

UK Capital Gains Tax 'Transparency' of Partnerships and Its Implications

A.1 INTRODUCTION

No discussion of 'tax transparency' in UK law can ignore the capital gains tax rules applying to all partnerships and to UK LLPs. These are mainly in sections 59-59A TCGA. Their approach is similar, but not identical to the treatment of 'bare trusts' in section 60 TCGA: *see* section 4.3.2.

A.2 SECTION 59 TCGA: PARTNERSHIPS

This reads:

> (1) Where 2 or more persons carry on a trade or business in partnership –
> (a) tax in respect of chargeable gains accruing to them on the disposal of any partnership assets shall, in Scotland as well as elsewhere in the United Kingdom, be assessed and charged on them separately, and
> (b) any *partnership dealings* [emphasis added] shall be treated as *dealings by the partners* [emphasis added] and not by the firm as such ...
> (c) ...
> (2) Subsection (3) applies if –
> (a) a person resident in the United Kingdom ('the resident partner') is a member of a partnership which resides outside the United Kingdom or which carries on any trade, profession or business the control and management of which is situated outside the United Kingdom, and
> (b) by virtue of any arrangements that have effect under section 2(1) of TIOPA, ('the arrangements') any of the chargeable gains of the partnership are relieved from capital gains tax or corporation tax in the United Kingdom.
> (3) The arrangements (so far as providing for that relief) do not affect any liability to capital gains tax (or corporation tax) in respect of the resident partner's share of any chargeable gains of the partnership.

(4) For the purposes of subsections (2) and (3) the members of a partnership include any person entitled to a share of chargeable gains of the partnership.

Subsections (2)-(4) override, for the purposes of taxing capital gains, *Padmore v IRC*, discussed in section 6.2.2. Of greater importance is section 59(1). This makes clear that if the partnership (including a Scottish partnership and a non-UK partnership) disposes of any of its assets, the partners are to be separately assessed in respect of gains 'accruing to them'. No further detail is provided on how the gains accruing to each partner in this way are to be quantified. Nor is 'partnership' defined.

The ambit of section 59(1)(b) is debatable. Read narrowly, it simply says that if the partnership itself deals with its assets, then that dealing is treated as being carried out by the partners themselves and not by the firm (which may or may not be a separate legal person). In short, the partnership is 'looked through' but only where the partnership itself deals with its assets. This narrow reading means that section 59(1)(b) adds very little to section 59(1)(a). It also risks creating a 'look through' rule under section 59(1) whose effect is narrower than the equivalent for UK LLPs in section 59A, discussed below. That would be a strange and unintended outcome. Hence 'partnership dealings' should be read as meaning 'dealings in connection with the partnership'. Section 59(1)(b) would then cover an asset acquisition or disposal by the partnership, as well as a partner's acquisition or disposal of its partnership rights, even if that involved no concurrent acquisition or disposal of underlying assets by the partnership. This reading would make clearer that, under section 59, the partner's interest in the partnership is not a separate and distinct asset for the purposes of taxing capital gains. This is the received wisdom.

Even if this broader reading is correct, section 59(1) does not 'look through' the partnership so as to treat partners as simple co-owners of the underlying assets. The phrase 'dealings by the partners' indicates that the partnership is not totally disregarded. Rather, its members are treated as dealing with partnership assets as partnership property. A partner's interest in partnership property is a special kind of proprietary interest even if the partnership lacks legal personality. It is not simple co-ownership (*see* section 5.2).

A.3 SECTION 59A TCGA: UK LLPS

This was enacted long after section 59 to deal with the taxation of UK LLPs. It dictates when a UK LLP is to be 'looked through' for the purposes of taxing chargeable gains. Where it applies, the UK tax authorities expect the outcome for UK LLPs to correspond to that for partnerships under section 59, although section 59A is worded differently from section 59. It states:

(1) Where a limited liability partnership carries on a trade or business with a view to profit –
  (a) *assets held by the limited liability partnership are treated for the purposes of tax in respect of chargeable gains as held by its members as partners* [emphasis added], and

(b) *any dealings by the limited liability partnership are treated for those purposes as dealings by its members in partnership* (and not by the limited liability partnership as such) [emphasis added];

and tax in respect of any chargeable gains accruing to the members of the limited liability partnership on the disposal of any of its assets shall be assessed and charged on them separately.

(2) For all purposes, except as otherwise provided, in the enactments relating to tax in respect of chargeable gains –

(a) references to a partnership include a limited liability partnership in relation to which subsection (1) above applies,

(b) references to members of a partnership include members of such a limited liability partnership,

(c) references to a company do not include such a limited liability partnership, and

(d) references to members of a company do not include members of such a limited liability partnership.

(3) Subsection (1) above continues to apply in relation to a limited liability partnership which no longer carries on any trade or business with a view to profit –

(a) if the cessation is only temporary, or

(b) during a period of winding up following a permanent cessation, provided –

(i) the winding up is not for reasons connected in whole or in part with the avoidance of tax, and

(ii) the period of winding up is not unreasonably prolonged, but subject to subsection (4) below.

(4) Subsection (1) above ceases to apply in relation to a limited liability partnership –

(a) on the appointment of a liquidator or (if earlier) the making of a winding-up order by the court, or

(b) on the occurrence of any event under the law of a country or territory outside the United Kingdom corresponding to an event specified in paragraph (a) above.

(5) *Where subsection (1) above ceases to apply in relation to a limited liability partnership with the effect that tax is assessed and charged –*

(a) on the limited liability partnership (as a company) in respect of chargeable gains accruing on the disposal of any of its assets, and

(b) *on the members in respect of chargeable gains accruing on the disposal of any of their capital interests in the limited liability partnership* [emphasis added],

it shall be assessed and charged on the limited liability partnership as if subsection (1) had never applied to it.

(6) Neither the commencement of the application of subsection (1) above nor the cessation of its application in relation to a limited liability partnership shall be taken as giving rise to the disposal of any assets by it or any of its members.

The last two lines of section 59A(1) are very similar to section 59(1)(a) in relation to partnerships. Section 59A(1) does not use the concept of 'partnership dealings' which appears in section 59(1). Instead, it treats dealings by the LLP entity itself (e.g., acquiring or disposing of assets) as if they had been carried out by the LLP members. It is not possible to give section 59A(1)(b) the wider interpretation suggested for 'partnership dealings' in section 59(1).

Hence section 59A(1)(b) does not cover the disposal of a member's interest in the LLP. However, section 59A(1)(a), which has no equivalent in section 59, applies a form of 'look through': the LLP's members are treated as holding its assets directly, but as partners rather than simple co-owners. Hence, section 59A(1)(a) treats the LLP's members as having the special kind of proprietary interest (*see* section 5.2) which partners in an English general partnership have in partnership property. Therefore, section 59A(1) does not treat LLP members as part-owning particular LLP assets in simple percentage shares. Both it and section 59 therefore differ from section 60 TCGA (*see* section 4.3.2), which does operate on the basis of deemed co-ownership. Section 60 does not, of course, apply to partnerships or UK LLPs.

Consequently, when taxing chargeable gains, a member's interest in a UK LLP seems to be disregarded as a separate asset from the underlying assets of the LLP. The member is deemed to part-own these as a partner under section 59A(1)(a). This is obliquely confirmed by section 59A(3)-(6) which dictates when and how the 'look through' in section 59A(1) ceases to apply. Section 59A(5)(b) indicates that, once section 59A(1) ceases to apply, each member's 'capital interest' in the LLP becomes a separate capital asset for tax purposes. That is logical because once section 59A(1)(a) ceases to apply, the tax fiction that it is a partnership, not a company, falls away retroactively.

A.4 STATEMENT OF PRACTICE D12 ('SP D12')

Therefore, sections 59-59A apply a form of 'transparency' to partnerships and UK LLPs but fail to spell out what this entails. In practice, the gap has largely been filled by Statement of Practice, SP D12, which has been updated quite recently. Important parts of SP D12 go beyond anything that sections 59-59A clearly require. Usually, SP D12 has tended to benefit taxpayers, but, in theory, a taxpayer could rely on the strict letter of sections 59-59A, ignoring SP D12.[921]

SP D12 is too detailed to be analysed in full here. However, it, and the associated HMRC guidance, explicitly treat partners as having fractional co-ownership interests in the partnership assets. A partnership interest is disregarded as a separate asset. SP D12's second paragraph states: '[Section 59A(1) TCGA] complements [Section 59(1) TCGA] in treating any dealings in chargeable assets by a limited liability partnership as dealings by the individual members, as partners, for capital gains tax purposes. *Each member of a limited liability partnership to which [Section 59A(1)] applies has therefore*

921. It has been suggested that SP D12 should be enacted as legislation: *see* Simon Yates: 'Partnerships and Capital Gains' [2008] British Tax Review 587 at 610. This has yet to happen and, if it did, would no doubt be backstopped by a 'targeted anti-avoidance rule' to discourage the tax planning for which SP D12 has been used in the past. There is further extensive guidance, with examples, on SP D12 in HMRC's Capital Gains Manual at CG27150 to CG28500 (accessed 12 July 2022). SP D12 also applies, in conjunction with section 59, to non-UK-resident income tax –'transparent' unit trusts which elect to be *treated* as partnerships under the rules for taxing non-residents on their capital gains from UK real property: *see* paragraph 8, Schedule 5AAA TCGA. This 'transparency' election is mainly designed to ensure a capital gains tax-free outcome for tax-exempt investors in the unit trust.

to be regarded, like a partner in any other (non-corporate) partnership, as owning a fractional share of each of the partnership assets and not an interest in the partnership itself.' This significantly expands what section 59(1) and section 59A(1) actually say, as does the statement at CG27150 of the HMRC guidance: 'The effect of the rules [i.e., Sections 59-59A] is that there is a disposal for [capital gains tax] purposes when either (i) the partnership disposes of an asset or (ii) one or more of the partners' fractional interests in a partnership asset is/are reduced.'

Section 1 of SP D12 invents a special, simplified valuation rule for a partner's fractional interest in a partnership asset. That value is a fraction of the value of the partnership's entire interest in that asset, *without* any discount for the size of the partner's interest. Section 2 of SP D12 provides non-statutory guidance on how to measure a partner's fractional interest in an asset. The starting point is (any) explicit statement about the partner's entitlement to share in asset surpluses at the relevant time. Failing that, one looks to the actual destination of such asset surpluses, in the partnership accounts and any related agreement. If asset surpluses are not allocated as such among partners, one looks to the partnership's ordinary profit-sharing ratio.

Importantly, SP D12 sets out how partners are to be taxed when partnership sharing ratios are adjusted, notably when partners leave and join the partnership. The aim is to minimise the risk that such adjustments (which are usually entirely commercial) trigger unfunded ('dry') tax charges because sections 59-59A deem part-disposals of partnership assets to arise. Section 4.1 of SP D12 states:

> In these circumstances, a partner who reduces or gives up his share in asset surpluses will be treated as disposing of part or the whole of his share in each of the partnership assets and a partner who increases his share will be treated as making a similar acquisition. Subject to [certain important exceptions, which are not considered further here], the disposal consideration will be a fraction (equal to the fractional share changing hands) of the current balance sheet value of each chargeable asset *provided there is no direct payment of consideration outside the partnership* [emphasis added].

Where that asset's current balance sheet value equals its tax base cost, there should (subject to the highlighted proviso) be no chargeable gain or allowable loss when sharing ratios change. A 'dry' tax charge is thereby avoided: *see* paragraph 4.2 of SP D12. Paragraph 4.2 also sets out important situations where this 'no gain no loss' approach will not apply (notably, if assets are revalued or the balance sheet value of a contributed asset – *see* below – exceeds the contributing partner's base cost).

Where a new partner makes a capital contribution to the partnership which is credited to that partner's current or capital account, that contribution is *not* treated under SP D12 as the cost of acquiring a fractional interest in existing partnership assets. Nor is it treated as consideration received by existing partners for reducing their fractional interests in partnership assets, in favour of the new partner. Instead, the contributing partner receives a base cost in existing partnership assets equal to its share of their balance sheet value. Similarly, repaying a retiring partner's capital account is not automatically treated as direct consideration paid to that partner for giving up its pre-existing fractional interest in partnership assets.

There are additional rules in paragraph 9 of SP D12 regarding lump sums and/or annuities paid to a partner on leaving a partnership. These relax what might otherwise be the strict capital gains tax analysis.

Paragraph 4.2 of SP D12 focuses on the current balance sheet value of *existing* partnership assets. It does not prevent a 'dry' tax charge if a partner contributes a chargeable asset (including non-Sterling currency) in return for a partnership share or an increased partnership share: *see* section 5 of SP D12. In that case, the contributing partner makes a part-disposal of the contributed asset equal to the fraction of it that passes to the other partners. Depending on the circumstances, that fractional interest will be treated as disposed of for its market value or (more likely) a proportion of the total amount given by the partnership for the asset. That proportion is the fraction of the asset passing to the other partners. In determining this amount, section 5 places excessive emphasis on amounts credited to the partner's capital account in respect of the contribution. It is unclear that credits to that account will always reflect the value of what is contributed. Section 5 also does not work well if the incoming partner's own profit share is not a simple fraction of profits but a variable amount determined by a formula which is hard to value upfront, e.g., an amount determined over time under a financial 'waterfall'. In such cases, the fraction passing to other partners is not easy to compute.

Strangely, section 5 does not address whether, when partners contribute assets to a partnership and receive a proportionate partnership share in return, taxable disposals can be avoided by relying on *Booth v Ellard*[922] and *Jenkins v Brown*[923] (*see* section 4.3.2.2). Arguably, those cases should apply because sections 59 and 59A TCGA apply, thanks to SP D12, in a similar way to section 60 TCGA. However, the argument would be stronger if SP D12 were set out in legislation. Moreover, an interest in a section 60 'bare trust' (*see* section 4.3.2) is a simpler proprietary concept than a partnership interest.

Neither section 3 nor section 5 addresses whether those cases prevent a disposal by any partner on withdrawing assets from the partnership in proportion to its partnership share. In fact section 3 ('Partnership assets divided in kind among the partners') is inconsistent with those cases.[924] The point has yet to be tested in litigation.

Important parts of SP D12 are unclear. Besides, the SP D12 approach to partnership 'transparency' is cumbersome and compliance-intensive, not least because it 'looks through' to underlying partnership assets, disregarding the partnership interest as a separate asset. It will require an adequate supply of information from partnership to partner about underlying assets, base costs and relevant balance sheet information. Each partner must keep track of its fractional interests in each of the partnership's capital assets, as well as its separate base costs in each of those interests (notably, its retained interest in chargeable assets contributed by it to the partnership).

---

922. [1980] STC 555 upholding [1978] STC 487.
923. [1989] STC 577.
924. Section 3 asserts that each partner who is not receiving the particular asset in kind disposes of a fractional interest in that asset at market value to the partner receiving it. So there is a potential 'dry' tax charge for the non-receiving partners. If that is correct, it may still be possible to postpone tax using section 165 TCGA holdover relief, if the partners agree.

These variables will change over time as the partnership acquires and disposes of assets and/or partners' sharing ratios change. Hence SP D12 is best suited to partnerships with a limited and fairly static membership, as well as limited changes in sharing ratios.

A.5 SCHEDULE 7AD TCGA

Because sections 59-59A (coupled with SP D12) are cumbersome, UK tax law has in one limited area adopted a less radical transparency approach when taxing partnership capital gains. Schedule 7AD TCGA applies where, for the purposes of an insurance company's 'long-term' insurance business, it is a limited partner in a 'venture capital investment partnership',[925] which need not be a UK partnership but whose 'sole or main purpose' must be to invest in unquoted shares and securities. In that case, section 59 TCGA is largely disapplied, and the insurance company's partnership interest 'is treated as a single asset'.[926] Therefore, the partnership interest is not 'looked through' and treated as a bundle of fractional interests in underlying partnership assets. The insurance company can acquire a tax base cost in that single asset.[927] It is treated as part-disposing of that single asset (and not the underlying partnership assets) each time it receives a distribution in respect of underlying securities (other than 'qualifying corporate bonds') disposed of by the partnership. It can offset part of its base cost in the single asset when computing gain or loss on that part-disposal. That offset will usually require it to value the part of the asset which remains undisposed of, using a modified version, in paragraph 6 Schedule 7AD, of the base cost apportionment formula in section 42 TCGA.

If the partnership does not make a distribution in respect of securities of which it disposes within one year of their disposal, then the insurance company is treated as receiving its pro rata share of the amount received by the partnership for those securities. Therefore, it is taxed on both distributed and undistributed partnership gains, with limited scope for deferral. If it is taxed on undistributed gains, there is no further charge when those gains are actually distributed. Schedule 7AD therefore achieves transparent taxation in respect of the underlying gains of the LP, which is not itself a taxable entity. This is achieved without fully 'looking through' to the underlying partnership assets.

This approach is less radical than sections 59-59A and is less compliance-heavy. If the insurance company sells its interest in the LP to a third party, it is treated as disposing only of its partnership interest, a separate asset in which it has its own separate base cost. It is not treated as part-disposing of each of the underlying securities (other than 'qualifying corporate bonds') held by the partnership, contrary to the

925. Defined in paragraph 2 Schedule 7AD. *See* HMRC Life Insurance Manual at LAM03600 to LAM03650 (accessed 12 July 2022).
926. Paragraph 3(2)(a) Schedule 7AD. Section 59 is not disapplied to the extent that the partnership holds 'qualifying corporate bonds', as defined in section 117 TCGA.
927. Paragraph 4 Schedule 7AD. This is what US tax advisers refer to as 'outside basis', to distinguish it from the partnership's own base cost ('inside basis') in partnership assets. Paragraph 4 is disapplied to the extent that the partnership holds 'qualifying corporate bonds'.

approach of sections 59 and 59A. Equally, if the partnership disposes of assets at a loss, a share of those capital losses does not flow directly to the insurance company partner. Instead, it may realise a loss in respect of its partnership interest, when the underlying asset disposal by the partnership triggers a part-disposal of that partnership interest under Schedule 7AD.

A.6 'AUTHORISED CONTRACTUAL SCHEMES' AND 'OFFSHORE FUNDS'

A similar approach to Schedule 7AD applies to two types of investment funds (one UK, one non-UK) which are 'tax transparent' for UK tax purposes. The first type is an 'authorised contractual scheme'[928] if it takes the form of a contract-based 'co-ownership scheme'.[929] 'Authorised contractual schemes' are a tax-'transparent' competitor to entities such as the Luxembourg 'fonds commun de placement'. They are not a 'company' within section 1121 CTA 2010. The second type of investment fund is a so-called offshore fund (e.g., a non-UK-resident unit trust scheme) where it is regarded as 'transparent' for UK income tax purposes.[930]

In either case, section 103D(3) TCGA provides that 'A unit in a tax transparent fund is treated as an asset for the purposes of [TCGA] and, accordingly, a participant's interest in the fund property is disregarded for those purposes.' Section 103D(5)-(9) makes various capital gains tax adjustments to reflect this treatment of the fund unit as a separate asset. Therefore, amounts chargeable to income tax on the unit holder (because unit holders are entitled to underlying fund income as beneficial co-owners) can be added to that holder's capital gains tax base cost in the unit. This avoids economic double taxation on the unit holder's taxable share of the fund's undistributed income (whose retention by the fund should boost the value of units).[931]

Where section 103D applies to an 'authorised' contractual co-ownership scheme which owns an interest in UK land, units in it will be treated not just as assets but as shares in a company,[932] in order to tax non-UK-resident investors on chargeable gains where they dispose of assets deriving at least 75% of their value from UK land.[933]

928. *See* section 237(3) FSMA.
929. *See* section 235A(2)-(4) FSMA. Scheme participants must beneficially co-own its assets as tenants in common, with the property being held on trust for them by a depositary. An 'authorised contractual scheme' can be set up, alternatively, as a limited partnership (*see* section 235A(5)-(7)). In that case, UK taxation of partners' chargeable gains will depend upon sections 59-59A TCGA. Therefore, investors' capital gains tax treatment differs significantly even though there is little substantive difference between an 'authorised contractual scheme' based on co-ownership and one which is a limited partnership.
930. *See* the 'transparent fund' definition in Regulation 11 Offshore Fund (Tax) Regulations 2009 SI 2009/3001, which turns on whether an interest in the fund entitles its holder to underlying fund income as it arises, as per *Baker v Archer –Shee*: *see* section 4.3.3.1.
931. Section 103D(3) suggests that *distributed*, taxed fund income can also be added to the unit holder's base cost, although there should be no economic double taxation of such income, if it is distributed promptly.
932. *See* paragraph 5 Schedule 5AAA TCGA.
933. An asset can only derive at least 75% of its value from UK land if it 'consists of a right or an interest in a *company* [emphasis added]' and at least 75% of the value of specified assets of that

Section 103D does not replicate those features of Schedule 7AD which ensure that treating an interest in the fund as a separate asset does not lead to deferral of tax on undistributed gains of the fund.

A.7 LIMITS ON THE TRANSPARENCY OF PARTNERSHIPS AND LLPS WHEN TAXING CHARGEABLE GAINS

While SP D12 provides guidance on how to apply sections 59-59A, there are key issues which it does not clearly address. In particular, can one use these sections to 'look through' a partnership or a UK LLP, so that a group relationship can be established between a corporate member of the partnership/LLP and a company whose shares are held by that partnership/LLP?

Suppose that Company A holds a 75% interest in a partnership or UK LLP which in turn holds directly all the ordinary shares of Company B. Are Company A and Company B 'grouped' for the purposes of corporation tax on chargeable gains, according to section 170 TCGA?

The practical answer should be 'yes'. HMRC published guidance confirms this, in the Capital Gains Manual at CG45110 (accessed 13 July 2022), if Company A has an interest in the capital of the partnership/LLP of at least 75%. There is some uncertainty about whether a 'partnership' for these purposes must be one without legal personality because there is a cross-reference to the guidance mentioned in section A.8. The legal basis for CG45110 is not specified but presumably, it is inspired by sections 59-59A, coupled with SP D12. In essence, this HMRC statement is concessionary because sections 59-59A are not this clear-cut, and SP D12 is not explicit. The 'look through' under both sections means that partners/members of the entity are treated as owning or dealing in its underlying assets *as partners*, and not as simple co-owners. As discussed, a partner's interest in partnership property is not a simple percentage interest in that property. So one cannot necessarily say that a 75% interest in a partnership/UK LLP equates to owning 75% of its underlying assets, even if the partnership lacks legal personality. Even if sections 59-59A did treat partners/members of the entity as co-owning its underlying assets, then that would leave each partner/member owning a fractional interest, but not all, of each underlying partnership asset (in the example above, part of each share of Company B). So technically, the partner/member would not own any of those partnership assets outright. Hence it would be harder to show that Company A owned 75% of the ordinary shares of Company B in order to establish a group relationship. This point has apparently been raised in the past by HMRC although it does not reflect their current practice.

---

company derives from interests in UK land: *see* paragraph 3 Schedule 1A TCGA. Hence, non-UK-residents investing in UK land via a 'company' are only subject to tax on chargeable gains if this '75%-of-value' test is met. By contrast, non-UK-residents investing in UK land via a partnership or UK LLP are subject to tax on such gains even if less than 75% of its asset value is derived from UK land, because of sections 59-59A TCGA. This places investment by non-UK-residents in UK land via 'companies' (including an 'authorised' contractual scheme based on co-ownership) at an advantage over equivalent investment via a partnership. *See also* fn 712.

If a partnership/LLP can in practice be 'looked through' to establish a group relationship, it should also be possible to show that a partner is beneficially entitled to profits on a distribution and assets on any winding-up of the company owned by the partnership. Hence the separate 'economic' entitlement conditions for group status should be met. The same should be true where a partnership/LLP can in practice be looked through for corporation tax 'group relief': *see* section A.8.

A.8 LIMITS ON THE TRANSPARENCY OF PARTNERSHIPS AND LLPS FOR CORPORATION TAX 'GROUP RELIEF'

HMRC published guidance is more detailed and arguably narrower for the purposes of corporation tax 'group relief' (which is separate from the 'grouping' rules which apply when taxing chargeable gains). It states that one can 'look through' a partnership or a UK LLP to demonstrate a group relationship, as defined in sections 131-133 CTA 2010: *see* the Corporation Tax Manual at CTM 80152 (accessed 13 July 2022). This says that 'A trading partnership in England, Wales or Northern Ireland has no legal personality and cannot own assets, so the assets of the partnership are treated as beneficially owned by the partners. This will generally be in proportion to the members' partnership shares, determined by the partnership agreement ... .' This guidance makes practical sense but glosses over the legal nature of a partnership share, even where the partnership lacks legal personality. It does not cover a partnership with legal personality nor an investment partnership.

The technical basis of this practice is less clear for group relief, which contains no equivalent of section 59 TCGA. Similarly, section 59 seems less relevant in relation to the corporation tax 'grouping' rules for 'loan relationships' and 'intangible fixed asset' in Parts 5, 6 and 8 CTA 2009.

In relation to UK LLPs only, section 1273 CTA 2009 operates like section 59A TCGA.[934] Section 1273(1) says:

> For corporation tax purposes, if a limited liability partnership carries on a trade or business with a view to profit –
>
> (a) all the activities of the limited liability partnership are treated as carried on in partnership by its members (and not by the limited liability partnership as such),
> (b) anything done by, to or in relation to the limited liability partnership for the purposes of, or in connection with, any of its activities is treated as done by, to or in relation to the members as partners, and
> (c) *the property of the limited liability partnership is treated as held by the members as partnership property* [emphasis added].

934. Section 1273(1)(c) is the corporation tax equivalent of section 863(1)(c) ITTOIA 2005 which was considered in *Bayonet Ventures* [2018] UKFTT 262 (TC): *see* section 5.2. As emphasised in that case, section 863 merely deems LLP members to be partners in a partnership. It does not disregard the partnership or UK LLP.

References in this subsection to the activities of the LLP are to anything that it does, whether or not in the course of carrying on a trade or business with a view to profit.

HMRC rely on the highlighted words to argue that '... for group relief purposes any ordinary share capital held by an LLP is treated as beneficially co-owned by the LLP members in accordance with each member's share in the LLP, and thus an LLP can be "looked through" to establish a group relationship'. The practical merit of this statement, which seems inspired by SP D12, is clear. However, it is concessionary. Section 1273(1)(c) only says that the LLP members are treated as holding its assets as partnership property. Given the nature of a partner's interest in partnership property, a LLP member cannot simply be treated as owning a share of particular assets of the LLP corresponding to its LLP interest. Hence the points in section A.7 about the legal effect of section 59A are also relevant here.

Besides, as there is no section 59 equivalent for corporation tax group relief purposes, it is that much harder to 'look through' a partnership other than a UK LLP, for such purposes. Unlike CG45110 (which is more ambiguous), HMRC guidance in CTM 80152 relies on the lack of legal personality of an English partnership as a basis for 'looking through' it. There is no guidance at all on how one can 'look through', for these purposes, a partnership with legal personality. This seems especially difficult, with no equivalent of section 59. In a Scottish partnership, partners do not beneficially own the entity's underlying assets.

A.9 LIMITS ON THE TRANSPARENCY OF PARTNERSHIPS AND LLPS FOR THE PURPOSES OF THE 'SUBSTANTIAL SHAREHOLDINGS EXEMPTION' IN SCHEDULE 7AC TCGA

A.9.1 A 'Substantial Shareholding'

Can one company own a 'substantial shareholding', via a partnership/UK LLP, in another company, for the purposes of the 'substantial shareholdings exemption' (SSE) from corporation tax on chargeable gains? The exemption is in Schedule 7AC TCGA? The main definition of a 'substantial shareholding' is in paragraph 8(1) of Schedule 7AC: '... a company holds a "substantial shareholding" in another company if it *holds shares or interests in shares* [meaning a "co-ownership" interest in shares] in that company by virtue of which (a) *it holds not less than 10% of the company's ordinary share capital. ...*' [emphasis added]. Strictly, it is hard to see how a company can 'hold' shares in another company merely by being a partner/ member of a UK LLP which owns those shares itself. This is especially true if the intermediate entity is a separate legal person, such as a Scottish partnership or a UK LLP. As discussed in section A.7, it is doubtful whether sections 59-59A 'look through' the partnership/LLP sufficiently to cure this problem. The UK tax authorities in practice take a more relaxed, concessionary position.[935] Elsewhere in Schedule 7AC, language has been added quite recently to address this issue for other, more limited purposes.[936]

A.9.2 SSE: Groups, Subgroups and Joint Ventures

Elsewhere in Schedule 7AC, concerns exist about whether shares or an 'interest in shares' can be owned via a partnership. These are discussed below. Paragraph 29 Schedule 7AC defines 'an interest in shares' as 'an interest as a co-owner of shares'. Paragraph 29(2) states that 'It does not matter whether the shares are owned jointly or in common or whether the interests of the co-owners are equal'. Paragraph 29(2) suggests that this definition of an 'interest in shares' is linked to the English law of co-ownership. In practice, the UK tax authorities take a more relaxed stance, as noted in the previous paragraph.

For SSE purposes, it can be important to decide whether the company whose shares are part of the 'substantial shareholding' is itself a member of a 'trading group' or a 'trading subgroup'. Paragraph 26 Schedule 7AC means that the group and subgroup concepts are based on section 170 TCGA, which defines a 'group' for the purposes of corporation tax on capital gains. However, the minimum required degree of affiliation is not 75% but just over 50%. Previously HMRC argued that this affiliation can only be traced through a partnership if it lacks legal personality. Current HMRC published guidance in the Capital Gains Manual at CG45110 (*see* section A.7) seems more generous and should apply whether or not a partnership has legal personality, at least if CG45110 is interpreted with the spirit of section 59 TCGA and SP D12 in mind.

---

935. *See* CG53009 of the Capital Gains Manual (accessed 13 July 2022) which states that 'Where shares are held through a partnership (including a Limited Liability Partnership where TCGA s59A applies), then paragraph 8(1) Schedule 7AC TCGA ... means that shares are treated as being held based on the proportionate interest in the partnership.' It is not entirely clear whether 'partnership' in this statement includes a partnership with legal personality, although the reference to section 59A TCGA suggests that it does, because partnerships are 'looked through' when taxing capital gains. If Schedule 7AD TCGA (*see* section A.5) applies to a life insurance company's interest in a venture capital LP, then the SSE does not readily apply, even if the partnership holds a 'substantial shareholding' in another company. This is because the partner can only accrue gain on the separate 'single asset' consisting of its partnership interest, which is not 'looked through' under Schedule 7AD. That partnership interest is not a 'substantial shareholding', even if it derives its value from such a shareholding. It is arguable that this 'single asset' is nevertheless an 'interest in shares', but this analysis does not fit easily with the scheme of Schedule 7AD.
936. Paragraph 3B(6) states that: 'Where the assets of a partnership include ordinary share capital of a company, each partner is to be regarded as owning a proportion of that share capital equal to the partner's proportionate interest in that ordinary share capital.' This deeming rule (like CG53009) is not very clear how one measures a 'proportionate interest'. It presumably treats a partner as owning underlying ordinary share capital to the extent of its partnership 'share', but does that mean its entitlement to income or capital proceeds or both? Paragraph 3B(6) goes further than sections 59-59A by equating a partnership share with ownership of specific partnership assets. It only applies for the purposes of paragraphs 3A and 8A(1), where it is used to work out percentage ownership (via a partnership) by certain tax-exempt institutional investors of a holding company which itself owns a 'substantial shareholding' in another company. Therefore paragraph 3B(6) has no bearing on the main definition of a 'substantial shareholding' in paragraph 8, which relates to the underlying shareholding in that other company.

The SSE also allows a corporate shareholder in certain joint venture companies to 'look through' the joint venture's underlying activities: *see* paragraphs 23-24, Schedule 7AC. This can help to show that the corporate shareholder is either a 'trading company' or a member of a 'trading group/subgroup', for SSE purposes. This 'look through' is only possible where the corporate shareholder has a 'qualifying shareholding', as defined in paragraph 24(2). If the corporate shareholder is not itself a member of a group, it can have a 'qualifying shareholding' in the joint venture company 'if, and only if, it *holds shares or an interest in shares* [emphasis added] in the joint venture company'. If it is a member of a group, it can have a 'qualifying shareholding' 'if, and only if, it *holds ordinary share capital* [emphasis added] of the joint venture company'.

There is no clear explanation for the drafting difference highlighted above. Apparently, a corporate shareholder which is a group member can only have a 'qualifying shareholding' if it directly 'holds' ordinary share capital and not just an interest in such capital. 'Looking through' a partnership may not suffice for these purposes.

If the corporate shareholder is not a group member, the reference to 'an interest in shares' means that a 'qualifying shareholding' can more readily be traced through a partnership but (?) only if it lacks legal personality. Also, given the nature of a partnership share, does a partner own partnership property 'jointly or in common', so that it has an 'interest in shares' (*see* above)? If the partnership has legal personality, this question becomes harder. In practice, HMRC guidance in the Capital Gains Manual (*see* CG45110 and CG53009) indicates that these issues are not concerns when interpreting 'an interest in a share'.[937]

A.10 CONCLUSION

Partnerships are the quintessential 'transparent' entity. The UK rules on partnership and LLP transparency when taxing chargeable gains are a fairly radical 'look through' but are cumbersome in compliance terms and can trigger 'dry' tax charges. The statutory rules underpinning this approach are limited and unclear, even more so when tracing affiliations between companies via intermediate partnerships and when applying the SSE. The void has been largely filled with non-statutory guidance. While this strives to give sensible practical answers and much of it is well established, it is largely concessionary, vague in parts and potentially hard to enforce against HMRC. Furthermore, HMRC practice in this area has been inconsistent. A legislative solution is needed.

If one were starting from scratch, a better 'transparency' approach to partnerships would be based on the less radical approach to 'transparency' in Schedule 7AD

937. *See also* Dominic Foulkes and Jonathan Cooklin: 'Analysis: Holding Shares through Partnerships: Some Observations' (5 October 2018) Tax Journal, Issue 1415, at 7. Statements in this article that SP D12 is broadly consistent with the strict legal position regarding the nature of a partnership interest are questionable, especially as the article only considers interests in English general partnerships and not in UK LLPs or partnerships with legal personality (as in Scotland). These too are covered by SP D12.

TCGA. By treating partnership interests as a separate asset for capital gains purposes and giving a partner an 'outside basis' in that asset, the complexities of sections 59-59A TCGA and SP D12 would be reduced. This would also deal comprehensively with tax planning where base cost has been 'shifted' tax-free between taxpayers by relying on the (concessionary) section 4 of SP D12. This planning was used to reduce the effective tax rate on 'carried interest' allocated by funds to fund managers. Section 103KA-KH TCGA now target such planning but only in relation to 'carried interest' arising in respect of individuals in the investment management industry.

Base cost in the partnership interest would be increased where the partner was taxable on undistributed partnership income. This avoids economic double taxation. No such adjustment is needed under SP D12 where the partner is treating as holding a fractional interest in underlying assets which represent that undistributed income.

Contributions in kind to, and distributions in kind from a partnership, would in principle be taxable under this approach, unless there was deferral relief. The non-disposal approach based on *Booth v Ellard* and *Jenkins v Brown* would not apply.

A Schedule 7AD-type approach would also need to be overridden in some cases. A 'look through' rule would be needed to trace relevant affiliations between companies via intermediate partnerships. The Schedule 7AD-type approach would probably need to be overridden to ensure that a non-UK-resident disposing of an interest in a non-UK partnership with a UK trade was taxable on its share of the partnership's unrealised gains on assets used in that trade. This is the kind of situation considered in the US in *Grecian Magnesite Mining* and later legislated for by Congress: *see* section 7.2.6.2.1.

APPENDIX B

UK Corporation Tax 'Transparency' where Partnerships hold Loan Relationships, Derivative Contracts or Intangible Fixed Assets

B.1 PARTNERSHIPS AND LOAN RELATIONSHIPS, DERIVATIVE CONTRACTS AND INTANGIBLE FIXED ASSETS

The UK corporation tax code contains special rules regarding 'loan relationships', 'derivative contracts' and 'intangible fixed assets'.[938] These rules aim to align more closely corporation tax treatment more closely with GAAP accounting treatment of the relevant assets and liabilities. It is increasingly odd that these rules apply only for the purposes of corporation tax, given how similar many large partnerships are, in substance, to companies.

The structure of these rules creates difficulties when dealing with 'loan relationships', 'derivative contracts' and 'intangible fixed assets' of entities which are 'transparent' for corporation tax purposes,[939] and, in particular, partnerships. These problems are most marked when an interest in a partnership is transferred between corporation taxpayers and that partnership holds intangible fixed assets.

938. Parts 5 and 6 CTA 2009 ('loan relationships'); Part 7 CTA 2009 ('derivative contracts') and Part 8 CTA 2009 ('intangible fixed assets'). Loan relationships cover most debts owed by and to corporation taxpayers, but the rules also cover other instruments and arrangements with 'debt-like' characteristics. 'Derivative contracts' cover a wide range of financial derivatives, e.g., futures, options and contracts for differences (including swaps). 'Intangible fixed assets' cover a broad range of non-circulating, intangible assets (as defined by GAAP), including goodwill.

939. Meaning that the entity itself pays no corporation tax but its members are subject to corporation tax as if they took part directly in the entity's underlying activities.

The source of the problem is that TCGA typically does not apply to items within Parts 5-8 CTA 2009,[940] even if those items are assets which would otherwise be capital assets. Hence if loan relationships, etc., are held by a partnership or a 'bare trust', sections 59, 59A and 60 TCGA are inoperative.

B.2 PARTNERSHIP 'LOOK THROUGH' FOR LOAN RELATIONSHIPS AND DERIVATIVE CONTRACTS

In the 'loan relationships' rules, sections 380-385 CTA 2009 (first enacted in 2002)[941] introduce a form of 'look-through', treating corporation taxpaying partners as if they were party to underlying money debts (but not all 'loan relationships') owed by or to the partnership. Similar rules apply to such partners in a partnership which enters into 'derivative contracts': *see* sections 619-621 CTA 2009. These rules 'look through' the partnership more comprehensively than the normal UK rules determining how a partnership's income (but not its capital gain) is taxed. Those normal rules, for corporation taxpayers, are in sections 1259-1260 CTA 2009. They do *not* treat partners as party to the underlying assets and liabilities of the partnership.[942] There is no radical 'look through' akin to section 59 TCGA. Instead, income profit or loss is computed assuming that the partnership is a company, even though it is not a taxable entity. A share of this profit or loss is then allocated to the corporate partner consistently with the partnership's sharing arrangements, under section 1262 CTA 2009. That partner is liable for corporation tax on profit allocated to it in this way.

If there are both UK-resident and non-UK-resident partners, then two computations of profit or loss are made under sections 1259-1260. The first assumes that the partnership is itself a UK-resident company and the second that it is a non-UK-resident company. The first computation is used to allocate profit or loss to each UK-resident partner. The second computation is used to allocate profit or loss to each non-UK-resident partner.[943] Those partners are then liable for corporation tax accordingly.

940. Parts 5-8 CTA 2009 ensure that profits and losses from 'loan relationships', 'derivative contracts' and 'intangible fixed assets' are typically income profits and losses, not capital gains and losses, for corporation tax purposes. There are limited exceptions which are immaterial for present purposes. Parts 5-8 CTA 2009 aim to cover exhaustively the tax treatment of 'loan relationships', 'derivative contracts' and 'intangible fixed assets', unless expressly provided otherwise: *see* sections 464, 699 and 906 CTA 2009. This means that TCGA is normally disregarded when taxing 'loan relationships', 'derivative contracts' and 'intangible fixed assets'.

941. Prior to 2002, there had been attempts to achieve tax advantages by exploiting the lack of such a 'look through': *see* the (obsolete) Statement of Practice 4/98.

942. Following *Investec Asset Finance PLC, Investec Bank PLC v HMRC* [2020] EWCA Civ 579, the effect of these rules seems to be that any trade carried on by the partnership is a separate taxable trade from the business activities of the partners (including any partners' separate trading activities) conducted outside the partnership. Income of the partnership trade computed at partnership level (and allocated to partners as described in the main text) is ignored when computing any separate tax liability of the partners from their activities outside the partnership. This avoids double taxation of partnership income.

943. Where partners are subject to income tax, not corporation tax, there are equivalent rules (in particular, sections 849-850 ITTOIA) for computing at partnership level the income profits and

The extent of the 'look through' in sections 380-385 and 619-621 CTA 2009 is uncertain. The rules could be clearer about a partner's basis in underlying money debts or derivative contracts of the partnership, and there is no equivalent of SP D12. However, these rules are not just a computation provision even if part of their role is computational and even if they do not totally disregard the partnership. In particular, if a corporation taxpaying partner sells at a profit an interest in a partnership invested in money debts, a court would probably regard that profit as taxable under Part 5 CTA 2009, on the basis of the partner's deemed part-ownership of those debts under section 381 CTA 2009.

B.3 PARTNERSHIPS: LIMITED 'LOOK THROUGH' FOR INTANGIBLE FIXED ASSETS

If a partnership owns intangible fixed assets, no rule treats a corporation taxpaying partner as owning a fractional interest in each of those underlying assets for the purposes of Part 8 CTA 2009. Furthermore, section 807(1)(c) CTA 2009 provides that 'the interest of a partner in a firm' cannot fall within the 'intangible fixed asset' rules, unless, under UK GAAP, it is treated as representing an interest in partnership property which is an 'intangible fixed asset' for Part 8 CTA 2009 purposes.[944] Such treatment under UK GAAP is not inevitable.[945]

This potential lack of 'transparency' can have important consequences if an interest in a partnership is sold from one corporation taxpayer to another. Suppose that A Ltd and B Ltd are partners in a partnership whose assets comprise valuable intangibles. They share profits in the ratio 30:70. A Ltd sells its 30% interest to C Ltd.

---

losses of the partnership, and for allocating them under the partnership's commercial profit-sharing arrangements. These rules do not 'look through' the partnership so as to treat partners as directly holding its underlying assets and liabilities: *see Bayonet Ventures LLP and another v HMRC* [2018] UKFTT 262 (TC) [2018] STC 297. Therefore they are less radical than sections 59-59A TCGA: *see* Appendix A. Can partners nevertheless 'cherry pick' specific items of income and expense feeding into the composite profit or loss computed at partnership level? This has been attempted in practice, e.g., in respect of low-taxed dividend income. An old statement in *Bucks v Bowers* [1970] 2 All ER 202 suggests, with minimal explanation, that this can be done by agreement. That statement had no bearing on the actual decision. Partners may purport to split between them different income sources feeding into the overall profit and loss calculation. However, if such allocations do not genuinely expose the relevant partner to the risk of its chosen income source failing to materialise, they look vulnerable to challenge.

944. Section 807(3) CTA 2009. Section 807(2) creates an equivalent exception for rights under a trust, which otherwise cannot be 'intangible fixed assets' for Part 8 purposes.

945. *See Armajaro Holdings Limited v HMRC* [2013] UKFTT 571 (TC), which focused mainly on the purchase of an interest in a UK LLP holding intangible fixed assets. Expert evidence showed that if a controlling interest in an English general partnership was acquired, UK GAAP would present this as acquiring underlying goodwill of the partnership on the basis of 'proportional consolidation'. The same GAAP accounting treatment was not possible when an interest in a UK LLP was acquired, because it is a separate legal person. This GAAP treatment was unaffected simply by treating the UK LLP as a partnership for tax purposes only. Hence the purchaser of the LLP interest could not amortise the underlying intangibles for tax purposes. As Crossley and Baldwin *supra* note at 18-09, had the case gone the other way, would the taxpayer have been entitled to tax amortisation on its LLP interest as well as benefiting from amortisation reflected in its share of partnership income from the underlying intangibles?

C Ltd has thereby 'acquired' a large slice of the underlying intangibles. However, the lack of 'transparency' means that C Ltd is unable to claim depreciation for tax purposes[946] in respect of those intangibles.

The corporation tax treatment of A Ltd is also odd. The potential lack of 'transparency' in Part 8 CTA 2009 means that it should not be treated as selling a slice of the underlying intangibles. Any profit it makes will therefore not be taxed as income under Part 8, even if that profit reflects growth in the value of 'intangible fixed assets'. That profit will not be taxed as capital gain either because of the way in which TCGA analyses an interest in a partnership. As discussed in Appendix A, section 59 TCGA, together with SP D12, treats a partner as owning a proportionate share in each asset of the partnership. One ignores the partnership interest as a separate asset and 'looks through' to the partnership's underlying assets. However, those assets are intangibles which ordinarily fall within Part 8 CTA 2009. To treat A Ltd as disposing, for TCGA purposes, of a 30% interest in the underlying intangibles would be at odds with the exhaustive nature of Part 8, as per section 906 CTA 2009. Subject to any contrary indication,[947] 'The amounts to be brought into account in accordance with [Part 8 CTA 2009] in respect of any matter are the *only* [emphasis added] amounts to be brought into account for corporation tax purposes in respect of that matter.' There does not seem to be a relevant 'contrary indication'. The fact that the amount 'brought into account' in this case under Part 8 is nil, rather than just negligible, should not prevent section 906 from applying. Otherwise, the corporation tax goal of dealing with most intangible fixed assets exclusively under Part 8 CTA 2009 would be undermined.

Part 8 CTA 2009 contains no 'look through' rule similar to those which apply to the 'loan relationships' and 'derivative contracts' of partnerships: *see* section B.2. Therefore, on selling a partnership interest, gains of the corporate seller attributable to underlying intangible fixed assets of the partnership may escape taxation under Part 8. The purchaser of that interest may not get effective amortisation relief for that part of the purchase price reflecting those intangibles.[948] This analysis is consistent with the way in which HMRC used to treat a disposal by a corporate seller of an interest in a partnership holding 'loan relationships' or 'derivative contracts': *see* paragraphs 13 and

946. Either on an accounting basis under section 729 CTA 2009 or by electing to write down at 4% per annum straight-line under sections 730-731 CTA 2009.
947. Section 906(2) CTA 2009.
948. There is inconclusive discussion of this issue in *Bloomberg Inc (UK permanent establishment), BLP Acquisition Holdings LLC (UK permanent establishment) v HMRC* [2018] UKFTT 205 (TC), especially at paragraphs 149-156. Both HMRC and the judge did not explore in detail the implications of section 59 TCGA being disapplied by section 906 CTA 2009, when an interest is sold in a partnership holding intangible fixed assets. Counsel for HMRC even suggested that a purchaser of a partnership interest would acquire a base cost in that interest for TCGA purposes, if the intangible fixed assets rules did not apply because of section 807(1)(c) CTA 2009. But how? In contrast to a company share, section 59 TCGA does not treat a partnership interest as a separate asset but 'looks through' (via SP D12) the assets underlying that interest. If they would be 'intangible fixed assets' within Part 8 CTA 2009, taxing a transfer of the partnership interest under TCGA would involve 'bringing into account an amount in respect of' those intangibles outside Part 8 CTA 2009. As discussed in the main text, this contravenes section 906 CTA 2009. There seems no way to 'switch off' section 59, and to treat the partnership interest as a separate asset for TCGA purposes, where the underlying partnership assets are 'intangible fixed assets' within Part 8 CTA 2009.

21 of the old Statement of Practice 4/98. Of course, that treatment no longer applies because of the rules (*see* section B.2) regarding a partnership's 'loan relationships' and 'derivative contracts'.

If the partnership earns income (e.g., royalties) from dealing with its underlying intangible fixed assets, then, for Part 8 CTA 2009 purposes, partnership profits from those dealings will be computed as income on the assumption that the partnership is a company subject to corporation tax[949] which owns those assets. That income will then be apportioned among partners subject to UK corporation tax according to the profit-sharing arrangements for the relevant period: *see* section B.2. There will be no tax on any such profits at partnership level. To that extent, the partnership is 'transparent' for Part 8 CTA 2009 purposes. However, this extends only to dealings of the partnership with its intangible fixed assets, but not to dealings by the partners with their partnership interests.

B.4 CONCLUSION

At a minimum, Part 8 CTA 2009 should include a 'look through' rule for partnerships holding 'intangible fixed assets' which is similar to the rules already applying to partnerships in respect of their 'loan relationships' and 'derivative contracts'. It is unsatisfactory and confusing that the current position depends on section 807 CTA 2009.

949. Sections 1258-1260 CTA 2009.

Bibliography

Avery Jones, John F.: 'Partnerships and Double Taxation Agreements: Padmore v IRC' [1987] British Tax Review 88.
Avery Jones, John F. et al.: 'The Treatment of Trusts under the OECD Model Convention' (December 1989) European Taxation, 379.
Avery Jones, John F.: 'Bodies of Persons' [1990] British Tax Review 453.
Avery Jones, John F.: 'Memec plc v IRC' [1997] British Tax Review 188.
Avery Jones, John F. et al.: 'Characterisation of Other States' Partnerships for Income Tax' [2002] British Tax Review 375.
Avery Jones, John F.: 'Taxing Foreign Income from Pitt to the Tax Law Rewrite: The Decline of the Remittance Basis'. Studies in the History of Tax Law: ed. John Tiley. Hart Publishing 2004, 15.
Avery Jones, John F.: 'The English Dreyfus Case: Categorisation of a French SNC for Tax Purposes in the UK'. Fiscalité et entreprise: politiques et pratiques: eds Mélanges en l'honneur de Jean-Pierre Le Gall. Dalloz 2007, at 325.
Avery Jones, John F.: 'The Revised UK-France Tax Treaty'. Bulletin for International Taxation (2008), 457.
Avery Jones, John F.: 'The History of the United Kingdom's First Comprehensive Double Taxation Agreement' [2007] British Tax Review 211.
Avery Jones, John F.: 'Defining and Taxing Companies 1799 to 1965'. Chapter 1. Studies in the History of Tax Law: ed. John Tiley. Volume 5 Hart Publishing 2012.
Azzi, John: 'Impact of the OECD Multilateral Convention to Implement Tax Treaty Related Measures to Prevent Base Erosion and Profit Shifting on the Taxation of Fiscally Transparent Entities under the Australia-UK Double Tax Agreement' [2018] British Tax Review 556.
Baker, Philip QC: 'The Application of the Convention to Partnerships, Trusts and Other, Non-corporate Entities' (2002) Gray's Inn Tax Chambers Review, Volume II, Issue 1, 1.
Baker, Philip QC: 'Beneficiaries of Trusts and Foundations' (2007) Gray's Inn Tax Chambers Review, Volume VI, Issue 2, 1.

Baker, Philip QC: '*The Commerzbank Litigation (1990)* UK Law, Tax Treaty Law and EU Law'. Chapter 15. Landmark Cases in Revenue Law: eds John Snape and Dominic de Cogan. Hart Publishing 2019.

Baker, Victor: 'Conservative and Unionist Central Office v Burrell (1981): A Case of Hidden Significance'. Chapter 12. Landmark Cases in Revenue Law: eds John Snape and Dominic de Cogan. Hart Publishing 2019.

Baldwin, Mark and Kiranoglu, Tulin: Country Report, United Kingdom: 'Cahiers de Droit Fiscal International: Qualification of Taxable Entities and Treaty Protection'. Volume 99b Stu Uitgevers on behalf of International Fiscal Association 2014, 835.

Bergedahl, Christopher: 'Hybrid Entities and the OECD Model (2017): The End of the Road?'. Bulletin for International Taxation (July 2018), 417.

Blanchard, Kimberly: 'The Tax Significance of Legal Personality: A US View'. Paper dated 3 February 2015 for the New York University School of Law, Colloquium on Tax Policy and Public Finance Spring 2015.

Blanchard, Kimberly: 'The Significance of Legal Personality for US Tax Purposes' (March/April 2016) Business Entities, 5.

Blanchard, Kimberly: 'What Is the Government's Appeal in "Grecian" About?' (10 August 2018) Tax Management International Journal, Volume 47, Issue 8, 546.

Boidman, Nathan and Kandev, Michael N.: 'Foreign Entity Classification and the Meaning of "Corporation"/"Société" in the Income Tax Act' (2009) Canadian Tax Journal, Volume 57, Issue 4, 800.

Brabazon, Mark: 'International Taxation of Trust Income: Principles, Planning and Design'. Cambridge University Press 2019.

Brabazon, Mark: 'After the Flood: Transparent and Hybrid Entities in Australian Tax Treaties after the MLI' (2019) eJournal of Tax Research, Volume 17, Issue 1, at 1.

Brabazon, Mark: 'The Oracle, Transparent Entities and Access to Tax Treaties' (2020) AT Rev, Volume 49, 250.

Brabazon, Mark: 'Non-discrimination and Transparent Entities'. Bulletin for International Taxation (2022), 76.

Bureau Francis Lefebvre, Loyens & Volkmaars, Oppenhoff & Raedler: 'Hybrid Financing in Belgium, France, Germany and the Netherlands'. IBFD Publication BV, Editions Francis Lefebvre 1996.

Chamberlain, Emma: 'Finance (No. 2) Act 2017 Notes: Section 33 and Schedule 10 – Inheritance Tax on Overseas Property Representing UK Residential Property' [2017] British Tax Review 594-605.

Chamberlain, Emma: 'Reform of Inheritance Tax' [2020] British Tax Review 184.

Clarke, Fiona: 'One Island, Two Systems: The Divergence of Trust Law in Scotland v England and Wales' (2019) Trust Quarterly Review, Volume 17, Issue 2, at 5-10.

Clayson, Murray: 'OECD Partnerships Report: Reshaping Treaty Interpretation?' [2000] British Tax Review 71.

Coustel, Anne-Sophie: Country Report, France: 'Cahiers de Droit Fiscal International: Qualification of Taxable Entities and Treaty Protection'. Volume 99b Stu Uitgevers on Behalf of International Fiscal Association 2014, 335.

Crossley, Damien and Baldwin, Mark: 'Taxation of Partnerships and LLPs'. Thomson Reuters/Sweet & Maxwell 2021.

Cullen, Felicity: 'Private Foundations: An Aspect of the Remittance Basis' (November 2008) Gray's Inn Tax Chambers Review, Volume VIII, Issue 1.

Morse, Geoffrey, Williams, David and Eden, Sandra: 'Davies: Principles of Tax Law'. 8th edition, Sweet & Maxwell.

Davis Polk LLP: Tax Reform and Transition/In-Depth Analysis of TCJA. TCJA Navigator – Final Bill (davispolk.com).

De Boynes, Nicolas and Howard, Andrew: 'Treatment of Partnerships in the 2008 France-UK Tax Treaty' (2009) Tax Notes International, Volume 54, Issue 5, at 401.

Debelva F., Scornos D., Van den Berghen J. and Van Braband P.: 'LOB Clauses and EU-Law Compatibility: A Debate Revived by BEPS?' (2015) EC Tax Review, Volume 24, Issue 3.

Derouin, Philippe: Note – 'Régime des sociétés mères et société de personnes interposée' (15 January 2015) Revue de Droit Fiscal, No. 3.

Eden, Sandra: 'The Obstacles Faced by the European Court of Justice in Removing the "Obstacles" Faced by the Taxpayer: The Difficult Case of Double Taxation' [2010] British Tax Review 610.

Du Toit, François: 'The South African Trust in the *Begriffshimmel?:* Language, Translation and Taxonomy. Rabels Zeitschrift für ausländisches und internationales Privatrecht'. Max-Planck Institute October 2015, at 852.

Fairpo, Anne and Salter, David: 'Revenue Law: Principles and Practice'. 37th edition, Bloomsbury Professional.

Fibbe G.K. and Stevens A.J.A. eds: 'Hybrid Entities and the EU Direct Tax Directives'. Wolters Kluwer.

Fibbe, G.K. and Stevens, A.J.A.: 'Internationale Fiscal Aspecten', Chapter 6. Belastingheffing van personenvennootschappen, Rapport van de Commissie Personenvennootschappen, 2020, 151 et seq.

Field, Heather M.: 'Checking in on Check-the-Box' (2009) Loyola L.A. Law Review, Volume 42, 451 http://digital commons.lmu.edu/llr/vol42/iss2/4.

Foulkes, Dominic and Cooklin, Jonathan: 'Analysis: Holding Shares Through Partnerships – Some Observations' (5 October 2018) Tax Journal, Volume 7, Issue 1415.

Frimston, Richard and Panico, Paolo: 'When Is a Trust Not a Trust? Continental Property Arrangements and English Real Estate' (2019) Trust Quarterly Review, Volume 17, Issue 2, at 25.

Gammie, Malcolm: 'The Origins of Fiscal Transparency in UK Income Tax'. Studies in the History of Tax Law: ed. John Tiley. Volume 4 Hart Publishing 2010, 33.

Gammie, Malcolm: 'The Archer-Shee Cases (1927) Trusts, Transparency and Source'. Chapter 6. Landmark Cases in Revenue Law: eds John Snape and Dominic de Cogan. Hart Publishing 2019, 139-160.

Gretton, George: 'Trusts Without Equity'. (2000) 49 International and Comparative Law Quarterly 599.

Hajjar, Ismael, Omar, Midya and Reisman, Suzanne: 'DIFC and ADGM Foundation Laws: A UAE/US Perspective' (2019) Trust Quarterly Review, Volume 17, Issue 2, 31.

Harle, Philip and Shiers, Rupert: 'Analysis: Anson, Transparency and Brief 15/2015' (16 October 2015) Tax Journal, Issue 1281, at 9.

Harris, Peter: 'Company, Person, Body of Persons, Entity: What's the Difference and Why?' [2011] British Tax Review 188.

Harris, Peter: 'Corporate Tax Law: Structure, Policy and Practice'. Cambridge University Press 2013.

Harris, Peter (barrister): 'French usufruits and S 43(2) IHTA 1984' (2018-2019) The Tax Planning Review, Volume 7, at 1.

HM Revenue & Customs: Consultation Document 6 June 2014: 'Inheritance Tax: A Fairer Way of Calculating Trust Charges'. https://www.gov.uk/government/consultations/inheritance-tax-a-fairer-way-of-calculating-trust-charges.

HM Revenue & Customs: Consultation Document 7 November 2018: 'The Taxation of Trusts: a Review'. https://www.gov.uk/government/consultations/the-taxation-of-trusts-a-review.

HM Treasury, HM Revenue & Customs: Consultation Document July 2022: 'Sovereign Immunity from Direct Taxation: Consultation on Policy Design'. https//:www.gov.uk/government/consultations/sovereign-immunity-from-direct-taxation-consultation-on-policy-design.

Honoré A.M.: 'Obstacles to the Reception of Trust Law? The Examples of South Africa and Scotland'. 'Aequitas and Equity: Equity in Civil Law and Mixed Jurisdictions: ed. A.M. Rabello. Hebrew University of Jerusalem 1997, at 793-818.

Howley, Simon: 'SDLT and Trusts' (22 October 2021), Tax Journal, at 15.

Infanti, Anthony C. and Moens, Bernard: Country Report, United States of America: 'Cahiers de Droit Fiscal International: Qualification of Taxable Entities and Treaty Protection'. Volume 99b Stu Uitgevers on behalf of International Fiscal Association 2014, 859.

Joint Report (2003) on Partnership Law of the English and Scottish Law Commissions (Law Com. 283; Scottish Law Com. 192) www.scotlawcom.gov.uk/publications/reports/2000-9.

Kent, Robert: 'Entity Classification: Oxnard Financing SA v Rahn and others' [1999] British Tax Review 125.

Kessler, James QC: 'The Quest for Fair Inheritance Taxation of Trusts' 1 (kessler.co.uk).

Kessler, James and Marre, Oliver: 'A Merry Dance' (20 March 2014), Taxation, 8.

Kessler, James QC: 'Taxation of Non-residents and Foreign Domiciliaries'. 18th edition, Key Haven Publications Ltd 2019-2020.

Lall, Tarlochan: 'Taxation and the European Economic Interest Grouping' [1993] British Tax Review 134.

Le Gall, Jean-Pierre: 'General Report on Worldwide Taxation of Partnerships'. Cannes Congress of International Fiscal Association 1995.

Loengard Jr, Richard O.: 'Tax Treaties, Partnerships and Partners: Exploration of a Relationship' (1975), Tax Lawyer, Volume 29, 31.

Loutzenhiser, Glen: 'Tiley's Revenue Law'. 10th edition, Hart 2022.

Loyens & Loeff: 'The Netherlands Brings Entity Tax Classification Rules in Line with International Standards'. 30 March 2021. https://www.loyensloeff.com/en/en/news/news-articles/the-netherlands-brings-entity-tax-classification-rules-in-line-with-international-standards-n22176/?utm_medium = email&utm_source = newsletter&utm_campaign = tax_classification_rules_30032021_en_en&msdynttrid = KeHeo2CbsS5LP7KLUYnCqJb45U6s5u5-cWsVGWRLBtg (accessed 1 April 2021).

Mason, Ruth and Saint-Amans, Pascal: 'Has Cross-Border Arbitrage Met Its Match?'. Thinker, Teacher, Traveller: Reimagining International Tax: Essays in Honor of H. David Rosenbloom: eds Kofler, Mason, Rust. IBFD September 2021, 355.

McGowan, Michael: '*HMRC v Lloyds Bank Leasing (No 1) Ltd*: The Troublesome Increase in the Scope of the "Sole or Main Object" Test' [2015] British Tax Review 649.

Merten, Martine: 'Taxation of Investment Funds Following the OECD Base Erosion and Profit Shifting Initiative: Part 1'. Bulletin for International Taxation (February 2019), 76.

Merten, Martine: 'Taxation of Investment Funds Following the OECD Base Erosion and Profit Shifting Initiative: Part 2'. Bulletin for International Taxation (May 2019), 252.

Molenaars, Michael L.: 'The Tax Significance of Legal Personality: A Dutch View' (December 2014) Tax Review, Issue 316.

Montagu, Gerald F.: 'Is a Foreign State a Body Corporate?' [2001] British Tax Review 421.

Montagu, Gerald F.: '*Anson* and Entity Classification Revisited in Light of Brexit: Can an LLC Constitute a "Body Corporate"?' [2016] British Tax Review 466.

Mortimer, Matthew and Hunt, Kirsten: 'UK Loan Structures: Changes to the Anti-hybrid Rules' (26 November 2021) Tax Journal, 10.

Nikolakakis, Angelo: 'Anson v HMRC: Sour Grapes and Maple Syrup: Has the UK Just Adopted Check-the-Box?' [2015] British Tax Review 538.

Nikolakakis, Austry, et al.: 'Some Reflections on the Proposed Revisions to the OECD Model and Commentaries and on the Multilateral Instrument, with respect to Fiscally Transparent Entities' [2017] British Tax Review 295.

Noll, Dr Bernd.: 'Foundation and Trust in Succession Planning'. Cross-Border Investments with Germany: Tax, Legal and Accounting – In Honour of Detlev J. Piltz: ed. Flick Gocke Schaumburg. Verlag Dr Otto Schmidt KG 2014.

Panayi, Christiana HJI: 'Cadbury Schweppes and Cadbury Schweppes Overseas (2006): CFC Rules under EU Tax Law'. Chapter 19. Landmark Cases in Revenue Law: eds John Snape and Dominic de Cogan. Hart Publishing 2019.

Parada, Leopoldo: 'Hybrid Entities and Conflicts of Allocation of Income within Tax Treaties: is New Article 1(2) of the OECD Model (Article 3(1) of the MLI) the Best Solution available?' [2018] British Tax Review 335.

Parada, Leopoldo: 'Hybrid Entity Mismatches and the International Trend of Matching Tax Outcomes: A Critical Approach' (2018) Intertax, Volume 46, Issue 12, 971.

Parada, Leopoldo: 'Hybrid Entity Mismatches: Exploring Three Alternatives for Coordination' (2019) Intertax, Volume 47, Issue 1, 24.

Parada, Leopoldo: 'Hybrid Entity Mismatches and the MLI: A Tax Policy Assessment' (2021) Intertax, Volume 49, Issue 10, 786.

Parrott, David and Avery Jones, John F.: 'Seven Appeals and an Acquittal: The Singer Family and their Tax Cases' [2008] British Tax Review 56.

Piccini Roy, Marilyn: 'Usufruct in Quebec' (2017) Trusts & Trustees, Volume 24, Issue 1, 17.

Pötgens, Frank P.G.: 'Income from International Private Employment', Books IBFD.

Prebble, John: 'Accumulation Trusts and Double Tax Conventions' [2001] British Tax Review 69.

Price, Toby and Hawkins, Alexandra: 'Practice Guide: Tax Transparent Property Funds' (30 October 2020) Tax Journal, Issue 1507, at 8.

Rust, Alexander: 'BEPS Action 2: 2014 Deliverable: Neutralising the Effects of Hybrid Mismatch Arrangements and Its compatibility with the Non-discrimination Provisions in Tax Treaties and the Treaty on the functioning of the European Union' [2015] British Tax Review 308.

Sanghavi, Druv: 'Structural Issues in the Income Tax Treaty Network: Towards a Coherent Framework'. Ipskamp Printing BV, 2018. ISBN 978-94-0280-972-5.

Schaffner, Jean: 'Droit Fiscal International'. Editions Promoculture 2005.

Schler, Michael L.: 'Initial Thoughts on the Proposed "Check the Box" Regulations'. May 1996, unpublished paper presented to the New York Tax Club.

Schulte, Dr Christoph: 'Legal Forms in German Corporate Law'. Cross-Border Investments with Germany: Tax, Legal and Accounting – In Honour of Detlev J. Piltz: ed. Flick Gocke Schaumburg. Verlag Dr Otto Schmidt KG (2014), at 415-426.

Squires, Sarah: 'Finance Act 2019 Notes: Section 13 – Disposals by Non-UK Residents Etc – and Schedule 1, Paragraph 21 – Schedule 5AAA to the Taxation of Chargeable Gains Act 1992 – UK Property Rich Collective Investment Vehicles, Etc' [2019] British Tax Review 278.

Sutton, Paul and McCormick, Jane: 'Scottish Limited Partnerships' (14 January 2008) Tax Journal, Issue 916, 26.

US Department of the Treasury: Technical Explanation of the Convention between the Government of the United States of America and the Government of the United Kingdom of Great Britain and Northern Ireland for the avoidance of double taxation and the prevention of fiscal evasion with respect to taxes on income and capital gains signed at London on 31 December 1975, as amended by the Notes exchanged at London on 13 April 1976, the Protocol signed at London on 26 August 1976 and the Second Protocol signed at London on 31 March 1977. https://www.irs.gov/pub/irs-trty/uktech.pdf.

US Department of the Treasury: Technical Explanation dated 2002 of the Convention between the Government of the United States of America and the Government of the United Kingdom of Great Britain and Northern Ireland for the avoidance of double taxation and the prevention of fiscal evasion with respect to taxes on income and capital gains. http://www.treasury.gov./resource-center/tax-policy/treaties/Documents/teus-uk.pdf.

Verhoog & Breuer: 'Hybrid Entity Issues in a Tax Treaty Context: OECD Approach Versus Actual Tax Treaties' Intertax, Volume 44, Issue 8 and 9, 684.
Van Hulten, Mart and Stevens, Ton: 'Is the Symmetrical Classification Method EU Proof?' EC Tax Review (forthcoming).
Wales, Christopher J.: 'European Economic Interest Groupings: Finance Act 1990' [1990] British Tax Review 335.
Warriner, Neil, Williamson, Michelle and Tolman, John: 'Analysis: LLPs, Groups and Stamp Taxes' (2010) Tax Journal, Issue 1053, 13.
Waters, Donovan W.M. QC: 'The Concept Called "the Trust"' (March 1999) Bulletin of the International Bureau of Fiscal Documentation 118.
Wells, Naomi: 'Staying Offshore' (17 January 2019) Taxation, 12 at 13.
Wheeler, Joanna: 'Chapter 2: Some Thoughts about Transparency, Attribution and CFC Regimes and Their Interaction with Tax Treaties'. The Aftermath of BEPS: ed. Wheeler, Joanna. International Bureau of Fiscal Documentation 2020.
Yates, Simon: 'Partnerships and Capital Gains' [2008] British Tax Review 587.
Yorke, Charles: 'Anson: Entity Classification Revisited' (8 July 2015) Tax Journal.
Zhang, Libin: 'To the Frying Pan: New Virtues of Subpart F Income over GILTI', Tax Notes, 2 July 2018, at 73.
Zweigert & Koetz (translated by Tony Weir): 'An Introduction to Comparative Law'. 3rd edition, Clarendon Press, published 1998, reprinted 2011.

Table of Cases (UK, England and Wales Unless Stated Otherwise)

Table of Statutory Provisions (UK Unless Stated Otherwise), EU Directives and Regulations, Tax Treaties and Related Documents

Statutes

Statutory Instruments (other than double tax treaties)

Statutory Instruments (double tax treaties)

Council Regulation (EEC) No. 2137/85

Extra-Statutory Concessions

Statements of Practice and HMRC Briefs and Notices

Australian Taxation Office Interpretative Decisions

Treaty on the Functioning of the European Union

Index

N

O

P

www.ingramcontent.com/pod-product-compliance
Ingram Content Group UK Ltd.
Pitfield, Milton Keynes, MK11 3LW, UK
UKHW020237290926
15470UKWH00002B/591

9 789403 537245